The Wind

in the

Trees

The Wind
in the
Trees

Thunder claps roared
The sky filled with light,
Antennas sent signals
The long, angry night

The messages distorted,
God is displeased,
Tomorrow our hope is
In the wind in the trees.

James E. Duffy

Endymion Publishing Company

Endymion Publishing Company

Copyright © 1997 by James E. Duffy

ISBN 0-9715569-0-3

Printed in the United States of America

Library of Congress Cataloging-in-Publishing Data

Duffy, James E., 1926-
        The Wind in the Trees
        James E. Duffy.
        p. cm.

ISBN 0-9715569-0-3 (hardcover: alk. paper)
1.Duffy, James E., 1926- 2. American Broadcasting Co.-
History 3.Broadcasters--United States--Biography.
5.Businesspeople--United States--Biography.   I. Title

He8689.8.D83A3   1997
384.55'092--dc21
{B}

Dedication

This book is dedicated to my grandfather, John Wheeler Adams, who started me in the right direction...

To my daughters, Marcia and Corinne, who also suffered the losses but kept their spirits and their heads held high...

And to all the broadcasters everywhere who helped create such a meaningful industry.

Table of Contents

Acknowledgements

Writing and publishing this book has been an unusual experience for me: therapeutic, exhilarating and, often, frustrating.

The rewarding and most gratifying moments of my experience, were working with so many wonderful people who encouraged me and made the completion of *The Wind in the Trees* possible.

I want to thank David Phillips, the talented British writer, who helped me sort out my thoughts in the early stages of the manuscript. I greatly appreciate the efforts and patience of my daughter, Corinne Duffy, who helped me collate materials from my ABC files going back to 1949.

My friends Bill and Eleanor Farber, Roger and Kate Semerad, the late Bob Loeber, Bob Jones and Pierce Quinlan were supportive and encouraging all the way to "get it on paper" and "keep going." My friend, Steve Steurer, was a great help with the early technical work.

A special note of gratitude to Ellie Trueman, the gifted chairperson of the Trueman Communications Group, for her insights, rewriting and guidance.

I want to thank Dawn Perusse of Corporate Solutions for helping me prepare the book for publication. Also, many thanks to Tabby Finch for a final shaping, focusing and editing.

Julie Baker of Workforce Skills Development in Cleveland, Ohio was especially helpful with encouragement and creative ideas that greatly enhanced the book. I am also grateful to John Hopkins and Jay Gardner for their long hours in editing.

Above all, I want to acknowledge the thousands of broadcasters, educators, literacy service providers and new learners for giving me the experiences and insights to make this all possible.

I sincerely hope that you enjoy this book and will find meaning in it. I hope you, too, will stop on occasion and listen to the wind in the trees.

Author's footnote:
An earlier version of this book entitled *Stay Tuned, My Life and the Business of Running the ABC Television Network* was printed in August 1997. Based on many grammatical and content errors by the publishers, all distribution was stopped. In the ensuing years, I have taken time to reassess what I had written in my original manuscripts and to analyze the continuing changes in the industry. I have rewritten, changed, deleted and added to much of the original work with a greater focus on the growing power and influence of media and what it portends for the future.

Introduction

The sounds of the wind in the trees were mesmerizing, and along with the lonesome and eerie whistles of distant trains, brought many dreams and visions when I was a child. I lived on my grandfather's farm in central Illinois and I would lie in bed at night and listen to the sounds; the winds sometimes would howl during a thunderstorm or bellow from a Midwestern blizzard over bare branches, but mostly the sound of the wind was gentle, almost whispering as it rustled the leaves.

Throughout my life, the sound of the wind has been a common denominator, an equalizer to place and distance, an almost prophetic force that seems to provide an anchor to my childhood, yet has also been the source of inspiration and reflection. I am certain that it was the solace of the wind that allowed me to lie in bed at night and dream about the future. One of those dreams was that I would become a broadcaster.

Broadcasting has fascinated me for as long as I can remember. It was difficult for me to fathom a stranger sitting in a room thousands of miles away talking to me over a box called radio. Or in later years, how pictures – even showing my beloved baseball games – could fly through the air and land in my living room. But the fascination and intrigue went well beyond the technology. It was puzzling, yet invigorating, to sort through all the visions and ideas that the programs and messages on those little boxes planted in my head.

My childhood dream of becoming a broadcaster never waned. Rather, it continued to grow and was fueled by my first real experience in the industry when I became a radio announcer in Beloit, Wisconsin, while I attended Beloit College. After graduating, I joined the American Broadcasting Company in 1949 and I knew then that my life would always be consumed with the power and the promise of the medium. I spent almost fifty years in the business and loved it every bit as much the day that I left, as the day I started.

I had the opportunity to work in every phase of the broadcasting profession, from publicity to programming, to sales, to affiliate services. I rubbed shoulders with politicians and presidents, movie idols and media superstars, great figures in the sports world, news writers and reporters, station owners and media moguls. Being in the right place at the right time with the infant ABC network, I rode the crest of a surging wave into the upper levels of broadcast management and became president of the ABC Television Network for an unprecedented fifteen years. That 46-year ride at ABC had incredible ups and downs as well as wild twists and turns that created, by any standard of measurements, an extraordinary experience.

The Wind in the Trees is my personal story, triumphs and tragedies, as well as the story of the people and struggles of the American Broadcasting Company; how it came to a leading position in the industry, first on its own, then with Capital Cities/ABC; and what that portends for the future in the stunning $19 billion merger with the Walt Disney Company. It also chronicles the advent of public service campaigns such as Project Literacy US, which were especially designed not only to address social issues, but also to cause action and bring about real change. The principal thread throughout the book is my love for broadcasting and my escalating concern for effective and responsible leadership to ensure it is a positive influence on our children, our values and our society.

For the past several years, various friends and associates, and even a couple of publishers, have suggested that I write a book about my experience and my vision for the future of the industry. In the aggregate, perhaps my experience can portray not only the growth and maturity of broadcasting, but can also serve as a bookmark to the direction, the responsibility and the consequences of management and oversight of media. In light of its ever-expanding power and influence, broadcasting, and especially television, will continue to shape our children, our attitudes and nearly every aspect of our world. The direction that the medium leads us simply cannot be left to chance or be the net result of another corporate mega-merger. Undoubtedly, among the most important issues of the present are effective, responsible, and ethical management, leadership and vision for the broadcasting industry.

James Edson Duffy
Stonewall Heights
Round Hill, Virginia
December, 2001

A kiss for Barbara Bush after presenting her award at the *National Literacy Honors* dinner, Washington Hilton Hotel, November 8, 1988

With President-Elect George Bush, Barbara Bush, and J.T. Pace, a PLUS *Learner of the Month* at the *National Literacy Honors* dinner.

One

The National Literacy Honors

"Literacy is the kind of freedom we should have for all Americans."
- President-Elect George Bush, November 11, 1988

The date was Tuesday, November 11, 1988. George Bush, the Vice President of the United States, and his wife, Barbara, were now President-Elect Bush and the soon-to-be First Lady. Even though seven days had passed, they were still flushed with the success of victory in the election for the new President of the most powerful country in the world. The couple, radiating happiness, standing in the ballroom of the Washington Hilton Hotel, was attending the first *National Literacy Honors* event held in our nation's capital. The evening was the apex in the Project Literacy US (PLUS) campaign founded by the American Broadcasting Company (ABC) and the Public Broadcasting Service (PBS) in 1985. PLUS was created to use the power and reach of broadcasting to issue a call to action for millions of adults to learn to read, write, or upgrade their basic skills. The extraordinary success of Project Literacy US passed all of our expectations. Hundreds of thousands of people had responded. PLUS, with its continuing messages on television and radio, had hit a national nerve. Barbara Bush had played a key role as the leader of the literacy movement. On this evening, she was to be honored by PLUS and the National Literacy Coalition.

Illiteracy, suddenly, was no longer America's hidden problem.

Hours after the Presidential election, the *National Literacy Honors* Dinner became the hottest ticket in Washington. The purpose of the dinner was to honor the outstanding national leader of the movement and a group of new learners representing the courageous adults who have stepped forward to overcome illiteracy. It had now also become a celebration of a political victory.

PLUS and the National Literacy Coalition hosted a reception for special guests just prior to the dinner. The President-Elect and

Mrs. Bush stood on one side of the room and greeted each of the guests as their photograph was taken. Among the notables were Vice President-Elect and Mrs. Quayle, Chief Justice Warren Burger, Senator Paul Simon, Congressman Tom Sawyer, Lee Iacocca, Ted Koppel, Secretary of Labor Ann McLaughlin, David Brinkley, Sam Donaldson, Governor Bill Clinton, Olympic athletes Evelyn Ashford and Terry Schroeder, Dr. Joy Brown, Governor Tom Kean, Dennis Weaver, Loretta Lynn and even Roone Arledge, the President of ABC News, along with a hundred others.

Peter Jennings, the managing editor and anchor of ABC's *World News Tonight*, was the master of ceremonies for the dinner. He was never better, setting a tone of dignity and yet warmth and humor for a special evening in Washington that, in truth, was one of a kind.

"We are here to remind ourselves, all of us, that the world we live in... runs... on... words." Peter said to start the evening.

The setting in the ballroom was spectacular. The tables were decorated with multicolored flowers accented by tiny dots of light, which the Bush people immediately latched onto as the "thousand points of lights" representing volunteers that the Vice President had referred to in his campaign speeches. It was a black tie affair, and the 150 tables were overflowing with dignitaries, educators, literacy service providers and Congressional leaders.

Loretta Lynn, in an elegant white gown, sang and then told the crowd, "I don't read that good today, but I read the Bible every night."

The since-departed Pearl Bailey was wonderful as she joked with a group of school children seated at the front of the stage and led them in singing an original piece written for the literacy movement called *Teach Me to Read*.

The most emotional moments came when the eighteen Learners of the Month from our PLUS campaign were each honored with a Literacy Honors Medal and a leather-bound commemorative book. Film clips with each of their stories, produced by Matt Zucker, ABC's talented director of PLUS, were shown on a huge screen. They were stories that really moved the audience.

Governors Clinton and Kean, whom I had met previously on several occasions, were the presenters of the awards to the new students. Each had a few words to say before making the individual presentations.

Bill Clinton, who had made his famous interminable keynote address at the Democratic Convention that previous summer, started his remarks with, "And in conclusion, I'd like to say...." The crowd roared.

When Tom Kean got up to speak, he looked over at Governor Clinton and said, "Are you sure you're through...." And the crowd roared again.

After Sherril Milnes of the Metropolitan Opera sang a spine-tingling rendition of *America, the Beautiful*, I, as the National Spokesperson for PLUS, was introduced to present the National Literacy Leadership Award. A raised platform had been placed at the back wall of the ballroom directly across from the stage and the podium where I was standing. An open aisle leading from the stage to the head table divided the room so that Mrs. Bush could walk to the stage to receive her award.

As I looked out, I could see the President-Elect and Mrs. Bush flanked by Jinx Crouch, the chairperson for the National Coalition for Literacy on one side and Peter Jennings on the other. The chairmen and their wives of the five sponsoring companies – Prudential Insurance Company of America, Bell South Corporation, the Olsten Corporation, Nabisco Brands, and Capital Cities/ ABC Inc. – were also seated at the head table.

I was surprised that I was not the least bit nervous as I approached the microphone.

> *All of us, each one of us, needs someone in our lives who cares,* I began. *The PLUS Learners of the Month and other learners across the country certainly illustrate that through their own experiences over the past few years. The recipient of the 1988 National Literacy Honors Award is a person who really cares. She cares about her country, our future, her family, and, very simply, she cares about people. She cared enough about the*

problem of illiteracy when it was America's hidden prob-
lem to step forward and do something about it. She cared
enough to travel to many places in our country to inspire
a more literate America.

I have been privileged to travel with her on some of
these occasions. I have seen the compassion and dedica-
tion and leadership and she has been instrumental in
bringing about a major literacy movement in the country.

I am privileged to present the recipient of the
National Literacy Honors Award, the wife of the Vice
President of the United States, soon to be the First Lady
of our land, and a dynamic, dedicated and caring
human being...Barbara Bush.

The ballroom erupted, not just with applause, but also with love. As Mrs. Bush walked down the center aisle, smiling and waving to people on both sides, the audience rose to its feet and kept applauding long after she reached the podium. I went down the five or six steps from the stage to greet her, and I took her arm to help her up the steps, but she wanted to go on her own, as much as to say, I'm young and active, I'll do it alone.

Mrs. Bush had her usual broad, warm smile as I presented her with a special *National Literacy Honors* Medallion, which, with rather shaky hands, I put around her neck and fastened in the back. J.T. Pace, son of a share cropper from South Carolina who had recently learned to read, joined me at the podium, and we presented the award: a specially designed writing box, made of dark mahogany with *National Literacy Honors* inscribed on a large gold scroll along with a special inscription to Mrs. Bush. Attached to one side of the top of the writing box was an antique quill. It was a beautiful and unusual award. After I presented it to Mrs. Bush and displayed it for the crowd, I kissed her on the check and offered congratulations from Project Literacy US and the National Coalition for Literacy.

She whispered to me, "Thank you. You're a nice man."

"How sweet it is," she said to the audience. "We could have been standing up here as losers tonight." There was another huge roar from the audience.

"I am really overwhelmed. It is really all of you who deserve the applause. You're all heroes to me," she said.

She quoted F. Scott Fitzgerald, "The essence of America is the willingness of heart." In her remarks she said that those people working to eradicate illiteracy were "shining examples of more than a thousand points of light," that her husband had talked about in his campaign.

"We are doing this for our children and our grandchildren," she said, "And for all of the generations of Americans to come." When she finished to a standing ovation, she asked the President-Elect to join her on the stage.

Again, there was a standing ovation and continuing loud applause from the audience as President-Elect Bush briskly walked to the podium.

"I feel lucky to be Barbara Bush's husband tonight," he said. "Literacy is the kind of freedom we should have for all Americans."

In his tribute to his wife he said, "Her drive and commitment is simply one of the thousand points of lights represented by all of you. You're it, all of you in this room, all of the literacy programs represented by all of you, all of the dedication, all the determination to help someone else."

I was sitting with Peter Jennings on the left side of the stage and when the President-Elect finished his remarks, he and Mrs. Bush came over to where we were now standing and shook hands. "Congratulations," he said. "This was a wonderful evening. You are doing so much."

Peter Jennings reintroduced Sherril Milnes and Loretta Lynn and they asked everyone to join in singing *The Battle Hymn of the Republic*. As I stood next to our new President and his gracious First Lady, singing together to a room full of leaders and great citizens from all across America, a chill went through my body. I was moved by the stirring words of the hymn but also by what the entire evening meant in my life. I had had many triumphs and tragedies. I had spent my entire professional career in broadcasting, starting out as an announcer, then a publicity writer, and finally as the president of the ABC Television Network for over fifteen years. I was a small-town boy standing on a stage in our nation's capital with the leaders of the free world and literacy was about to become an issue of national importance, spearheaded by the First Lady and fueled by an innovative television public service campaign.

As the music reached a crescendo, I had to fight back tears. I thought back to where it all began, back to those days on the farm in Moweaqua, Illinois when I listened to my grandfather, John Wheeler Adams, weave stories about Abraham Lincoln and the growth and beauty of America. I know he would have been inspired by this evening and I know he would have been proud.

Two

The Old Homestead

The smell of freshly cut alfalfa was delicious. It must have permeated most of Christian and Shelby counties. It was 1934 and it was late spring. As I trudged up the dirt road on my way home from school, my whole world was a half a mile down the road at my step-grandfather's farm, known throughout central Illinois as The Old Homestead. A Model T Ford rolled by leaving a small track of dust as it headed away from town. Then the familiar clopping of an approaching horse and buggy caused me to look up. I had to shield my eyes from the bright afternoon sun to see the stern-looking Amish couple from Stonington coming down the road. Looking neither right nor left, and not even acknowledging my presence, they moved on in their methodical way. I smiled to myself, knowing that even though the world was changing, some things would always remain the same.

Still shielding my eyes, I looked for the large white farmhouse off in the flat distance. For three years that house had been home for my sister and me, and I loved it. The Old Homestead was special.

The Southern colonial style house, constructed in 1854, featured four huge pillars fronting twelve rooms plus a screened-in summer kitchen with a smokehouse in the back. It had a formal living room that extended across the entire front of the house with oak floorboards and polished chestnut moldings dressing up all the doorways. At one end of the room was a ceiling-to-floor stone wood-burning fireplace. A magnificent curving chestnut staircase was at the opposite end, leading gracefully to the bedrooms on the second floor.

Outside, the huge front and side lawns were shaded with large oak and black walnut trees and splashed with an assortment of flowering bushes: large peonies, roses and azaleas. Along with its chicken coops, a three-seat outhouse, hog sheds, corn cribs and a buggy shed

7

that now housed a 1933 Chevrolet, the farm's most distinctive feature was a twenty-stall circular sale barn that was a stopping-off point in the cattle drives from Texas to Chicago or New York in the late eighteen hundreds. The land consisted of one square mile, 640 acres of rich Illinois soil.

The owner of The Old Homestead was a native son, perfectly suited to the central Illinois farm community: my grandfather, John Wheeler Adams. "Wheeler," as he was called, was widely known in those depression days as being "money poor, but rich in land and heart."

Wheeler Adams was proud that he was a direct descendant of the American pioneers John and John Quincy Adams. More importantly, he was a man of his time, strong in spirit, a worker of the soil. And he was a teacher. "A day's work is a day's pay," he would say. "Work hard and never give up. Life is a great game, so make yourself fit: be a poor loser but don't let the other fellow know it." These were lessons I learned from John Wheeler Adams that I carried with me throughout my life and career.

A horse and rider were coming in the distance as, again, I had to shield my gaze from the sun. The rider pulled up when he saw me.

"Hey, young fella, ain't you Wheeler's boy?" he asked in a friendly voice.

I recognized the man from playing on the Methodist church softball team. "No sir, I'm his grandson," I replied.

"Well, he's right proud of you," the man said. "Says you're gonna be a great lawyer one day."

I gazed up trying to get a closer look at the man but he was silhouetted against the sun. I paused before answering, "No sir, I want to be a radio announcer like Franz Lockes of the St. Louis Cardinals."

"He's a good one," the man chuckled as he started to ride off. "You be a good one, too. The best there is, hear?"

I nodded and continued to walk toward the big house with the outbuildings and the sale barn getting closer. I caught the hum of a tractor in the distance. It joined the zinging noise of the newly erected telephone lines along the road. I stopped a minute to breathe in the scene. The meadows were bright green, highlighted by the orange and gold of the afternoon sun. It was a moment my mind would revisit many times in the years to come. I saw Grandpa Adams in the front yard waving at me. I smiled. It was good to be home. I started to run for it was also time for *Jack Armstrong, the All-American Boy* on the radio.

As I drew closer I could sense that Grandpa Adams was out of sorts. He was half running towards me, yelling as he came.

"What in Sam Hill have you been up to?" the old man asked.

"Hey, Grandpa, what's the matter?"

Wheeler Adams looked at me closely. "The principal called Mother on that dadgum talk box and said you was a-swearin' at him. That don't sound like you. What's going on? I'm tellin' you, she's in there fit to be tied. She wants me to get a hickory switch!"

I wasn't surprised that Grandma was angry.

My mother, Corinne Saphronia Longenbaugh Duffy, was a nurse at Macon County Hospital in Decatur and only came to the farm on weekends, sometimes every other weekend. I would go with my sister, Marjorie Ann, sixteen months my senior and now a ripe nine years old – to visit mother at the hospital on occasion. We had a loving and caring relationship with our mother, but when we were on the farm we were under the strict and steady rule of Grandma Adams with Wheeler Adams trying to smooth out the rough spots.

Helen Jordan Longenbaugh Adams, in her mid-fifties, was a pillar of strength and propriety. She was a tall woman, carrying herself even taller than her five feet nine inches, and she was large. She had a full head of white hair in tight curls and wore her round steel rims close to her face. She had a beautifully modulated voice that came to fruition in the Methodist church choir. But when she looked at you with her very clear blue eyes, her head would nod slightly, the early effect of Parkinson's disease. Helen Adams was a person to be reckoned with.

She was widely acclaimed in the small community of Moweaqua. She had spent her entire life in the central Illinois farming area and was fiercely proud of her American heritage, which went back to the War of Independence on her father's side. Her great-grandfather, James Jordan, was a soldier in that war and an American pioneer. Helen had married her first husband, Joseph Edson Longenbaugh, in Moweaqua. They had six children: twins who died at birth, a son, and three daughters including my mother, Corinne. Joseph Longenbaugh, an esteemed citizen, an educator and the local newspaper editor, died of typhoid fever in his early forties.

Helen Adams was a survivor. After her husband's death, she became the editor of the local newspaper, *The Moweaqua News*. She was also the postmistress for the area; and she founded and fervently perpetuated the first Woman's Christian Temperance Union chapter in Christian County. The latter proved to be a most unfortunate circumstance for my father, Harold Francis Duffy, a dashing traveling shoe salesman who came from a hard-drinking, bingo playing, Irish Catholic family in La Salle-Peru, Illinois. The religious factor, Methodist versus High-Mass Catholic, resulted in a head-on collision for Harold Francis and his mother-in-law, only matched by their widely divergent views on the subject of alcohol, since Harold would have a toddy or two and even, on occasion, three or four more. Helen Adams' convictions were so rigid that Marjorie and I, and everyone else for that matter, were forbidden to use the word root BEER in her presence! I have often wondered how my grandmother would have tolerated the hard-drinking antics in the newspaper and broadcasting businesses several years later.

As my grandfather anxiously questioned me, I could feel Grandma's presence at the side porch screen door.

"We've been waiting for you to come from school," she said in a very calm and even voice.

Wheeler Adams put his arm around me and started walking away from the house towards the barn. "We're talkin'. We'll be there directly," he said over his shoulder.

The old man limped as he walked quickly, the lingering effect of having been kicked by horses and milking cows and cut by the hand plow. He had a habit of expectorating slightly every three or four seconds, and now this was accelerated by his concern.

"What did you do, boy? Maybe we can fix it. It just ain't like you to get into these here scra—"

"It wasn't a big thing, Grandpa. We were playing our last second-grade softball game and we wanted to win real bad because the captain of the other team was Bobby Cheatum. He's a bully. Remember I got into a fight with him last year?"

"Go on, go on. Where did that damned principal come into it?"

"Well, it was the last inning and the score was tied. I hit a double with two outs. My friend, Alan Ayres, came to the plate, and he's a good hitter."

"Good, good, you got a double. Good boy," Wheeler said, getting into the action of the game.

I paused and looked at the ground. "Alan hit a ground ball into right field and Bobby Cheatum was catching. I slid into home plate and knocked him over, and I saw him drop the ball. I thought we had won the game because I was safe."

I paused again. The old man was practically grabbing me. "So you won. Hey, you did good."

"No. They called the game because of bad language. The umpire called me out," I said quickly.

"What?" Grandpa was beside himself. "Well, who in Sam Hill was the umpire?"

"The principal, Mr. Sturges."

"Well, why did he stop the game?"

I took a deep breath. "Because I called him a blind son of a bitch."

The old man did a double take. He was stunned. He sprayed tobacco juice to the side. "Jumpin' Jesus, why would you do that? Well, we're in for it now...." his voice trailed off.

"I know I was wrong, Grandpa. But I was safe and I didn't think it was fair. Besides, I didn't think it was that bad. I hear you saying 'son of a bitch' all the time."

Wheeler Adams looked startled. He shook his head. "Well, don't say that too loud or I'll take a lickin' with you." He wiped off his chin and looked toward the house. "C'mon boy, let's go face the music."

The confrontation with Grandma Adams went better than I had expected. The hickory switch lay threateningly within easy reach as she spoke. I didn't believe she would really use it and she didn't. She did ask Grandpa to wash my mouth out with soap and he handled that later by having me put the tip of my tongue on the bar of Ivory soap. He reasoned that I "might get the runs" if I got too much soap in my mouth.

I came to attention when Grandma suggested that, as punishment, the annual trip to Sportsman's Park in St. Louis for a Cardinals baseball game be canceled. Now it was getting serious. Every summer for the past two years our uncle, Karl Longenbaugh, and my cousin, Scotty, would drive in Karl's 1930 Model A Ford to St. Louis and watch the beloved "Gas House Gang" – Dizzy and Paul Dean, Ducky Medwick, Pepper Martin, Frankie Frisch, Ripper Collins, Wild Bill Delancy and all the players on the "best team in all of major league baseball." Jay Hanna "Dizzy" Dean was my first athletic hero. Already at the age of eight I could see myself as a radio sports announcer. I was so struck with the game of baseball that I would give an out-loud play-by-play account of my own games hour after hour using cutout pictures of players from the various teams, placing them in their respective positions using the big Oriental rug in the West Room as the ball field. The Cardinals rarely lost a game in the Duffy league. Dizzy Dean would pitch most games and was incredibly undefeated, striking out most of the opposing hitters and even occasionally hitting a game-winning home run.

In the warmer weather, I would arrange a baseball diamond outside just to the west of the smokehouse and would play simulated games hour after hour, sometimes into the evening so that the back porch light would have to be turned on in order to finish the game. As the pitcher and all the fielders, I would wind up – or "stretch" as the occasion allowed – and throw a hard rubber ball against the stone base of the house. The wall was the "batter." A strike zone was drawn onto the stones and a ball that was "hit" back to me and caught on the fly was, of course, an out. A ball caught on the first bounce, thrown back to the wall and caught by the "first baseman" was a ground out. A ball hit out of reach was a single at a certain distance, a double a little further out in the yard, a triple if it was on the fly to the garden fence. If the ball was hit out of the park, over the wire fence into the vegetable garden, it was a home run. The only home runs ever hit in my Old Homestead League were by Cardinal players.

Unbeknown to the teams in play, Wheeler and Helen Adams would often stand quietly on the back porch and listen as I announced the games and would wink and hug each other as their beloved St. Louis Cardinals ran up a huge lead on the despised Chicago Cubs – even with the Cub ace, Lon Warneke, pitching. Grandma Adams interrupted one game when she let out a loud yell as Dizzy Dean hit a long ball homer into the lettuce patch and startled me so badly that I couldn't finish my "call" for the momentous occasion.

My sister, Marge, had outgrown dolls and started to notice boys in her classroom, thought that her little brother had lost his way, babbling about baseball with some imaginary figures on the lawn, and announced that the entire affair was "stupid." Her opinion did not impress or deter me, of course, since I knew that girls were not supposed to know about such important things as baseball and monumental figures like Dizzy and Paul Dean.

When I wasn't playing my own games, I would listen in the West Room through the static to Franz Lockes announce the Cardinal home games over station KMOX on the Philco radio, the only radio receiver in the house. And when the date was picked for the annual trip to St. Louis, I would literally count the days and be so excited I couldn't sleep until we were driving out the driveway.

So Grandma Adams' threatened punishment came as a shock. The thought of not going that summer of 1934 was unbearable.

Actually, Marge, bless her, saved the day. She walked into the kitchen just when things seemed to be at their most difficult and the St. Louis trip seemed to be seriously threatened. She had stayed after school and the principal had given her a note suggesting that our *parents* come to school the next day for a meeting to determine how to handle my "outrageous" conduct. The note Marge presented to our grandmother irritated Helen Adams considerably since Mr. Sturges knew that our mother was in Decatur and that Grandma Adams was responsible for our well being as well as our behavior. This lack of recognition of authority was well timed because it stopped all the talk about canceling the baseball trip.

Dutifully, Wheeler Adams drove us to school early the next morning. The school building, originally constructed in 1890 and added on to on three occasions as needs dictated and more farmers settled in the area, was known affectionately as the Little Red Schoolhouse. It was an American education original in contrast to today's sprawling, multi-classroom, modern school buildings with gymnasiums and auditoriums – some even with radio and television studios.

The meeting with Mr. Sturges, principal of Moweaqua Elementary and High School, was to the point. He suggested a student gathering at recess and a public apology and that the incident then be forgotten.

Mr. Sturges was a slight man in his mid-thirties with a receding hairline, thick horn-rimmed glasses and a perpetually serious, almost calamitous look on his face, with an intensity about him that made one want to move away rather quickly. On this bright May morning he had asked that, during the recess period, all classes in the elementary school line up to witness a special and serious occasion. Now the dreaded time had come, and Gerald Sturges stood stiffly and most officiously on the top of the steps in the front of the red brick schoolhouse. I stood next to him on the steps, staring solemnly down on my classmates and the other students who gaped back with a mixture of glee, curiosity and skepticism. I noticed my sister with her third-grade class trying to slip into the back row so she could avoid as much of the embarrassment as possible. And I also saw good old Grandpa Adams standing out by the road for moral support.

As I looked around at the mix of young faces staring up at me, I couldn't help but feel a sense of sadness for most of the kids. Many, especially the boys, were dressed poorly in faded bib overalls and frayed shirts and even went barefoot. Several of these children had lost their fathers or uncles in the horrible Moweaqua mine disaster on Christmas Eve in 1932 when an explosion of methane gas blew through the tunnels and killed fifty-four men. I remembered the eeriness of the torchlights off in the distance for three or four nights as families kept the vigil, praying for survivors. The depression had devastated this farm community, like most of the nation. Some kids came to school without enough to eat for lunch. One boy in particular brought only a small bag of prunes each day. I often shared my sandwich or cold fried chicken, prepared by Grandma Adams, with him. We soon became friends. Then one day the boy didn't come to school and I never saw him again. Some time later I learned that he had died of typhoid fever in the epidemic that killed a dozen or so kids in the Moweaqua area.

Nervously, Mr. Sturges started his little ceremony.

"Boys and girls, we had a rather unpleasant and distasteful incident at the end of the second-grade softball game yesterday afternoon. James Edson Duffy here indulged in some unsportsmanlike behavior and used profanity. It was serious enough that I was forced to call the game and award the victory and the class championship to Bobby Cheatum's team."

The principal's words were drowned out by a mixture of cheers and boos and nervous laughter. As he droned on, I thought about the entire incident and knew I was wrong, dead wrong, in swearing and questioning the voice of the principal. I had been certain I was safe at home because Bobby Cheatum had dropped the ball. I knew in my heart that we had won the game, but I also knew it wasn't worth this scene.

"...And so I have asked James Duffy to come before all of us and apologize and take his just punishment," the principal concluded as he looked down at Moweaqua's version of John Dillinger, who at that very time was America's Public Enemy Number One.

There was a distinct pause in the proceedings. I was flustered but not frightened. I looked up at the principal and then down at the students and finally off in the distance at Grandpa Adams. I could hear the faint sound of the laughter of the high school students playing ball on the other side of the building.

Finally I spoke in a soft voice. "I didn't mean to cause a problem. I'm sorry to my teammates and to you Mr. Sturges. I'm sorry."

The principal smiled slightly and said, "All right, now step forward and hold out both hands."

I was not expecting to be punished with the ruler, but it happened from time to time at the school so I raised my arms with the palms up. Mr. Sturges smartly smacked my hands a half a dozen times. I bit my lip and tears welled up in my eyes, but I was determined not to cry. It really hurt, but I managed to hold back the tears as I looked out toward my grandfather.

In today's society, I expect that the slapping of a youngster by the school principal would bring about law suits against the principal, the city and probably the Board of Education – plus coverage by every newspaper and radio and television station in the area. But in those depression-ridden days in rural America in the nineteen-thirties, punishment came with misdeeds and was accepted accordingly.

Apparently satisfied that his mission had been accomplished, Mr. Sturges dismissed the classes and told them they had ten more minutes for recess. The crisis was over. My classmates came over to lend their support and pat me on the back. One of them, Joy Smith, a pretty little girl who sat behind me in school, even kissed me on the cheek.

My hands were still smarting as I walked out to the road where Grandpa had been waiting.

"Are you all right, boy?" Wheeler asked as he knelt down and put his arm around me.

"I'm okay," I answered. I looked deep into the old man's blue eyes. "Did I embarrass you, Grandpa?"

"Naw, you can't embarrass an old goat like me. I was just concerned for you. We make a pretty good team and I just want you to understand all of this. You know you shouldn't have cussed at Mr. Sturges or anyone else. Even though I cuss from time to time, it don't make it right."

Wheeler Adams looked out at the road and then back at his grandson. He was silent for a moment. He could hear the school bell ring in the distance signifying that classes were about to resume.

"Jimmy, I want you to learn that there's a time for cussin' and a time for havin' fun and a time for lovin' and all like that. But that's more for when you're grown up. Swearin', really, is using words cause you don't know what other words to use. I didn't get to high school 'cause I had to work the fields when I was young. So I didn't get to learn many good words. But that don't have to happen to you. You can go on through school and go to college and learn all the right words, the good words, and be a great lawyer. You don't need to be cussin'... not much anyway." He squeezed my shoulder and patted me gently.

"Thanks, Grandpa," I said, and I hugged him.

"Let's take a look at those hands," Grandpa said as he turned the palms upright. "Lordy, he gave you a smack. Them welts have got to smart a bunch."

The old man gently folded my hands into his. His jaw muscles tightened as he looked back at the school. "Jimmy," he said. "That guy Sturges might not be blind but that's about all he ain't. That dumb sum of a bitc –"

"Grandpa!" I scolded. "That's how this whole thing started."

"I know," the old man laughed. "Anyway, I'm proud of you. And you should know this whole thing saved me some skin too."

"What do you mean?"

"Well, Mother has been raising holy Ned with me ever since Monday night when I drove her and them church cronies of hers to a service."

Wheeler Adams started to laugh. "Just before I got to the church, I spit some tobaccy juice out the window, and she was fit to be tied."

"I've seen you do that before, Grandpa."

"Yeah, but not with the window closed," he said starting to double over. "Ha, ha, ha, ho ho, ho.... What a mess. They couldn't get out of there fast enough....Anyway, she let up on me when you did your thing. So thanks."

Wheeler patted me on the shoulder again and limped toward his shiny black four-door Chevy sedan still laughing and quite ready to go home.

As I watched him go, I couldn't hold back the thought that John Wheeler Adams was a great man, even if he did think I was going to be a lawyer instead of a broadcaster. Grandpa Adams and Dizzy Dean were truly great men!

The summer of 1934 was a happy time for Marge and me. Cousins Helen Jean Woods and Scotty Longenbaugh from Jacksonville, Illinois came to stay at the farm for almost three weeks. It meant a lot of playtime in the circular barn and a lot of cowboy and Indian shoot-outs while galloping on broomsticks over the meadows and through the back woods. There was plenty of baseball, too. Scotty and I formed the two-man "Edson Boys" baseball team (Scott's middle name was also Edson). We invited town boys out to the farm to play us, and under our unique rules for two-man baseball, we beat them every time. The playtime didn't shorten our work time, however. All of the youngsters had chores, including helping to clean the house and weed the vegetable garden. We also helped Grandpa milk the cows and strain the milk in the early mornings and feed slop to the pigs in late afternoon. But in-between the appointed chores, we played and laughed and sang and told stories that were funny, even if there was some question as to their accuracy. We grew as children of the "thirties" in the wholesome and invigorating environment of the farm.

And, of course, a farm isn't a farm, unless there is a dog. I had my dog, Jack, a handsome silver German Shepherd who apparently ran away from the circus when it came to town, and he found his way to The Old Homestead. Jack did his chores with Grandpa Adams, rounding up the cattle and protecting the chickens and other animals from predators, but mostly he played with me and created my life-long love affair with the canine species. I have had several German Shepherds and a variety of breeds since, but I always remember Jack with great fondness.

For me the highlight of the summer was the trip to St. Louis to see my beloved Cardinals. Uncle Karl chose a day when Dizzy Dean was pitching, and both Scotty and I were awestruck and still wildly cheering as the "Great One" out-pitched the masterful Carl Hubbell of the New York Giants. The Cardinals won in a low-scoring game. It was a day to cherish forever, and we talked about it for years afterwards.

It was an important summer, also, for Marge and me, because we spent some needed time with our mother when she came to the farm on weekends and on two overnight visits to the Macon County

Hospital where she worked in Decatur. Corinne Duffy, "Code" as her peers affectionately called her, was a beautiful young woman with a peaches and cream complexion and an even disposition, who always seemed to see humor in the most trying of circumstances. Her sunny outlook made her a marvelous nurse since she cheered up everyone around her, especially the aged and incapacitated in the old folks' wing of the county hospital.

Corinne was well schooled, having attended Illinois Normal University in Bloomington for two years, the Arizona School of Music in Phoenix for a year and then having gone into nurse's training, she became a registered nurse in Decatur. It was here that she met and married the tall, dark, lean, and handsome Harold Francis Duffy. Harold was glib and filled with Irish charm, and he shared her sense of humor with his own teasing and subtle observations. Unfortunately, he also had the curse of the Irish, which had not been really noticeable in their courting days. Harold Francis, like his forbears, fancied the taste of liquor. It almost ended their young marriage after a series of unpleasant episodes at their lovely home in Mendota, Illinois. Harold would come home after a few days on the road while selling to shoe stores for the Hamilton Brown Company and create havoc with his drinking.

Marge and I, as toddlers, would hide in a closet and hug each other while our father chased our beloved mother through the house, cursing and threatening all sorts of dire happenings.

As is so often the case, Harold was a perfect gentleman when he was not touched by John Barleycorn. He was a hard worker with an intense drive to better himself and his family, and he was a loving father. He was protective of Marge as his very loved and only daughter. He introduced me to the world of sports, and together we listened to the Notre Dame football games on the radio on Saturday afternoons and shared stories about the immortal Knute Rockne and the All-American Irish running back, Frank Shakespeare. My dad also bought me a green jersey with Notre Dame and a large number seven emblazoned on the back, along with shoulder pads and a funny leather helmet. Neighbors would chuckle at a tow-headed four-year-old wearing the odd-shaped helmet with a football tucked under one arm, dancing back and forth down the lawn avoiding imaginary tacklers.

My father's drinking problem reached a pitch one particular weekend when Helen Adams visited us in Mendota. Harold came home from a trip absolutely fried and he and the mother-in-law of Woman's-Christian-Temperance-Union fame stood toe to toe, Helen Adams arguing the evil of liquor and Harold Francis slurringly defending the rights of man.

The whole scenario, rather comical in parts but still threatening, reached an unceremonious climax around midnight in the midst of a thunder and lightening storm when Harold got his handgun from the closet and ordered everyone but the children off the premises. I still remember my grandmother standing in the driving rain on the front porch with her arms thrust to the heavens, shouting in a quivering voice, "Our Father in Heaven, save us all. Save my daughter and her children."

The next morning Helen Adams was on her way back to Moweaqua and within a few days, Mother had packed her belongings and we were all on our way to the farm, where we would stay until we could get our lives straightened away.

Harold was filled with remorse and pleaded with his young wife not to leave him and ruin his life. He argued that he was really ill (which he was) and that he would take every step necessary to see that liquor never touched his lips again. But it was to no avail, and Marjorie Ann and I said good-bye to our dad, not knowing if we would ever see him again. Harold was devastated and in a week or so left Mendota and went back to the Duffy home in La Salle-Peru, Illinois. After palling around with his younger brothers, Charlie and Leo, for a few weeks and getting some sound advice from his brother, Edward, to straighten himself out, Harold set out to seek his fame and fortune selling shoes in Chicago.

Meanwhile, Corinne, who was very resilient and always looking on the optimistic side, made a pact with her mother and step-father that she would get a job and provide for the kids and help financially as much as possible. Both readily agreed, and Wheeler Adams took both us youngsters under his wing as if we were his very own.

Corinne did get a job as a nurse at the Macon County Hospital outside of Decatur. It was a pleasant place but during the era of the great depression, the poor got poorer. Many more needy and ill people came to the county facility than could be accommodated. Still, Corinne cheerfully plunged into her work, bought a used 1931 Ford roadster with a rumble seat and commuted to the farm on most weekends to be with her children.

As fate will often have it, the unpleasant circumstances that led to the separation of our parents and our estrangement from our father, brought us to an environment that was nourishing and supportive, one that would help establish a solid foundation of values and morality at a critical time in our young lives.

John Wheeler and Helen Adams were upstanding, religious, law-abiding and respected members of their community. They had a strong sense of spirituality, fundamental honesty and compassion that they would, by their very care, instill in their two youthful charges. They exemplified the steely fiber of giving and sharing that was so prevalent in rural and small-town America. If anyone in the town, or as far out as a horse or the old Chevy would take them, had a problem, Grandma and Grandpa would pitch in to help; whether it was rebuilding a barn, bringing food to neighbors who had a stretch of bad luck, or paying respects to a family when a member had died.

I will not forget one morning when my grandfather told Marge and me that we were all going over to Obid, just east of Moweaqua, to help out some neighbors. "Jed Workman died last night," Grandpa said. "You two go play with those grandkids, while Mother and I try and settle down the others."

Grandma saw to it that Grandpa drove us to church every Sunday. Marge and I would attend Sunday school in the basement of the old Methodist Church and giggle, as Grandmother's contralto would rise above all the other voices at hymn time during the services in the chapel above us. Importantly, our grandparents had time to spend with us, in the kitchen, working the fields, doing chores in the barn, or in the evenings sitting before a wood fire in the West Room.

The evenings became family time when Wheeler Adams would settle into his favorite rocker with the coal bucket, which he used as a spittoon, at his side (much to Helen Adams' dismay). He would tell stories of the prairie life in central Illinois at the turn of the century. He would describe living in a one-room log cabin out on the prairie where his mother had to sit in the doorway at night with a shotgun in her lap to keep the wolves away. Helen worked on her crochet quietly on the other side of the room as Wheeler would spin yarns about the great cattle drives from St. Louis and how his aunt's white slipper was stepped on by Abraham Lincoln at a dance in Springfield. Her only contribution would be an occasional, "Oh, Wheeler!" when she felt he was waxing a bit over-imaginative in his tales. But the old man would continue and fill the minds of two fascinated youngsters sitting at his feet with visions of history and people and events.

Marge and I were fortunate that the folks on my father's side of the family were also decent, loving and giving people. We would visit the family home in LaSalle-Peru for two or three weeks in the summer when things were quiet at The Old Homestead. Our mother gave her consent to the visit, even though she was still angry with our dad.

The Duffys were a large family with my grandfather, James, as the titular head of the family, but our grandmother, Anne, was the one who set the rules and settled most of the problems. There were four boys, Harold Francis, my father, the oldest; then Edward, Leo and Charlie. There were three daughters, Florence, a beautiful young woman who would pass away in her early thirties; Marie, and the youngest, Katherine. They were all good-hearted, fun-loving folks, all with a touch of the Irish charm and wit. All the boys, with the exception of Ed, but including Grandpa, acquired a hankering for whiskey as they grew into manhood. The Westclox Factory in Peru, a manufacturer of mid-priced clocks and watches, was the main source of jobs for the family, especially the girls, and most all of the family, with the exception of Grandma Duffy, became Westclox employees at one time or another.

During the depression years, the boys in the family drifted from one job to another, taking whatever might be available. My father worked on President Roosevelt's Civilian Conservation Corps (CCC), wielding a shovel and a wheelbarrow wherever needed. Grandpa tried to make a go of a cement block business in his garage behind the house, making blocks and selling them, but building was at a standstill in the early thirties, and Grandpa's too-frequent absences on drinking binges hindered what small chance of success the business had.

Two of the biggest days of the week on our visits to LaSalle were Wednesday nights for the bingo games in the basement of the church, and Sunday mornings for the interminable High Mass at the huge and almost frightening St. Patrick's Cathedral on Ninth Street.

Grandma Duffy was the Queen Bee at the bingo games, having a gay old time calling out the numbers and winning all kinds of glassware, blankets and sundries that her household desperately needed. Marge and I had fun too, getting caught up in the excitement of all of it. We couldn't talk about the bingo games when we returned to The Old Homestead since gambling was forbidden by the strict Methodist religion.

As a matter of fact, the entire religious scene became rather difficult, at least for me in my learning years. When Marge and I were in LaSalle, the Catholics would whisper, not directly to us but we would overhear, about the no fun, uptight Methodists in Moweaqua. When we were on the farm, we would overhear the rumors about the Catholic Monastery south of Moweaqua where the priests did strange things to young boys. We did not pay much attention to any of it, but as I grew older the idea of religious prejudices from those seeds that had been planted became distasteful. As youngsters, we would dutifully attend Sunday School at the Methodist Church in Moweaqua, then squirm and survive the long masses in LaSalle, trying to figure out why there was so much kneeling and standing.

Grandma Duffy was a loving and giving person and was very concerned about our welfare when we were in her charge. I almost undid most of that caring one morning when, in my grandmother's presence, I reached behind a cupboard and with a gag penny nail that slips under your finger, pulled my hand out screaming that I had put "a nail all the way through my finger."

Grandma Duffy turned pasty white and collapsed on the kitchen floor, out like a light. I was scared to death and had to run next door to get my Aunt Margaret, Ed's wife, to revive her. Grandma, of course, did forgive me after a deserved scolding. That was the last of my practical jokes.

Despite Grandpa Duffy's seeming shortcomings as a provider, I had great respect for him because he was so kind to everyone. He became widely known for feeding breakfast to the drifters who would come through on the Illinois Central Railroad. These people, mostly men, were called "hobos" in those days. I would get up with Grandpa at the break of dawn, and we would find eight or ten hobos quietly waiting near the back door. Grandpa would fry some eggs and bacon, or cornbread or what ever he had for them, and they would go sit on the curb in front of the house and eat, then wash their plates off at the water pump in back, thank my granddad and be gone.

"Why, do you do that, Grandpa?" I asked. "Isn't that a lot of work?"

"I do it because those people are hungry, and we have plenty of food for all of us," he replied.

Not a bad thought for the world we live in today where so many of us have so much, and so many more have so little.

Marge and I visited the Duffys on occasion, Marge more than I, even after we moved away from central Illinois, although not as often as we returned to The Old Homestead, because the latter had been our home.

At The Old Homestead, the medium of radio was our mind's eye and ear to the distant world. We all joined Grandpa Adams around the old Philco stand-up set and listened through the crackling static to news about a new government developing in Germany lead by a house painter named Adolph Hitler. We listened to reports about the desperate job situation in America, the exploits of Pretty Boy Floyd or Baby Face Nelson or the notorious John Dillinger and the crime wave running through the country. The crime reports became so vivid that Marge and I pictured a carload of gangsters wheeling into our driveway in the middle of the night. On certain nights we would listen to *Lum and Abner* with Grandpa. He thought Lum and Abner were the funniest people alive. He loved their homespun humor, and he would rock back and forth in his chair and just roar, and then expectorate a stream of tobacco juice into the center of the coal bucket. Grandma was fit to be tied.

Jack Armstrong, the All-American Boy, was my favorite show. I would listen every day after school and throughout the summer months and live the radio adventures of Jack and his sidekick, Billy, in my fantasies. But my all-time favorite on the radio was Franz Lockes and his descriptions of the Cardinals games. I remember the seventh game of the 1934 World Series when Dizzy Dean beat Schoolboy Rowe and the Detroit Tigers, 11 to 0. Grandma Adams and I cheered and hugged each other all through the game and for hours afterwards.

During the school year, Wheeler Adams would help us prepare for our schoolwork, especially Marge, since she was a year ahead of me. He would make homemade flash cards with equations or words on them. Hour after hour Marge would respond. Meanwhile, I sat alongside Marge and learned much about mathematics and words to the point where Wheeler would have arithmetic and spelling contests between the two of us. Grandma Adams made sure we read and read a lot, both aloud and in the privacy of our rooms. Our fare included the Bible, of course, but also such classics as *Little Women, The Call of the Wild*, and *The Little Shepherd from Kingdom Come*.

In later years, both Marge and I would come to realize our good fortune in spending our weaning years in such a wholesome, stable and giving environment as The Old Homestead. In the mid-nineteen thirties, America was just crawling out from a devastating depression that had severely changed the fortunes and lifestyles of millions of people. Franklin Delano Roosevelt had been elected by a landslide in 1932 and announced the New Deal, creating the "alphabet soup" of government agencies to fight the desperate situation that prevailed in America. Congress passed the Emergency Banking Act and the Reforestation Relief Act, establishing the Civilian Conservation Corps (CCC) and many other initiatives to put a nation back on its feet.

The Old Homestead was an oasis from all of the turmoil of the 1930s, providing a healthy environment and lots of good food and warmth. But it wasn't all easy. The winters were cold and snowy and blustery but Grandma Adams would bundle us up with extra sweaters, ear muffs, mufflers and mittens. We would walk the three-mile round trip to and from school every day, the only exception being when the snow got so deep that nobody could move and the school was closed. Those days were few, but became very special events because Grandpa Adams would build a huge fire in the West Room and the family would roast chestnuts and even play a game or two of Rook in the evenings.

The young people today with all their computer-based games, movies, television, cellular telephones and the Internet, would probably scoff at our simplistic upbringing. But for us it was wonderful.

The aura of the Adams' farm, with all of its sights and sounds and smells, would stay with us well into adulthood. The cawing of the crows in the trees at sundown on a summer evening was haunting; images of fireflies lighting up the entire lawn in the darkness as we chased after them to put them in a bottle to make our flashlights, indelible. The sounds of the wind in the trees, the hum of a distant tractor and the eerie whistle of the far-off train passing through, painted untold visions and dreams and became symbolic of a simple, yet euphoric time.

The memories of The Old Homestead are many and infectious: the many happy days playing in the haylofts and stalls in the sale barn; skinny dipping on warm afternoons when the water ran high in Flat Branch Creek: watching Grandpa Adams walking toward the barns in his uniquely gimping style, carrying buckets of feed and spitting every fifteen seconds or so as he grunted along. Perhaps the most permanent and meaningful memory is of the black walnut tree that stood magnificently just to the west of the house. It was a huge tree, hundreds of years old, that spread majestically in all directions. Grandpa would often take a few minutes before starting his chores to sit under the tree in his rocking chair, read his paper, and then nod off with his glasses falling off his nose. Marge and I, and whoever else was visiting, would quietly run in circles around his chair and buzz like flies to see if he would wake up. He knew what we were doing and occasionally would grunt and scare us away. The walnut tree became a symbol of security, support and contentment. I still have dreams, good and peaceful dreams, about that wonderful walnut tree. It became the genesis of an almost spiritual bond with trees for me.

In the early summer of 1935, when our mother was on the farm, we overheard our mother and grandparents talking, even arguing, about the possibility of her getting back together with our father. After a week or so, during one of my mother's weekend visits, we were told we would leave in mid-September and move with our mother to Chicago.

My parents had decided to reunite, since my father had regained his health and had made a solemn vow to keep liquor to a minimum. He had a job in Chicago and while the wage was small, it did provide a new beginning and an opportunity to bring the family back together.

Wheeler Adams helped pack up our belongings and early on a Saturday morning, drove us to the Illinois Central Railroad Station in Decatur some seventeen miles north of Moweaqua. Marge and I sat in the back with our mother and reflected on the life we had enjoyed at The Old Homestead. We wondered, with a natural sense of excitement, what life might hold for us in the large and rather frightening city of Chicago.

It was raining, and the paved road was slippery as Grandpa Adams gamely hung on to the wheel of his Chevy. Grandma Adams wailed hysterically when the dangerous contraption would slide off to the side. When we arrived at the station, my grandparents had tears in their eyes as they put an unhappy-looking threesome on the Illinois Central train.

Wheeler Adams pulled me off to the side and whispered to me softly, "Remember what I taught you, Jimmy. Work hard and never give up. Come and see me if you ever need anything. I'll take care of your dog and your pals. You take care of yourself and your mom and Marge."

The old man started to choke up a little, but he continued, squeezing my shoulder as he talked. "Learn everything you can and I'll look to the day when you plead your first case as a great lawyer. I'll be right here waitin' for ya. I'll see you next summer. You know I love you. Square your shoulders and go on now."

As the train chugged out of the station, I looked back at my grandparents and vowed I would return every chance I could. And I did, every summer vacation until my junior year in high school.

Three

The Greening Years

Chicago was much more than Mom, Marge and I had expected – not necessarily bad, just more. The city was big and noisy and dirty with papers blowing about on the busy streets. The big double-decker, open-top buses spewed huge clouds of exhaust as they stopped and started in the bumper-to-bumper traffic. There were people of all ages and shapes and sizes every place we looked, some even spoke in languages that we had never heard.

The newly pulled-together Duffy family lived in a two-room apartment on Lawrence Avenue and Sheridan Road. It was a very busy corner on the north side of Chicago. Mom would take Marge and me down to the intersection to watch the people bustling about and the traffic moving in and out, honking horns and creating havoc. We would walk two blocks west on Lawrence Avenue to the famous Aragon Ballroom where we learned the great bands of the era played live every Friday and Saturday night. These were the big-name bands lead by Claude Thornhill, Hal Kemp, Eddie Howard and even Lawrence Welk. It was a long way from the open spaces of the farm, or even the peaceful quiet of small-town LaSalle-Peru. But we were excited. And as a couple of unsophisticated kids, we learned something new every day and gradually became acclimatized to city life.

Our school situation was adequate at best. Mom enrolled us in an inner-city elementary school west of Sheridan Road and two blocks to the south. Since we were put into classes that had started the first of September and with inner-city kids, mostly Black, our classmates took great glee in having a couple of hicks – and *white* hicks at that – in their midst. Our already tenuous relationship was considerably worsened when one evening my mischievous sister dumped a bag of water from our fourth-story window on a bunch of kids who had been teasing us. The leaders of the group somehow blamed me and threatened to break my face if they ever caught up with me. It made for some speedy escapes and varying routes home from school for a week or two, but my face stayed intact and I gradually adjusted, all the while missing the sanctity of the farm.

My father worked in the shoe business for the Edison Brothers Company in downtown Chicago. He was an assistant manager of one of their stores featuring women's shoes. He took the bus into the Loop six days a week, so we didn't see much of him except Sundays, when we would take excursions to the parks or museums or to Lake Michigan beaches.

After three months, my mother found a larger apartment in a neighborhood that she felt would be more suitable for us. It was not that far from the Sheridan and Lawrence area, but it was in a neighborhood with more space between the smaller apartment buildings and even some private homes sprinkled in. Subsequently, Marge and I did very well in school and gained some new city friends who seemed a bit more active and worldly than our pals in Moweaqua. We were allowed to go with our friends to the movies on Saturday and Sunday afternoons at the Oriental Theater on the northwest side of town. Along with the short subjects like *Pride of the Marines* with Grant Withers, we saw classics like *The Professional Soldier* starring Victor McLaughlin. And we were introduced to show business when the Oriental Theater, along with others in Chicago, began presenting live stage shows featuring great performers like Jimmy Durante and introducing new talent such as a gorgeous blonde named Betty Grable, Harry James, the trumpet king, and a fabulous drummer named Buddy Rich. Marge and I were really taken with the magic of the live shows and produced some of our own skits and songs that we played for Mom and Dad, even neighbors, on occasion.

I got a part-time job for a few weeks as a door-to-door *Liberty Magazine* salesman. I made a few sales in the neighborhood, but made the mistake of accepting merchandise instead of the required nickel a copy. The sticks of Fan Tan gum and Bullseye candies were tasty but didn't satisfy the man who was in charge of the neighborhood route. All in all, the Duffy family started to settle in Chicago fairly well, and Marge and I almost started to like the big-city lifestyle, when suddenly we had to move on.

Being with the Edison Brothers Company proved to be a transient situation for Dad, and all of us, because we moved to a new location every year or so when Harold Francis transferred to new stores in new cities. I guess he was good at his job, because the executives at the headquarters in St. Louis kept moving him to places where their store was not doing well.

First we moved to Milwaukee, Wisconsin. We lived in a shared rental house off North Avenue next to an apartment building that was reputed to have been a hideout for Public Enemy Number One, John Dillinger.

Marge and I attended the elite Maryland Avenue public school on the east side of Milwaukee and did well socially and with our schoolwork, despite the lack of proper clothes and, on occasion, a scarcity of food. One time I was sent home from school because the soles of my shoes had worn through and my classmates were poking fun at me and creating a disturbance because the masking tape that my mother had used to hold the shoes together had unraveled. Toward the end of the month, before my father's paycheck would arrive, we would collect soda and beer bottles, and with the refunds, buy speckled apples and day-old bread. A big bowl of Spanish rice appeared on the dinner table two or three times a week. The German neighbors on occasion would bring in meals of bratwurst and sauerkraut.

In the fall of 1937, after some very happy days in Milwaukee, the family moved to Oak Park, Illinois. My father was named assistant manager of Burt's Shoe Store on Lake Street in the lovely suburb directly west of Chicago. We children entered Whittier Elementary School in a neat and pleasant neighborhood on the north side of Oak Park.

For Marge and me it was our fourth school in three years and it was difficult for us because we could not establish lasting friendships. At best, we would meet some nice kids and then have to leave. Moving so often did bring Marge and me much closer since we had to depend on each other in so many ways. And we learned to share. If Marge got a candy bar or I was fortunate enough to buy a soda, we would split it in half – I don't mean just in half, I mean precisely in half. It made for a very supportive relationship. With Mom's guidance, and despite my father's occasional drinking bouts, we had a loving atmosphere in our several homes.

There was more moving to come, but we all immediately liked Oak Park and wanted it to be our long-term home.

Oak Park is one of the most attractive suburbs in all of America. It was especially so in the late thirties and early forties, when, despite the effects of a war raging in Europe and the South Pacific, people's lifestyles seemed more controlled and less complicated. With its immaculate streets bordered by well-clipped lawns and lined with oak trees, some of which formed a perfect archway, Oak Park was the largest village in the world.

Marge and I liked the Whittier School and our new classmates immediately, even though I was embarrassed on my first day, when the more sophisticated suburban kids laughed at the knickers I was wearing when I was introduced to the class. My teacher, Miss Gent, sent a note home suggesting that my mother might want to get me some long pants, since the knee-length britches were long out of style in Oak Park. In today's public school environment, kids wear everything from blue jeans to short pants to clown suits and I suppose my knickers might be considered cool. But in those days, it was embarrassing. Still, the kids were friendly and helpful. It was an uplifting change from the adventures in the Chicago schools.

It was here, too, that I met my first love. She was an unusually pretty, blue-eyed blonde named Georgeane Bach. Despite being two inches taller than me, she seemed to like me and I determined that she was the nicest person I could ever meet. When we grew up we would surely be married. This young beauty dazzled me. To me, she was Alice Faye, Betty Grable and Lana Turner all wrapped up in one. Georgeane and I would pass love notes in class; it got to the point where Miss Gent intercepted one of the notes and decided to send a letter to my mother advising her that I might be in trouble with a severe case of puppy love.

My parents rented a small two-bedroom brick home close to the street on busy Chicago Avenue, about twelve blocks from downtown Oak Park where my father worked. The house was abutted on one side by a two-story building with a candy store in front. It was a long way from the rolling green prairies of Grandpa Adams' farm where Tom Mix and Buck Jones would often ride on their broomsticks until dusk.

I made up for the loss of the farm in other ways. The small living-room radio was a good companion. Bert Wilson and Bob Elson were the Chicago baseball announcers. I would often listen to the Chicago Cubs games, waiting breathlessly for my beloved Cardinals to come to town. Gradually, I began to root for the Cubs and became a full-fledged fan when my man, Dizzy Dean, was traded to Chicago in 1938. Reading, literature and writing were also important to me throughout my school years, an interest that had first been engendered by my grandparents. It was while I was still at elementary school that I became interested in the American Civil War. It was also at that time that I wrote my first book.

> *One of the most unusual friendships in the Jungle was that of Jerky the long necked giraffe and a little gray chattering squirrel who we shall call Mike. Now Mike was a very busy little fellow gathering nuts as he chattered and jumped from limb to limb....*

So began the story *A True Friend in Uncle Bim's Animal Tales* by James E. Duffy, with illustrations by James E. Duffy. The cover bore the legend: "The Duffy Publishing Company, Chicago, Illinois," and "Made in the U. S. A." Inside there was a dedication: "To my Mother and Father in memory of my happy childhood."

On the back of the little book my mother wrote, "Jim wrote this at age 11. His first dream was to become a writer. As you can see from the front of the book he figured he'd have to have his own publishing company to make that dream come true. He always was a realist."

Georgeane was, in a way, the cause of my first genuine fistfight. In the eighth grade, George Hunt, a former Whittier student, now in his first year of high school, had started hanging around Georgeane. He made it known that I was to stay away from his "girl friend" and that the next time he saw me, he was going to beat me up.

Late one afternoon, after a softball game in the schoolyard, I saw George Hunt leaning against a tree in front of the school. I walked rather quickly down Augusta Boulevard toward my home, not anxious for trouble, since Hunt, while not bigger, was older and had a reputation of being a tough guy.

"Hey, you," he yelled just as I reached the front of the north Oak Park Fire House. "I've been looking for you." And with that he tackled me and started pummeling me with his fists.

I tried to protect myself as best I could. Finally I struggled to my feet, and, with my eyes closed, started swinging back as hard as I could. After I couldn't feel any of his blows landing on me, I opened my eyes. George Hunt, with blood on his cheeks, stood with his arms at his sides.

"I hope that teaches you a lesson," he said halfheartedly.

The next day, Georgeane told me she was proud of me for defending her, and she kissed me on my black-and-blue cheek.

After graduating from Whittier in June of 1940, I spent the summer at The Old Homestead. Grandpa and Grandma Adams seemed to be getting much older, but they were still active on the farm and in the community. It was always a thrill to go back to where I had spent so much of my childhood. However, I was heartbroken during this visit when Grandpa told me that Jack, my German Shepherd, suddenly disappeared after the circus had been in Moweaqua a couple of weeks before my visit. Maybe it was the same circus that he had escaped from to be my best friend. It took me months to get over the loss of my pal.

In the fall, I entered Oak Park River Forest High School with the rest of my Whittier classmates, including Georgeane Bach. It was a rather overwhelming experience suddenly being thrust into a school with almost four thousand students. I enjoyed my occasional walks to school with Georgeane. She became very popular and, much to my chagrin was constantly being asked on dates by upper classmen. She remained very friendly and helpful and would always ask me to dance at the Coke Dances after the football or basketball games.

It was during this time that I got my first lecture on the birds and the bees from my father. One summer afternoon my friend,

Don Madsen, and I rode our bikes down to Ridgeland Commons, a park in central Oak Park, to watch a softball game. When the game was over and we were about to leave, I noticed my mother, father and Marge sitting in "Old Nell," our 1937 Oldsmobile obviously looking for me. Mom and Dad had long unhappy faces, and I was certain there had been some kind of a tragedy.

"Can you take Jim's bike home?" my father said to Don Madsen. "Get in the car," he said to me rather sternly. Nobody, not even Marge, said a word on the drive home.

When we got home, Dad said he wanted to have a talk with me on the front steps. After flustering around for a few minutes, he said, "Your mother found a prophylactic in your pants pocket. What's going on?"

"A what?" I asked.

"A prophylactic. A rubber." he said. "Have you been fooling around with Georgeane?"

Boy, don't I wish, I thought. I explained that my second cousin, Harold Giles, who was a junior in high school, had given it to me when I visited Moweaqua earlier in the summer. He had suggested I keep it in my wallet because a time would come when I might need it. The time had not come, but it did make a neat tell-tale ring in my wallet.

My dad seemed relieved. "Whenever you feel that urge, ah, you know, ah Jim," he stammered. "Run around the block and get rid of the energy, or go down in the basement and hit the punching bag for awhile."

"Okay, Dad, I will," I said. "Thanks." We shook hands and that was that.

My father was basically a very nice man. He was a hard worker, sympathetic to others' needs and an extraordinary salesman. He was also fun with a teasing, wry sense of humor. In his earlier days, he was known to sing a few Irish ditties after a couple of drinks, although he did not have a particularly good voice. Mom would be love struck with his rendition of *On The Rocky Road To Dublin*. Then, a few drinks later, an argument would break out. My dad's drinking pattern, then and in later years, was unusual and disturbing. There is little question that he was what we now call an alcoholic. In those days we didn't know what the word meant. We always knew when he was getting snockered. First, Mom would get upset, then, when he raised his glass, his pinkie finger would stand out, extended upward. A strange, faraway look would come over his face, and an argument with Mom would usually ensue. Finally, Harold Francis would call his mother in LaSalle and tell her how much he loved her. It was only in later years that I realized how Irish he really was.

I am fascinated to this day about the diverse reactions to my dad's drinking. My mother, despite all of her great humor, would be angry and hurt. Her mother, my grandmother Adams, would have just as soon put him in jail. His mother, my grandmother Duffy, would want to put him to bed with the admonition "boys will be boys." My own feeling was that I wished the drinking didn't cause so many problems. While he disappointed and embarrassed us at times, I still loved him because he was my dad.

My freshman year was an interesting one at Oak Park. I did only average work in my studies, but I played intramural sports and gained some wonderful new friends: Bob Loeber, Bill Farber, Phil Young, Ray Zumbrook and Joe Mikolas, among others, would become life-long friends. And I also maintained a very solid relationship with Georgeane. Then, we moved again. This time back to Milwaukee in 1941, where we lived in a lovely, small rented house on North Oakland Avenue. I entered East Division (Riverside) High School for my sophomore year. Perhaps it was the frequency of the moves that gave me the idea that I had seen enough of life to justify setting forth an account of my existence to date. Whatever the reason, at the age of fifteen, I felt I had lived long enough to write my autobiography.

*The early sun was shining brightly on Decatur, Illinois. It was a very crisp, cool morning in April when I was born at five o'clock in St. Mary's hospital...*begin the story. Milking cows at the crack of dawn in Moweaqua, my father's illness, moving here and there, basketball, baseball and volleyball, best friends at school, strep throat and fevers of 104°...until I felt I had covered the entirety of my existence. It ended, *from that day on April 2, 1926 until this day in June, I feel that*

I have only seen a portion of the great adventures in life. And like all youth, I am anxious to continue it.

My interest in radio stayed with me. My dad and I would listen to the Green Bay Packers football games and other sporting events. It intensified on Sunday, December 7, 1941, when the game between the Chicago Bears and the Packers was interrupted with news bulletins that the Japanese had bombed Pearl Harbor. Our country was being attacked. Our family, huddled close to the radio, listened late into the night to the continuing news reports about the destruction in Hawaii. The next day we listened somberly as President Roosevelt's voice came over the small receiver with his declaration of war on the Japanese Empire.

It was also while we were in Milwaukee that I had my first taste of professional journalism. In the summer of 1942, at age sixteen, I took a job as a copy boy and cub reporter at the Milwaukee *Sentinel* morning newspaper, working on the 6 PM to 2 AM shift.

I had a little desk in the copy room where the Associated Press and United Press International machines chattered constantly as the seemingly endless streams of news from around the world would come down the "wire." The ticker might be from UPI Paris with a story about the war, or something from London or New York. I used to stand over the machine and tear these off, reading them as they came in. I would edit them to some degree if they were not readable or if there were grammatical mistakes. Then, I would distribute them to the proper desks.

Very young and very impressionable, I had an opportunity to see the different elements of the newspaper, including being able to watch the enormous presses. I would sit there fascinated as the freshly inked papers rolled off and were bound, ready to be sent out in trucks for early morning distribution.

On occasion I would go along with a senior reporter to City Hall and then be assigned to write three or four paragraphs on the story that we had picked up: robbery or murder, or whatever it was. Being an avid sports fan, this job gave me a chance to meet the sports columnists who were heroes to me. Red Thisted was one of them. He was an older fellow, probably in his late forties, and was widely quoted. It fascinated me that these journalists were mostly heavy drinkers and would come back from dinner smelling of whiskey, but would sit and write and manage to meet their deadlines. Bill Tracy, the city editor, who was a very articulate, fast-moving man, took the time to tutor me, because I did have an interest in writing and he wanted me to stay on.

I got a paycheck of something like $70 for a forty-hour week. Out of this I had to buy my own clothes, and the rest went to help the family. While most of my fifteen- or sixteen-year-old friends were shooting baskets or hanging out, I was learning a lot about things that I wouldn't otherwise have come in contact with, including the progress of the war and the process of government from my visits to City Hall.

The *Sentinel* building also housed its sister communications outlet, radio station WISN. When I got a break from my copy boy duties, I would visit the radio studios and watch in awe as a newscaster delivered the evening news, barking into a circular microphone in the small, enclosed studio. As I looked through the glass, I fantasized about what it would be like to be on the air and talk to hundreds – maybe even thousands – of people all at the same time. It took me back to The Old Homestead League at Grandpa Adams'.

When my shift ended at two o'clock in the morning, I would take the streetcar home. That taught me a few things too. I would look out and see the brownstones and the old houses along Oakland Avenue that represented the German and Polish heritage in Milwaukee. On the way, I became fascinated with the people – not many, because it was late – who got on my streetcar. I especially remember one elderly Black fellow. I don't know where he was going, but he wasn't in good shape, probably from alcohol. He sat slumped, and looked depressed and dejected. He looked over at me once and smiled, wanting to strike up a conversation, but he really wasn't capable of it. I remember wondering how a person could get to that stage in life. This was the forties and there was segregation in Milwaukee – not like in Birmingham, but segregation nevertheless. I knew that he was underprivileged and didn't have the opportunities that I did. It left an impression on me.

It was also the summer of 1942 when I experienced real heartbreak in my young life. My mother got word that a motorboat in the Fox River in Illinois had killed Georgeane Bach near her parents' summer home. I was devastated. My parents and I went to the funeral in Oak Park. When I returned home, a letter arrived that Georgeane had written to me just before she was killed. She told me that she had broken up with a boyfriend, really missed me, and was looking forward to a visit in Milwaukee. I kept that letter. It took me several years to put Georgeane Bach's place in my life into perspective.

As difficult as it had been to leave Oak Park in 1941, it was equally difficult for me to return when my father was transferred back from Milwaukee in the summer of 1943. Marge and I had a very special time during our two years in Milwaukee, especially at East Division High School. Marge had become extremely popular for she had blossomed into a dark-haired, blue-eyed Irish beauty and was much in demand among her classmates, especially the young men, who kept our phone ringing most evenings. I had found many new friends and was especially thrilled to have played on the varsity basketball team for two years.

When I returned to Oak Park High School after Labor Day in 1943, I reflected back on my freshman year at this institution which had seemed so large and threatening at the time. The school had some 3,800 students, and for a country boy from Moweaqua, it was a little overwhelming. I had gone out for the freshmen basketball team with some eighty other hopefuls, but I was only five feet six inches, and despite my developing ability to shoot and score, I had been cut in the second round, much to my disappointment. In Milwaukee, however, I had grown some four inches the summer of my sophomore year and made the varsity team. I played a lot of basketball in my junior year.

Now, as I stood in front of the school observing the students of OPRFHS (Oak Park River Forest High School), the "doopers" (dear old Oak Parkers), hustling up the two curving stairways leading to the front door for the first day of school, I felt a sense of excitement, but not intimidation. I was, after all, a senior with some rank and privilege. And having grown taller – I was now six feet two inches –

I was hopeful of a good basketball season as an Oak Park "Huskie," and a successful and fun-filled senior year. I still hadn't gotten over that Georgeane wasn't there, but I knew life had to go on.

I had been warned by several of my friends that it would be very difficult to make the varsity basketball team since most of the team had played through the previous three seasons and would be hard to supplant. Moreover, ten of the fifteen-man squad also played football and were recognized as the jocks by the students and the coaches.

When the call for fall basketball tryouts was issued, I was the first one in line. Henry Scott, the varsity coach, greeted me with some enthusiasm. Apparently, my transfer records showed that I had played basketball, and Scotty was very aware of what I had done, or at least the promise of what I might do.

During the course of the fall I was thrilled to work out with others who had played the previous year and a couple of other transfer students. The large Oak Park field house with its raised hardwood floor in the center of an oval dirt track resonated every afternoon with bouncing basketballs and the shouts and grunts from hard-fought scrimmages. Coach Scott was very encouraging, complimenting me on three or four occasions on my drive and footwork and my ability to score.

"You've had some good training, Duff," he said. "Who was your coach in Milwaukee?"

"John Hafey," I told him.

"Well, he taught you well," he said. "Good fundamentals."

My head was in the clouds. I knew I could play with the Oak Park varsity. The local paper, *The Oak Leaves*, had a couple of columns about how Coach Scott could put a "strong team on the court without even using his regulars from last year. Some new faces, including Jim Duffy, a high-scoring forward from Milwaukee...has brought a new feeling of excitement...."

Then football season came to a close and the "veterans" joined the practices. After a couple of weeks, it became obvious that I was not going to get much playing time, since Scotty was trying to whip his late comers, his regulars, into playing shape for the first game late in December.

The only media coverage for the regular season games was through the local *Oak Leaves* or maybe a line in the Chicago papers. Unlike today, there was no radio coverage since Oak Park did not have a radio station. Television was unheard of. Although, I played well in the scrimmages, I wasn't surprised when Scotty called me in after practice late one afternoon and gave me the bad news.

"Duff, I think you can be a heck of a ball player, but I think you need to play regularly. With this squad, you aren't going to get any time at all. I'm going to send you down to the junior varsity where you will get to play and you can have some fun. Who knows, if you really get hot and prove yourself, we may call you up later in the season."

I was disappointed, but I wasn't crushed. I could see it coming. I thought Coach Scott had been very fair to me. What I thought was unfair was that I could be back in Milwaukee and maybe, just maybe, leading the team to a city championship. But, as Grandpa Adams used to say, you deal with what is. I resolved to move ahead and star on the jayvees and get the opportunity to play and prove my talent against the varsity in scrimmages.

Some forty young men went out for the junior varsity, including those who were cut from the varsity. My first day of practice, I met the new coach, Russ Foug. He was a science teacher and knew very little about the fundamentals of basketball beyond putting the ball in the hoop. In the next two weeks, I was confident that I had played very well in the scrimmages, showing some decent passing and scoring often.

When the list was posted for the jayvee fifteen-man squad, I hardly bothered to look since I was sure I had made the team and felt I would undoubtedly be among the starting five.

My eyes glazed over when I could not find my name as I read down the list. I read it over four times. I couldn't believe it. There had to be a mistake. The realization suddenly overwhelmed me. Russ Foug had cut me. Now I was crushed. Dick Hemingsen, who had made the squad, saw the look on my face, "Jesus, Duff, you've been screwed," he said.

I dashed back into the locker room and approached the coach.

"Mr. Foug," I stammered. "My name is not on that list. I don't understand."

"Oh, yes, Duffy," he said. He waited for a long moment. "I'm sorry. You seem to be a good enough player, but something is missing. I thought others better deserved a place on the team."

"Missing? What's missing? I don't...." I tried to respond, but he had turned away and was walking out of the locker room. I sat stunned in front of my locker. I had failed! How could I tell my folks?

I wanted to put my head in my hands and cry. But I couldn't. I finally cleaned out my locker and, with my spirits lower than the bag I was carrying, started the walk home. It was dark outside. It was a long, slow and painful journey home.

My father was working, as he always seemed to be, but when I got home, my mother listened patiently as I told her what happened. I have never been much for tears, but that night, I cried long and hard because I was so convinced I was a good basketball player.

My mother finally said, "Well, Jim, if you believe in it that much, go in and see the coach again and tell him exactly what you think and why you feel so strongly about it."

And somewhere in the back of my head, Grandpa Adams' farm-spun credo came back to me: "Never give up."

The next morning I went in to see Mr. Foug in his office, and in a polite but determined way, told him that I sincerely believed that I could play rings around any player on that team if only given a chance. I asked him to give me that chance.

Foug was a stoic sort. He looked at me for what seemed like a very long time. Then he said slowly, "All right, if you have the courage to come in here and ask for what you want, then here's what I'll do. You can come and practice with us for the next two weeks, but you'll have to wear your gym suit. I'm going to pass out the uniforms tonight and there are only fifteen. I hope you won't be embarrassed. I'm willing to give it a try if you want it that badly."

I thanked Mr. Foug profusely and could hardly wait for practice. I was more determined than embarrassed when I took the court that afternoon and was met with a lot of good-natured kidding about my pasty white gym outfit while the rest of the team donned their orange and blue practice uniforms. Still, I sensed a feeling of respect since I had played with and against each player during the fall practices.

Little by little in the next two weeks, I moved up in the scrimmages, getting a little more playing time each day. One day during the second week, we had a scrimmage with the varsity team and I scored often, still racing around in my white gym suit.

I did not dress for the first game. But the next week, a kid dropped off the team and I was issued a uniform. I made the trip for a game with Maine Township High School on the following Saturday.

Maine scored early on our starters, and in the middle of the first half, Russ Foug told me to go in at forward. On the first play, I scored on a pass-and-cut out-of-bounds play and went on to be the game's leading scorer. After that, I started every game and led the team in scoring for the season.

In one game at Morton (Berwyn, Il.) High School, I stole the ball at mid-court and had a wide-open lay-up when I spotted Hemingsen, my teammate, streaking down the far side. I gave him a perfect bounce pass and he scored. The guys on our bench went berserk.

Later, Billy Farber, my friend and teammate, said, "That's great stuff, Jimmy. The guys will love ya for that kind of team play."

When the season was almost over, Scotty came over to me after a game and congratulated me and asked me if I wanted to come up to the varsity for the last couple of games. I told him that I really didn't. I wanted to stay with my own team.

On the Friday before the last game, Coach Foug asked the team members to vote for a team captain (there had not been an official captain for the season). You can imagine how I felt when he called the team around him and announced, "It gives me a very special pleasure to tell you that you have voted Jim Duffy as captain of your team. I think he has made all of us very proud this season."

In truth, being the captain of a junior varsity basketball team is certainly not very distinguishing in the scheme of life's many challenges. But it was very important to me because it was a defining moment in my life. In retrospect, I wonder what would have happened had I not gone back and asked for a second chance. I know my confidence would have been shattered and my self-esteem shaken. The important thing to me was I did not give up. I knew I never, ever would give up on myself. It was a lesson learned that I tell people, especially young people, whenever I feel it is appropriate. It was useful for me in my later work with Project Literacy US and the many people I met who had limited skills. It is never too late to learn to read. Never give up! It had so many applications.

The remainder of my school year was most enjoyable and even rewarding. I became adept at public speaking in my speech classes and even came to hold my own with acknowledged academic types in class debates. My simulated radio broadcasts from my childhood gave me a sense of confidence and established a foundation of sorts. My interest in literature, going back to my grandmother's training back on the farm, brought surprising recognition.

The school's English students were advised that as part of our assignment for our final senior class essays, we could write about Mark Twain and his works. The school had been notified that one, but only one, student essay, selected by the English Department faculty, could be submitted to the National Mark Twain Essay Contest.

The idea of writing about Mark Twain and the Mississippi River appealed to me since I had read a lot of Samuel Clemens' books and I saw the adventures of Tom Sawyer, Huckleberry Finn and Becky Thatcher as being akin to my experiences with my cousin Scotty on Flat Branch (about one hundredth the size of the Mississippi River, but nevertheless adventuresome). And I had been fascinated with the Mississippi River and its power and mystery ever since the times Uncle Karl, Scotty and I would drive across the bridge to St. Louis for the Cardinals baseball games.

I reflected a great deal on the compassion of Clemens' works as I sat at the dining room table in our apartment one night. I thought about the young people in a simpler time, working the magic of the mighty river and I started to write:

> *The call of 'Mark Twain, Mark Twain' floated and*
> *echoed across the wide muddy river as the barges and*
> *riverboats and the paddle wheelers moved slowly, even*

rhythmically down the waters of the mightiest river in America. The Mississippi was alluring, dark and moody, swirling and shifting, always moving southward to the great ports before it. It was here that Samuel Langhorne Clemens, better known as Mark Twain, painted the word pictures of his America, playful and tempting, to a nation that had been ravaged by a civil war.

Of all of the writers who emerged from that war with a promise for a new America, Mark Twain is the most remembered and most engaging with his amusing and picturesque stories of life on the Mississippi. The adventures of Tom Sawyer and Becky Thatcher and Huckleberry Finn and his friend, Jim, became our stories and our dreams, conjuring up visions of the mighty river and its beckoning to sail on and on to ports unknown. His wonderful characters taught us the meaning of friendship and brotherhood long before it was approachable. Black and white. White and Black.

Mark Twain's greatness came because he was an accurate and clear-headed observer who understood what he saw and knew how to relate his impressions with humor and compassion. And those observations and his writings have become timeless.

I went on to briefly describe Mark Twain's writings about the new western frontier and how his works had touched my life. I related my awe and affection for the mighty Mississippi River and how it symbolized our youthful visions of America – *rugged, always moving, and filled with beauty and mystery.*

It was a four-page piece. I had no illusions about my essay being selected to represent the school, even though I was pleased with it and felt it accurately described my feelings. I was surprised when one of the English teachers announced to our class that Richard Quetsch's (he was a straight-A student) had been selected for the national contest, but that they also decided to send mine as an alternate, despite the fact that that was against the rules.

I was even more surprised a couple of weeks later when it was announced that I was a winner in the National Mark Twain Essay Contest. I would like to say I was THE winner, but I'm not sure that only one prize was awarded. I do know that I was presented with a beautiful, leather-bound set of Mark Twain's books, was honored in front of the student body, and became the object of many approving looks and comments from members of the faculty.

It was a great way to enter my graduation ceremonies. Now all I had to worry about was going into military service since the war in Europe and the Pacific was still raging. I had volunteered for the Army Air Corps in March, 1944. I would be inducted shortly after graduation. I had kept up with war news through the newspaper and radio reports. Edward R. Murrow and the CBS news team from London were exceptionally articulate and professional and further whetted my ambition to get into journalism and broadcasting.

Meanwhile, during the few weeks after graduating, and before I was inducted, I worked at the Mars Candy Company, located just north of Oak Park. I wore a white uniform with a white cap and gloves and was stationed on the side of a circular metal track that, every minute or so, would push out long wooden boards filled with piles of rejected candy bars. Out of habit, I would occasionally reach out and eat a candy bar. It became so frequent, that by the end of the day, I would be nauseated. It got to the point in going to work, when I got off the bus two blocks from the factory, I could smell the sweetness of the sugar and syrup and almost became sick. I was saved by Uncle Sam.

Four

The Air Corps and College Years

On July 9, 1944 my folks and Marge drove me to the Fort Sheridan Army Base just north of Chicago, and, after tear-filled good-byes, dropped me off at the imposing, large iron gates. My great saga of World War II was under way. I knew absolutely no one in my indoctrination group, although I did meet a kid with a good sense of humor named Jack Drennan from Berwyn, Illinois, who helped keep my spirits up with his rebellious but innocent shenanigans. On the second day, Drennan was in front of me in a long line of nervous young men waiting to have blood tests. When Drennan stepped up for his turn at the needle, he started to giggle and then did a beautiful swan dive and passed out on the floor. The medical officers bumped into each other trying to get to Drennan's prone body, until Jack opened one eye and said mischievously, "Is it all over?" The place broke out in laughter as the medical people pulled Drennan to his feet and mumbled something about "insubordination" and "disciplinary measures." But even they started to smile when they looked at Drennan's pale innocent face and round blue eyes between his jug ears. It would be one of many incidents that Drennan would pull on Uncle Sam's Army during the next few months. And I was almost always on the scene, if not actively involved in the action. It was Drennan and Duffy – he was always next to me in line, giggling, farting, whistling, whatever, wherever we went for a year and a half until we went to Sheppard Field, Texas, where Drennan became one of the worst drill instructors in the history of the military.

After ten days of indoctrination at Fort Sheridan, we were shipped to Amarillo, Texas Air Corps Base for our basic training. Our flight instructor was a bone-tough professional soldier named Otis Van Meter who took no lip or nonsense from anyone, especially from his troops. At the end of our training, however, he did accept a rather substantial collection of five-dollar bills from his "boys." Private (he kept getting busted from Sergeant) Van Meter made it known that the funds were for his poor, lil' ol' sick mother back in Kentucky. We learned later that at the end of every one of Van Meter's thirteen-week training sessions, the instructor's "lil' ol' mother" grew very ill and was in need of funds.

We had more than three battle-simulated, Van-Meter-beaten, months at Amarillo Air Corps Base, and we became soldiers. Despite our bitching behind his back and our secret ambitions to punch him out, we all learned to respect Otis Van Meter. He taught us well, and we took great pride in our precision marching drills on Saturday morning inspections on the parade field in front of other flight squadrons and the base officers.

In mid-October of 1944, we were suddenly put on a troop train and headed to an unknown destination, south and west of Amarillo. It turned out to be the quiet town of Hobbs in the southeast corner of New Mexico, not far from the famous Carlsbad Caverns. Prior to our arrival, the Airs Corps Base at Hobbs did not exist. We became its first occupants, as the engineers resurfaced and lengthened a small landing field in the sandy desert and erected barracks, officers' quarters, a PX (our military general store), a field hospital and all the accouterments that go along with a first-class air base in war time.

The town of Hobbs, as I recall, was a hot and dry desert crossroads with some small stores, a barbershop, a state liquor store and some sleepy-looking, dirt-covered cowboys wandering around. There was a USO Club formed for the servicemen, and it became, far and away, the classiest spot in town. The rest of Hobbs consisted of a small motion picture house, some old cars on the dusty streets, and a lot of abandoned machinery and used tires lying around for local color. If I recall, there was a 5,000-watt radio station in the town, but the southwest Texas country music it played was so bad, that, despite my love for radio, I couldn't listen. I don't think anyone else in the area did either. The town had so little to offer that, after we had established the base, the townsfolk came in droves to the Air Corps Mess Hall for Sunday brunch. It was the highlight of their week.

We had now officially become aviation cadets, and Hobbs was to provide the second phase of our flight training and teach us about airplanes.

It was a rather fascinating experience since a good many of the planes that we were assigned to were Flying Fortress B-17 bombers that had been returned to the States after flying missions overseas. My assigned plane was the famed *Pistol Packin' Mama*, which had flown scores of raids over Germany in the early years of the war. I was in training to become a bombardier since I had been disqualified from pilot's training due to a minor operation. The truth of the matter is I had my right breast removed because of a non-malignant tumor when I was fifteen years old and that surgical removal brought me immediate fame as "Johnny One Tit." As Drennan told everyone, "I don't want some guy with just one tit piloting my plane." I did fool them, however, on occasional night training flights, when the pilot would let me take the controls.

My experience at Hobbs, New Mexico and the Air Corps was rewarding in several ways including making it possible for me to go to college on the GI Bill of Rights issued for veterans. As it turned out, to also it helped build my career in journalism and broadcasting.

Happily, in the new civilization that we had formed, there was a base newspaper, *The Hobbs Bomb Buster*. After reading a few copies of this publication, I decided I could bring some reportorial genius to the paper based on my experiences with the Milwaukee *Sentinel* and my success in the Mark Twain contest. I had earlier proposed that we establish a base radio station, but the officers didn't share my enthusiasm for show business, so I opted to use my journalistic skills instead.

"What kind of writing can you do?" a *Bomb Buster* editor asked.

"Most any kind of writing that you need," I said rather cockily.

"Yeah, I'm sure," the sergeant said. "Look, why don't you write a column about the happenings on the base? You know, a gossip column: who's doing what to whom. And make it funny if you can."

So I became a *Bomb Buster* reporter. *Here, There and Everywhere* was the not very original name of the column. I wrote all the good things that happened to the aviation cadets and service personnel, on and off the base, including upcoming dances at the USO, newly found girlfriends, news of babies born back home, and any kind of high jinx that was in keeping with my newfound breezy writing style. Drennan, of course, frequently made the column, as did most of my close pals.

One Jack Drennan item stands out in particular. It became a well-known fact on the base that it was a serious mistake to assign Drennan and Duffy together to any significant duty. One evening the alphabetical pairing once again worked against the military system when Drennan and I were posted as sergeants of the guard over our particular flight squadron for a 24-hour watch. The responsibility consisted of making certain that all functions were executed properly, that all cadets were back on the base for lights out and were in their beds and accounted for, and that any problems of any kind were reported promptly to the officer of the day.

It was about two-thirty in the morning as I sat in the day room reading and falling half asleep when I suddenly realized the other sergeant of the guard had disappeared. I started to panic.

"Drennan, where the hell are you?" I yelled. The next thing I heard was an unmistakable voice booming over the parade ground loudspeakers.

"ATTENTION ALL SQUADRONS. NOW HEAR THIS. NOW HEAR THIS. FALL OUT. WE'RE MOVING OUT. WE'RE MOVING OUT."

Lights suddenly popped on everywhere as barracks doors flew open and men came stumbling out in their underwear and nightshirts and mumbling, "What in the Christ is going on?"

Drennan couldn't be stopped. "FALL IN. FALL IN. GET YOUR FLIGHT BOOTS. LET'S GET MOVING. WE'RE MOVING OUT."

I was absolutely dumbstruck as I watched and heard all of this. I did two false starts, first one way and then the other trying to get to the door. I finally fell over the coffee table and made my way outside. An MP Jeep roared up, and the officer of the day bounded out, demanding to know what was going on. I stumbled and stammered and, I swear, I had visions of Drennan and me in front of a firing squad. All of a sudden, Drennan appeared out of the darkness, hysterical with laughter that his idiotic practical joke had gone so well. The officer of the day saw absolutely no humor in any of it. We were briskly hauled down to MP headquarters. They threatened both of us (even though I had nothing to do with it) with courts-martial and dishonorable discharges and all kinds of threats that can come at three in the morning. Suddenly the officers stopped and realized that the troops were still lined up on the parade grounds, ready to ship out, and then they started to laugh.

The officer of the day took us back to the barracks, and through the public address system dismissed the troops, explaining that there had been a misunderstanding. We got off rather easily. We were assigned to KP (cleaning up the slop around the mess hall) for a month, although when the full story became known, several cadets threatened to castrate Drennan. If I remember correctly, I kind of encouraged them. Most of all, "The Jack Drennan early-morning caper" made great reading in *Here, There and Everywhere.*

After the Battle of the Bulge in February of 1945, the Aviation Cadet program was suspended and our flights were all shipped to Sheppard Field in Wichita Falls, Texas for reassignment to permanent party personnel. We had the rich choice of becoming cooks, bakers, drill instructors, or joining the 925th Air Corps Guard Squadron (Military Police).

I chose the guard squadron and soon found myself escorting squads of American prisoners to various clean-up chores on the base, serving as a stockade guard, and even working the lonely shifts in the guard towers with a sawed-off shotgun. While trying to stay awake during the long hours of the night, occasionally seeing imaginary shadowy figures trying to climb the stockade fences, I would read books by the dim tower lights and even memorize poetry. Byron, Kipling, Keats and Shelley were recited in the most unlikely places. As I reflect back on those slow-moving hours in the towers, I realized that I had no entertainment props as we do today, no portable radios or tiny-screen TV sets to help me while away the time. All I had was an occasional book, my poems, and my own thoughts. Maybe it wasn't all that bad.

I was in a guard tower in the late afternoon of April 12, 1945, when Chief Officer Captain Hairline's voice came over the stockade loudspeakers. "Attention all prisoners and members of the Guard Squadron. I regret to inform you that the President of the United States, Franklin D. Roosevelt, died today from a heart attack. Let us all pray for him and for our country."

The news came like a rifle shot. I couldn't wait to be relieved in the tower so I could get to the day room radio and get all of the particulars. It meant, of course, that Harry Truman, the Vice President, would now be President. All of us wondered how Roosevelt's death would affect the war effort.

As the weeks wore on, three of us in the Guard Squadron Flight became prison sergeants, even though we didn't have the rank of sergeant. We were in charge of some 300 prisoners, all American soldiers, who were serving time for everything from being AWOL, to slapping an officer, to committing murder. We worked with old line and very tough staff sergeants who were in charge of the stockade, but we still had considerable responsibility keeping the prisoners in line, since we worked face to face with them inside of the stockade and without any kind of weapon. I witnessed a great deal of violence and inhumanity in that stockade, including prisoner-conducted kangaroo court sessions that led to much bloodshed. They were experiences that opened my young eyes a lot wider and taught me lessons I wouldn't forget.

One of my closest friends, who worked with me in the stockade, was Art Schroeder, who had been with Drennan and me since our induction at Fort Sheridan. Art was as tall as I, straight as a ramrod, with broad shoulders, light blond hair and bright blue eyes – he looked like a young Burt Lancaster – and was as straightforward and honest as people come. If you were marching into battle you would want Art Schroeder at your side.

Art had a great sense of pride about soldiering, some of which rubbed off on me. We both were promoted to Private First Class at the same time and were selected as two of the eight-man team of the Honor Guard, which meant that at military funerals on the base or in Wichita Falls, we would line up in full dress Military Police uniforms, scrubbed and polished to perfection, and fire the precision rifle salute after *Taps* as the casket was being lowered into the ground. I still get chills thinking about the echo *Taps*, where a bugle off in the distance would answer the *Taps* from the cemetery, followed by the sharp, jolting snap of rifle fire. It all seemed so final. And I guess it was.

The guard squadron and stockade experience, which lasted almost a year, taught me a great deal about human nature. In the later months, I was assigned to travel cross-country and retrieve prisoners who had escaped from the stockade or had Sheppard Field as their assigned base. It called for some anxious moments, since I was dressed in full MP regalia including a sidearm. The prisoner most often was in handcuffs. It brought crowds of the curious, especially at train depots or bus stations. One very early morning, I remember coming out of a coffee shop across the street from the train station in Lawton, Oklahoma with a prisoner handcuffed to my wrist, only to find myself staring into the barrels of a circle of eight shotguns. I guess the local sheriff's office thought we were the James Boys reincarnated.

I was discharged on October 28, 1945 as an Aviation Cadet/Private First Class, which was probably an entirely new classification in the US military. I was given the option of staying on for pilot training in glider school. I politely and quickly declined and headed home to search for a college to further my education. My eighteen or so months of military service proved to be a very valuable experience as I believe it would be for most young people, war time or not. I had never been away from home before, and it gave me a sense of discipline, responsibility and maturity that I simply would not have learned otherwise.

Drennan, Schroeder, Bob Loeber, my high school friend, and I spent the winter months of 1945-46 traveling to college campuses throughout the Midwest, trying to locate the institution of higher learning that could accommodate our various talents and worldly ways, now that we had the GI Bill after having won WWII. I was particularly interested in schools that had strong journalism and radio courses since my military experiences had not dampened my media ambitions. We had actually enrolled at the heavily populated University of Illinois at Champaign-Urbana, until Drennan kept ringing the bell at the information desk when we showed up to sign our admission papers. He yelled, "Barkeep, step forward immediately. You have thirsty people here." The "Fighting Illini's" interest in us subsided after that, and we were skeptical of the very large campus and the army-like atmosphere with thousands of ex-GIs enrolling.

Drennan and I settled on Beloit College, an attractive and welcoming school, that sat high on a hill overlooking the Rock River in Beloit, Wisconsin, about 120 miles north of Chicago. The school's Liberal Arts curriculum and small enrollment of approximately 1,000 students seemed most appealing and I was advised that there was a campus radio station and good courses in English composition and journalism. Beloit College sounded right for me!

Beloit epitomized the blue collar, rugged, small-town midwestern culture that unfolded in America after World War II. The city rode on the shoulders of the manufacturing companies, the Beloit Iron Works, Fairbanks Morris, and others that had emerged during the war and continued in the industrial expansion. Beloit was, and is, as resilient and tough as the river that runs through its center, the Rock River, flowing urgently, angrily, at times, south into the Mississippi. In the mid-seventies, Margaret Mead, the distinguished anthropologist, speaking at the dedication of Beloit's Godfrey Anthropology Building, was said to have remarked, "Beloit is America in microcosm."

One of the proud features of the city, although it is not often acknowledged, is Beloit College, sitting high on a hill, amidst the Indian mounds on the west bank of the river. The college, founded by Yale University religious leaders in 1847, is the first institution of higher learning in the state of Wisconsin. It has maintained an enviable tradition and academic standing through the years and is regarded as having one of the best liberal arts programs in the Midwest, if not the country. Along with that, it enjoys a beautiful campus with many oak and walnut trees standing tall on a rectangular campus with a stately four-story, white pillared Middle College Administration Building standing directly, per its name, in the middle. I came to appreciate Beloit's traditions and beauty only after being away for several years. When Drennan and I decided to enter Beloit College, frankly, we did not do it because of the school's great tradition, or its physical beauty; we decided Beloit was the school for us because the ratio of girls was 3 to 1, along with certain classes that appealed to me as I have mentioned. Truthfully, Drennan had difficulty pronouncing the name of the college (Bee-loy-t). "Below what?" Jack kept asking.

The supposed maturity we had gained in military service was not really in evidence when Drennan and I arrived on the Beloit campus in January of 1946. As a matter of fact, our first appearance was so flamboyant that it probably made the college administrators rethink their policies for admitting ex-GIs. With his discharge money Drennan had purchased a shiny, black, four-door, skinny-tired 1917 Dodge. We immediately decided that the proper way to inaugurate that beauty was to make the trip to Beloit to enter college. Adorned with derbies, canes and loud bow ties, we drove from Oak Park to Beloit early that January morning, the old squeak horn blasting all the way up US Route 20 until we arrived in Beloit. We had a wonderful time on the highway with people honking at us and cheering us on. Thank goodness, it was a warm winter day, without ice or snow, so we rolled right along, fully prepared for our adventure in higher academia.

Our first problem came when Drennan decided to drive not only to the school, but also directly onto the campus on a rather wide sidewalk that was not intended for automobiles. With his derby sitting straight on his head and his usual insipid smile, Drennan drove right through groups of cheering students, past Middle College, where the school president, Dr. Carey Croneis, was quartered, on around to the girls' dormitory at the far end of the campus and right up onto the dorm steps. We got a rousing reception, of course, from the cheering female students. The difficulty came when the Dean of Women arrived and scolded us unmercifully about our lack of "comportment and respect." It was reminiscent of our dressing down from the officer of the day after Drennan's Hobbs Air Base caper. The students kept cheering, some even booing the dean, and Drennan, with his innocent face and Irish charm, calmed the woman down and convinced her we were two innocent soldiers who desperately wanted an education and had merely lost our way (if not our minds).

As much as my many adventures with Drennan kept me on my toes and laughing, it was at Beloit that my interest in writing and announcing came together and set me on the serious highway to a career. Beloit was also exceptionally friendly and informal, and the faculty and advisers would welcome discussions when students had difficulty with their subjects. I struggled during my first year with some of the required subjects such as mathematics and science, but as the year moved forward, I became more confident and started to appreciate and understand the benefits of a liberal arts education. Beloit had some world-class professors: Ivan Stone in government, Kirk Denmark in drama, John Eels in English, and Andrew "Bud" Whiteford in anthropology, are a few with whom I came into contact.

After a full year at college, my newly gained maturity was not in evidence when I got married at the tender age of twenty with only a $75 war bond and my monthly GI Bill payment as my financial base. My life took a serious turn toward a sense of responsibility, much to Drennan's chagrin.

I had met an extremely attractive girl named Betty Jane Zuehsow shortly after arriving at Beloit. Betty had attended Oak Park High School and lived around the corner from my folks' apartment, but we had never met until we came to college. Betty was a very classy young woman and a good athlete, but rather reserved and independent. She was an only child and was sheltered by her parents, even to extremes by her mother.

My Sigma Pi fraternity brothers and other campus friends, including Drennan, of course, pleaded with me not to get married, pointing out all the good times that were ahead for me as a bachelor. Betty was very popular, and I'm sure her friends counseled her in a like manner.

Betty and I were married in the First Congregational Church in Oak Park on February 7, 1947. My Air Corps buddy, Art Shroeder, was my best man, and my sister, Marge, was the Maid of

Honor. I knew as I stood in the reception line following the ceremony, accepting the best wishes of family, friends and relatives, that I was not ready for the responsibilities and obligations of marriage. Betty and I were both just twenty years old and we had to have our parents' written consent to marry. I am amazed that Mrs. Zuehsow ever allowed it.

After a one-night honeymoon at the Palmer House in Chicago, we traveled back to Beloit and set up our home in a three-room unit in a Quonset hut, one of several similar buildings, near the campus with other ex-GIs and their wives. One of our neighbors was a tall and engaging fellow who had been a great basketball player at South Shore High School in Chicago. His name was John Ensar Harr. He was married to a very attractive blonde, named Barbara. We became fast friends. Jack was also attracted to writing, was somewhat of a romantic, and shared my interest in literature. Many stanzas of Keats, Shelley, Kipling and Byron where recited in the coming years in every quarter of the campus, just as they had been at Sheppard Field.

Betty worked as an assistant in the Anthropology Department, and I worked at the Fairbanks Morse factory in Beloit in my off hours from school to supplement my GI stipend for a few months. The work at Fairbanks Morse was tedious and comical at times. I worked on three twelve-inch circular-disc cutting machines that were stationed in a triangle. When I hit the foot lever to start the first machine, I would move to the second and put the disc on the cutting spindle, hit the foot lever, and so on. After four or five trips of going the full circle, I would be so dizzy I could hardly stand up. The old-timers, some of whom had worked on the machines for twenty-five years, would double over with laughter. One time, they caused so much commotion that a supervisor came over and chewed me out for disrupting the rhythm of the workers. My stint in the factory was short term at best, but it did bring in some needed capital when Betty and I were starting out.

In mid-May of 1947, I received some very bad news. Mom called and told me Grandpa Adams had passed away. He was 87 years old. The service was to be held the following Monday at The Old Homestead. I took a train back to Chicago on the weekend and the folks, Marge, Betty and I drove in "old Nell" through the flat and familiar countryside of central Illinois to the land that we loved near Moweaqua. It was a sad time. There were hordes of people, immediate family, relatives, friends and neighbors, all coming to pay respects to a grand old man. John Wheeler Adams was one of a kind. He was not only my mentor, but also my inspiration and I loved him deeply.

I did well in school my sophomore year thanks to Betty's help and the guidance of friends in our Quonset hut community. Before the semester ended, I decided to forego any further career at Fairbanks Morse and Jack Harr and I launched a campus hamburger delivery business. Our enterprise, which, incidentally, operated out of our kitchen, closed down after a couple of weeks when our weary hamburger-frying wives pleaded with us to stop. This was mostly because too many customers had complained, with some justification, that our "burger specials" were the "size of a quarter and cold to boot." McDonald's we were not. Besides, we had a higher calling.

During the summer, Harr went to work for the Beloit College Public Relations Office under Art Hudson, an experienced veteran from the Associated Press and other major news organizations. He had worked with the legendary Edward R. Murrow and other renowned radio reporters in London during World War II. He was hired by Beloit College to bring a broader visibility and identity to the school.

Early in my junior year, Harr suggested that I talk to Art Hudson about joining him and another student named David Mason in the newly formed Beloit College News Service, an operation whose purpose was to publicize the college's academic and athletic achievements throughout the Midwest and nationwide.

Hudson, a tall, tough but good-humored sort, and I hit it off immediately, and he became a mentor to me, one of those often-unsung people whose guidance makes a major difference in lives. I went to work as a writer at the nifty salary of seventy-five cents an hour and, along with Harr and Mason and a very gifted photographer named Bob Miller, launched a new and unprecedented era for college publicity, especially for a small school.

Beloit already had a fine reputation academically as one of the best liberal arts colleges in the country, but it was the entrance of a new basketball coach, Dolph Stanley, that brought it to national reputation athletically.

Dolph Stanley made a name for himself before he came to Beloit in the winter of 1946. He had taken his Taylorville High School team of 1944 to the Illinois State Sweet Sixteen Basketball Tournament undefeated and won the championship going away. Many members of that team followed Stanley to Beloit and brought an unprecedented era of recognition to the sleepy Wisconsin town and its college. They were supported and publicized by the team of Hudson, Harr, Mason, Duffy and photographer Miller. We got stories and pictures of the Beloit stars on the wire services and in newspapers across the nation.

Stanley's teams gained notoriety because they usually won by large margins. They were well coached and played a very high-scoring, flamboyant style of ball that always had the crowd in a frenzy. Jack Harr and I (Mason worked more on academic news) literally lived with those teams, traveled with them to many cities in the country, including the small-college NAIB tournaments in Kansas City, and publicized them to a fare-thee-well.

Several players on Stanley's Beloit teams went on to gain national recognition. Johnny Orr, the captain of the 1949 team, was an All-American, played professional basketball, became the head coach at the University of Michigan and, finally, the head coach and legend at Iowa State University ("Here's Johnny," they announced at every home game). Johnny Erickson, a scoring leader on that same team, became the head coach at the University of Wisconsin. Ron Bontemps, a sophomore on the 1949 team, went on to become an All-American and the captain of the 1952 United States Olympic Basketball Team.

It was an era that any Beloiter will well remember because the school and its basketball team gained such national fame that it became an embarrassment to the rest of the schools in the conference. Beloit was asked to withdraw from the conference in the mid-fifties.

I got totally caught up in my work with Beloit athletics, especially the basketball teams since I had played basketball. Harr and I were instrumental in a write-in contest to give a new nickname, "the

Buccaneers," to the Beloit teams. The name served us well as writers, with our references to "the swashbuckling Buccaneers of Beloit College," "the Golden Bucs of Beloit," "Beloit's Bucket Brigade," and so on. Our stories, sometimes by-lined, about the Beloit athletic teams – especially basketball – appeared in publications across the country.

Harr and I made some money too, supplementing our $75 a month income from the college news service by becoming stringers and reporters for newspapers and wire services in the area or for the hometown papers of schools that were playing Beloit. For instance, on a given Saturday in the winter there would be a swimming meet in the morning, a wrestling competition in the afternoon and a basketball game that night. Jack and I would cover all the competitions and write short separate stories for each event, which we would wire to our assigned publications. He would send his story to one paper in a given town and I would send mine to the other. We got three dollars a story, and at the end of the month, we would split up our treasure of $150 to $200 and have a celebration at the Victory Tap saloon in downtown Beloit. It was becoming big-time business and we loved it.

At the end of my junior year, I became an announcer, which further assisted my income and, more importantly, my career. I had done well in my schoolwork at the college. I struggled with science and mathematics in my first two years, but thrived on college classes in literature, history, journalism and public speaking. Toward the end of the year, I was asked to make an extemporaneous speech in one of my speech classes. I startled the professor by rattling off a play-by-play of an imaginary basketball game, much as I had done with the baseball contests on the lawn at my grandfather's farm.

Afterward, John Clark, the speech professor asked, "Jim, did you memorize that call?"

When I told him that I had not, that it came to me quite naturally from my childhood days, he couldn't get over it.

"You should get into radio," he said. "You have the voice for it and with your ability to ad-lib you might be a natural. Why don't you go see Don Dobson at WBNB?"

Don Dobson was the publisher of the *Beloit Daily News*. He had obtained a license for an FM station in 1947, figuring that the higher frequency and clearer tone modulation would be the radio wave of the future. Dobson was right, but he was twenty years ahead of his time. Few, if any, of the good townsfolk of Beloit were interested in buying a separate FM receiver, especially when they had two AM stations in town. The dilemma came during the basketball season when WBNB carried the college games. Most people solved it by leasing an FM set for a given night or for the season and returning the sets when the basketball season was over. That resolution did not provide a large or stable audience for WBNB on a year-round basis.

I knew Mr. Dobson from my College News Service work, so I called him and asked for an audition. He was most cordial and suggested I meet him the following week at WBNB's studios, which were in a tiny white frame building in an empty prairie about four miles outside of town. I took the Beloit bus to the end of the line and walked the additional couple of miles to the broadcasting building. I was really primed for my big audition.

Dobson greeted me warmly, and rather awkwardly reached up and put his arm around my shoulder (he was half my size). He walked me from his office to the small glass-enclosed studio. An engineer sat at the console outside the glass looking directly into the studio.

When we got to the studio door, I expected Dobson or someone to hand me a script or a news story or something to read for my audition.

"What would you like me to do, Mr. Dobson?" I asked.

Without a trace of a smile, he said, "I want you to go in there and be funny."

He pushed me into the studio, closed the door and for the next fifteen minutes watched, along with a very bored engineer, peering through the glass as I stammered and stumbled my way through one of the worst ad-lib, hopefully funny, routines of all time. Have you ever been asked to tell a few jokes to an audience when you don't have any jokes in mind? That's how it was. Somehow I got through it, and Mr. Dobson thought it was pretty good, although I knew he couldn't have been very impressed. Anyway, I got the job. My pay was $1.50 an hour – double what I was making at the College News

Service. I literally skipped back to the bus stop like a small child. I now had two jobs: one with the press and one in radio. Surely, I was on my way to becoming a media mogul.

I worked the rest of that summer at WBNB as a disk jockey, news reporter, floor sweeper and general handyman. And it was lonely. The audience for WBNB-FM was so small that I became concerned whether anyone at all was out there listening. One Saturday evening in the middle of a prerecorded *Candlelight and Music* program, I opened the microphone and said, "Hey, all you great listeners, I'd like to talk to someone. If anybody's out there listening, please give me a call. I want your comments and suggestions." I gave the telephone number on air. No one called. I take it back. I did get one call. It was Mr. Dobson. He said, "I've got a suggestion for you. Cut out that crap!"

My work with the station was, for all that, a useful and memorable experience. I still occasionally cup my hand to my ear and in deep, well-modulated tones, say, "This is Station WBNB, the voice of southern Wisconsin."

From this experience I was able to realize my childhood dreams and do the *real thing*: announce a live athletic event. Early in the fall, Beloit had a football game at Carleton College in Northfield, Minnesota. WBNB asked me to do the play-by-play. I was thrilled because the game was going to be piped into the Student Union Building on campus and I could display my prowess as a sportscaster to the student body, as well as the handful of people with FM sets in town.

Strangely, I wasn't really nervous about the assignment. Despite the fact that I had never announced a real game, I had announced hundreds of imaginary games at The Old Homestead. And I had studied the rosters carefully and stayed awake for a week conjuring up possible plays or situations that I would have to announce and explain.

Dave Mason was to be the statistician and occasional color man for the game. We drove up to Northfield, Minnesota the night before, loaded with excitement about the upcoming big game.

Late the next morning, we went out to the football field, a typical small college stadium with wooden bleachers on each side and an old-fashioned paint-chipped scoreboard with hooks for the numbers that some fortunate youngster would post as the game progressed. The announcing booth was a long, open-air, wooden room with a table and three chairs. On the table sat a microphone along with a glass of water.

At game time, the bleachers were three-quarters filled, with most of the folks bunched up on the home team side of the field. A few Beloit students and followers, who had made the long trip, cheering lustily, sat on the other side.

I opened in fine fashion. "Good afternoon ladies and gentlemen, this is Jim Duffy along with Dave Mason, speaking to you from high atop the Carleton College Stadium in Northfield, Minnesota. It is a beautiful, crisp, fall day here in Minnesota, and we have two great football teams ready for the start of the Midwest Conference football season. The swashbuckling Buccaneers of Beloit and...."

It all seemed to go very well as the game got underway. I followed the plays carefully and tried to explain with the proper enthusiasm what was happening on the field. In retrospect, I probably asked too many inane questions of Dave Mason, which brought back similar inane answers.

"Wow, Dave did you see John Hanifan sidestep that tackler? Wasn't that something?"

"Yes, Jim," Dave replied. "That was something. That was really something."

"Yes, that was something, Dave," I would say and then continue. And I probably got too excited when Beloit threatened to score. "Look at Hawley's legs churn, he's going right over the middle," I would scream. "He scored I think. Dave, is it a touchdown? Did he score, Dave?"

"No, Jim, he didn't score," Dave would say. "I don't think it's a touchdown."

"Thanks, Dave. Folks, I guess Hawley didn't score. There goes Hanifan...Yes! Yes! YES! A TOUCHDOWN!"

In the third quarter disaster struck, my voice got harsh, I tried to clear my throat and I started to gag. Frantically, I motioned for Dave to take over the microphone as I lunged for the glass of water and spilled most of it all over the table.

"Jim," Dave said calmly grabbing the microphone, "I think this is a good time to reflect on how these teams have prepared for this game...."

"Thanks, Dave," I said finally in a high-pitched voice sounding like a young Michael Jackson. I got back into the game. Somehow, we got through it and did just fine, except that I knew I had been a little hysterical and didn't announce the game as professionally as I knew I could.

When I got back on campus, a couple of students said, "Way to go, Duff. Boy, you sure got excited," which I knew was not exactly a compliment. But Art Hudson was terrific. He gave me the little pat on the back that we all need when we aren't quite sure of ourselves. "That was just great, Jim," he said. "You're going to be a fine sportscaster one day."

I went on to do many play-by-play games for WBNB, covering football, some basketball, the local softball leagues and even the track meets. But I will always remember that crisp fall day in Northfield as a milestone in my career.

Radio in the late forties provided great stimulation for me. I joined the Beloit College Players on WBNB and appeared on several live dramas, including a mystery story, *Watermelon Like Wine*, which I had written. And I listened to as much radio as I possibly could between my college courses, the Beloit College News Service, and my newspaper stringer assignments. One particular program was my favorite. It was called *Johnny Madero, Pier Twenty-Three*. Jack Webb starred as a breezy but down-in-the-mouth private eye working the waterfront.

I thought the writing was colorful. In a flat, low-pitched voice, Webb, the detective, described an unusually sexy lady's entrance to the bar: "She walked in with a wiggle that would make a worm blush. She was wearing an ice-blue dress, but I knew it was twenty degrees warmer inside."

Radio announcing, sportscasting in particular, was very exciting for me. I remember a conversation that I had with Dr. John Eels, the head of Beloit College's English Department, when Harr and I were invited to his home for dinner one evening. Dr. Eels was a very tall, thin, erudite gentleman with a small head and a rather large behind. He was delightful to be with and basked in the world of Chaucer, Shakespeare and other classics.

"James, what career will you pursue when you finish college?" Dr. Eels asked me as he peered over his round, steel-rimmed glasses.

"I would like to get into broadcasting, Dr. Eels," I said. "As you probably know, I have been doing some work for the local radio station, and I am really quite taken with the idea of sportscasting."

Dr. Eels looked rather shocked and made a statement that would make every practicing or would-be sports announcer in America shudder. "James, don't waste your life on the trivial," he said. "You have far much more to offer beyond describing the silly actions of young men in short pants chasing a ball around a field. The world needs thinkers and visionaries to help solve many of the problems in the years ahead. I hope you will rethink that ambition."

At the time I didn't take it very seriously, but I have thought about Dr. Eels' statement many times in the ensuing years. I have watched sports figures, both players and announcers, become national celebrities and "role models" while the nation's teachers, social workers and service providers continue with their very meaningful work, often unsung and underpaid. I did have the growing conviction that leaders in broadcasting should be visionaries and that they can play an important role in helping to solve some of society's problems.

Still, I wanted to continue to try my hand at announcing. After graduation I traveled to several cities and radio stations in the Beloit area to audition, including WISN in Milwaukee and the state's most powerful station, WTMJ. One station I visited, WKOW, the CBS radio affiliate in Madison, Wisconsin gave me a lengthy interview and a live audition. I was asked to read a news report that had the names of some small towns in the area like Waunakee, Mukwonago and Wandiwego. I butchered some of the pronunciations so badly that I was positive I wouldn't get the job.

Lo and behold, the following week, I received a phone call. Station WKOW offered me a job as a staff announcer.

But as fortune would have it, a few weeks earlier, I had met a dynamic executive who would change the course of my life. His name was Elliot W. Henry, Jr.

Ell Henry was something of a growing legend in the publicity business, even at the young age of thirty-six. Since graduating from Beloit College, Henry had hustled to make his mark, first representing and selling fraternity publications and then joining radio station WLS, "The Voice of the Prairie Farmer," as a press writer and eventually publicity manager, and finally was appointed press chief for the American Broadcasting Company's Central Division when the company was formed in 1943.

The fact that Henry had attended my alma mater turned out to be a stroke of fortune for me. In May of my senior year, Ell and his wife, Florence (better known as "Corky"), visited the campus where Corky, who had been the first Beloit Track and Field Relay Queen in 1939, was to be honored at the 1949 relay event. Jack Harr and I, representing the Beloit College News Service, were stationed in the press box covering the relay events for a series of newspapers in the Midwest. I also announced some of the track events for radio station WBNB from the enclosed, if not sufficiently soundproof, press booth. Art Hudson had made Harr and me aware of the potential visit of Henry and other press dignitaries weeks before the relays. As a matter of fact, we had looked for the important ABC representative at the reception prior to the evening games. Much to our disappointment, Ell Henry did not make an appearance.

Midway through the relay festivities while Harr was tabulating and organizing results for press stories and I was on the microphone, the door to the press booth flew open. A smiling, but rather anxious-looking man with wisps of hair on his balding head, announced that he was in need of a telephone for some urgent press calls. Obligingly, Dave Mason, assuming that this might be the fabled Ell Henry, directed him to a telephone at the far end of the booth. With his official relays program clutched in his hand, the fellow proceeded to make a series of collect calls on the results of the track and field events, including comical names of people who weren't even in the races. We became concerned when the caller's voice started to rise in volume and might be heard in our broadcast. Hudson finally came to the rescue and took the man to a front row seat in the stands.

Later we learned that Ell's press box visit was a gag for his friends and probably for us. The collect calls were to his pals around the country, most of whom were very annoyed, and most of whom had never heard of Beloit Relays. When the track meet finally ended and Corky Henry had been duly recognized and her husband introduced to the crowd, Hudson, Mason, Harr and I gathered around the Henrys and found them to be gracious and charming. With a twinkle in his eye, the fun-loving Ell apologized for his disruption and had everyone laughing hilariously as he recounted his friends' reactions to the collect calls.

We invited the Henrys to join us at Beloit Country Club for a reception, but they politely declined. Ell shook hands, congratulated and thanked us all, and vowed he would be in touch.

The very next week, without telling me, Art Hudson called Henry, and with an extraordinary recommendation, asked him to consider me for a publicity position with ABC. Ell said he might be interested since his chief writer, Craig Claiborne, was leaving to go to chef's school in France. I could hardly believe it when Hudson told me I might be getting a call. A few weeks later, I received the call from Station WKOW in Madison offering me a job as an announcer. On that very same day, Ell Henry called me to come to Chicago for an interview.

Five

Television in its Infancy

I stared down at the grayish-green Chicago River curling its way south with an unpalatable stew of bobbing bottles, candy wrappers and driftwood. Watching the water swirl under the Madison Street Bridge, I wondered if it was true that this was the only river in the world that flows backwards. I looked up at the building on the east side of the river standing like a huge majestic throne in judgment of all it surveyed: the river, the *Daily News* Building, and all of Chicago's West Side. The Civic Opera Building was one of the city's tallest and most prominent structures in the late nineteen-forties. Some thirty-eight stories high, it was the home of the Chicago Opera House and the Civic Opera Theater, scores of offices and businesses, as well as a few restaurants and bars, including the exclusive Electric Club on the very top floor. And most important to me, this imposing structure was the headquarters of the American Broadcasting Company's Central Division.

On this early-summer morning in June, in bright sunshine and a slight breeze blowing, I sensed the electricity of the nation's second-largest city as its people, all shapes, sizes and colors, hurriedly passed by, some scowling and even muttering and some looking pleasant, but most with no expression. I was neither perplexed nor frightened by Chicago. As a matter of fact, I had been fond of the city ever since we had moved there when and I was in the fourth grade. Later, in my senior year in high school, my friends and I would travel into the city to watch the Cubs baseball or Bears football games or to visit the Loop for dances and other occasions. My more romantic side appreciated the sprawling metropolis, as Carl Sandburg had described it, "Stormy, husky, brawling, City of the Big Shoulders." Besides, Chicago was a famous programming center for radio shows, and now, I had read, was a growing area for the new medium: television.

69

Still standing on the Madison Street Bridge, I looked at my watch for the tenth time and steadied myself for the upcoming meeting. It was ten minutes to eleven. I felt my nervousness grow as I walked across the bridge. The appointment was for eleven. I took a deep breath and headed up the Civic Opera steps. Pausing at the glass board in the lobby, I noted that ABC's offices were on the 15th and 16th floors. I stopped as I saw my reflection. I looked good, I thought – very presentable – in what my parents would call my Sunday best. As a matter of fact, I was wearing the gray gabardine suit that I had worn, under my robe, of course, for my graduation from Beloit College just three weeks earlier. I also wore the same red suspenders and bright red tie, feeling that the whole attire might bring good luck. I was taking no chances with this interview, having started at the crack of dawn to catch the early morning train from Beloit so I would have plenty of time. I took one last look at the reflection in the glass and smiled. I felt ready for business on this bright day in June 1949.

The young and rather attractive receptionist smiled as I came through the double glass doors to the executive office on the 16th floor.

"Good morning," said I with a smile. "My name is Jim Duffy. I have an eleven o'clock meeting with Mr. Ell Henry."

The receptionist smiled back and thanked me. I felt her eyes examine me as she picked up the telephone to relay the message. After a few minutes, a shapely and pretty young woman walked toward the reception area from down the hall. "Wow! What a pair of pins," I thought. As she got closer, I noticed that she wore glasses and had one eye that was crossed, but she was still very attractive with her sensational figure, her short brown hair and nice smile.

"You must be Jimmy Duffy," she said taking my hand. "I'm Doris Lydel, Mr. Henry's secretary. We have been waiting for you."

She took my arm and started to guide me down the hall.

"I think you'll love this place," Doris cooed. "Everybody is friendly around here. It's just like a big family."

"Well, I sure like it so far," I said with a smile. "There is one small problem. I don't have the job yet. This is just an interview."

"I know, I know," said Doris laughing, "But Craig Claiborne is leaving and...." She pushed me away and looked me up and down. "You sure look like the ABC type. You'll like Ell Henry and I think he'll like you."

I was starting to hope that all of ABC was as friendly as Doris Lydel. When we came to a bank of offices on the right, we entered the small secretarial room; Miss Lydel motioned for me to go through an open door to the left.

"That's Mr. Henry's office. Go right in. And good luck," she said, winking with her good eye.

Ell Henry's office was a long, dark, narrow room with a desk in front of the room's only window, a leather chair at the end of the office and a long brown leather couch on the wall to my right. I squinted and I wasn't certain if anyone was sitting behind the cluttered desk, even though a small lamp illuminated it. Finally, as my eyes became accustomed to the light, I could make out the tufted hairs on the top of a balding head. The publicity director of the ABC Central Division sat hunched over his desk, staring intently at the papers scattered on the surface.

"Hello, Mr. Henry," I said. "I'm here for my interv...."

"Hiya, kid!" Henry interrupted without looking up. "Sit down, I'll be right with you," he said as he waved at the couch.

I sat rather uncomfortably glancing occasionally off to my right at Henry. I could hear phones ringing in the outer office and the sweet Miss Lydel taking the messages. I could also hear Ell Henry muttering softly to himself. Occasionally, Henry's cheek would twitch and his left foot would tap the floor as he wrestled with an apparent problem.

As I looked over again at the man sitting there, still deep in thought, I started to smile at the nonsense of the relays' scene. Suddenly, Ell looked up, leaped out of his chair and charged around his desk with his hand extended.

"Hey, Jimmy, it's good to see you. You look great. Thanks for coming in."

"Well, thank you, Mister Henry," I stammered as I struggled to get up from the depths of the couch. Ell's sudden movements had startled me, and I half lunged to shake the outstretched hand. "I hope I didn't interr...."

"No problem, kid. That's great," Henry exuded. "Let's go."

"Where are we going?"

"We're going to lunch. Up at the Electric Club." And he breezed out the door. I looked at my watch. It was eleven thirty-two.

Ell Henry was obviously well known and well liked. As we walked down the hallway to the elevators, several people waved and smiled at him. A couple joked with him about the power of the press. It was important to Henry that he be popular and widely recognized, but, in reality, this was more from a business than a personal standpoint. Many people in broadcasting, and business in general, were highly skeptical of the need for publicity and public relations activity. In the late nineteen-forties, the separation of line and staff functions had not been fully defined. To many people, if you weren't involved in making the product or selling it or directly related to the profit or loss bottom line, you were superfluous. But Henry knew, and so did a growing number of executives, especially in the volatile and changing business of broadcasting and particularly the new world of television, that enhancing the visibility of programming and personalities through promotion and creative exploitation would bring new listeners and viewers in ever widening circles across the country. Ell Henry, in his role as public relations director, at least for ABC in Chicago, had access to all areas of broadcasting, network and local, that would help him create a vision of things to come. Ell Henry was about to introduce a young hopeful from Beloit to this fascinating world.

As we emerged from the elevator on the top floor, the elegance of the Electric Club immediately struck me. Rich walnut paneling lined the walls, even in the elevator hall, and became more handsome and distinct as we walked into the foyer of the club with its soft Oriental rugs. Ell Henry was obviously at home in the club. He stepped quickly to the bar on the left-hand side of the corridor, a paneled room, with walnut, which had seven or eight tables and a small bar with six stools off to the right.

"Hey, Pete," Henry greeted the bartender. "How is it, man?" Henry's voice was friendly and alive. As a matter of fact, I thought he spoke with something of an English lilt, almost a cross between Cary Grant and Tony Curtis imitating Cary Grant.

"It's great, it's great, Mr. H." the bartender responded with a smile while taking a look at me.

"Say hello to Jimmy Duffy, the pride of Beloit, Wisconsin," Henry said. "Pete's the best bartender in the entire Midwest, maybe the entire country. Makes the best martini in America. I'll have one, Petie, maybe more. What'll you have, kid?"

"I'll have the same as Mr. Henry," I said, smiling at the bartender.

"So you had a good trip in?" Henry asked almost absentmindedly as he looked into the hall at guests walking by. "Tell me about Jim Duffy," he said, even before I could respond about the trip from Beloit.

I had thought many times about what I would say in the interview since I first received the phone call. Ell Henry knew something about me from our chance meeting in Beloit, and from the clippings and materials I had sent him. So I began by telling him about my interest in journalism and broadcasting, describing my job as a writer with the Beloit College News Service and the *Beloit Daily News*, and as a reporter/stringer for newspapers and wire services around the Beloit-Rockford area. I told him how I loved broadcasting, especially being on the air and described my experiences covering the Beloit football and basketball games and my stints as disc jockey and news reporter.

"But I've always wanted to write, Mr. Henry," I said. "I won a national Mark Twain essay contest at Oak Park High School in 1944. I even wrote for the base newspaper when I was in the Air Corps, and then, of course, I did a lot of writing at Beloit."

"I got the stories you sent me," Henry said as he motioned to Pete for two more martinis. "Mostly sports by-line stuff. It's pretty good. We have an opportunity here for a good writer, a PR man, and that's what I want to talk about."

I nodded and listened intently as Henry described the job and the qualities he was looking for. Henry's assistant, Craig Claiborne, was leaving in a couple of weeks for Paris, and his job was open for the right person. The position was for a publicity writer who would cover all shows originating from ABC Chicago, for both radio and television. Covering the shows meant getting to know the talent, producers and staff, attending the broadcasts or telecasts, looking for the positive angles on the cast or incidents on the shows that would make good copy to enhance the reputation and audience of the programs. Further, the writer would be the *Daily News Report* editor, meaning he or she would edit all the copy about network programs coming in on the news wire from the other ABC offices in San Francisco, Los Angeles, Detroit and especially New York. New York, of course, was the source of the greatest volume of stories since it was the headquarters for the network and the seat of the network's programming operation.

The editor/writer would write news or feature stories about the Chicago-originated shows, prioritize them with the other edited stories, make all corrections and send the package to Central Typing. From there the copy would be mimeographed and bound and sent to the mail room for distribution to all newspaper and magazine editors and columnists in the Central Division area. All employees in the Central Division (Chicago) office received copies as did the executives in the other four cities where ABC owned radio and television stations.

Henry sailed through that part of the assignment rather quickly and matter-of-factly. I gulped and choked slightly on my martini.

"Is that every day, Mr. Henry?"

"Every day but Saturday and Sunday for the *Daily News Report*, kid," Henry smiled. "And at times we expect to see you on Sunday to cover *Super Circus*." Henry stopped and looked directly at me: "You know, *Super Circus* is telecast on Sunday from the Civic Opera Little Theater downstairs?" It was a question. I nodded though I knew nothing about silly circus, or whatever show Henry was talking about.

As Ell Henry described the responsibilities of the position, I realized that ol' sweet Pete, the bartender, had put two more large stand-up martinis in front of us. I also realized I was getting a delightful warm glow, and that maybe this was the third time Pete had rerefreshed us. I was starting to have a fine time listening to this experienced and charming man of the press who epitomized show business and who maybe, just maybe, would soon be my boss. I also knew I had to get a signal to Pete to give me a pass on the next round if I was going to make it through the day.

"And there is some entertaining that goes with the job. My assistant (the new writer) is expected to take newspaper columnists and magazine editors to lunch or dinner and sell them stories on *Breakfast Club* or *Super Circus* or *Studs' Place*, or whatever," Henry stated. "And all the major stars come through here, Hope and Crosby, Martin and Lewis, Godfrey, ...you name it...this is the crossroads of America...if they're going to appear with Don McNeill on *Breakfast Club*, we go meet 'em, search them out, keep them happy so we can get good photos and good column notes. It's a fun business, and we have to stay on top of it all the way. You understand, kid?"

"Sure, yes, I do," I said as my head nodded too many times. I was feeling good. But I was staying with it. Other people had noisily gone past the bar and into the dining room. I shifted on the barstool and decided to stand up, just to see if I could. "What's the matter, have to pee?" Henry asked.

"No, no, I'm just stretching," I answered as I felt my left leg wobble.

"Oh, and kid," Henry continued at his staccato pace, "I expect my employees to be loyal. No surprises. Always shoot straight. The publicity business is a wormy game. You can't trust everyone. Somebody's always looking for an angle. So we've got to trust each other. And we've got to be clean-cut, dress right and have the right attitude. You seem to be just fine in that regard, Jim. And, oh, my man has got to know how to drink. We go to many places and meet many important people. We've got to handle our booze and always be alert. You never know when a big story is right in front of you."

Beads of perspiration were starting to show on Henry's almost bald forehead. His lips twitched once or twice, but he was smiling and his eyes twinkled, a man obviously happy in his mission, at least for the moment.

"Give us two more here, Petie," Henry said. "We're making progress."

Henry quickly got up from the bar stool so that he could be on a more even eye level with me, even though I was four or five inches taller. He scraped his shoe on the gleaming oak floor and then continued. "The guy that has this job has a marvelous opportunity. You learn all facets of the business. You're a PR man so you can go where you want. You see things other people don't see." Henry paused, concerned that he wasn't making his point. It sounded like he was selling the job, and he knew he didn't have to.

"What I'm really trying to say, is that this writer's job is unique because it gives a broad view of broadcasting, especially with the start of television, for anyone that's interested in the long run for this business."

I nodded and started to respond knowing Ell Henry was coming to a key point.

He took a sip of his martini, looked up and then asked with some deliberation, "How do you see this new thing called television, Jimmy? Do you think it has a future?"

I had given some thought to the new medium, which was barely a year old, nationally at least. I did not know a great deal about it. Radio was my first love and primary interest. Television had hardly reached Beloit, Wisconsin, and, frankly, I was in the same position as so many curious Americans in that I still couldn't figure out how anyone could "get a picture to fly through the air into the home."

"Well, I think it's fine," I answered, struggling to sound serious and sober. "I've only watched a couple of times down at the Victory Tap in Beloit. The screen seemed pretty small and the reception wasn't too good. Little figures bouncing around."

"What programs did you see?"

"One was a wrestling show that was really funny, it..."

"That's our show," Henry interrupted. "*Wrestling from Rainbow Arena* with Wayne Griffin. We carry it every Wednesday night at ten o'clock on WENR-TV. That's ABC's locally owned station on Channel 7. You'll have to go out there some night. It's crazy: women throwing their bras in the ring, yelling and screaming. It's phony as hell, I mean the wrestling matches, but people seem to love it. The wrestlers are full of shit, but Wayne is great."

"I'd like to do that," I said. "People in Beloit seem to be more interested in radio. More of the guys at the Victory Tap were watching people play shuffleboard than watching the wrestling on TV."

More little beads of sweat appeared on Henry's forehead, and his lip twitched again. He studied his almost empty martini glass. "The medium is just getting started," he said softly. "We just started our half-assed network schedule last fall and there are still only a few thousand television sets in the whole Chicago area. But it's coming. New York is getting very excited about it. The real promise, our people say, is when the price of sets goes down, and television gets into people's living rooms. Earl Mullin, my publicity boss in New York, says it's going to revolutionize the entertainment business. Some say it may eventually put the motion picture business, and even radio, out of business. What do you think?"

I tried to clear my head. This was serious stuff. Ell Henry was checking me out pretty good, smack in the glow of Pete's wonderful martinis. And two more had suddenly appeared on the bar. I knew I couldn't finish mine.

"I don't think it can put radio out of business," I answered. "Radio reaches too many people – millions, I guess, and it stretches all across this country." I paused. "Radio is a personal medium. The idea of sitting in a chair in a studio and talking to people in their homes about things that affect their lives is powerful...."

"You've got a point," Henry cut in. "Don McNeill is sure powerful on radio. *Breakfast Club* is one of the most popular shows in any medium. And look at Godfrey and Tommy Bartlett. And Jack Benny and Fred Allen and on and on. Television has the potential to change all that."

"It probably does." I said, still trying to hold a steady, serious tone. "If it develops great programming, and advertisers can sell their products on TV, it can change radio and movies and a lot of things, but I don't see it eliminating all of it."

"I read a story the other day that said television will be the most potent marketing and advertising sales tool that history has ever known," Henry said. "And its programming can be so powerful that it can influence people's life styles...both bad and good."

"Maybe so," I replied. "But it sure has a long way to go." I suddenly realized that I was hungry, really hungry, and the lunch hour was long gone.

Suddenly, Henry pushed away from the bar. "OK, kid, now let's see if you can write. Thanks, Pete. See you later, probably tomorrow," he said with a wave and headed toward the elevators.

I was startled. I glanced at the bartender, who was grinning. "Howaboutalittlelunch?" I called after Henry in a suddenly squeaky, high-pitched tone.

"You had your lunch." Henry chuckled. "Olives and peanuts. We're too busy to eat. This is show business. Food comes later." He ran his hand across his forehead straightening out the two or three hairs that were still in front. His lips twitched again, but he was smiling and obviously still happy. His finger stabbed at the elevator down button.

Everybody in this place grins, I thought, struggling to keep up with Ell Henry as we swung through the doors of the ABC Central Division reception room. The bartender was grinning, people on the elevator were grinning, the pretty young receptionist was grinning, and I could swear Doris was not just grinning, but laughing when we got to the publicity department office.

"Wait here." Henry shot over his shoulder as he continued into his office.

I felt rather awkward as I stood in front of Doris Lydel's desk. I didn't think I was crocked, but I knew I should be petrified with all of the martinis. My eyes were probably red and I wondered if my hair was mussed.

"Did you have a nice lunch?" Doris asked in a low whisper.

"Yeah..., yes, it was good," I said as I shuffled my feet and tried to look businesslike. "The olives were exceptional and plentiful," I added. I *grinned* back at Doris.

Ell Henry came flying out of his office with a handful of papers.

"Here you go, kid," he said. "Sit over there at that typewriter and see if you can write this story for me. That machine works doesn't it, Doris?"

Doris got up and wiggled over to the desk a few feet from hers and examined the typewriter. "I think it's fine, Mr. Henry. Here is some paper and carbons. Sit here, Jim."

I tripped as I turned to go toward the desk, but I didn't think anybody noticed. I knew I was still a little tipsy.

Henry was all action. The little fuzz hairs on his forehead were standing straight up and his eyes sparkled. "Here's what I want you to do, Jim. These are notes about Bardie Patton. He's Phil Patton's son. Phil is the producer of *Super Circus*. Bardie plays Scampy the Clown on the show. The kid is probably spoiled, but he's pretty good in that clown suit. What I need is a feature story bio on him. Couple of pages. Read these notes and see what you can do." Henry paused and asked softly, "Are you okay, Jim?"

I nodded. "Yes sir, I'm fine," I said, glancing through the papers. "Just damned hungry," I added under my breath. I was not awed by the situation. I had written many features at Beloit and was confident of my imagination and ability to write a good story. But I was troubled by the fact that I was starting to feel a little nauseous. The olives were indeed plentiful and green. "My God!" I thought, "I can't throw up on the typewriter." I stared off into space for a few seconds, and then it passed. I quickly read the notes on young Patton, put the paper and carbons in the typewriter, and started to type swiftly in my hunt and peck two-finger style. I knew Doris was watching me, but I wouldn't be distracted. Somehow my mind came together and I picked up the pace on the machine.

Watching a circus is one of a kid's biggest thrills, because there's nothing like clowns, canines, camels and cotton candy wrapped into one thrill-packed afternoon. And when you can be smack in the middle of that big top tempo every Sunday afternoon, it's an even greater thrill. Just ask Phillip Bardwell Patton, ABC-TV's 11-year-old find.

Bardie, as he is commonly called, finds himself mixed with animals and acrobats every week in his job as Scampy, the mischievous little playmate to Cliffy the

*Clown Soubier on the hour-long video circus. As Scampy,
Bardie has been an integral part of Super Circus since
May of this year.*

*He literally fell into the role when a midget, origi-
nally slated for the part, failed to appear. Bardie stepped
in on a moment's notice, and the response from the studio
audience, as well as viewers from the East through the
Midwest, has been so positive that he has been signed as a
regular. Despite his youth, Bardie is no newcomer to
show business....*

I continued the story, wrapping up Bardie's brief bio, and making up some quotes from Soubier praising the young man's natural
abilities and comedic sense. The story was just short of two pages. I
proofread it and made a few spelling corrections. Then I looked up
and winked at Doris who was watching me intently. She winked
back with her good eye and buzzed her boss.

Henry's lips kept twitching as he read the story. He was more
than pleased. He was smiling. "Good, good, Jim. I couldn't have
done better myself. You have a good style. Let's go in the office."

We didn't even sit down. Ell stuck out his hand and said, "I
want you to go to work for me. Craig leaves the first of August. Can
you start on Monday, July 19th? That will give you ten days or so to
work with Claiborne and learn the ropes."

I thought of all the things I had to do: resign from the radio
station, move to Chicago with my young wife, and find a place to
live. That would be a problem. I had just about a month. What did
I expect? I wanted the job. I had better ask about salary and benefits. Of course, I could start. This was Mecca. The American
Broadcasting Company. I tried to be cool, but I was really excited.

"Oh, the starting salary will be $375 a month plus an expense
account," Henry smiled. "And you'll have your own office, not that
crummy desk you were working at. We're moving down the hall in
a couple of weeks, so it will be a whole new deal by the time you get
here. The company is working on an insurance plan so that will be
coming. What do you say? Would you like to work for ABC?"

"You bet I would, Mr. Henry," I responded, squeezing the outstretched hand. "This is great. Thank you very much. I won't let you down. I'll work very hard."

Doris kissed me on the cheek as I left the office. I grinned at her. I grinned at the pretty receptionist and anyone else who would look at me. I was smiling all the way back to Beloit.

The blue and silver bus was rumbling into view about four blocks down on Washington Boulevard in Oak Park. It was 6:45 in the morning, a hot and uncomfortable summer morning in the greater Chicago area. I waited for the bus that would take me to my new position with ABC. It was Monday, July 19, 1949, and the new adventure was beginning. The sun was glistening on the oncoming bus. I looked at the three other early-bird passengers also waiting for the trip into Chicago. All three looked displeased with the day and with the weather, and probably with their jobs, I thought, as we all climbed onto the bus and headed east toward Lake Michigan.

As the bus rattled on through the nearly empty streets of Oak Park, past Austin Boulevard and into Garfield Park, I felt a growing sense of the excitement – not totally without trepidation – that began with my meeting with Ell Henry. This was my first day of work with the great American Broadcasting Company. I was to meet Craig Claiborne at Don McNeill's *Breakfast Club* program between 7:30 and 8:00 at the Civic Opera Little Theater. I glanced at the *Breakfast Club* kit that Henry had sent to me, but I couldn't concentrate. I really didn't want to read, and besides, I had read it three times over the past few days so that I would be completely familiar with this show that Henry had touted as one of the most popular and important in all of broadcasting.

As I looked out the open windows of the bus, watching early risers watering the small lawns that dotted rows and rows of three-story gray Chicago West Side townhouses, I thought back on how easy the transition had been from Beloit to this new ABC adventure. Betty and I had packed up our few belongings from the small suite of rooms we had rented on a week-to-week basis in Beloit. We sent them parcel post to Betty's parents' apartment at the corner of Kenilworth

Avenue and Washington Boulevard. It was the very corner where, conveniently, I would catch the bus for work. I had given the required two-week notice at the radio station, WBNB – "the voice of southern Wisconsin." Don Dobson seemed genuinely excited about my break into the big time. He not only wished me well, but also said I could always come back to the station if things didn't work out, and with his arm half-way around my shoulder, he said in a confidential whisper, "You're a nice-looking fella. Get in front of the camera in this new television. That's where the big payoff will be."

I chuckled as I thought about the conversation. He might be right. Frank Reichstein, the crusty and rather slovenly, but wise, sports editor of the *Beloit Daily News*, had told Jack Harr and me the same thing on our trips through the Midwest when we covered the Beloit College basketball team. After a couple of beers at the bar of the Cornhusker Hotel in Mt. Vernon, Iowa, or some other small-town America hostelry, Reichstein would regale us young reporters with stories of the astounding feats of former Beloit athletes and his own prowess as a general news and sports reporter and editor. And he would invariably end the evening with his overview of the coming power of television.

"Sight, sound and motion, boys," Reichstein would say. "One picture beats a thousand words. You guys are young. When you get out of school, head out of little ol' Below-it and ride the big wave. Television will revolutionize sports. Get in front of the camera early and make some big money." Jack and I would nod our heads in unison and agree that Frank was probably right. Then we would look to the next night's game and the more immediate and pressing problems at hand.

The sight of Skid Row on Madison Avenue brought me back to the present. Despite the early morning hour, several derelicts were wandering the streets. Others huddled in doorways, cradling the bottles of "midnight express" fine wines and sleeping off their misery. Speaking of misery, I reflected on the move to Betty's parents' apartment during the past week. It was to be a very temporary measure, but it presented some major problems. The Zuehsows were fine but strange people. Henry, Betty's father, was a very gentle man who had worked for the Great Western Railroad as assistant treasurer for twenty-some years. He was a veteran of most of the major American battles of World War I, finishing as a top sergeant and highly decorated for his bravery. He had become a quiet man due to shell shock, received first in the battle of the Argonne Forest in France and also in some later battles. It affected his hearing which served him well, strange to say, after he married Euhlah Jane Beach, a tall, strong, dominating woman from Texas who claimed to be a direct descendent of Davy Crockett.

Prior to marrying Henry, Euhlah had played piano in upscale movie theaters for silent pictures and later sang from the stage following the movies. Her small stint in the spotlight left her bitter since she didn't get quite enough applause, ever, and decided to take it out on Henry when he talked her into marrying him and leaving show business. Euhlah Jane Beach Zuehsow, with her white hair perfectly coiffed and bulging blues eyes, ruled everything, including Henry, of course, who became less and less of a challenge to her day by day. She hovered over Betty, their only child, with constant illusions of evil men trying to seduce her or force her into compromising situations. She had Henry standing guard wherever Betty went.

I shook my head out of that reverie as the bus pulled up to Wacker Drive and Washington Boulevard. Stepping out into the morning sunlight, I noted the long line outside of the Civic Theater: folks, all kinds of folks, young and old, waiting for the doors to open to Don McNeill's *Breakfast Club*.

As I hurried across the street, the theater doors opened and the crowd that had been spilling onto Wacker Drive started to move excitedly into the home of the *Breakfast Club*. The live sounds of Eddie Ballantine's orchestra tuning up for the show drifted through the doors as I headed for the cast entrance to the left-hand side of the theater.

"Hey, are you part of the show?" a youngster yelled at me as he started to go in.

I blushed and smiled, "Yeah, kind of, I guess. Enjoy the show."

"Wow! How about that?" I thought as I walked down the long hallway that would take me backstage. "I am part of this show and many more to come with ABC."

As I reached the backstage area, there seemed to be people everywhere, scurrying around getting ready for the live broadcast that would go out over some 350 radio stations across America. I was looking anxiously for Craig Claiborne since I was starting to feel uncomfortable, if not in the way, when I heard a friendly voice say, "You must be Jim Duffy, our new press man."

I turned around to see the smiling face and the outstretched hand of a slightly older man, balding, with glasses and a relaxed, friendly air about him.

"I'm Fred Montiegel," the man said. "I do public relations and publicity for Don McNeill Enterprises. Welcome. It's nice to have you aboard. Craig told us you would be stopping by this morning. He'll be here directly. He's a super guy, but he's his own man and doesn't always show exactly on time. But he'll be here. Let me show you around."

I nodded and shook hands and was relieved to be under somebody's wing as Montiegel and I walked on stage.

"Don's on vacation the whole month of July," Montiegel said, "So he isn't here. Don Ameche is filling in as toastmaster this week. This is his first day, and he's back in the dressing room going through his notes. You'll meet him later."

My God, I thought, Don Ameche, the movie star. Alexander Graham Bell (Ameche had starred in the movie) right here on this stage. A handsome, dark-haired young man with a great smile came walking up.

"What have we got here, Freddie, my man?"

"Jim Duffy, meet Johnny Desmond," Montiegel said. "Jim's our new press man for ABC working with Ell Henry. Craig's leaving, you know. Johnny is the show's dynamite sing...."

"Hey, that's great," Desmond said. "Jimmy Duffy, huh?" He stepped back and looked me over very carefully, especially my hairstyle. "Good luck," he said.

"Thanks, Mr. Desmond," I said. "I'm pleased to meet you. I listen to you...."

"Let's knock off the mister stuff. It's John," the singer interrupted.

"Okay, John," I responded. "What I started to say was that we used to listen to you all the time when I was in the Air Corps down in Texas. Sergeant Johnny Desmond was, or, ah, is very special. It's a real pleasure to meet you."

"Jim, this is Patsy Lee," Montiegel said. "Patsy is our female vocalist and does a terrific job."

Patsy Lee was a pretty young lady in her late teens with a twinkling, perky look about her, and rather sexy I thought, as I shook her hand. I later learned that she came from California, had a mother who was with her almost everywhere she went, and dated a guy who worked in business affairs at ABC.

"Cliffy, Cliffy," Montiegel yelled at a tall, blond fellow hurrying across the stage. "Come over, I want you to meet Jimmy Duffy." "Can't now," the man said with a wave. "Welcome. We'll talk later."

"That's Cliff Petersen," Montiegel explained. "He's the producer of the show and a great performer. He plays Uncle Cliffy, the Swede in comedy sketches, and he sings duets with Patsy or Johnny. You'll like him. He's a great guy and always cooperative."

Montiegel and I, now standing off to stage right, were joined by a slim and very stylish young man with a warm tan and a smile, almost a grin, on his face. I was immediately taken with his dress. He wore a soft gray plaid suit with a stark white shirt, a plain but bright red tie and a pocket-handkerchief.

"Hi. Ah'm Craig Claiborne," he said with an unmistakable Mississippi drawl.

"Ah'm sorry ah'm a little late. Ah know you're Jim Duffy because Ell described you to me. Ah see you're in good hands with ol' Fred here. Anyway, welcome, and let me show you the treachery ah've been going through and you now inherit."

I liked Craig Claiborne immediately. He had not only a stylish look about him, but he seemed totally relaxed and full of good humor.

Craig introduced me to the rest of the *Breakfast Club* cast: Fran Allison, who played Aunt Fanny; Sam Cowling, the rotund little man who provided the show's main comic relief; Eddie Ballantine and even members of his orchestra, some of whom were famous in their own right as featured performers with various big-name bands of the day. Ballantine, I learned, was a member of the studio orchestra when McNeill started the *Breakfast Club* in the early thirties.

I wasn't nervous or star struck, but I suddenly realized that here I was, two months out of college, standing in the middle of some of the biggest names in broadcasting, people who were famous all around the country.

Don Ameche came onto the stage and the audience – now seated in the filled theater – started to applaud. As Claiborne took me over to the broadcast table where the toastmaster sat, Ameche, looking very dapper and tanned, suddenly smiled and extended his hand to both of us.

"I'm Don Ameche," he said. "This is my first day and I'm a little nervous. Let's hope it goes well."

As Claiborne made the appropriate comments, I did become star struck, a feeling I would soon lose in the morass of talent that I would have to deal with in the coming years. For some inexplicable reason, I felt my lower lip start to quiver as I tried to respond to the introduction.

"Mr. Ameche. Good luck. I, ah, loved you, ah, in the movie with the, ah, telephones...."

Ameche let out a roar – a friendly roar of laughter. "Thanks," he said. "Let's do the show."

"Good morning, Breakfast Clubbers, good morning to you...."

Ell Henry had not exaggerated about the popularity of Don McNeill's *Breakfast Club*. The program had become a radio institution in the sixteen years since a tall and rather shy young man from Sheboygan, Wisconsin came up with the format while en route from Milwaukee to Chicago in 1933 to take over a little-known show called *The Pepper Pot* on the original NBC Blue Network. McNeill's idea was have a "call to breakfast" via radio to all good folks across America, sprinkled with songs, humor, guest celebrities and most of all, good old-fashioned corn. McNeill changed the name to *Breakfast Club* shortly after he took over the reins, broadcasting from a Merchandise Mart studio. Year-by-year the *Breakfast Club* grew in popularity.

In 1941, the Federal Communications Commission ordered RCA to divest itself of one of its NBC radio networks, the "Red" or the "Blue." In October 1943, General David Sarnoff, the Chairman of RCA, sold the Blue Network to a group headed by Edward Noble, Chairman of the Lifesaver Company, for $8 million. It was the beginning of the American Broadcasting Company. Don McNeill's *Breakfast Club*, as ABC's feature attraction, became one of America's favorite entertainment institutions.

The hour-long program attracted major celebrities who visited the *Breakfast Club* during a stay-over in Chicago at the Ambassador East Hotel, or the finery of the Blackstone or Congress or Drake Hotels. They exchanged quips and gags and sentiment with McNeill and his cast. Bing Crosby, Dick Powell, Perry Como, Bob Hope, Milton Berle, Cary Grant, Joan Blondell, Phil Harris, Alice Faye, Dean Martin, Jerry Lewis and a thousand other stars visited the show. Audiences flocked to the studio to get tickets to the live production so that they could see and participate with Don, Sam, Aunt Fanny and the stars in person. When the program moved out of the Merchandise Mart into larger hotel facilities, and then the Civic Opera Theater, tickets were even more in demand with long lines winding around Washington Boulevard and Wacker Drive.

McNeill was the heart and soul of the show; as well he should be since he had created it. He epitomized the heart and soul of America – the great Midwest, down to earth and friendly. He was understanding and honest. He and the *Breakfast Club* represented Norman Rockwell's America.

McNeill tells of the time, "I was walking though the audience and said, 'Is Norman Rockwell here?' There Rockwell was just sitting in the audience."

The show was unfancy Rockwell style and, yes, corny. Audiences loved it.

"Corn is sentiment, sincere and unashamed," McNeill has stated. "Corn is the familiar, the tried and true. Every normal person likes corn. Cynics and sophisticates think they hate corn..., but the tombstone of many a sophisticate bears a corny epitaph."

The *Breakfast Club* was loaded with corn, starting with McNeill's or his guest toastmaster's invitation for folks in every corner of the nation to "march around the breakfast table," opening each quarter hour of the show. I joined with the rest, marching and clapping hands as Don Ameche, Sam Cowling, Desmond, Cliffy, even the show announcers, Bob Murphy and Don Dowd, marched around the broadcast table on center stage along with members of the audience who had come up on the stage. Fran Allison, as the lovable chatterbox Aunt Fanny, dished up her share of the pone with her letters from Nettie – "Dear Fanny: Poor Ophie Hackitt is all sick, allergies. She's worse since she got her new plate. I guess she must be allergic to teeth. She was without them for so long...."

The regular features that were planted and grew through the years were the substance of the program that the audience related to and adored. The inspirational *Moment of Silent Prayer* when McNeill would ask the audience, "Each in his own words, each in his own way, for a free world united in peace, let us bow our heads and pray!" started during World War II, on October 28, 1944. Legend has it that less than a year later – May 7, 1945 – a few minutes after Don and the audience had said their usual prayer for a "world united in peace" – an excited newsman interrupted the program with the announcement that the Germans had surrendered. To Breakfast Clubbers, their prayers had been answered.

Memory Time came a few years later: the thoughtful moments when Don or his guest host would read nostalgic poems or essays selected from thousands of submissions sent in by the national audience. One favorite of McNeill's was *Why God Gave Us Grandmas*, and among the favorites of audience members were *When Pa Is Sick* and *When Ma Is Sick*, along with *The Kid Who Always Struck Out*, penned by McNeill himself.

THE KID WHO ALWAYS STRUCK OUT

There's usually one on every team from every neighborhood.
A boy who can't quite make the grade; a lad misunderstood.
His heart and soul in every play, he tried for every fly,
But he just can't field like the other boys; the ball goes zooming by.

And when his turn comes at the plate, the other side will shout
"Put 'em across – this guy can't hit!" He's the kid who always strikes out.

You'll never know the bitter pain nor the teardrops in his eye
As he stands there lost and awkward as that called third strike goes by.

Each game for him is a bitter draught, no fun and laughter there.
He wants to be like the other lads without a worldly care.
But his whole world crashes at his feet, he's a mass of gloom and doubt.
He'd like a hole to crawl into, each time that he strikes out.

His teammates somehow seem to sense that he can't quite make the grade,
There's indifference there, a sickly grin and then smiles so quickly fade.
He could stay home – all alone, and give up the game of course,
But he wants so hard to be one of them; it's a constant driving force.
So he grits his teeth and buoys his hopes, he's the last kid each side chooses.
Then it starts again – his bungling hands, and of course his ball team loses.
You watch the kid. You can't help admire the spirit in that breast
As he stumbles on and fluffs again and fails his every test.

And you somehow feel there'll come a day in another world perhaps
Where he'll get a chance and come flying through like the other lucky chaps.
In the Great Beyond you can see him grin as the angels cheer and shout –
For that home run he's smashed o'er the Pearly Gates – the kid who always
struck out.

On the public service front, McNeill turned the power of radio to a number of issues, proving that national communications can reach and influence. One feature, the *Sunshine Shower*, started in the late forties, were segments where audience members were saluted for performing good deeds in their communities. It was the forerunner of a latter-day American promotion of community service and volunteerism.

McNeill also created his famous 1945 *Christmas in July* broadcast for twenty-five recently returned serviceman who had been in battle during the traditional wartime Christmas seasons. Christmas in July stands as one of the all-time high points in *Breakfast Club* history. Not only did it receive national attention, but also it represented one of the most heart-warming moves by an entertainment clan in America, which had been at war for almost four years.

Don McNeill's *Breakfast Club* stayed on the air for 35 years, 1933 to 1968, airing every weekday morning from 8:00 AM to 9:00

PM Central Time, calling millions of Americans, in various states of somnolence, to breakfast. The program was a package of laughter and tears, nostalgia and happiness, triteness and trivia, and music and songs. It was all about being wholesome and being family.

McNeill became a national icon, his popularity transcending show business.

He died on May 7, 1996, at the age of eighty-eight.

As I stood off stage watching the cast members perform their magic for a cheering in-house audience and millions of listeners all around the nation, I felt a shiver of excitement. Ameche brought the program to a close and the audience stood in unison cheering and clapping. I felt myself wanting to cheer too. I looked at Montiegel and Claiborne standing next to me and they were as cool as the day was warm. I guess it's business as usual, I thought, but I was still pleased with my own sense of exuberance. Cliff Petersen, behind the glass in the control room, gave the thumbs up sign to Ameche and the cast. Ameche looked weary and relieved that his first stint as toastmaster of America's favorite morning program was over. He was good, but a little stiff. He knew he was not Don McNeill.

I joined the others as they went onto the stage to congratulate the cast and especially Ameche. "Whew, that was tough," Ameche said with a big smile. "It's not like shooting a movie. Hope it was okay."

Everyone nodded and shook his hand. The cast and Ameche went to the broadcast table to accommodate the long line of admirers from the audience who wanted autographs. As I looked out over the huge theater from the stage, I empathized with how performers must feel. I walked over to the standing microphone in front of the control booth and fantasized that I was Johnny Desmond, singing "Laura." The lights seemed to fade and a hush fell over the audience as I....

"Hey, you. Hey, Red," a voice called from down front. I snapped out of my dream and looked down at the face of the same young man who had greeted me in front of the theater before the show. The kid had a big smile and gave me the okay with his thumb and forefinger in a circle. "It was a great show," he said. "Thanks."

"Thank you." I replied. I was part of show business!

Radio was reaching its zenith. I was awed by the effects that it could create and by the fact that one man with an idea could become a national idol, a leader in the humdrum, day-to-day living of the ordinary man in the street. Don McNeill affected the lives of people he never met, yet they felt they knew him personally. He spoke to them every morning out of the little box that sat in their dining room or kitchen. I have often reflected on those heart-warming days with Don McNeill and his *Breakfast Club*. And I have pondered, how did we get from such value-filled, all-family entertainment of yesteryear to the cynical, suggestive and often-obscene contemporary material delivered by radio talk show hosts and shock jocks today?

Back in the late nineteen-forties, radio was king and its performers and programs didn't have to sensationalize to get an audience.

Six

A New ABC is Born

Craig Claiborne kept me moving at a fast pace in the following two weeks, meeting people, providing as much information as he could about the ABC Central Division, the two ABC-owned stations in Chicago, WENR-TV and Radio Station WENR, the people both inside and outside the company, and the broadcast business in general. Most importantly, he taught me how to garner information from the producers and key contacts at the assigned shows in order to write stories for the *Daily News Report*.

I took a real liking to Craig. He was extremely helpful and good-natured and seemed to be very popular with all the people we met. He had an ingratiating manner with his soft Southern drawl, his stylish dress and obvious self-assuredness. I was told that he came from a wealthy aristocratic family in Mississippi, attended a prestigious prep school, and graduated from the University of Mississippi. He was a bachelor, lived in an apartment on Chicago's fashionable Near North Side, and had the reputation of being an exceptional host and master of cuisine. According to Ell Henry, Craig "mixed the best stand-up Beefeater martini in North America." He lived with a young man in the advertising business in Chicago who was equally stylish and friendly and somewhat effeminate. Appearances and gossip had it that they were lovers, but it didn't seem to affect Claiborne's popularity or his standing at ABC. As much as he liked his publicity job, Claiborne told me he wanted to expand his horizons and perhaps make a career of blending his writing skills with his love of cooking. He went on to do just that, gaining international renown as the food editor for the *New York Times* and the author of several best-selling books.

I also liked the new office set-up for the publicity department. It was in the hall of the Civic Opera Building on the sixteenth floor on the left as one approached the glass doors to the main ABC offices. It had a large main office as one entered with two desks for writers and two more desks for secretaries, one occupied by the curvaceous Doris Lydel. Toward the back of the room to the right was a nice-sized square office that belonged to Ell Henry and at the back wall was a doorway that led to a rectangular smaller office that had been Claiborne's, and which I would now inherit. It was a comfortable room, not apt to win designer awards, but functional, with a large window that looked out across the Chicago River at the *Daily News* Building. The room had a high ceiling and was painted a medium green that looked rather dirty at certain times of the day. In front of the window was a somewhat worn wooden desk with a telephone and in and out boxes. Four dark-green file cabinets stood against the far wall in the front of the room near the door. An old Underwood typewriter on a stand was pushed off to the side of the desk. "It's not much," I mused. "But it's mine. My first office...or at least it will be when Craig leaves."

Working as a press representative with ABC afforded me the opportunity to see all facets of the broadcasting business: radio in its matured but transitional state, and television, growing and changing every day. I visited and interviewed the programming people, the researchers, the salesmen and especially the writers, directors and talent for both radio and television, including the locally produced shows and those that were fed out to the network. I learned what the respective functions were and watched in the studio while the actors, producers, directors and technicians worked so that I could better understand how the system functioned and translate that into the stories that I would write.

It was a fascinating time to be in the television industry because it was during its earliest stages and every day brought new experiences and challenges. The unique, casual "Chicago School of Television" was created and became popular with the ever-growing television audience. Chicago had a dominant place in television from the late forties into the mid-fifties, picking up the legacy that the city enjoyed for so many years from its creativity in radio. Chicago television nurtured original and live programming such as *Garroway At Large; Kukla, Fran and Ollie,* created by the genius of

Burr Tillstrom; *The Wayne King Show*; *Super Circus*; Studs Terkel's *Studs' Place*, and the soap opera, *Hawkins Falls*. It even produced one of the medium's first live talk shows, *The Bob And Kay Show*, featuring the rotund Bob Murphy and the winsome Kay Westfall, airing locally on WENR-TV.

Being a press representative was consuming and invigorating. I had the opportunity to lunch with and get the real inside views of Chicago's highly regarded newspaper columnists: Irving "Kup" Kupcinet and Bill Irwin of the *Sun Times*; the fiery Janet Kerns from the *Herald Examiner*; and, especially, Larry Wolters and Tony Remineh of the influential *Chicago Tribune*. These people had their fingers on the pulse of what was happening in all media, especially the quickly expanding TV industry, and were very helpful to me. Wolters was the dean of the broadcast columnists and was especially helpful. An older, thoughtful, soft-spoken man, he pointed out many of the pitfalls of the public relations game and encouraged me in my writing. I remember one luncheon where we talked about the astounding growth of television and he observed, "Be careful and vigilant as you work in this business of TV. It is growing so quickly that its leaders may become expedient. That may be harmful to its potential and to the audience."

My job also had its frustrating and anxious moments. These seemed mostly to spring from the over-inflated egos, the hallmark of some, but far from all, of the performers and producers.

I was told that a new game show had been created as a pilot for a possible network time period and would originate from a Chicago ABC studio. I was assigned to write up a brief publicity piece on it for the *Daily News Report*. The program was not in production so the facts I was given were rather sketchy. I did have the game format and the fact that there were to be five celebrities on the panel including Myron (Mike) Wallace, and other Chicago performers. Wallace was a brash young man whom I had observed delivering the Peter Pan Peanut Butter commercial on the *Green Hornet* radio program on occasional visits to the Merchandise Mart studios.

Wallace was married to Buff Cobb at the time and the two were local celebrities of sorts. I didn't know them and certainly would not have guessed that Mike would go to New York and become an "icon" in the television world on CBS's *60 Minutes*.

I wrote an announcement piece on the proposed show, described its purpose and at the end listed the panel members in alphabetical order, Wallace being listed last.

The day after the story was released, I received a phone call.

The caller growled, "Who wrote the story on my new show in the Daily News Report?"

I said, "Who is this?"

"This is Mike Wallace."

"Well, this is Jim Duffy, and I wrote it," I said.

"Let me tell you something, Sonny, I am too well known in this business to only get a God-damned mention at the end of the story. We have hopes that this thing can be a big hit...."

I said, "Mr. Wallace, I worked with the data I was given and that's the way I saw the story...."

"Where are you? Because I am coming up and I am going to punch your face in," was the reply.

I thought for a moment and then said sharply, "Well, listen carefully, Mike. I am on the 16th floor of the Civic Opera Building and when you get off the elevator, turn to the right, I am the first door to the left and I will be in my office waiting for you. And, Mike, I have a suggestion for you: bring your lunch, because it is going to be a very long afternoon for you."

I hung up the phone and sat there and waited for him. He never showed up. But he did call Ell Henry a few days later and tried unsuccessfully to get me fired. Years later we were at a private party and I reminded Wallace of the incident. He just good-naturedly smiled and shook his head.

On another occasion, Ell Henry burst into the office and announced in frantic tones that a major, major ABC-TV celebrity from New York was coming through Chicago the next day, and we had to take care of "the man" and his wife (or lady-friend). The man was Bert Parks, the always tanned, pearly-toothed star of ABC's *Stop The Music*, who would later gain fame as the long-time host of the *Miss America Pageant*.

Henry had devised plans for hosting our noted star that made our heads spin. He had set up a noon luncheon with Parks and John Norton, ABC Vice President of the Central Division, at the Pump Room (in the celebrity booth) at the famed Ambassador East Hotel. I was ordered to get a limousine, bring our freelance photographer, Ray Ellingsen, buy a bouquet for Parks' lady-friend, and meet the Twentieth Century Limited train due in from New York at 9:00 AM at Union Station.

Meanwhile, Henry was making arrangements for an afternoon reception in Parks' honor at the Electric Club with Chicago's movers and shakers. He was considering taking Bert and his lady-friend to Howard Street to hear George Shearing for some late-night jazz if the occasion warranted it.

Henry's instructions to me were clear. "Don't be late meeting the train. And make sure that Ray gets some good shots when you greet Parks and hand the lady her flowers. Take them to the Ambassador East in the limo and get some pictures in the suite, if you can. This guy is a pain in the ass, so don't let him intimidate you."

Ellingsen and I were parked outside of Union Station with the limousine a good hour before the train pulled into the station. I had purchased a very pretty bouquet of orchids that was wrapped in cellophane and tied with a bright purple bow.

"Ray, be sure and get some pictures as Parks and his lady are walking toward us down the ramp and especially as I hand her the flowers," I said anxiously.

Shortly after nine o'clock, Ellingsen and I were peering down the ramp watching the hordes of people piling off of the Twentieth Century Limited that had just pulled in on track number nine. Suddenly, from the mass of people, a single dominant figure emerged. He was tanned and wore a double-breasted camelhair topcoat and he was, with arms swinging, striding mightily toward the exit. Behind him, almost stumbling, was a slender blonde lady dressed in a tight black coat with fur at the bottom. She wore a small black hat that she was clutching with one hand to keep it on her head as she took multiple itsy-bitsy steps trying to keep up with the super star.

"LET'S GO," I thought I heard Parks bellow.

"Let's go," I said to Ray Ellingsen. "It's them."

"Mr. Parks, Mr. Parks," I greeted him as he walked toward me. "Welcome to Chicago. I'm Jim Duffy with the ABC Central Division. These flowers are for Mrs. Parks."

He didn't even break stride. Barely glancing at me, he took the lovely bouquet of orchids with the bright purple ribbon, grunted, and pitched them in the nearest trash bucket.

"Were those for me?" the lady yelled as she accelerated her tiny steps trying to keep up.

"Let's go," he bellowed again. "Let's go."

I was stunned. I just froze in my tracks for a second or two and headed for the trash bucket to retrieve my flowers.

"Jim, Jim," Ellingsen yelled. "Let's go catch them at the limo."

"Did you get any pictures?" I panted as we raced for the front of the train station.

"Yeah, I got a beauty of that asshole throwing away your flowers," Ray said.

We got to the front of the station just in time to see a camel-hair coat disappear in the limousine and roar off down the street. "Jesus, Ray, the son of a bitch stole our limousine. Now what?"

We stood looking at each other for a minute or two and then I said, "Let's grab a cab and see if we can beat them to the hotel."

I hailed a cab, told the driver we were with the Secret Service, gave him twenty dollars and told him we had to get to the Ambassador East Hotel in the fastest ride of his life.

It was no use. Traffic was terrible. When we roared up to the hotel, the limo had already dropped off our TV star and was pulling away. When the driver saw me, he stopped the limo and yelled, "Hey, kid. You owe me. That bastard didn't even tip me."

"Send a bill to him," I yelled back. "And thanks for waiting for us."

When I got in the hotel, Parks had already checked in. I called the suite but a "Do not disturb" order had already been put on the phone.

Feeling very defeated, I called Ell Henry to report our failure.

"Jesus, kid," he said. "They're probably up there screwing or something right now. Break down the door and have Ray get some pictures." Then he giggled. "It's okay. Come on back to the office. It won't be the last time. It's show business, kid." He giggled some more. "Oh, by the way, I don't think the company will pay for the flowers since you failed to deliver them." I could hear him laughing as he hung up.

It was one of many episodes where I wrestled with egos, including my own. Ell Henry was right. It was all part of show business.

Part of my new role in show business was entertaining visiting newspaper columnists and, on occasion, celebrities from ABC programs who stopped off in Chicago while traveling between New York and Los Angeles. One of my favorite people was Jerry Devine, the founder and producer of the popular radio program Your *FBI In Peace And War*.

Jerry visited the Windy City on several occasions, and we became great friends. On one trip, I met him at the Ambassador East Hotel where he introduced me to Robert Mitchum and Jane Russell, two young actors who were in Chicago for the movie premiere of *My Kind of Woman*. When I shook hands with Ms. Russell, fresh from her sizzling triumph in the movie, *Outlaw*, she scowled and acted as if I were a total waste of time. Mitchum, on the other hand, was extremely friendly. At the time, he was the new heart-throb for RKO Studios and much in demand. Mitchum called me later, invited me to the premiere and asked if I might be interested in being his publicity agent in Hollywood. I declined on both counts, having hardly gotten settled in my job with ABC.

The evening entertaining, while not excessive, did put somewhat of a strain on the home front. Betty and I were still living with her parents and were anxious to find our own place. Betty didn't seem to mind my being away from home and even declined when she was asked to join us for special business occasions. Her mother, however, was a different story. I'm sure Mother Zuehsow preferred that I *never* show up at the apartment. Her demeanor made it clear that she resented me being there, especially sleeping in the same bed with her daughter.

One morning at breakfast, having found some apartments for rent in the area newspapers, I told Betty that I would try to get home early so that we could get serious about finding a place.

Mother Zuehsow overheard our conversation. She riveted me with her large blue eyes and said, "James, I see that you have circled a basement apartment that you might be interested in."

"No, I am not especially interested in any of the apartments until we have a chance to see them."

"My daughter will not live in the basement," she snapped.

"Well, of course not, Mother Zuehsow," I said as pleasantly as possible. "But I do think it's important for us to see what is available and at what rates."

When I arrived home that evening, I was greeted at the door by a wide-eyed Mother Zuehsow. "If you take my daughter to see a basement apartment, your clothes will be on the back porch when you return."

Henry Zuehsow sat in his chair in the living room shaking his head.

"Let's go, Betty," I said

We looked at several apartments in Oak Park and the adjoining community of Forest Park: a first floor garden apartment which we agreed wasn't right for us, and two or three others that we considered.

When we returned to the Zuehsow apartment, I found all of my clothing on the garbage cans on the back porch.

"Well, I guess she meant it," I said to Betty. "Look, let's not make this into World War III. Why don't you tell your folks that we're going to the Carleton Hotel for a night or two until we rent our own place."

Betty stared at me and said softly. "You go ahead. I'm going to stay here. I think my parents need me more than you do."

I was stunned. I gathered up my belongings and went around the corner to my own parents' apartment. Mom and Harold Francis were really upset, but neither said much. In retrospect, I wish they had said, "Jim, maybe you should reconsider your marriage with Betty." Divorce, in those days in my family, was unspeakable and unacceptable.

I kept very busy with my work and after a few days, Betty called and apologized. Mother Zuehsow, through Betty, sent a note of apology and invited me for dinner.

Betty and I finally got a one-bedroom apartment on Garfield Avenue in Oak Park near the "El" tracks. It was an older brick building with creaky stairs and stained hall carpets, but several young couples lived in the building, and our lives took on a happier outlook.

Jay Edson Duffy, our first child, was born on February 25, 1951. He was a robust eight-pound five-and-a-half-ounce scrambler and brought much joy to my life, along with some anxiety. Even as a tot, Jay always seemed to be moving. One time he literally took my breath away when I saw him on the sill of our third floor apartment window. He had pushed the screen out and was headed for a free fall when I grabbed him by the ankles. Between the new baby and my job in broadcasting with television coming on the scene, I, too, was moving most of the time.

In the early days of television, the programs, even the commercials, were all live. After a program aired, a recording called a kinescope or "kinnie" (it was a film made directly from the television monitor) would be sent around the country to stations that didn't pick it up on a live signal. The quality was usually pretty poor, but it was the only means of distribution at the time. It was done on a "bicycling" basis, where kinescopes would be sent out to say twenty stations to be aired and after the air dates were completed, those stations would send the kinescopes on to twenty other assigned stations and so on until that particular show's distribution was completed. The result was that a particular episode of a show would be shown, including the commercials, at different time periods and on different days, sometimes two months after the original airdate. This created a nightmare for the researchers trying to track an audience for the show. It was worse for advertisers trying to key a certain date for a national promotion for their product. The human error factor was always in play. The ABC Sales Service Department was bombarded with calls from station managers, "Where the hell is my episode of *Super Circus?*" In tracking down the culprit in the "bicycle" chain, the answer would invariably come back, "Well, gee, we put it in the mail on Tuesday...."

With today's advanced technology it is hard to imagine that kind of rudimentary process. But, for all its shortcomings, it worked: the viewers kept watching and the advertisers kept buying.

Today, of course, the majority of network entertainment shows are pre-recorded, allowing the luxury of editing before the viewer ever sees them. Some critics say much of the freshness and spontaneity of TV's live performances is lost in today's more controlled environments. Certainly, live production was one of the factors in the magic of the Chicago School of Television and the often referred to Golden Age of Television. For sure, the hilarious bloopers from the live era are missed.

Super Circus was one of early ABC Television's most popular shows. It featured tall, handsome Claude Kirchner as the ringmaster; gorgeous, blonde, nineteen-year-old Mary Hartline as the circus beauty and sometime band leader; Cliffy and Scampy the clowns; and lots of animals and circus acts.

The program premiered in 1948 and was tested for three weeks without an audience before its first telecast on October 2nd. It played every Sunday afternoon before a live audience, and was telecast to the homes of the growing number of Americans who had TV sets and to bars and other public places where sets were rapidly increasing. Early every Sunday afternoon outside ABC's Civic Theater, a block-long line would form of children waiting for the show with their accompanying parents (adults were not admitted to the show unless they were with children).

Many of the people who constructed *Super Circus* went on to fame and fortune in the ensuing years as television grew. Greg Garrison, the handsome director of the show, later produced and directed the *Sid Caesar Comedy Hour* and Dean Martin's variety shows. I ran into Greg some years later at Caesar's Palace in Las Vegas and I swear he looked more like Dean Martin than Martin himself. Grover Allen was a floor director on *Super Circus*. He became one of the top directors in Chicago. George Paul, a fill-in director on the show, is now one of ABC News' most sought-after producer/directors. And members of the *Super Circus* band were understatedly incredible. Many, as with members of the *Breakfast*

Club orchestra, were feature musicians with the big-name swing bands of the era.

Writing about *Super Circus* became a regular part of my life.

I remember the time a well-trained pelican appeared on the show. Suddenly the pelican took off from its trainer's shoulder and headed for the balcony, much to the hysterical amusement of the theater audience. The pelican zoomed around and finally landed on the upper balcony rail and refused to come down. Go to black!

And I remember the time three motorcycling chimpanzees were featured. They were doing very well, cycling in a circle to the music of the *Super Circus* band, when one of them spotted Mary Hartline waving her baton, supposedly leading the musicians. The chimp got off his bike and threw it at the lovely Miss Hartline. Mary screamed, and ducked, and the motorcycle went crashing though the bass drum. Go to commercial!

That was a minor mishap. The chimps had nothing on Tom Pack's elephants. Three of the pachyderms were booked on *Super Circus* a few weeks later.

I remember it well because I was there in the studio, as I was for practically every telecast. Usually the elephants were relieved before they were to go on stage. Apparently it was overlooked on this occasion. Again, Mary Hartline, her golden locks flowing, was riding on the shoulders of the lead elephant. The pachyderms were doing their act, marching to the music, holding each other's trunks, when the lead elephant suddenly stopped. He defecated mightily right on the stage. The other animals followed their leader. Ms. Hartline had to dismount and before she knew it, she was ankle deep in elephant manure. The cameramen showed shots of the big top tent, the studio balcony, the studio audience (which was roaring with laughter), whatever they could to avoid pictures of a messy, distressed Miss Hartline. It got so bad that the trainer and stage hands had to get the elephants out of there and clean up the mess before they could continue the telecast.

One of the perks for working on the *Super Circus* crew, I was told, was that there was a crew restroom adjoining Mary Hartline's dressing room. Apparently, several peepholes were engineered peering directly into Mary's changing quarters. The descriptions that came from certain members of the crew would make a grown man's shoes squeak. Mary, for a time, was married to "Pappy" Stokes, the Chicago network program director. He was easily thirty years her senior and always epitomized the punch line of the old joke: when his doctor warned an elderly fellow about too much sex, the old fellow replied, "If she dies, she dies."

Equally humorous moments in those early days involved the commercials – especially by used-car dealers – because commercials were also live. There were stories of car dealers who would intentionally try to sabotage their competitors' live announcements.

One of the examples involved the not-too-popular Sabini brothers. Legend has it that from time to time, one of the Sabinis' competitors would sneak into the showroom and remove the distributor caps from the cars slated for television showing.

The story goes that one always smooth-talking Sabini brother was over-modulating in his best, but affected, tones, "Here, ladies and genelmen, we have something spectacular for you. Let's bring in this indescribably buful yella Lincoln convertible." Nothing happened. So he continued to talk, "This is a sensational aumobile...What a beauty...She'll be here in a secon...." The car wouldn't start. The offstage grinding of the starter could be heard over the air. Sabini started to get noticeably irritated. "Push it out, push it," he whispered, and then cursed as his assistants failed to push the "beauty" onto the set. The director finally had to go to black and return to the movie. It was no big loss for the Sabini brothers. Television had them selling more cars than they had ever imagined.

The most popular and successful of all the local programs sponsored by automobile dealers was *Jim Moran's Courtesy Hour*. Moran was a tall, blond fellow with a nice smile and an honest face. For one hour every Monday night, he would present a live talent show with special guests on WENR-TV. At the commercial breaks, he would sell his automobiles on behalf of his dealership, Courtesy Motors. The talent often wasn't that good, but it really didn't matter. Moran sold thousands of automobiles, including one to me. It was the first car I ever owned.

In a very different vein, another example of the uniqueness of live television was a regular ABC program called *Studs' Place*. I wrote an article on the show in an edition of *TV Times*, a forerunner of the later *TV Guide*:

> *Studs' Place is not a variety show with dancing girls and choral groups. And it is not a dramatic show with synthetic contrived plots. It is a program with normal people, surrounded by common tables, and common chairs, and plenty of emotion.*
>
> *Studs' Place's credo is that honest human relationships make for good televiewing. That theory has made the program genuine and alive to the critics and TViewers because we all have experienced the essence of emotion...heartaches...warm companionship...moments of exuberant happiness...moments of throbbing despair. These are the concerns on Studs' Place.*
>
> *On a recent telecast, the principals of the show discussed labor pains with a prospective father while his wife was in the delivery room. It was one of the first such discussions on television.*
>
> *The program's principals, Studs Terkel, Chet Roble, Win Stracke, and Beverly Younger, do a great deal in making Studs' Place authentic. Studs, Chet and Win play themselves on the show. Only Beverly and Studs have acting backgrounds. Chet and Win were brought to the show for their musical talents, but their naturalness and simplicity before the cameras have brought them tightly into the speaking format.*
>
> *Before each show, at rehearsal, the actors are presented with a story outline, not a script. The personalities take it from there, inventing their own dialogue as the story progresses.*

The *Studs' Place* shows were all live, put out over the airwaves, warts and all. Considering the fact that there was no script, no memorized lines, the risk of bloopers was great, but so were the opportunities for spontaneous ad-lib masterpieces, and it was these moments that far overshadowed any distraction of an unpolished performance.

One lesson I learned during that period – and the industry learned it too – was that good radio does not necessarily translate into good television. ABC and Don McNeill Enterprises made a major effort to take the highly successful Don McNeill's *Breakfast Club* and translate the popularity of its star and cast into a different format on *Don McNeill's TV Club*. The TV venture was to be the centerfold of ABC's prime-time schedule in the early fifties. The telecast was scheduled to air at 8:00 PM Central Time on Wednesday nights. We had to build a huge publicity and promotion campaign around it. The show was produced with a far more elaborate set from the same studio as the radio *Breakfast Club*. I helped put together an enormous reception in the Electric Club prior to the premiere show. We all had high expectations. McNeill was brilliant; he was warm and corny and funny, but the elements just didn't translate from radio to television, in the same way the legendary *Fibber McGee and Molly*, also all-time radio favorites, never really made the move over to TV. Some radio performers, however, did make the transition to the newer medium: Jackie Gleason did to a large degree, Bob Hope certainly did, but in a different format. We were all learning. There was a TV perspective, a visuality, that had to be carefully taken into consideration and the same old cornball kind of joke that worked on radio often fell totally flat on television.

It was apparent early on that the new visual medium would grow into one of the most influential factors in our society. It would be a means of reaching almost every person in the country, forcefully and instantaneously. I could see the power it held, the power to change what people thought and what they did. And it became fairly clear that these changes could be either beneficial or destructive. Television's influence would depend totally on management's sense of responsibility. Television would depend on the people who created the programs, how the scripts and story lines were crafted, the executives who made the decisions on what programs would be on the air, and also the television viewing audience.

I hoped then that the various players in the broadcasting game, myself included, would acknowledge television's power, and live up to those responsibilities.

Until 1952, my job was to publicize ABC Central Division's radio and TV programs. Then one day in May of that year, I received a phone call from John H. Norton, Jr., the vice president of the Central Division. He told me that Dean Linger, the promotion manager, was being promoted to New York and asked if I would be interested in taking that job. The word 'promotion' was somewhat misleading since the job had responsibilities far exceeding promotion and exploitation. Advertising, marketing, and promotion, as we know it today, were probably a better description for the department. The responsibilities included creating and placing all media advertising for print, billboards, radio, television and other specialized advertising vehicles. The office also was responsible for producing sales brochures and research analysis for the programs in the Central Division. And the promotion people wrote all of the on-the-air copy highlighting the shows from the Central Division. The job sounded like quite a challenge and an opportunity.

I was twenty-six years old, with three years' experience at ABC. I figured I was ready to broaden my horizon and run my own department, so I accepted the job with great enthusiasm. It turned out to be an exceptional learning experience. With help from my staff of two writers and a secretary, I was introduced to the intricacies of advertising. I learned layouts and copy appealing to different listening or viewing segments of the audience. I learned how to create and structure programming and research brochures for the sales departments. One of my old pals from Beloit College, Bill Hohlman, came to work for me as the manager of research and we had some fun sorting out the media statistics.

I learned how to deal with sales and copy people; station promotion representatives from around the country; and, most importantly, ABC's large staff of executives from New York, Detroit, Los Angeles and San Francisco.

My new job involved some unusual adventures, too. One of them was participating in the annual Christmas Parade in downtown Chicago. In November 1953, just after Thanksgiving, our department was responsible for creating a colorful ABC float, to promote our stations, programs and personalities. Ell arranged to have Bob Hope featured as part of the presentation. The famous comedian, along with other ABC celebrities, greeted Santa Claus and waved at tens of thousands of onlookers as we wound through the streets. Ell and I, of course, rode along with the reporters and photographers. It was a long, but very exciting and successful day.

On another front, we were responsible for tying in merchandising ideas with local and national sponsors. One episode involved the Ralston Purina Rocket, a thirty-foot Star-Wars type of vehicle that a fellow named Don Cole, from the Gardner Advertising Agency in St Louis, brought to Chicago. We worked with the Chicago Police and parked the rocket on various streets over a two-week period. Kids came from every part of the city and suburbs to walk through the fascinating vehicle from outer space. It was great visibility for the Ralston Purina Company and for ABC.

As the promotion manager, I was a department head and, consequently, sat in on all executive staff meetings and got an inside look on how the company was doing and its plans for the future. It was in those staff meetings, held every Monday morning, that I realized the seriousness of the potential merger of United Paramount Theaters and the American Broadcasting Company. The merger had been agreed upon at special meetings of the stockholders of both companies on July 27, 1951, but there were serious concerns from the Justice Department's Antitrust Division that caused long delays and much speculation that the merger would never happen. It was a frustrating and debilitating time for the company and its employees since ABC was reportedly almost out of fuel financially. Yet it had to be business as usual in a multi-million dollar organization, which embraced the exploding new industry of television. It created fascinating conversation and speculation for all of us.

On Monday, February 9, 1953, the announcement came down the line that the Federal Communications Commission had approved a new company after 93 days of hearings and 19 months of waiting. We had new bosses and the company had a new name:

American Broadcasting - Paramount Theaters, Inc. (AB-PT). We were puzzled about what it all meant. It didn't help when United Paramount Theater President Leonard Goldenson and his key executives and the top officials from ABC New York, including ABC President Robert Kintner, came to Chicago for meetings with ABC employees. The principal owner of ABC, Edward Nobel of Lifesaver Company fame, did not attend. All of the Central Division employees gathered in the Civic Opera Theater after a *Breakfast Club* broadcast and heard how we were "all going to work together and how great the future looked." As in all such circumstances, there was much emotion and skepticism about the intruders in our company.

Leonard Goldenson paid $25 million for ABC against the recommendation of most of the members of the United Paramount Theater Board of Directors. At the time of the merger, ABC had 355 radio affiliates, including five owned radio stations, 14 primary television stations (five of which were owned), and assets of some $29 million.

In early 1953 there were 159 commercial television stations on the air. CBS had 74 affiliates, NBC had 71 and ABC brought up the rear with 14.

Despite the competitive disparities, later years would show that Leonard Goldenson made one of the outstanding purchases in the history of broadcasting.

In Chicago, we did not realize just how difficult the merger would be. Because of the complication of station ownership changes, much confusion was created for the viewers, and certainly for our promotion and publicity departments, when station call letters and channels changed the day after the merger. Our lives were further complicated when the entire staff from Channel 4, the former CBS-affiliated station, descended on us en masse to occupy offices right down the hall in the Civic Opera Building. These people were now to be employed by ABC's Channel 7 (with the call letters WBKB, formerly at Channel 4) and work with the rest of us. It was as if the enemy had infiltrated our lines and they did the very same jobs that we were supposed to do. It meant that there were two complete (and unfriendly to one another) sets of management and staff – sales, programming, and engineering – running the AB-PT Central Division. Fortunately for Ell Henry and me, the new folks in our midst did not have publicity and promotion departments, partly because they ran a local station operation and the station manager handled whatever had to be done, and partly because they "didn't believe those functions were necessary," I was told.

I do know that when members of the new AB/PT management team were taking a tour of our facilities and stopped in my office, the head of engineering made a point of asking me what I did as the manager of promotion.

I carefully explained my responsibility for all newspaper advertising, sales promotion, and exploitation of the national and local programs for both television and radio in the Central Division.

He looked at me sourly and said, "And we pay you for that?" He left my office as quickly as he had arrived.

And I said, "Yeah, just like they pay you for screwing up all the pictures that go out over the air." But I said it when he was down the hall and couldn't hear me, thank God.

The worst part of it was that I reported to two bosses and had to get approval from both for final advertising layouts and for any unusual expenditure of funds. It was almost impossible. John Norton was ABC's head of the division and John Mitchell was the new VP of the division under the AB/PT banner. It was very uncertain as to who would finally win the top position or if there was a possible realignment that could include both of them. The two men were very competitive and did not like each other. If you found yourself in a room with both of them, it seemed to get very chilly if not downright frigid.

I finally figured how to get an approval if I was on deadline to get a newspaper ad placed for *A Date With Judy*, or whatever show we were promoting. I would take the ad layout to Norton and rather breathlessly say, "Mr. Norton, I have a 5:00 PM deadline on this ad. It is a good clean ad, lots of white space. I think it will be effective, and I need your approval."

"Has Mitchell seen it?" Norton would ask.

"Yes, sir. I don't think he likes it," I would answer.

"Run it," he'd snap.

Then I would go in and see John Mitchell and give him the same pitch.

Mitchell was a little slower in his deliberations. He would study me for a while to see what kind of game I might be playing. Finally he would ask, "Has Mr. Norton seen the ad?"

"Yes sir, I don't think he likes it at all," I would say with a straight face and my fingers crossed.

"Then run it," Mitchell would say, and I was free to proceed with the job they were paying me to do.

This little game was very nerve wracking. I didn't like it at all. It went on – not every day, but far too often – for nearly two months.

Finally one Friday early in May (I labeled it "Black Friday"), the word came out that Sterling "Red" Quinlan, the general manager of the new operation, was calling people into his office and dismissing them from the new company. I was stunned. People I had worked with for the past four years, some who had been with ABC since 1943, were being fired. The report was that, by the end of the day, 29 people from the former American Broadcasting Company had been released in Chicago.

I wondered when I would get the call. At about 3:00 PM, Quinlan's office called with the message that he wanted to see me. I squared my shoulders and headed for his office wondering all the way what the severance pay might be and when I should make the phone calls to the two companies that had offered me jobs in the past few weeks. One of them, incidentally, was NBC.

Closer to home, Ed Smith, director of sales for the ABC Central Division Radio Network and a good friend of Ell Henry's, had, on several occasions, planted a seed that I should get into broadcast sales. He told me to give him a call whenever I was ready, as he was interested in naming me an account executive (salesman). I was intrigued by the idea.

Red Quinlan, who turned out to be a friend and terrific executive, got up and greeted me warmly when I came into his office.

"This has been a long and terrible day for us, Jimmy," he said. "But I just wanted you to know that we took to two guys in this place like a duck takes to water. Ell Henry is one of them and you're the other. We want you to stay on as promotion manager in the new company."

I was really surprised since I had expected the worst. I thanked him and told him I was flattered but wanted to think about it since I had had some recent offers.

"You do what's best for you," Red said. "But a piece of advice. Don't leave the broadcasting industry. It's going to be dynamite."

Quinlan was right with his advice. I had no intention of leaving the industry.

The early fifties were a meaningful time to be in broadcasting. They saw the birth of network television programming and, at the same time, radio broadcasting in all its glory. Many talented and innovative people were in front of and behind the cameras and microphones. Every day was a new experience and a new adventure. I, of course, look back on the fifties with great fondness. It was a beginning for me. I met many wonderful and unusual people along the way during those early years.

The Chicago ABC executive staff was eclectic and strange, but stimulating as I reflect on it. There were many very able and professional people, but I remember the following three as being the most colorful. The Central Division's manager of purchasing was a dark-haired, dark-eyed, slinky and very sexy woman in her thirties named Mary. It was rare when a visiting executive from other ABC offices did not have his eyes on her. After the AB/PT merger Mary was dismissed. The new executives were shocked to find huge warehouses stacked with paper products – toilet paper and paper towels – that ABC had purchased from Mary's husband's company. All I know was that at the company Christmas parties, the exotic Mary was terrific, a good dancer, a good sport and loads of fun.

One of the most colorful characters on the ABC management team was the chief engineer for the division whom everyone knew as The Chief. He was a brawny, beefy-faced, energetic and macho man who put in more time at the Civic Opera Bar than at the engineering office. He was famed and loved for the fact that when there was a strike by the broadcast unions, The Chief was there, day and night, to direct his troops and keep the stations and network on the air. He set a record of 72 hours without sleep. I worked with him during one broadcast engineers' strike, on cameras and on the station-break microphones, and I was astounded because he was indefatigable. The Chief was an institution in his day. He died tragically in a swimming accident a few years later, after he had left ABC.

There were several others, but probably the most eccentric was the financial officer for the Central Division, named Frank. Frank was a quiet man, small, undistinguished and more prone to stay in his office with his calculations than mix with the rest of us at the Civic Opera Bar. Frank had an assistant: a stoic, rather unattractive, but well-endowed younger, blonde woman, who spent most of her time in Frank's office. I was always fascinated that Frank was in his office with his door closed when I came to work, when I went to lunch, and when I went home for the day, no matter the hour. I never thought too much about it except, when on rare occasions, I would see his assistant in the hall, and she would give a sheepish grin and look very relaxed. Frank and his blonde assistant controlled all of the division's financial data. It was no surprise to most of us that when the merger with United Paramount Theaters happened, the new company fired Frank and his assistant. The new management was astounded when they found only blank pages in the financial ledgers. Frank had all the data in his head, backed by the statistics of his assistant. There was no way AB/PT could trace the financial history of the Central Division unless they hired Frank on a handsome retainer to bring them up to speed. They did. Supposedly, when the new company cleared out Frank's desk, while they did not find the financial records, they did find some whiskey bottles and risqué magazines. I always admired Frank for his privacy, even when it was fodder for off-color jokes.

And there was, of course, my man Elliot W. Henry, Jr., who rounded out the Central Division team and guided me.

Ell Henry was an extraordinary mentor to me. I have always been grateful to him for giving me an opportunity and getting me started in the broadcasting business. He went on to become the vice president for public relations for the ABC Western Division and a prominent figure in California broadcasting. Ell and I corresponded and visited on many occasions until he passed away in late 1994.

Seven

Broadcast Sales and Public Service

In retrospect, I should have recognized that "Black Friday" represented a serious crossroads – even potential opportunities in new directions for my career. I should have thoroughly explored all the options that might have been available to me, within the reconstructed company, with other networks or stations, or even with advertising agencies where I had been offered positions based on my work with the *Breakfast Club*. I probably should have more seriously considered doing some outside sportscasting work that had been offered by small radio stations in northern Illinois or even investigated announcing jobs at the ABC local television and radio stations that might have satisfied some of the 'ham' in me that I tasted mightily in my work at WBNB in Beloit. I could have at least followed through on the advice of Frank Reichstein, Don Dobson and others to get in front of the camera. I thought about all of these, but I wanted to move on, and quickly.

The Monday morning following my meeting with Quinlan, I went in to see Ed Smith about the account executive's spot he'd offered me with the ABC Radio Network.

It was strange that I would consider going into the sales field. I had acquired an aversion to the idea of selling when I worked part time at my dad's shoe store in Oak Park selling ladies' shoes. Smelling feet and putting up with the insults of complaining, disgruntled customers turned me off. But selling radio, I reasoned, would be different.

I felt very comfortable speaking in front of groups of people, making improvised remarks or presentations (as far back as my high school speech classes). I had made a few presentations to all of the employees in the Central Division about our activities in the promotion department. After one presentation, Jim Stirton, the distinguished VP in charge of television sales, stood up and said amidst some laughter, "Jim, you can sell used cars for me anytime." I wasn't sure it was the kind of image I wanted, but there was little question that I was tagged as the sales type.

Being an account executive with a major network had certain panache to it, especially at my young age. And the compensation, as Ed Smith laid it out to me, was sensational: $12,000 a year plus commissions. This would allow Betty and me and our young son, Jay, to move out of our rented apartment near the "El" tracks in Oak Park and move into a house of our own.

After cleaning up my business in the promotion department, I joined radio network sales on April 1, 1953, the day before my 27th birthday. The sales offices were located in the southwest corner on the 15th floor of the Civic Opera Building. It was a large bullpen located directly across the hall from the network television sales office. Unfortunately, Ed Smith resigned from the radio network a few weeks after I joined the department. A former CBS executive named Don Roberts replaced him. Roberts was cordial, at best, and I had the distinct feeling during the first year that he resented my age and inexperience.

I was the youngest salesman in the department by at least twenty years with the exception of Pat Rastall, a former CBS salesman. The differences between the people in the two sales departments – radio and television – were really a sign of the times. The radio salesmen were much older and looked a little worn out and content to wait for their pensions to kick in, while the television people were young, aggressive and alert. Each one had a sharp sense of humor. The television salesmen's big joke was that they were going to get a large plastic bubble and put it over the radio operation and donate it to the Smithsonian Institution.

Rastall was somewhat of a savior for me because he was a very sharp young guy who helped me over the rough spots during the first few weeks. It wasn't long before Pat and I became known as "the joy boys of radio." We developed a song and dance act as "the joy boys," and while the television sales people thought it was great, our radio crew, including the boss, didn't see any humor in it.

Speaking of inexperience, I had no idea how to make a one-on-one verbal sales presentation, although I had written several presentations in my promotion job and, as I described, loved to make speeches or presentations to groups of people. What was required of me now was mostly one-on-one sales calls where I had a radio program to sell to a buyer. My job was to convince that person that sponsorship of this particular program would benefit the sale of his or her product. Quite an intimidating task when you haven't done it before.

My first sales call was a disaster. I called on an agency representative for Drewry's Beer, and instead of casually discussing the radio possibilities for his client, I found myself pacing in front of his desk, waving my arms as though I were making a major oration.

The bemused executive finally stopped me and said, "Slow down, son. You don't have to preach to me. Sit down and tell me what you have to sell."

I started to learn about media sales and how to sell. The old-timers around me seemed to have the attitude that radio was on the way out and TV was on the way in, and they rolled their eyes at my enthusiasm and ambition when I would go out on a call. One morning as I headed for the door with my briefcase under my arm, one of the old-time salesmen stopped me and asked me where I was going in such a hurry. I told him I was taking a taxi to the Leo Burnett Agency on Michigan Avenue, where I had an appointment.

"Can that crap," the old-timer said. "Take the bus up to Michigan Avenue and put in for the cab on your expense account. You're screwing it up for the rest of us."

This was the same old-timer that I would see headed for Grant Park near the lakefront a couple of mornings a week. Legend had it that he would sit in the park and feed the pigeons when he was supposed to be making sales calls. It wasn't too long before he got to feed the pigeons full time, when he was summarily "retired."

I was determined that I would not get caught up in that defeatist attitude. I had the sincere belief that radio remained a far-reaching and influential medium. So I applied the old adage, as corny as it sounds, "You've got to see 'em to tell 'em and tell 'em to sell 'em." Much to the chagrin of the geriatric crew, I got in my gray two-door 1951 Chevrolet and traveled around my territory, which was Indiana and central and southern Illinois, and literally knocked on doors. I would always call first: "I'm in your area. I want to come in and introduce myself and see how we can help you sell more of your product. I'm with the ABC Radio Network."

I guess this just wasn't done at the time, but I found the advertisers extremely receptive. It laid the groundwork for a lot of business in later years.

For the first nine months I didn't sign any business at all. I was starting to question my ability to sell, as I'm sure Don Roberts was also. But by making face-to-face sales calls and buying lunch for key buyers, I made a lot of contacts. One of these buyers, an older lady – older to me at the time – by the name of Evelyn Vanderploeg, with the Lillienfield Advertising Agency, sort of mothered me. One day she told me over lunch, "The Realemon Company is interested in a buy; the proposal you made is taking hold. You may want to go see them."

This was my chance. I made my appointment at the Realemon Company and gave my presentation on *Breakfast Club* to the company president and his advertising department.

The next day, Evelyn called me and said breathlessly, "Congratulations. You have an order."

My first sale. I was delirious: a quarter hour once a week in Don McNeill's *Breakfast Club* from a good, reputable client. Chuck Lillienfield, the president of the agency, had the order written up and sent over by messenger to me with a copy to Don Roberts.

Charlie Ayres, the vice president in charge of the ABC Radio Network, was in Chicago that day and was in a meeting with Roberts when the ordering letter arrived. I was really proud of my accomplishment and buzzed Roberts to see if I could interrupt their meeting.

Roberts had a big smile as he opened the letter and then his face turned sour and he said, "What the hell is this?" and threw the order on the desk in front of me.

"It's the Realemon order, Don," I said, starting to panic.

"Yeah, well you sold it for the time cost only. The order is invalid."

I looked at the letter and could not believe it. The order was for $3,500 a week, which, indeed, was the time cost only. There was supposed to be a program charge on top, making the full order $6,500 for the quarter hour sponsorship. I was certain I had made that clear to the agency and just knew it had to be in my written proposal.

Charlie Ayres was a crusty old sort. (He really wasn't that old. He just acted grouchy and old.) I heard him make grunting disapproving noises.

"Let me call the agency right away," I said.

"No, sit still. I'll call Lillienfield, that conniving bastard," Roberts said. "Let's see what's going on here."

I listened red-faced and anxious as Roberts and Lillienfield had a conversation with a lot of "uh huhs" and "oh, I see" from Roberts and it ended up with Roberts telling Lillienfield that Charlie Ayres was in town and wanted to come over and see him.

Ayres and I went to see Lillienfield and his agency people. I defended myself mightily and showed them the written presentation with the costs outlined. It was resolved when Ayres and Lillienfield sat silently and exchanged little pieces of paper with figures on them. Ayres finally nodded and the Realemon Company had the order at a discount price. I believe the final figure was $5,000.

"Hey, Charlie," Lillienfield said just before we left. "Advertising is a tough business. Never send a boy to do a man's job."

I was humiliated but, nonetheless, it was my first sale. I also learned a very valuable lesson. Always, triple-check your figures in your presentation and reiterate them in your meeting with the client. And always read an ordering letter before you take it to your boss.

In the next few months, business really started to come my way, thanks in great part to my practice of making client calls. One day I got three large orders all on the same day; one from the Aero Mayflower Moving Company with the largest order in radio news in ten years; another from Ball Brothers and their mason jars in Muncie, Indiana for sponsorship of Don McNeill's *Breakfast Club* in Review on Saturday mornings, a program we had created especially for them; and a renewal from the Bankers Life and Trust Company for *Paul Harvey News*. Suddenly the television network sales department became interested in my services.

If only all my sales efforts had gone that way! I made a presentation where a key executive at an agency, after an obviously heavy lunch, fell dead asleep in the middle of my pitch and another, where the bulb in the projector exploded when I punched up the most important slide in my proposal. But, all in all, I was getting far more than my share of business for ABC Radio. It was at the time that advertising was growing rapidly into a very large business.

Selling advertising and the resulting commercials that are presented on the air are what make the American over-the-air broadcasting system possible.

Bing Crosby said of broadcasting, "Well, I'd say it's pretty good considering it's for nothing." Consider that without paying any bill or subscription fee, without being hit up for donations, in fact, without any apparent cost to you at all, you can turn on the radio or television and tune in to a variety of stations and enjoy entertainment, news or sports programs. This is obvious when you stop to think about it. The average viewer or listener often doesn't stop to think about it. After all, this is America, and it is a society based on commercialism and profit. There is no such thing as a free lunch. How can there be such a thing as a free radio or television program? The stations and the networks are run as profit-making corporations with owners or shareholders who expect to make significant financial rewards from their activities. But it's free to you and me. Modern miracle? No. Someone is paying for it. The people paying are the advertisers. They are underwriting the entertainment, news, sports, documentary or other type of program with their advertising dollars, and in return for this, you and I get to hear a predetermined amount of their message about the products they want us to purchase. In the end, of course, it is you and I who really pay for this system by buying a variety of goods and services that the advertisers present. If the advertisers failed to see sales results from their commercials, they would move away from broadcast ads and eventually the system of commercial television and radio, as we know it, would simply fold. A new system would undoubtedly be devised to take its place.

Over-the-air commercial broadcasting, while it has exploded in its growth, has changed little over the years in terms of its basic system. Cable and Pay TV emerged in the nineteen-eighties and created some competition in terms of programming and revenues, but neither system could match the vast national coverage of commercial broadcasting. Cable and Pay TV lacked the foundation of commercial broadcasting, localism, wherein stations in cities across the country present local news, sports, weather and traffic reports as well as national or regional programming.

Advertising was, and still is, the backbone of commercial broadcasting, nationally and locally, and, although there are a great many complexities involved, they all derive from the simple formula of programming with commercial inserts.

A good example: in my radio selling days advertisers would fight to sponsor Paul Harvey's news show. Harvey's first job was as a news announcer with Station WENR in Chicago in 1944. Fifty-seven years later, he is still ABC's leading radio personality, with millions of listeners. And his listeners trust Harvey and believe him when he endorses and delivers the commercial for a product. Most importantly, they purchase the product.

Harvey, as you probably know, has that unmistakable sense of importance and drama in his voice. He has the wonderful, dramatic flair of pausing… and making a point, pausing…and then finishing with a flourish.

It was during the decade of the fifties that I became involved in my first real work in community service. It began in 1953 when Betty and I and young Jay, now three years old, moved to Glen Ellyn, Illinois, a lovely, peaceful suburb twenty-three miles west of Chicago. We bought our first home, a small three-bedroom, Queen Anne Cape Cod at 669 Pleasant Avenue. It was a delightful little house with two bedrooms downstairs and a large, dormer-windowed room upstairs that was ideal for children. We had a single-car garage with a screened-in porch off the back. In later years, the porch became a playhouse as our family grew and youngsters from the neighborhood came to visit. I became a legitimate commuter, using the Chicago Northwestern Railroad on a daily basis, at least when I wasn't traveling.

We had adjusted to the trials and pleasures of exurbia for about a year when our second son, Terry Beach, was born on August 5, 1954. He was an adorable, tow-headed little fellow who could break your heart just looking at you. While Jay was outgoing and verbal, Terry, as he grew, was quieter and more introspective. From the time Terry was born, there was an instant bonding with Jay that lasted throughout their abbreviated lives. They were brothers in every sense of the word. As I look back on my life, one of my most heart-filling joys as a father and a human being was to play with Jay and Terry, love them and watch them as they grew from toddlers to boys. Those moments now seem so long ago. Yet, they are indelible in my mind.

Also on the personal side, I began to pursue my long-time interest in singing when a high school friend, Joe Mikolas, invited me to take vocal lessons with him in Oak Park. Camille Mikolas, Joe's mother, had reputedly been with the Boston Opera in her younger years and had been training her son for some time. Most Tuesday nights I would stop off at the Mikolas house in Oak Park on my way home from work, and for an hour or two, Mrs. Mikolas would have me vocalize and eventually sing some simple arias and even some show tunes and popular ballads. It got to the point that on weekends, Joe and I would be in demand to sing at piano bars and restaurants in the area. Eventually I sang, on occasions, in some small clubs under the name of Johnny Holiday, and I enjoyed it immensely. Singing, like speaking and acting, is a great release from the stresses of life for me.

One Saturday afternoon in 1954, I was raking the fall leaves on our small front lawn when a fellow named Kink Pilkenton stopped by and asked if I would be interested in joining the Jaycees, the Glen Ellyn Junior Chamber of Commerce. He explained that the Jaycees were a volunteer national service organization that used the talents and abilities of men under thirty-five years of age in community service to better their respective towns or cities, their states and the nation. I was reluctant at first, but Pilkenton explained that the Glen Ellyn chapter was just two years old, had recruited about eighteen members and was looking to build a large and effective organization that we could all take some pride in and have a lot of fun while we were doing it. "Besides," he said, "It is the quickest way I know to meet people in this town that we hope you'll call home for a long time."

The work of the Jaycees was useful and personally gratifying because it got us into the heart of the community, and along with its needs, we learned a good deal about the town itself. We met many of the leaders and residents of the community as well. Neighborhood clean-ups, paint-ups, get out the vote campaigns, and charity fund drives were organized by the Jaycees. A highlight of every year was the Saturday before Christmas when the entire group would take children from the local orphanage into the Marshall Fields' store in downtown Chicago. We would spend the entire day with the youngsters visiting Santa Claus and the toy department. The joy was in giving out gifts to each child at a luncheon in their honor. This was a fun trip, not just for the kids, but also for each of us because we got to know the individual youngsters. Many of us stayed in touch with the kids at other times of the year. As I look back, this type of charity effort was a predecessor to many of the comprehensive mentoring programs we have for inner city kids today. Importantly for each of the Jaycees, the effort blessed us with the spirit of giving and set the tone for the holiday season with our own families.

I eventually became the president of the Glen Ellyn Jaycees and toward the end of my tenure, we organized a Village Fair to raise funds for community charities. This was a weeklong activity held in an empty parking lot and field near the center of town. It included rides for the kids and booths with all kinds of games for everyone, at a price, of course. The local merchants set up display booths and auctioned their wares. There were bake, taffy and fudge sales, too. It was really quite an event that turned out most of the town. As the highlight of the fair, I organized a contest to select the *Fairest of the Fair*, a write-in competition with the local newspaper, including ballot boxes at the fairgrounds, to select a young woman and her court who best exemplified the spirit and beauty of Glen Ellyn.

The Junior League and a team of faculty from the high school nominated young ladies, sixteen to twenty years old. The contestants' pictures were put in the paper and the finalists were featured with large blow-up photos at the fair. The announcement of the winner came in the afternoon at the final Sunday at the fair.

I had searched mightily to find the proper celebrity who would help me crown the winner. Ell Henry finally came through for us. It so happened that Clint Walker, the rugged six-foot-six star of the new ABC Television Network show *Cheyenne*, was going to be in Chicago that weekend on a promotional tour for the show. Walker was brought to my home that Sunday morning, met my children, and turned out to be absolutely delightful. That afternoon at the fair, I was going to have Walker ride a horse from a couple of blocks from the fairgrounds, up through the crowd, and dismount at the stage, but the police, for safety reasons, would have none of it.

At the appointed moment on that bright, breezy afternoon, we had the final six contestants take the stage. I walked up the steps of the platform and approached the microphone. We had promoted the fact all week that "Cheyenne" would be part of the ceremonies. A couple of thousand people had arrived to see the TV star.

I welcomed everyone and, as I introduced the young ladies, built up the suspense as to who would be chosen as the Fairest of the Fair. Finally I paused and said, "As often happens, we advertised the fact that Clint Walker, the star of ABC's show *Cheyenne* would be with us today. Well, unfortunately, he couldn't...."

A large groan rose from the crowd as I continued... "Wait a minute," I said. "There's a disturbance at the back of the crowd. Who is that coming through the crowd?"

The audience turned and a wave of cheers started and then built to a roar as the tall, tanned, handsome cowboy in full dress, John Wayne style, came ambling through the crowd.

"That's him. That's Cheyenne," I heard one kid say, "Wow!"

Other youngsters tugged at his sleeve as the cowboy made his way to the podium.

Walker was terrific as we announced the Fairest of the Fair, a very attractive young woman who turned pale and almost passed out as "Cheyenne" put the crown on her pretty head and then kissed her on the cheek.

I was elated because the fair was a success, and especially because of the appearance there of Clint Walker. We raised over $10,000 for Glen Ellyn charities. The appearance of a television celebrity had helped us do it.

The event reinforced my belief, even in those early days, in the power of television and radio and its personalities. It was a lesson in the benefits that can be derived from harnessing just a little of that power to help society or some small part of it. In this case, it helped raise much-needed money for charity.

This was a lesson that influenced the later course of my career.

As I mentioned, my role in revitalizing the Central Division's radio network sales had not gone unnoticed by television network sales management. In early November 1955, I got a call from the vice president in charge of TV sales for the Central Division's office, asking me to come and meet with him. Jim Beach, one of the key executives who came over to ABC in the merger, was a redheaded Irishman who was known for his hard-driving managerial style and his quick temper. If you screwed up with Beach, he might fire you on the spot but would invariably hire you back. He had a great sense of humor and was fun to be with at any one of his many haunts in the party-prone Windy City. The word was that he would party and have fun with his salesmen but strictly on his terms.

Beach enjoyed the reputation of having an "in" with Mayor Dick Daley and the Chicago Police Department. One story has it that when he would barrel down Edens Expressway at 80 miles an hour in his yellow Lincoln convertible going to work in the morning, the police would occasionally pull him over. Jim would be sitting there with a folded twenty-dollar bill clenched in his teeth.

"Can't talk," Beach would say when the police approached him. The officer would gently remove the obstruction from his mouth and go about his business. Jim would drive off to downtown Chicago.

"I wanted to see you, kid," Beach said as I sat down in his large office. "I'm expanding the department and I've got a spot for a young guy like you on the sales team. You've done a hell of a job in radio and now it's probably time for you to get your feet wet in television."

I wasn't that surprised. I knew all of the TV sales people who worked right across the hall and I liked them, and as a matter of fact, spent more time with them at lunch or after hours than I did with the older radio group, with the exception of Rastall. I started to respond to Beach, but he wanted to continue,

"Television is really expanding, Jim. This is the medium of the future, and ABC is making some breakthroughs. Leonard [Goldenson] has broken down the barrier for TV production from the movie guys, and we now have a series from Warner Brothers on the air, as you probably know. There are plenty of opportunities here. We have a great sales team. I think you'll fit right in. I want you to go to work for me. What do you say?" He came around the desk with a big smile and his hand extended.

I said, "Yes," but with the condition that I work out the details on leaving the radio network and finalize the accounts I was working on. I was reluctant to leave radio because I was just getting into a real groove with my clients of selling the intricacies and effectiveness of the audio medium. But I knew Jim Beach was right on every score about the power and growth of television.

Television was growing fast in the mid-fifties. In 1950, some one hundred television stations were broadcasting programs several hours a day to about five million television sets in homes across the country with the concentration in the major cities. In 1953, there were roughly 160 commercial stations. Going into 1956, approximately 450 television stations were on the air, many of them 18 hours a day, airing programs to thirty-seven million television sets in all parts of the country.

Leonard Goldenson did indeed break down the barriers with the motion picture producers by virtue of his friendship with many studio heads from the United-Paramount Theater days. An even bigger factor was his persistence and utter belief in the future of television and the fact that picture studios and TV could be compatible and serve one another extremely well. Goldenson's initial success was with Jack Warner, whom he had been pestering for two years. Warner's studio produced an hour-long series for the ABC fall schedule in 1955 entitled *Warner Brothers Presents*. Three shows, *Cheyenne, Kings Row*, and *Casablanca*, rotated on Tuesday nights and became the lead for other Hollywood studios to get into production. *Cheyenne* became a hit and started the action-western-adventure trend that brought about such shows as *Wyatt Earp, Maverick, Sugarfoot, Lawman, Rifleman* and several others on ABC in the next few years.

Ironically, Goldenson also persuaded Walt Disney to come into television by taking a financial interest in the new Disney theme park and becoming a partner of sorts for TV production. In 1954, a one-hour prime-time Walt Disney program premiered and became extremely popular. In the fall of 1955, *The Mickey Mouse Club* came on the air in the late afternoon every weekday.

All across the country youngsters began wearing Mickey Mouse caps with floppy ears and singing "M. I. C. K. E. Y M. O. U. S. E." in front of their television sets. (I am sure many readers of this book were among that audience.) It was an exciting time for the new medium. The early ABC/Disney partnership was prophetic with the two companies destined to become one and the same some forty years later.

Beach was also right in that he did have a great sales team with Hal Wettersten as sales manager; Stan Meigs, Jack Reilly, Bill Gillogly, Dick Cahill and George Drace as account executives, and Doug Streff and John Grace in the sales service department. These people were recognized as the best media salesmen in the Midwest. And there were opportunities. Advertisers were starting to feel the sales power of the sight, sound and motion (color was soon to come) of television. Advertisers became increasingly receptive to ideas and had steered their agencies accordingly. Some advertising agencies realigned their media and broadcast buying departments to benefit from the remarkable marketing capabilities of television.

Don't get the idea that selling television was easy. It was not, especially at ABC. I found that out from the day I started as a TV account executive the day after Thanksgiving, November 23, 1955.

Beach assigned me to the Pabst Blue Ribbon beer account handled by the Leo Burnett Agency. Pabst sponsored the *Wednesday Night Fights* on the ABC-TV Network and was obviously an important piece of business for the Central Division. A new senior account executive from New York had come to Chicago to handle the Pabst account at the agency. His name was Lester Malitz, and he had a reputation for being really nasty.

I made an appointment to meet Mr. Malitz and when I arrived, I found that his younger assistant, Bud Wolfe, was also in his office. Malitz, who was a large, gruff, imposing-looking man, greeted me rather curtly and asked me to sit in a low chair immediately in front of his desk. As I looked across and then up at Malitz, I realized that he had elevated his chair so that he looked down on his visitors. And he slanted the Venetian blinds so that the morning sun was directly in my eyes. I was blinded. I could not see his face in the glare of the sun. His voice boomed down on me from out of the blinding light, "If you're going to handle this account, Mr. Duffy, let's find out what you know. Recite the list of ABC affiliates carrying the Wednesday Night Fights. I want the call letters and the channel numbers starting from the top."

I heard Wolfe snicker, obviously enjoying the pig-sticking.

I waited for a minute and then got up and moved to the side of his desk out of the sunlight. I said as I reached into my briefcase, "Here is the list of stations from the program sheet. If you want someone to read them to you, have your boy here do it. Unless you can be a gentleman, I'm not interested in working with you on this account." And I left his office.

On the way back to the ABC sales office, I thought for sure my career with TV was over. To my surprise, Malitz had called Beach before I got back to the office and apologized and offered to buy us both lunch. I did handle the Pabst account and found Lester Malitz to be a decent man, although difficult at times, from that day forward.

Aside from the unusual personalities, and Malitz was not the only one, there were reasons that ABC television was difficult to sell. The ABC Television Network, despite some exciting new programs, lagged way behind CBS and NBC in the number and quality of affiliated stations. Consequently, we were invariably lowest in the audience circulation figures.

I found very quickly that television was sold strictly on ratings, by the numbers, and there were few opportunities to use creative salesmanship the way we had in radio. Because of the smaller audiences, ABC seemed to be last in line for most advertising buys. Still, I determined that the same formula that I had used in radio could work in television. I got into my same little gray Chevrolet and traveled into my territory – Indiana, central and southern Illinois, and southern Michigan – to knock on doors and find some smaller advertisers and bring them into the medium. As in radio, it took some time, but eventually we brought in a number of sales, including good orders from the Helene Curtis Company, Maybelline, the Toni Company, and Black & Decker. I also played a prominent role in the Kellogg Company's purchase as a major advertiser in *Walt Disney Presents*.

There was a frenetic pace in selling television because the pressure was always on to "get the order." The network was extremely costly to operate and the only way to stay competitive and build for the future was to pay the increasing costs of programming. The sales department was the only avenue to bring in revenue through more sales...and more sales...and more sales.

Being in a branch office of the company made sales more diffi-cult. Chicago, like Los Angeles and Detroit, was an "outpost." The major decisions were made in the New York headquarters. The first opportunities for selling the new schedule or a new program were in New York. This would drive Jim Beach crazy. He would constantly be on the phone bitching that "his boys" didn't have the same imme-diate data and materials as our New York counterparts.

This also meant more pressure on us because Beach would drive us harder to get orders and "show those greedy bastards in New York." It was stressful, but it also brought some occasional laughs.

George Drace was one of the TV sales department's most col-orful characters. "Georgie" was the only bachelor among us, and his late-night activities often made him late for our morning sales meet-ings. Beach, of course, would go berserk, always threatening to fire Drace, and, as a matter of fact, did on a couple of occasions, only to hire him back the next day.

Georgie also had a nonchalant manner that made people who didn't know him think he was not motivated and didn't care. This also drove the highly aggressive Beach up the wall. Drace also was the quintessential Chicagoan and had perfected the "Chicago mum-bles" long before the later-day "Da Bulls" or "Da Bears" lingo.

At the end of one particular week, Beach warned all of us that he was having a very important sales meeting at 8 o'clock on Monday morning. Anyone who showed up late could start looking for a new job. Beach wheeled on Drace and pointed his finger directly at him.

"That means you, Mr. Night Life. YOU be on time."

Drace brushed it off. "Hey, Jim, no pralem. Got da message. No pralem."

On Monday morning at eight sharp, the entire sales staff, with the exception of "Georgie" Drace, sat stiffly in Beach's office as he started his meeting. Beach did not say a word about Drace's absence. All of us kept looking at the clock on the wall and the closed door in Beach's office.

Finally, at 8:50, the door opened and a disheveled and perspiring Drace flew into the office with his arms waving and babbling in triple time. He headed right for Beach's desk.

"Hold it, Jim. Hold it. Don't say nothin'. I can explain it. Let me tell you what happened."

Beach didn't say a word. He just stared at him. The rest of us all held our breath because we were sure Drace was a dead man.

"Ah, see, ah," George started to stammer. "Ah, see, I had this date and I got home a little late and I knew I had this meeting this morning and I couldn't find a parking place...."

Beach just stared at him.

"I parked the car on the street around the corner. When I went to get the car this morning, I saw that the car was parked on a hill, and, ah, the car looked like it was out of gas. But, see, ah, it wasn't really out of gas, just almost. See because it was parked on the hill, the gas stayed at one end of the tank, and, ah, I couldn't get it started."

Beach very calmly said, "Why, then, George, didn't you back the car down the hill to a level spot so you could start your car," his voice growing in intensity, "So that YOU COULD GET TO THIS GODDAMN MEETING."

"Oh, no, I couldn't do that, Jim," Georgie said. "It was a one-way street!"

Beach exploded. The rest of us could not contain ourselves any longer. We laughed till our sides hurt, some even rolling on the floor. It was so bizarre that even Beach laughed. Drace was fired on the spot. Jim hired him back the next day.

This was the same George Drace who, a few weeks later, caused more consternation on a sales trip to New Orleans. Beach had not heard from George in two or three days and finally out of exasperation late one morning asked Margie, his secretary, to get Drace on the phone.

"They're ringing his room," Margie called out to Beach.

Just as Jim picked up the phone, he heard the familiar tones of one Georgie Drace say rather sleepily into the telephone, "Ah, room service, ah, send up a pitcher of orange juice and a double order of bacon, some blueberry pancakes and, ah, a big pot of black coffee."

There was dead silence on the phone. Then Beach erupted.

"Jesus Christ, Georgie. It's eleven o'clock in the morning. What in hell do you think...."

"Oh, ah, Jim," Georgie interrupted. "Oh. Hi. Ah, ya see, Jim, I had a late-night meeting and, ah....

"Get your ass back here and fast." Jim yelled. "Get the first plane and don't stop off anywhere. You are in big trouble, buster."

"No pralem, Jim," Georgie said. "I'll be there before you know it." And then he paused and said, "Oh, and, ah, Jim, maybe you better cancel the breakfast order."

Drace, of course, was fired the next day. But this time he wasn't hired back until two days later.

Despite all of the nonsense, believe it or not, Beach was a good leader. Drace and the rest of the staff were excellent sales people and wrote orders far beyond their rightful share based on the low ABC ratings.

The medium of television grew and changed in several different directions in the fifties. Chicago, known for its program creativity in those early days, gradually was diminished as a major entertainment producer when many performers and producers moved east. New York, known for its early news dominance, became the programming center with game shows and the advent of live, hour-long dramas. Later in the decade, Hollywood studios produced western and action-oriented film shows for television and the West Coast became the production capital. In the mid-fifties, the advent of live drama from New York brought an exciting and evolving time to television programming that helped develop some of the great writers in the medium. The era became known as "The Golden Age of Television."

Paddy Chayesky became television's most celebrated playwright with his classic *Marty*, followed by *Middle of the Night*, *The Bachelor Party*, and *The Catered Affair*. Robert Alan Arthur wrote his memorable TV dramas, *A Man Is Ten Feet Tall* and *Shadow of the Champ*, starring Eli Wallach, Jack Warden and Lee Grant for *Philco Playhouse* in 1955. Other writers who went on to great fame include Tad Mosel, Horton Foote, Gore Vidal, Reginald Rose and Rod Serling. Many of the award-winning dramas, written especially for

TV, went on to acclaim as motion pictures or on Broadway, such as *Twelve Angry Men*, *Requiem For A Heavyweight*, *The Miracle Worker*, *Days of Wine and Roses*, and *Patterns*.

Television in the early years was a spawning stage for many unknown or little-known actors and actresses, some of who went on to become celebrities in TV, the movies or Broadway. The list of success stories could fill a third of this book. Some recognizable names include Eva Marie Saint, E. G. Marshall, Jack Lemmon, Teresa Wright, John Cassavetes, Vivian Blaine, Tony Randall, Elizabeth Montgomery, Jack Palance, Julie Harris, Leslie Nielson, Sidney Poitier, Thelma Ritter, Martin Balsam, John Forsythe, Grace Kelly, Steve McQueen, James Dean, Kim Stanley and on and on. And it was the era of the great TV directors: Arthur Penn, George Roy Hill, Delbert Mann, John Frankenheimer, Robert Mulligan and more.

Many industry leaders in the ensuing forty-five years have claimed that the classy description 'Golden Age' is a misnomer and that, while there were a few superior plays, most of the live dramas were junk and inferior to the taped and filmed series which later replaced them. It is an argument not easily made. All I know is that the shows were very exciting when they were telecast in the happy days of the fifties, and that the vast majority of them were on either CBS or NBC. Unfortunately, I did not have the pleasure of selling them from my ABC sales outpost in Chicago.

Meanwhile, in the mid-fifties at the ABC New York headquarters, there was much rumbling about dissension between corporate management and Robert Kintner, the president of the TV network. The last vestige of the former ABC management was gone on October 22, 1956 when Kintner resigned and Goldenson appointed a young and very bright numbers whiz named Ollie Treyz to lead the television network into a new era. Kintner went on to become the president and finally chairman of NBC. Treyz, who was talented but unpredictable and undisciplined, proceeded to provide some successful and exciting moments for ABC. However, his style, and in particular his tendency to make misleading or false promises on behalf of the company, left bad feelings and scars, especially on the advertising front, that affected the company and me in later years.

In 1958, Treyz brought the wrath of the Federal Communications Commission down on ABC when the network programmed a racy TV version of *Bus Stop*, the earlier theatrical movie that starred Marilyn Monroe. The mistake was that the movie was aired at an early evening hour when many youngsters were able to watch. A national uproar from parents, politicians and church groups ensued. Those outcries were the forerunner of the violence and permissiveness debate of more recent years.

At that point Goldenson had just about had it with Treyz. It wasn't long before Tom Moore was named the president of the TV network.

For me, the two years in Chicago TV sales were hard work and rewarding if not entirely fulfilling. And as with all of the other jobs in my career with ABC, I gained invaluable experience.

I certainly learned what it was like to be in the sales "trenches," to be on the street with a bag under my arm and make the calls, be rejected, come back again, and keep creating and never give up. I also learned that the branch offices play a tremendously important role in the success of the entire network operation. I vowed that if I ever had the opportunity, I would see to it that all offices had equal access to materials and up-to-the-minute details on all sales materials. I learned further that there is much gratification in selling, in starting out a project from the beginning and following it through with meetings and presentations until you finally get the trophy – the order.

Another thing I gained from being a salesman was a clear understanding of the entire financial underpinnings of the business – the dynamics at work in providing the viewing public with the programs the network thinks they want, and the slavish adherence to the ratings system which is the sole measurement, right or wrong, of the popularity and success of programs. More on the effects of ratings will follow.

I also learned that in the network television distribution system there was no controlled growth whatsoever – no blueprint for expansion of one of the nation's major industries. Neither the Federal Communications Commission nor any other body – private or public sector – had a blueprint that outlined how the system should grow and develop. There was no plan that called for X number of stations in 1950. Then X number in 1955. X number in 1960. And so on.

Further, there was no plan to allow for three networks or four networks, each having station lineups of X number of stations or a plan for X number of independent stations.... There was none of that. Growth was strictly based on the needs of the players in the developing system, the magic of supply and demand of the marketplace. The television industry grew in an unguided manner, complicated by the vagaries of ultra high frequency (UHF) and very high frequency (VHF) licenses granted to station operators by the FCC and restricted on occasion by the regulations of the FCC.

Supply and demand provided the excitement in the growth of television. Inherent in this growth was the fact that your program had better be very good or you were not going to get distribution. And if you didn't get distribution, you were not going to sell it to anybody, or you were not going to get sufficient returns to keep producing that program. That was the battle in those early days in television. It is still being waged to this day.

On my birthday, April 2, 1957, I received an unexpected telephone call from my patron saint, Si Siegel, advising me that the company was making some changes in radio and that it was time for me to get into management. Three weeks later, I returned to radio as director of network sales in the ABC Central Division. In many respects, I welcomed the return to radio.

I was torn because I was making great strides on the television side, but I was still down the list in terms of seniority. I knew it would be a long time before I could get any kind of a promotion. I still had a real affinity for radio harkening back to my childhood days on the farm. I reasoned that I could run my own shop and build my own team that would certainly broaden my experience. My salary was to be an astronomical $17,000 per year.

The financial factor was especially appealing because our family was growing. Betty was pregnant with our third child and I was becoming more and more involved in the Glen Ellyn community. Our daughter, Diane, a raven-haired beauty, was born on June 5, 1957 and a year and twelve days later, on June 17, 1958, her sister, Marcia, a pink-skinned, very pretty redheaded little girl came into our world. This was an especially tough time for Betty with four small children to care for and a husband who was moving up in the business world and traveling a great deal. In retrospect, it would have been a good time for long-range counsel, because our lives and interests were moving away from each other. In retrospect, Betty deserved and would have been much happier with a husband who had a nine-to-five job in the area. I would have been much smarter to have spent more time at home.

As director of sales for the ABC Radio Network in the Midwest, I was more and more in demand on the social scene. Betty simply didn't seem interested in joining me for the business functions, and, as a matter of fact, avoided a role in our expanding community activities. I was often invited to attend special functions hosted by companies who were doing business with ABC. Occasionally, I was asked to attend their annual conventions and give keynote speeches.

These were often fun occasions and certainly expanded my horizons. I wished that Betty could have joined me on at least the more pleasurable trips. When I returned from such functions or trips, I had mixed feelings of elation and guilt. It bothered me that she was home with a house full of little children while I was away enjoying myself. I eventually discussed it with her but nothing really changed and our discussions did not strengthen our faltering relationship.

The Central Division Network sales offices were moved from the Civic Opera Building to the much more convenient Stone Container Building at the corner of Michigan Avenue and Wacker Drive, right in the middle of the area where the largest advertising agencies were located: The Leo Burnett Company, J. Walter Thompson; Young & Rubicam, Batten, Barton, Durston & Osborne, Ruthrauff & Ryan, and several others. We moved into newly decorated offices on the fifth floor of the building, again, right next to the network TV sales operation. Jim Beach had an office the size of a dance hall and his secretary, Margie, had an office immediately in front of it that was larger than any salesman's office. Wettersten, the sales manager, joked, "You have to genuflect and be blessed by Margie before you get in for an audience with the Pope."

John Grace in sales service quipped, "The city of Chicago plans to hold the next political convention in Beach's office."

I had a very nice office about one fourth the size of Beach's with a large walnut desk and two chairs in front of it and a sofa and cock-tail table off to one side. My office faced Michigan Avenue and was at the end of a long rectangular area that included five good-sized sales offices and a sales service office, plus ample room for secretarial space and file cabinets. It was a far cry from the bullpen offices that we worked out of in the Civic Opera Building and seemed in keeping with the multi-million-dollar business that broadcasting had become.

In assigning my new managerial role, Siegel told me that the company was planning some different programming ideas in the near future. I hired some promising staff, and we rapidly got to work selling high volumes of business.

In 1958, Siegel's promise of a new idea for radio came to fruition when it was announced that Robert Eastman, the founder and pres-ident of the Eastman Company, a well-known radio station represen-tatives group, was coming to ABC with an innovative *Live and Lively* concept for the network. The new format was to consist of Don McNeill's *Breakfast Club* leading off five daily hour-long shows, all live, each with full orchestras, male and female vocalists, guest celebri-ties and bright, lively music in keeping with the "good times" of the fifties. Each show would feature a major star as host such as Herb Oscar Anderson, a "hot" New York City radio personality following McNeill. Jim Backus, the actor and voice of Mr. Magoo, and Bill Kemp, a popular local broadcaster, would be in the afternoon and Merv Griffin, singer and budding entrepreneur, and Jim Reeves, the country/western singer, would be featured in the evening.

This concept hit the radio industry like a whirlwind. ABC invested $5 million in the programs with high expectations. Those of us who were in the business, especially in sales and affiliate relations, knew it was doomed from the outset. It looked great on paper and sounded like the coming of the new media order, but it was flying in the face of the realities of the broadcasting system in transition. Radio, being dominated by television in the home, was now going more and more out of home and was a more transient medium. Audiences wanted shorter bites of news and entertainment, not longer ones, and affiliated radio stations were simply not willing to give up huge chunks of their program time for musical shows. *Breakfast Club* was an exception. It had become an institution and was the foundation piece for some 355 stations every weekday and had been for 25 years. Clearances (local stations putting a network program on their schedule) for the other *Live and Lively* programs were predictably miserable, especially in the late afternoon and the evening time slots.

We tried mightily to sell it and, by having the whole sales team using my earlier-day strategy of making personal calls to every conceivable client in the Midwest, we did get some sales on our rate card. But we were at the same competitive disadvantage in radio that I had experienced in television: limited distribution for the programs. The entire effort, with the exception of *Breakfast Club*, was canceled after nine months and I was appalled to find out later that the New York *Live and Lively* sales staff was selling the weaker-distributed shows for as little as $100 a minute. That was one-twentieth of what we were getting in the Chicago office for the same programs.

The failure of the entire *Live and Lively* endeavor symbolized the change which radio was undergoing as a result of television's growth and predominance in home entertainment.

Shortly after the Eastman project went off of the air, our Chicago office suffered a different and very sad loss. Marty McGeohan, one of our salesmen, who had had several heart attacks in past years, dropped dead in the elevator of the Pure Oil Building a couple of blocks from our office. The police asked me to come and identify his body and then notify Marty's wife. It was a very tough and emotional assignment.

It was a sad time, too, because after the cancellation of *Live and Lively*, I was called to New York and told I would have to severely cut back on my staff. I returned to Chicago with a heavy heart and dismissed an assistant in sales service and three members of the sales staff, including my old pal from high school, Bob Loeber, who had been the last sales person hired. They were all terrific about the unhappy situation and understood. Loeber teased me about it later, but also told me he had been looking for a way to get out of the cold Midwest. He headed for California and became a very successful radio and television syndication salesman and executive in Los Angeles for many years.

The failure of *Live and Lively* created a loud thud in the industry and to those of us working in radio, it was a chilling reminder that radio was not only in a state of transition but, perhaps, in its waning days as a national entertainment and information source. I thought very seriously about my options and had quiet conversations with several people whom I had grown to respect and trust.

One such person was my good friend and lawyer, John Healy, also an ex-Beloiter, who had counseled me in my career since I arrived at ABC.

"Stay the course," he said. "This company has invested too much in you to let you get away. Radio isn't dead. It's just finding its way in the wake of television's accelerating growth. ABC is a young company and television and radio, too, are fledglings in the overall communications era that is coming on. There will be an important place for you."

Healy's words were encouraging and probably what I wanted to hear, but working in an atmosphere of uncertainty on a daily basis made the future rather hazy.

The weeks that followed the cancellation of *Live and Lively* were difficult for the ABC Radio Network and for all of us who were trying to keep it alive. We made a number of outstanding sales for the *Breakfast Club* and *Paul Harvey* and the other shows, but it was a struggle. Advertisers were skeptical of making long-term commitments to programs on a network that might be discontinued.

Then one sunny day in early April 1960, I received a telephone call from Si Siegel's office requesting that I come to New York for an important meeting.

Eight

The Big Apple and Big Business

There are moments in all of our lives that are filed away in our minds and souls and come back years later with such clarity and brilliance that it startles us. As the American Airlines Electra banked over the southern tip of Manhattan and headed up the East River, I knew with all of my being that what I was feeling and seeing would be among those moments. It was in the early spring of 1960. Dusk had overtaken the greater New York area. A light rain had fallen in the early afternoon and had cleansed the great stone canyons. As the millions of lights from the bridges and buildings and byways of the most dynamic city in the world began to sparkle on the darkening canvas, they created a magical scene. I felt a growing sense of excitement as I gazed at the scope of this powerful city, the now lighted Empire State Building, the Chrysler Building, past Broadway and into Central Park. The music from the Sinatra movie, *On The Town*, rushed to my head, "New York, New York, What a Wonderful Town."

For me, like most Americans, the sixties were a great time to be alive. I had enjoyed a very satisfying career with the American Broadcasting Company for the past eleven years in Chicago. Suddenly, I had received the phone call to come to New York to discuss the possibility of working in the fascinating city that now stretched out below me.

It was at a time when our country was alive and moving. We had experienced a post-World-War-II decade of unprecedented growth and prosperity in the fabulous fifties. Now America wanted more and different. A young Massachusetts Senator, John F. Kennedy, had made a strong showing in the nation's first Presidential primary just a few weeks earlier. He would soon be calling for the torch of freedom to be passed to a "new generation of Americans." I was part of that new generation. You could feel the energy as the country was swinging into a new era of uncharted changes, societal and otherwise, that would bring it to new heights – and almost to its knees – both at home and across the world. The sixties would be a decade of bullets in Dallas and Vietnam, a Civil Rights movement, riots in our major cities and journeys into space, even to the moon. But for now, America was ready to surge ahead, to swing on and reach up, and to step out....to rock and roll.

As the plane touched down at La Guardia Airport, I tried to contain my excitement. Just as the country was ready for change, so, seemingly, was I. The light rain that had fallen could not dampen my spirits, or the style of the streets of Manhattan, and certainly not the avenue that would become Broadcast Row, Sixth Avenue. The nation's prosperity had fueled a bonanza in broadcasting that was bringing it new reach, influence and power.

At the corner of 54th Street and Sixth Avenue, Howard Cosell, the ever-present lawyer turned sportscaster, postured in the lobby of New York's Warwick Hotel, holding court for all who would listen. Cosell knew most of the habitués who frequented the city's famous watering spots like Toots Shor's, The Stork Club, Mike Manuche's, the 21 Club, the Dorset Hotel and the Warwick bar. This was the same Cosell about whom James Michener, in his book *Sports In America*, would later write: "Into the bland and almost sophomoric world of television sports coverage came this rasping, opinionated, logorrheic, knowledgeable gadfly of whom a jealous critic once said, 'Howard is the only man in the world who changed his name and put on a toupée to tell it like it is.'"

Now, with his toupée glued neatly in place and the smoke from his nine-inch panatela curling in circles to the ceiling, Howard was fascinating a group of beleaguered tourists when he noticed me swing through the revolving doors, luggage and all, heading for the reception desk.

"Hey, Duffer," Howard bellowed for all to hear. "Hey, Redhead, what in the hell are you doing in the big city?"

I acknowledged Howard as the controversial figure headed toward me with cigar smoke billowing behind him. I had a fondness for Cosell, which was not a commonly shared feeling among broadcasters at the time. But Howard was a unique figure who could create controversy at a moment's notice. He was intelligent and quick and extremely forthright, even fun to be around...well, sometimes.

"Hello Howard," I returned his greeting. "I'm in town for a couple of meetings. I'll be here a couple of days. It's no big deal."

The fact is that the next day's meeting was a big deal – a very big deal. The meeting concerned the future of the ABC Radio Network. Television had built a powerful base through the previous ten years but radio had been diminished, especially ABC Radio.

It was decision time for ABC management on the future of the ABC Radio Network. After the expensive *Live and Lively* program failure, and the network literally in limbo for over a year, there was much speculation that ABC would discontinue the network

The radio network still had programming, even strong, popular shows: Don McNeill's *Breakfast Club*, Paul Harvey, Cosell's *Speaking of Sports*, hourly news reports plus whatever other sponsored features it could get. Goldenson wanted to pull the plug on the radio network and get on to the business of the television network which was struggling and disadvantaged, but showed promise. Siegel wasn't so sure.

Bob Pauley, a bright and highly principled salesman in the network, had approached Goldenson and Siegel and challenged them to make one more try with some new faces and a dedicated, recommitted effort. Siegel liked the idea. He envisioned how Pauley and three or four other young people in the network (including me, I was to learn) could make quite a team. I knew that Siegel had been following my career for some time and was starting to see a bigger future for me in the company. Siegel was impressed that, under my leadership, the Chicago office was bringing in over 60% of the ABC Radio Network's gross sales even in the bad times. He wasn't pleased that I had promptly reported those figures in the trade press, but he conceded that it showed some aggressiveness and a badly needed spark. Si Siegel was intrigued by the idea of a new force of "young Turks" with style and commitment. He finally convinced Goldenson of this and named Pauley president of the radio network. He then placed the call to feel me out on becoming the national sales director in New York.

I fully understood the significance of such a move and had considered what my reaction would be to the next day's meeting. I was a born and bred Midwesterner, and it would be difficult to leave Chicago. My family was still very young, and I wondered if the tough New York environment was the right place for them. Still, New York was electric any time, and especially in the spring of 1960. I was encouraged by comments that the suburbs in Connecticut, New Jersey and Long Island were great places to raise a family. It seemed to make sense – a new network, a new challenge, a new decade, a new environment. Besides, television was continuing to boom and that, too, quickened my interest. I had read that there were now some ninety million television sets in the country. The quickly exploding TV medium had sight and sound and motion and was still growing strong.

Television had a captured audience, millions of potential buyers sitting in front of the screen waiting to be entertained and informed. From my experience as a network television salesman, I fully understood the advertising and marketing potential. It was intriguing. Radio was still exciting and challenging, also, in that it cried out for change. First things first.

Of course, I was not about to – could not – share the possible management changes with Cosell, even though Howard was a growing force within the radio network.

I checked into the hotel and, after exchanging pleasantries and a few barbs with Cosell, I accepted his invitation to have a quick dinner at the Warwick bar. I promised myself that it would not turn into a late evening knowing the importance of the next morning's meeting, but I enjoyed jousting with Howard and I was excited by the fact that he had invited Cus D'Amato, the manager of the former heavyweight champion of the world, Floyd Patterson, to stop by after dinner. Patterson had lost his heavyweight championship to the unheralded Swede, Ingemar Johannsen, in June of 1959. The rematch was set for June 22 at the Polo Grounds. ABC Radio would cover it and the excitement was starting to build, especially in New York.

The dinner, which I paid for (I can't remember when I didn't with Howard), was pleasant enough except for Howard's incessant bleating that "The Big Apple's too big for you, kid. If you ever consider New York, stay where you're at," etc., etc., but Howard is Howard and I understood all that. Cosell did broach the subject of the possible radio moves.

"I hear Pauley might be taking over the radio network."

"I heard that rumor," I answered. "Maybe tomorrow's meet...."

"And that you might be taking over sales," Howard interrupted. "How about it, kid? Wouldn't that be something? Remember what I told you about the big city...."

I cut him off. "Howard, I really don't know what's going on. I may learn something tomorrow," I said with a smile, "And I have every confidence that you'll have the whole story before the rest of us."

Howard had one last comment. Bob Pauley was a strong Cosell supporter even in the early days when most ABC management thought he should stick to practicing law, preferably some place away from New York. Cosell and Pauley were neighbors and maybe even friends.

"Pauley is a prick." Howard said, then broke out in his forced and staccato laugh for the entire restaurant to hear.

The meeting with Cus D'Amato was memorable, to say the least. D'Amato had brought his dog, a huge and handsome Great Dane, and could not stay in the restaurant. He asked if we would mind taking a stroll over to Fifth Avenue. It was a nice reprieve. The rain had stopped and the air was fresh. As our foursome started uptown on Sixth Avenue, I somehow found myself paired with the Great Dane while Howard and D'Amato walked up ahead. The small gray-haired manager/trainer talked quietly, almost confidentially to Cosell. He then began to display animatedly the peek-a-boo style that Patterson intended to use in the rematch.

"Floyd is smart," D'Amato whispered in gruff tones. "His speed and his mind will win back the...." and his voice trailed off.

I half-stumbled along behind them, holding on to the dog's leash, as I strained to hear what was being said.

As we turned east on 55th Street heading toward Fifth Avenue, passers-by were amused by the odd-looking quartet: a bent-over, older man jabbing and weaving in peek-a-boo fashion while the taller man with a cigar nodded and a younger man and a nonplussed large, large dog brought up the rear. Once we moved on to Fifth Avenue, the Great Dane got more into the swing of things, pulling me to the curb and then back around to the storefronts. D'Amato and Cosell were oblivious, deep into the fight for the heavyweight championship, Cus silent, jabbing and shuffling, Howard strutting and blowing smoke. I was relieved when the odyssey finally ended in front of the Warwick Hotel. As Howard and D'Amato said their good-byes, the evening came to a damp but riotous climax. I shook Cus D'Amato's hand and thanked him for the stroll and then stood dumbstruck as the Great Dane moved close to his walking companion and casually lifted his leg and slowly relieved himself up and down my pant leg.

Cus D'Amato was aghast, but Howard started to double over. "Ho, ho, ho...That's a sign of things to come in the Big Apple. Ho, ho. They're going to pee all over you, kid."

There was more to come. And it was worse. After Cus D'Amato, full of apologies, shuffled away, Howard, enjoying himself immensely, announced that he had missed the last train to Pound Ridge, New York.

"Come on, kid, I'll buy you a nightcap," Howard said magnanimously. "You could probably use something wet. Ho, ho."

And then he let the hammer drop. He asked if he could bunk in my room for the night.

I had booked a small simple room with twin beds. The hotel was sold out so I couldn't move to a suite or have Cosell get his own room. I had had more than enough of Howard for one night. Besides I was dying for a long, hot shower, mostly for my still-moist right leg. The serious fact was that I had several notes that I wanted to review for the next day's meeting. Most of all, I wanted to sleep. But Cosell persisted, and after shuddering over the unthinkable that the room could have had a double bed, I relented.

Howard made himself immediately comfortable, stripped to his BVDs and undershirt, propped himself up on one of the twin beds, broke out and lit another of his huge cigars and proceeded to pontificate on the evils of sports, New York City, radio and television and repeated over and over the particular inabilities of "the Redhead," "the Chicago kid," to have any future in the largest city in the world. The drone went into the morning hours as I, trance-like, tried to doze in a room filled with smoke and the nasalized proclamations of Cosell. I rolled and tossed and simply could not sleep. After reevaluating my career and my life, I finally told Cosell to "shut it down."

The dawn was bringing a new day. I stared at the ceiling where the cigar smoke from a now snoring Cosell and the words, "They're going to pee all over you, kid," hung thick and heavy.

I dragged myself out of bed at 7:30, sluggish from my lack of sleep, and headed for the shower. Cosell continued to snore up a storm. I tried to concentrate on the meeting, now just two hours away, that could make a significant change in my career and my life.

After showering and hurriedly getting dressed, I quietly shut the door and went down to the coffee shop for a roll and coffee. I stopped by the newsstand for some Murine to clear my still-stinging, smoke-filled eyes. I grabbed a cab and headed for ABC headquarters on West 66th Street.

Siegel's office was on the fourth floor of the executive building, a narrow six-story reconditioned edifice that was remarkable for its drabness. I arrived at his office at about 8:50 and was surprised to see Si sitting alone reading the morning paper. His secretary was not there, nor was anyone else on that part of the floor, although I could hear voices coming from the other side.

"C'mon in," he yelled when he saw me outside the door. "How are you, Jim?" he said. "Nice to see you. Have a good trip in?"

Siegel was a financial wizard, a problem solver, and he had a reputation for being very tough. He was bald and had a rather droll aura about him, but in a tight situation he could wither an underling with a sharp stare and seemingly cold eyes. The fact was, as I would learn, he was a very gentle man with a delightful sense of humor and cared a great deal about his people.

I had not been in a meeting alone with Siegel until that morning. I was rather on edge from the previous night's lack of sleep.

"Thanks, Mr. Siegel," I said shaking his hand. "I had a good trip in but kind of a long night. I met Howard Cosell at the hotel and he missed his train to Connecticut and wanted to talk half the night."

Si gave me a slight grin. "You can have a long night with Howard in just the first few minutes."

The meeting was brief and to the point. I was surprised. I thought Siegel might take me in to see Leonard Goldenson, but he didn't. Siegel explained what the company wanted to do with the radio network: give it a real charge and build a team. And after explaining the Pauley move and what my compensation would be ($22,000 a year plus an additional commission based on performance), he said, "We want you to come to New York as the national director of sales for the radio network. I think it will be a good move for you. Think about it and get back to me."

I didn't have to think about it. I had been thinking about little else since I got his initial telephone call. I swear I was thinking about it when D'Amato's dog was using my leg as his personal fire hydrant. During the night, I had thought about the complications of moving Betty and my young family. Would the lifestyle on the East Coast be beneficial to them? My relationship with Betty was strained, at best. Would the move to a new environment improve or destroy that situation? Betty and I had discussed the possible move privately and then with the kids. Betty was somewhat reluctant but said she was game. Jay, ten, and Terry, six, full of adventure, cheered wildly, and the girls, three and two years old respectively, not really knowing what it was all about, joined the cheering. I knew it was an extraordinary opportunity for me. I hoped and prayed it would be for every member of the family.

I officially became a New Yorker, in the first week of May, 1960. Betty and the children stayed behind until we could sell the house in Glen Ellyn and Jay and Terry could finish the school year. Meanwhile, I would scout the vast New York area to find a suitable place for us to live.

My first night in the big city was not exactly orchestrated by the Welcome Wagon. I had rented a room at the show-business-flavored Mayflower Hotel on Central Park West, a few blocks south of the ABC buildings. When I arrived at my new "home" following my first day at work, I was greeted by three of New York's finest dragging a screaming gentleman through the lobby and out the front door. When I got to the sixth floor, a large, blonde woman was standing in her doorway across from my room, hysterically screaming, "I hope they castrate the son of a bitch. He lied to me. He stepped out on me." She reached out toward me.

I meekly went into my room and, after cleaning up, immediately left to meet Bill Cummings, advertising manager for Sylvania, for cocktails at the Park Sheridan Hotel on Seventh Avenue. As I strolled down Central Park West and then turned east on Central Park South, I noticed a young Black man carrying a cleaning bag over his shoulder, whistling as he dashed along the busy street. Suddenly, the young man brushed against a burly Hispanic man, and after exchanging heated words, they started fighting and ended up wrestling in the gutter. I gingerly stepped around them and hastened down toward Seventh Avenue. When I turned the corner, I saw a Chinese gentleman passed out in the middle of the sidewalk. Rush-hour pedestrians stepped over him and around him, hardly noticing, as though he were a cardboard box. I started to move toward the man to see if I could help when a policeman approached and waved me away. When I told Cummings my experiences, he laughed and said, "Welcome to a typical night in the Big Apple."

I started to wonder if Cosell's warnings might hold some truth.

The offices for the radio network were in an unimposing two-story white concrete building at the corner of 66th Street and Columbus Avenue. The address was 77 West 66th Street. In retrospect, the address seems strange, since many years later the handsome new Capital Cities/ABC headquarters building, about fifty times larger, was erected just to the east of that building with the same address.

Our radio offices were up some wooden steps and down the hall to the left on the second floor just beyond the personnel department. We would often have to stumble through job applicants who flooded the halls outside of the personnel offices in order to get to our department. I felt sorry for some of the people who were applying for work. Some of the personnel people were rather aloof and filled with the power of being able to reject other human beings. At times, I heard them humiliate applicants during the interviews. I would stop by unannounced on occasion, poke my head in the offices with great authority, and make an arrogant personnel clerk explain the proper conduct in interviewing. They really didn't know who I was, but I had let the word get around that I was very close to Leonard Goldenson. I appeared to be doing this in fun, but I really wasn't. I didn't care for people who pulled rank on others. It seemed to be an accepted practice in personnel.

As the decade of the sixties began, despite television's growing dominance and the recent uncertainties about radio's position, I still felt radio had a promising future – IF the networks and local stations could come up with programs that would appeal to an ever-expanding mobile population. Radio's penetration was extraordinary. Over 98% of American homes had more than one radio; some 43 million automobiles were radio equipped, and there were millions of portable sets being carried to places of recreation and work.

Competition from the other networks was considerable: CBS still had its strong lineup of daytime serials; NBC had a new fast-paced concept on weekends called *Monitor* to go with its serials and game shows, and the Mutual Radio Network had a far-reaching news presence with its over 500 affiliated stations, many in very small markets. All four networks and hundreds of local stations were trying to adjust to the changing medium and the need for "different" programming.

In early September 1960, the family packed our portable belongings into our new, white Chevrolet station wagon and made the long trek to the East Coast. I had found a very nice three-bedroom home on Lancer Road in Riverside, Connecticut, during one of my many house-seeking travels that summer. The house was in a lovely neighborhood with lots of young children and the North Mianus Elementary School practically in the backyard. After discussing it, Betty and I decided to rent it for a year and then look further in the greater New York area. We grew to love Connecticut with its rocks and streams and woods, and a year later we bought a wonderful house on Mimosa Drive near the Mianus River in Cos Cob, just a mile away from Lancer Road.

The new house was a tri-level four-bedroom with a large screened-in porch on one side. The house sat back on a deep lot with a well-landscaped front lawn. Behind the house was more lawn, perfect for swings sets and slides with woods and large boulders at the far end of the lot. The kids were ecstatic. I might have been too if I could have spent more time at home and enjoyed it.

In my new job as the head of national sales, I traveled a great deal to our sales offices in Chicago and Detroit. I also spent some time in Denver and Los Angeles with Bob Pauley, where we developed ABC Radio West, a regional network to supplement our national offerings in the Western states. We also inaugurated a series of regional meetings for our radio affiliates so that they could better understand and cooperate with our new programming plans. I implemented the same strategy in our sales efforts that I had used in Chicago: get to the advertiser with your story in person, and get to him often.

We were told later that some clients, especially in the East, couldn't believe our determination – and our enthusiasm—for what they considered then to be the dying medium of radio.

My personal enthusiasm was dampened somewhat in the spring of 1961 when my mother called and told me that her mother, Helen Adams, had passed away. Grandma Adams had suffered from Parkinson's disease for several years, and, finally, died of natural causes in Jacksonville, Illinois on April 11, 1961. She was 86. My mind reeled back to my childhood with my grandparents at The Old Homestead in Moweaqua. Grandpa Adams was my hero, my mentor, as I have written. But my grandmother had had a very strong, positive influence on my sister and me and lived an exemplary life filled with love and faith. I was very saddened and felt small and vulnerable.

The ABC Radio Network new program concept, *Flair*, came on the scene in May of 1961 like a fresh breeze in spring. It was designed per Bob Pauley's plan to do something "new, creative and appealing" for the changing radio audience. *Flair* was all of that! Our radio network management quintet, Pauley, Ted Douglas, Jack Mann, Bill Rafael and I, had met for many months, often late into the night, searching for the new radio format.

It did evolve, and when the pieces fell into place, we all knew immediately that it was right. I believe the basic idea belonged to Rafael, the colorful and talented vice president of programming. As I look back, *Flair* combined elements of NBC's *Monitor*, and television's later-day *Entertainment Tonight*, but was simpler and breezier in a fast-moving format leaning more toward entertainment than news.

Flair was a fifty-five-minute program (network news was at 55 minutes past the hour), and aired initially at 1:00 PM (Eastern Time) to all ABC Radio affiliates, and was repeated every hour until 5:00 PM. The local affiliates could choose the best time locally to air the show. The program consisted of a fast kaleidoscope of information, music, personalities, sports, public service, comedians, news and anything that was emerging on the American scene that was fresh and different. No program segment was more than two and a half or three minutes long and the upbeat musical bridges kept the program moving at a fast pace. The individual segments were taped every day and then edited around the program "host," in a stylish manner by Rafael, his assistant, Maury Benkoil and the ABC engineers.

The host, or emcee of *Flair* was a young man who had recently starred in the Broadway hit, *Bye, Bye, Birdie*. His name was Dick Van Dyke. The personable, gangly Van Dyke was fun to work with. We took him on a couple of sales calls to introduce the new *Flair* concept. I don't think he fully appreciated the sales area because, when I was in the middle of my presentation, he would give me that surprised, befuddled look that became so familiar on Rob Petrie whom he played on the later TV *Dick Van Dyke Show*. But on the air, his natural enthusiasm carried the show and gave it a sense of innovation and vitality. *Flair* went into the field searching for the stars of the future. For instance, in one program, Van Dyke introduced a young female singer who was getting rave notices at The Village Gate, a Greenwich Village bistro in New York. He played a segment of her rendition of *Cry Me A River*, with some tones so high and crystal clear that listeners came right out of their chairs. She, of course, was Barbra Streisand.

Comedians often came on *Flair* with short monologues that became the talk around office water coolers that afternoon or the next day. For example, Jonathan Winters taped a piece that became a classic concerning a couple, Biff and Buffy, with affected Connecticut lockjaw, who bought "his and her" yachts and raced each other around the bay for recreation on weekends and "visited their gatehouse to see how the poor folks lived." Even old Henny Youngman visited the program on occasion, firing off his one-liners: "Doctor, Doctor. I think I have a rejection complex. The doctor says, 'Next!'"

Herb Granath, one of our sales people who eventually became a major executive with Capital Cities/ABC, tells the story about the time that Sammy Davis, Jr. visited *Flair*. Davis, the diminutive and very talented song and dance man, was at the height of his popularity. We were all amazed that we could afford to get him. Granath asked him about it.

"Hey, man, I'm doing this for scale," Sammy said with a big smile. "I love radio. You know why I love radio? It's the only medium where I can play a six-foot-five-inch white man."

Many well-known news people started or enhanced their careers with *Flair*. One of the most successful was a little-known reporter working for ABC Radio News, who in later years became one of the more famous among radio and television news people. His name is Ted Koppel. Ted's first news job was on *Flair* reports. Another reporter who got a jump-start at *Flair* was Charles Osgood, who went on to fame at CBS with his *Osgood File*.

Flair grew to have a lineup of over 200 affiliated stations. It became a key part of our network sales picture. The program appealed to the more mobile, out-of-home listeners, in the automobile or at the beach, who were now becoming the core of radio's total audience. Radio appealed to any number of national advertisers who wanted to market to the younger, active generation.

It was the job of the affiliate relations department to convince individual ABC affiliated radio stations to include the new *Flair* concept in their program schedules. I was delighted to work with the affiliated relations people, Earl Mullin and Frank Atkinson, because they did a superb job and they taught me a lot about working with local stations. I would occasionally travel with Mullin, and it was always an adventure because Earl was one of the funniest men in America telling stories about the people and the bewildering problems during his earlier days at ABC. I remembered Mullin in those earlier days, because he was the publicity director for ABC New York, Ell Henry's boss, when I joined the network

Flair became an important part of the ABC Radio Network schedule along with Don McNeill's *Breakfast Club* (then in its thirtieth year), *Paul Harvey News* in the morning and the evening, Howard Cosell *Speaking of Sports*, *Tom Harmon Sports* for United Delco, and five-minute news shows every hour throughout the day.

Flair gave ABC a new sense of purpose with the radio network, and its growing success led Leonard Goldenson on at least two occasions to have Pauley and me talk about our progress to the ABC Board of Directors. It was infinitesimal compared to the need for success on the TV side, but Leonard liked our spirit and seemed proud to show us off to the outside directors. In later years, I often have thought how relaxed Leonard was in presenting the radio story versus the intensity of the television discussions. Television's higher stakes demanded maximum intensity.

All of us took great pride in our programming vision with *Flair*. While the rest of the world probably wasn't as aware of the importance of the program as we were, those of us who worked on it felt that *Flair* made us different. It was one of the sales leaders at the network that helped us grow from $6 million in gross sales when I came from Chicago in 1960 to over $13 million when I left for the TV network in 1963. It also helped save the radio network at a time when ABC management was considering eliminating it. That "save" for the company became extremely important, financially and otherwise, five years later.

One of the reasons *Flair* became a sales leader and helped save us is that our small band of warriors at ABC came up with a new measurement system for national radio. The truth is that we were instrumental in doing away with the Nielsen Rating Index for radio because of its inaccuracies and out-of-date methodology.

In the early sixties, Nielsen's radio (and television) Rating Index was *the* way the popularity of individual programs was measured. The Nielsen Company placed 1200 audimeters (approximately 942 working on average in any given week) on radio receivers in homes of families, selected by the Nielsen Company, all across America. It was a ridiculous system for measuring the audio medium.

With the surging dominance of television viewing in the American living room, radio had become a medium of mobility. It was clear that radio listening had moved into other rooms in the home through smaller portable radios. The old stand-up Philco at my Grandpa Adams' farm was now a relic. Most importantly, radio listening had expanded beyond the home into automobiles and to the beaches and many other public places. Yet, the Nielsen Company continued to measure only in-home listening. Their attitude was, "if it's good enough for TV, it should be good enough for you." The Nielsen ratings were a nightmare for our sales people. The only acceptable measurement to agencies and advertisers was the Nielsen Radio Index, which no longer provided any realistic approximation of how many people were listening to particular programs. The Nielsen rating system was a major factor in causing the near extinction of network radio.

With the advent of *Flair*, we very quickly devised a marketing campaign based on the slogan, "Homes don't buy automobiles (or bread or hamburgers, etc.). People do!" *Flair* was tailored for the younger mobile market. We created and delivered countless presentations across the country based on the fact that people are influenced when they are listening in their cars or to their portables in a "growing mobile America." The outdated Nielsen in-home audimeter system was useless to us. So we canceled it, despite the screams and curses from the TV researchers (fearing Nielsen would take retribution against ABC television).

We immediately hired Sidlinger & Company, a market research firm that we had been talking with for months, to do a monthly "people-oriented" survey and report. Acceptance of the new numbers did not fit easily into the traditional minds of some agencies and advertisers, but we did an all-out sales blitz to "sell the sizzle" of our changing medium. And it proved successful. In time, agencies and advertisers accepted the Sidlinger numbers.

At this same time, the Nielsen Company had come under scrutiny in Washington for alleged "flaws and inaccuracies in its radio ratings." It was reported that some of the field representatives would change the internal workings of the audimeters to make their own lives easier by cutting down the number of stations that would be recorded by the audimeter and, in doing so, created a false impression of the listening habits within the Nielsen homes. Bob Pauley and I, again much to the chagrin of the TV researchers, testified in front of a United States Senate Hearing Committee, chaired by Senator Oren Harris. Based largely on the testimony of former field representatives, a determination was made that the Nielsen Company was inadequate, if not fraudulent, with its radio ratings. In due time, the Nielsen Company ceased measuring radio listening.

In order to take advantage of radio's growing mobile and more personalized audience, ABC introduced four different networks in 1968 that set the stage for the powerful radio industry that exists today. The four networks were (1) The American Information Network for Talk Radio, appealing to older audiences; (2) The Contemporary Network for the younger rock and roll audience; (3) The Entertainment Network for broader listening audiences; and (4) an FM Network designed for easy listening stations. ABC eventually programmed seven different networks and became the acknowledged leader in the industry by every measure. When I was with the radio network in 1963, ABC had a lineup of 350 stations carrying Don McNeill's *Breakfast Club*. In 1995, the combined Capital Cities/ABC networks serviced over 2,300 radio stations.

ABC's vision in radio's transitional stages laid the foundation for the far-reaching industry that continues today to grow year by year. Specialized networks and stations dealing in general news, farm news, business news, sports and music continue, and new talk radio formats come on the scene every year. With its ability to reach into every corner of the country, and, indeed, the world, major American advertisers wanting to break into the European market, the Far East and certain Third World countries are now embracing radio. Radio is also playing an increasing role in education through distance learning for the more isolated and disadvantaged students, especially young people, in this country and more frequently around the world. Radio, the once dying stepchild to television, has emerged as a major player in the communications superhighway in the 21st century.

In April of 1963, I received a call from Tom Moore, the president of the ABC Television Network, asking me to consider becoming the vice president in charge of sales for the television network. I was flattered, but I was also wary. I was having a grand old time in radio, and the incessant pressure and stress of Chicago television sales was still fresh in my memory.

On top of that, word was on the street that the ABC-TV Network was in deep trouble from the former management's deceptions with stations and advertisers, giving ABC little credibility with clients or their agencies. Frankly, I was put off with the idea of uprooting my career once again. Still, it would be a tremendous challenge for me. The words kept echoing in my mind, "Television is the place to be."

Along with those echoes was the conviction that TV had the reach and power to be a catalyst in helping to bring about awareness of our nation's growing social problems. Working to formulate and create a blueprint for television's impact upon our social problems had great appeal to me. I found myself thinking of the possibilities and considering another career transition.

Nine

The Trauma and Triumph of TV Sales

Strangely, from the moment Tom Moore called, I had to continually fight my attitude about returning to television network sales.

I was extremely happy with the radio network and the last thing I wanted to do was return to the wild, disorganized and stressful circus of television sales. My experiences in Chicago had given me a taste of the pressure, but I knew that would be nothing compared to the constant backbiting and demand for sales quotas that I would be walking into as the head of television network sales in New York.

My attitude became really pronounced when Tom Moore asked me to see Julie Barnathan, the vice president and general manager of the television network at the time. I honestly believe that Tom wanted the meeting just for the record since he and Barnathan got along like bad blind dates. Barnathan was a short, raunchy, enthusiastic, near-genius Brooklynite who came out of the research department in the mid-fifties and had made an impression on both Goldenson and Si Siegel. I had known Julie from his research days. As a matter of fact, he had helped me with the big Aero Mayflower Moving Company radio sale in 1954. I thought Julie was brilliant, but not as the general manager of a TV network. My meeting with him was very predictable.

"Jeez, Jimmy, I can't see you running the sales department. My man is Ed Bleier, and I'm making no bones about it."

I couldn't help but think as I watched Julie animatedly tell me his feelings that he must know Tom Moore doesn't share his affection for Bleier. I was sure Moore made that clear in his conversations with Goldenson.

"Maybe we could consider you for a salesman's job," Julie continued with a straight face.

He was serious. He felt radio salesmen really didn't have the right stuff for the big show.

"Thanks, Julie," I said flatly. "I'm really not interested in a salesman's job, and as a matter of fact, I'm really not interested in being the head of sales for the TV network. The only reason I'm sitting here is because Tom and Si asked me to talk to you. I'll tell them what you said. See ya." And I left.

I didn't give much thought to the television prospect in the next three weeks, sincerely believing and hoping that it had gone away. Then in the middle of an important presentation to try to win over a powerful CBS radio affiliated station in San Antonio, Texas, I received an urgent message to fly back to New York immediately. I had a sinking feeling. All of my earlier concerns came flooding back.

When I went in to see Si, he was smiling. "Leonard isn't going to let you get away. He really wants you to take the television job. He's waiting to see you."

I walked slowly across the fourth floor of ABC headquarters trying to build my enthusiasm for leading a sales charge for the expanding television medium. I knew there was no way out.

Leonard was also smiling when I got to his office. He got up from behind his huge desk and shook my hand.

"Thanks for coming back, Jim," he said. "This is important to the future of the company. You have done an outstanding job with the radio network. I want you to do the same kind of work for the TV network. I want you to give the whole TV sales operation the same sense of class and style that you brought to radio. Many of the people there now won't know what you're talking about. But just do it, and do it your way." Goldenson told me how strongly he felt about the future of television and the role that ABC could play. He reiterated his belief in radio, but he left no question that TV was the medium of the future and the place for me to be. He paused and looked me straight in the eye and said, "I want you to do this."

"Well, Mr. Goldenson, I'm flattered with this kind of recognition," I answered, still working to overcome my misgivings. "And I certainly want to do what you and Mr. Siegel feel is right for the company. I have sold network television in Chicago, as you know. And I honestly believe that we, ABC, need a different selling philosophy, a top-level approach to the heads of major companies that will eventually bring respect. The bargain-basement mentality has to go. I don't know if the company can afford or tolerate that approach because it will take time."

I hesitated for a minute because I knew that my decision would have an enormous effect on the rest of my life. I could hear the clock ticking on the chairman's desk. I took a deep breath and said, "I will take the job, but I do have several concerns. When I was a salesman with the TV network in Chicago, I felt that there was a good deal of expediency in television. Because of the power of the ratings, I feel that the programming is often sensationalized and lower in quality than it can be. That programming represents this company and all of us who work here. I feel strongly about it. I will take the job, and I'll give it everything I have, but I don't want to be a voice in the wilderness on the programming issue."

"Television is a new medium, Jim. It is finding its way. I'll back you in your beliefs," Leonard said. "You will have help in what you want to accomplish. You might look at a young fellow in sales proposals. His name is Fred Pierce. He is very bright and has a good future with the company. Congratulations."

We shook hands and I walked out of his office. Feelings of relief, trepidation, bewilderment and some jubilation swept over me. But the thought remained, "What the hell have I done now?"

I went home that night and said to Betty, "I think I'm about to walk into the lion's den." She treated the promotion with indifference. By this time, Betty was into her own routine of taking care of the children, keeping an immaculate house, reading her many novels, and listening to music into the wee hours of the night. We did very little as marital partners, except, on occasion, take our growing family out for dinner or to the movies or an amusement park. I spent a good part of my weekends, when I wasn't traveling, playing football or basketball with Jay and Terry and doing yard work. Betty had grown very disenchanted with my show business life-style and would sharply criticize me, privately and publicly, for my quest for what she termed 'Elysian Fields.' It created several arguments and made for a less than happy home life. I was looking for understanding and support. She needed someone who was home more often and perhaps less ambitious. In retrospect, I understand her frustrations. But that's the way it was, and our relationship continued to deteriorate.

The announcement was made that I would be joining the television network as the vice president in charge of sales in May 1963. It created quite a stir among my radio network colleagues. I know they were pleased with my recognition. I also think they felt a sense of pride that my promotion was a tribute to what the entire radio division had accomplished.

One evening, after I had packed up my belongings in my office, a group of some forty employees and friends from the radio network gathered in the Gaslight Club on East 56th Street to celebrate my making it to the big time. The Gaslight Club was one of my favorite haunts in New York. I had been one of the first members to be issued a key when the founder, Burton Brown, an advertising executive, opened the original Gaslight Club in Chicago in the mid-fifties. The New York club was in a classy three-story brownstone, styled after the roaring twenties, with food and piano bars and lots of singing and fun at almost any time of the day or night. It was a place where many New York sports celebrities would drop by and dazzle the out-of-towners. One night we met half of the New York Giants football team, who were out on the town. Another evening I had the pleasure of meeting the famed Yankee Clipper, Joe DiMaggio. I would often take clients to the Gaslight for a bit of relaxation. The radio network sales department celebrated many sales around one of the Gaslight's pianos.

This particular celebration was, of course, very special for me since I was leaving people with whom I had worked closely and whom I would sincerely miss. As a matter of fact, they were the center of my life in New York, with the exception of my family and a few friends in the southern Connecticut area. It turned out to be a fun-filled evening with lots of stories and laughs about our bringing the radio network from the steps of the gallows to a place of respectability in the broadcasting world. Some, I think, shared my anxiety about going back to the world of TV. I overheard a couple of the younger people talking about it.

"It's really kind of amazing that they would pick somebody from radio to run the whole TV sales operation," one of them said. "I'll bet they'll try to eat him alive."

The speeches were wonderful, most of them funny, some emotional, but all were extremely sincere. Bob Pauley was very complimentary about working as a team and admonished me to "hold on to my principles at any cost." Ted Douglas, Jack Mann, Earl Mullin and Herb Granath all spoke. Cosell told the dog peeing on my leg story for the twentieth time and predicted an "inglorious continuation of a career of mediocrity on the television side." Tony Rocco, whom I had hired when he came to Manhattan from Buffalo, NY in 1961, had become a close friend, and he was especially hilarious with his remarks. He also had a perceptive warning. After telling a few jokes involving our adventures and a very funny dissertation on, "Why did they pick this guy? Why not me?" he said, "Watch yourself and behave yourself. They think, act and dress different over there."

They presented me with pictures, funny cards and signs. My favorite sign, because I found it to be very relevant to our business, reads, "Whose food I eat; whose wine I drink, his songs I sing." Toward the end of the evening, I was presented a handsome plaque for my new office with my picture emblazoned on the front. It had an appropriate inscription. Along with some flattering words, the inscription read, "DON'T FORGET, RADIO PUT TELEVISION IN BUSINESS." It was signed on the back by all the people in the radio network. The plaque and its significance have remained with me throughout my career.

As I stood and looked at the circle of familiar faces, I couldn't help but marvel at how important they had become to me, and how my life had changed in New York in just three short years. Along with the sales, affiliate relations and programming people, I saw Bob Holmgren, the network business manager; Don Shlosser, the promotion manager; several engineers and secretaries and clerks from all the departments. I thanked them all for attending and caring, told a few funny stories of our adventures, and emphasized how much the previous three years had meant. I assured them I would try to carry on their tradition at the television network. "Most of us will be together again," I said. "Either I will be back here, or you will be over there."

The first day on the job justified all my concerns. It was Monday, June 17, 1963, and it was one of those clear blue sky, balmy days in New York that occur about seven times a year. As I got out of the cab at 7 West 66th Street, I noticed again how unpretentious, even tacky, the building looked. The ABC headquarters in those days was not the tall and ominous-looking skyscraper that dominates Broadcast Row today. The main building was a former riding academy that Leonard leased in 1953, and it housed the TV studios. Some pundits claimed you could still smell some pungent horse odors when certain prime-time programs were aired. At the east end of the structure was a six-story building that became the executive offices as well as offices for the programming, news and sales departments. ABC Sports, formed in 1960, had its offices in temporary quarters on Fifth Avenue.

The ABC executive building had a small, narrow lobby that led to two very small and slow elevators in the back. When a client's representatives and advertising agency people would visit for the screening of a new television show, they often had to ride these elevators in shifts, much to my embarrassment.

The sales department offices were on the fifth floor. On this particular morning, as I got off the elevator, I was met in the hall by stacks of cardboard boxes that I practically had to drop kick my way through. I turned right to head for my office at the front or downtown side of the building. There were rows of desks and chairs in front of small cubicle offices on each side of the aisle as I snakehipped my way to my new quarters. I could feel the secretaries' heads turn as I walked by. I noticed a couple of sales people peek out from behind their cubicles.

"Is that the guy?" somebody whispered.

I had asked my secretary from radio, Alva Goodall, to move with me. She was sitting at her desk outside my office when I arrived. She smiled and then rolled her eyes, as if to say, "What have you gotten me into?"

My office was a long, narrow room with an upholstered sofa against one wall and a small, rather scarred desk at one end with a window facing 66th Street.

Half windows ran the length of the interior wall to my left looking out over the sales department. Across the shorter wall, a window looked into the office of Ed Bleier, the vice president and general manager of the department, who would now be reporting to me. The windows were covered with some dingy green curtains that you could pull aside and peek through if you wanted to see if all the troops were working or see who was meeting with Bleier.

This particular morning, I peeked out from behind the curtains to see groups of sales people collecting in the aisles exchanging notes. I made the safe assumption that the notes were about their new, young, fair-haired, Chicago-born, radio-bred boss. I felt like a chicken at a snake farm. Alva doubled over with laughter as she saw my eyeball peeking out from behind the curtain.

Ed Bleier greeted me very warmly. I must say he was helpful and a perfect gentleman during the early weeks of my indoctrination, despite the fact that he probably felt I was usurping the position he deserved. On this first morning, he came in, closed the door and filled me in on the structure of the sales department and what accounts were working. He offered to take me on a brief tour to meet the sales people. I had heard that the Eastern Division sales staff had been divided into two distinct and competitive teams, one consisting of the younger folks and the other the older, veteran sales people. Selling media of any kind is difficult enough without creating a dog-eat-dog atmosphere in your own house. This concept ran counter to my selling philosophy. Ed confirmed that, indeed, it was the structure and that it had been his idea. We were just about to go on the tour of the offices when the door burst open and a red-faced Ed Sherick, the man I replaced and now the VP in charge of programming, returned to his old office, fit to be tied. He didn't even acknowledge me. He turned to Bleier and started screaming, "God damn it, Ed, I got a call from American Tobacco this morning and they claim your sales guys have fucked up their order, and I got a hold of Julie...."

Just then the door flew open again. Julie Barnathan blustered in yelling at the top of his voice. "Jesus Christ, Ed, you can't fuck up an order like this here. Holy shit, you think we can toss business away...."

Bleier jumped off the couch and started to defend himself. There was a cacophony of screaming voices, all three executives shouting like madmen while I'm sure the entire sales staff, if not half the neighborhood, thought the new guy in town was being eaten alive. I sat behind my new desk and tolerated the insanity for about sixty seconds. Then I slammed my hand against the desk as loudly as I could. Suddenly the room was quiet. The three men, looking like something from a Three Stooges movie, stopped in mid-sentence and stared at me.

"That's enough. If you want to fight, go out in the alley," I said softly. "I don't do business this way. That's the last screaming session that will be held in this office or on this floor as long as I am here. If this is a decision for the sales department to make, then Ed write me a brief memo with the particulars, and I'll make the decision. See you two later."

Sherick and Barnathan left as fast as they came in, only more quietly. It certainly wasn't the last screaming session on the fifth floor in the months that followed, but it set the tone for a major change. I thought for sure I had gotten off on the wrong foot with three important and effective company executives – despite what the shouting scene might indicate. They never said a word about it, and I believe the new guy from radio might have gained a measure of respect.

It was time to get acquainted. I called a meeting of everyone in the sales department – the managers, the salesmen and woman (ABC had the first network saleswoman: a marvelous lady named Helen Guy), the sales service people, development and proposals people, as well as the secretaries and clerks. The meeting was in a television studio on the first floor where I had chairs arranged auditorium style.

I informally introduced myself despite the fact that I had known many of them from my TV days in Chicago. I then proceeded to tell them where I came from and how I felt about my new assignment and what I expected from them as a staff and as individuals. I tried to make it a motivational session that would start to establish a spirit of teamwork; something I felt was missing in the department.

I closed with a story I had heard Paul Harvey use to end his speeches on several occasions. I had used it myself as a motivational message to end speeches (always crediting Paul Harvey, of course). It never failed, after a quiet moment, to get a rousing response, often standing ovations. As I looked out into the hundred or so faces staring at me, some smiling, some stony, but most just curious as to how I was going to run the operation, I decided "the bird story" should be told.

The story, without all the histrionics and dramatic pauses, involved two aggressive, unscrupulous and overly ambitious young men who moved into a small town in the Midwest. They began scheming to take over the town with their greedy and often underhanded methods. The character of the once peaceful town started to change. Its economy faltered, the attitude of the people, once neighborly and supportive, changed, and families started to move away. The young men were energized by the town's disintegration. They increased their efforts to dominate the community. The only obstacle in their way to total dominance was a wise old man who lived up in the hills. The old man had the total respect and love of the townspeople.

The young men were perplexed until finally one of them said, "If that old man is as wise as people say, let's show him up. Let's go up and talk with him. We'll catch us a bird along the way, and I'll hold the bird in my hands and we'll ask him if the bird is alive or dead. If he says the bird is alive, I'll crush it in my hands and kill it. If he says the bird is dead, I'll open up my hands, and the bird will fly away. That will show him!"

The next day the two young men trudged up the hill and captured a live bird for their confrontation. When the old man opened his door, they challenged him.

"Tell me, old man, what's this I have in my hands?"

The old man paused and finally said softly, "It's a bird."

"Well, if you're as smart as all the town folks say, tell me old man, is the bird alive or is it dead?"

The two men smirked and glanced confidentially at one another.

"The old man didn't answer for a long time. He looked them both straight in the eyes and he finally said, "It is as you will, my son."

I looked out at my new sales team and they stared back rather wide-eyed, even disbelieving. I concluded, "And it is as you WILL. Each one of you, over the next few weeks and months and years, can make this the best sales department in all of network television. I know you will. Thank you."

There was dead silence in the room. It seemed like an eternity. My audience of sophisticated New Yorkers didn't know what to do.

Finally, a voice in the back said, "I don't know, Marshall, what do you think happened to that bird?"

The room erupted with laughter. The tension was broken, but it was very clear that my motivational message had missed the mark. Various sales people kidded me about the story for years afterward, saying, "Hey, Duff, whatever happened to that bird of yours?"

Still, I think they all got the underlying message that it was not going to be business as usual and some changes were in the offing. I quickly discontinued the competitive two sales team concept in the New York office and installed a single sales manager with responsibility clearly spelled out for the Eastern Division. I also discontinued the late-night sales meetings that had apparently been a matter of course under the previous management. They would have the staff half-asleep and hostile when they weren't actually nodding off. I believe in hard work, but I also believe if you can't accomplish what you set out to do in the course of the working day, then there is a real problem in your management strategy and style. The blank look of fatigue on most of the salesmen's faces reminded me of some of the prisoners of war who were in a compound at Sheppard Field during the war.

I also included the management of the sales offices in Chicago, Detroit, and Los Angeles in our monthly sales meetings. And twice a year, I would bring the entire sales staffs from around the country to New York for motivational meetings and screenings of new programs.

Little by little, attitudes began to change, and the spark of a spirit of working together began to ignite.

As often happens in a growing medium, the involvement of management in decisions in all facets of the network was immediate. There were several trips to Los Angeles with advertisers and agency representatives to view shows that were in production for the fall season. I was asked my opinion on casting and story lines on many occasions. Without my Chicago TV network sales experience, I would have been absolutely lost.

In contrast to my radio experience, sales came quickly. On my first trip to Los Angeles as the head of TV sales, I helped wrap up a schedule for the Maybellene Cosmetic Company and assisted Tom Moore in securing a renewal from the Kaiser Company for sponsorship on alternate weeks of *The Greatest Show On Earth* on Sunday evenings. The thrill of the sale was obtaining the renewal in a meeting with the great ship builder, Henry J. Kaiser himself.

Memories of the importance placed on television program ratings, and the fanaticism with which these were regarded, came rushing back to me very quickly from my TV sales experience in Chicago.

I had been at the television network as the head of sales for about three months. The new television season had premiered when I received a call late one September afternoon from Tom Moore's office. He said it was important for me to be at the research department offices that evening, and we would get an advance look at the new season's Nielsen prime-time ratings.

It seemed ironic to me since, as I described earlier, I had been instrumental in bringing about the cancellation of the Nielsen Radio Index. It was inconceivable to me that the audimeter system that the Nielsen Company had devised could ever properly measure a medium as mobile as radio or as swiftly growing as the television medium.

The audimeter was a small box that sat on the radio or TV and recorded when the set was on and what station it was tuned to. Originally the recording was made on slow-moving film. Field representatives of the Nielsen Company would come and gather the results. To compensate the Nielsen family home for its efforts, the audimeter would spit out a couple of quarters once a month.

These audimeters, along with a diary system where members of the household were supposed to record their listening or viewing habits in a book, were used to measure the numbers of viewers (or listeners) of respective programs. The networks conducted their business by analyzing the numbers for their programs and selling advertising on the basis of these results.

In 1991, Nielsen replaced the audimeters and diaries with people meters, which is the measuring system for television viewing that is used now. The people meter is a box with eight buttons that sits on each TV set in a Nielsen home and is wired into each TV set and VCR in the home. Each family member is assigned a different button and is supposed to press it when he or she starts and stops watching TV. The box records time and channels including VCR activity and correlates it with the individual family members. Nielsen's computer headquarters in Florida calls in to the box daily and downloads the information. Field representatives record information on each member of the household including data on household age, race, and income. Nielsen also increased the number of homes used for the sample from 1200 to 4000 to measure an estimated 95,000,000 television homes. Nielsen also raised the pay to $50 for signing up and $2 per TV set per month for being a participating family.

Taking the figures recorded by the Nielsen homes and factoring the percentages of people watching particular programs at particular times derive the famous "ratings." Thus, if a program has a 20.5 rating, that means that 20.5 percent of all the homes in the country with television sets (or radios in those earlier days) were determined to have watched (or listened to) that program for at least six minutes. Multiply the rating points by the number of television sets in homes around the country, and then multiply that number by the number of viewers per set for the program, and you get the number of people watching that particular program according to Nielsen.

Nielsen also extracted demographic information from the audimeter and diary records. For example, the Nielsen numbers might show the percentage of white females (or black males) between the ages of 25 and 35 who watched a certain program on a certain night. Nielsen ratings also make assessments on children's

Saturday morning television viewing. The survey also assesses how many people in a certain income bracket or age bracket listened to a respective network's news program. And so on. With the people meter, there was no need for the diaries because the button system kept track of who was watching, what was being watched and for how long.

One point of breakdown was the fact that the census information on which these demographics were based can be as much as ten years out of date. The result is, while a survey might indicate that a middle-class white family with three children lives in one particular Nielsen home, the truth may be that an African-American couple with no children has moved into the home in the ensuing ten years. And national demographics are also changing so that the percentages are applied against outdated data. Oops! And all of this measures a very mobile, constantly changing population of growing economic importance.

There is another significant failing of the Nielsen system. While it is quite easy to find a representative sample of houses to install the people meters in, only 55% of those chosen accept the offer from Nielsen. The remaining 45% are made up of substitutes, which may not meet the demographic breakdown originally intended.

There are a number of other factors, which result in an incredibly error-prone method of measuring success in the television industry.

Now, here I was, fresh from radio and less than one year in the television sales job, on my way to the research department to get TV ratings that I had found so misused and so misrepresented. It was the same Nielsen system that had failed in radio. And this pitifully small sample (1,200 audimeters) was being used to measure the viewing habits of over 40 million television homes in 1963. Like it or not, the Nielsen ratings were a principal tool I had to utilize in an attempt to lead the network to the Promised Land.

When I finally arrived at the research department offices, I couldn't believe the large number of people that had gathered. Research was housed on the second floor over the A & P grocery story on Broadway. The cramped quarters were cluttered with papers, coffee cups, research books and old typewriters. Almost everyone from the television network was there for the ceremony of revealing the new season ratings: Tom Moore, Ed Sherick, Julie Barnathan, Ed Bleier, most of the programmers, most of the sales people, John Gilbert, the VP for affiliate relations and his crew, all of the researchers, Fred Pierce, then in charge of sales proposals, and probably some freeloaders from Clancy's saloon across the street were there. And to my amazement, right in the middle of the action, was Leonard Goldenson.

The center of attention was the far right-hand corner of the room. Seymour Amlen, a young expert in audience research, sat hunched over his telephone, which was hooked up to an open line in a phone booth outside Nielsen's offices in Evanston, Illinois. The research department had flown one of its specialists, who had a friend working for Nielsen, to Evanston to get copies of the network ratings as soon as they were available. The specialist's assignment was to call all of the information to the waiting executives in New York. The ratings in 1963 were tabulated for the full National Nielsen Index, where ABC was always behind because of the lesser number of affiliated stations carrying its programming, and for the Multi Station Nielsen Index (the MNI), where ABC had more stations and could be more competitive. The MNI calculated ratings in the top seventy cities in the country. It was in the latter report where ABC had hopes of giving an indication of strength against the competitive programming. As I looked at the chaotic scene, what everyone seemed to be overlooking was the fact that the sales department had to sell to national advertisers on the national ratings, rarely on the MNI.

Expectations ran high as the executives milled around noisily and occasionally glanced at young Amlen. I kept thinking that if fiery Jim Beach from Chicago had been there, he would have cracked open a couple of bottles of whiskey. But this was not party time. The stakes were too high. It was a rather warm evening, and people were starting to perspire in the non-air-conditioned room. Then a hush fell over the crowd as someone yelled, "He's on."

There was a mob scene around poor Amlen as he struggled to write down the numbers on the prearranged sheets. Top television executives, including the president of ABC, were hopping up and down trying to get a closer look at the scribbled numbers. There were screams of anguish as each night's figures came in. "Oh my God, Monday looks like a disaster," or "Oh Christ, looks like CBS is running away with it." There was a lot of hushing and pushing. Once Amlen lost his cool – and his pencil – because he couldn't hear the fellow trying to communicate from the phone booth in Illinois.

As it turned out, the numbers were not all that bad. A couple of new shows seemed to be showing great promise, including an adventure series on Tuesday entitled *The Fugitive*, starring a young actor named David Janssen. Sunday evening, anchored by *The Greatest Show On Earth*, performed well. When the long evening was over, and I wearily got on the train heading for my home in Connecticut, I could not help but think that the gospel according to Nielsen is upon us, and there is a long and very difficult road ahead.

The reason that evening stays with me is that it illustrates how fervent broadcasting executives (or at least the majority of them) are about the industry bible – the Nielsen ratings. Networks base their entire operation around these figures as if they were scientific fact. Yet to me, the ratings system and the way it is used, represent one of the medium's most obvious, and, in many ways, most destructive shortcomings. It is incomprehensible to me that through all of these years, an industry as powerful and important as television cannot or will not devise a reliable and realistic method to measure the popularity and distribution of a product that reaches virtually every home in America.

The Nielsen Company is really not at fault. They calculate and deliver the data that television and advertising industries request and employ. From the inception of the service, Nielsen has clearly stated that its ratings are to be used as an indication of program popularity. It is the network, agency and advertising researchers and executives who manipulate the figures with a childish faith in the system's accuracy. Rating numbers, with acknowledged large margins of error, are multiplied many times over to determine, "cost per thousand homes in the average minute" (CPM) or any number of "cost per thousands" based on demographic categories, age, education, income levels, location etc. The more a rating number is multiplied, the greater the margin of error and the less accurate the final figure. In some smaller demographic categories, e.g. children's shows on Saturday morning, the margin of error is often larger than the original rating number. The rating can completely misrepresent the viewing audience. Yet, the CPM has become the standard of selling and buying advertising time. In the contemporary practice of selling television "by the pound," as I like to call it – selling a number of spots in different programs – where the total gross ratings for the total of the shows, or the cumulative factor for a particular demographic category, are the criteria, the inaccuracies and margins of error are exacerbated even further.

Several different research companies have tried to compete with Nielsen through the years, but they have always been shot down and have disappeared, mostly through lack of funding and advertiser and industry support. Every broadcasting executive in the country has at one time or another violently "cursed" the ratings because they have "destroyed" his or her program or time slot or ability to compete. But ratings have the devil's touch: a measurement is essential, and when the measurement shows that you're winning, you're unlikely to complain about the system of measurement, even if you know that it is inaccurate. The same people who rail against the system when they're losing become its strongest advocates when they're winning.

The problem with the measurement of program popularity is no small matter. Incredibly good programs can be discarded because of low ratings; careers and fortunes of actors, actresses, directors, producers and the entire program creative team can be made or broken based simply on these numbers. Advertisers and the industry base their decisions on these questionable figures. The selection of programs chosen to be shown to viewers all over the country is based almost exclusively on the rating system.

Nonetheless, in the early sixties, the medium of television rolled steadily forward, locally and nationally, growing in impact by the day, and collecting more and more advertisers along the way. It was quickly living up to its promise as the greatest sales and marketing vehicle ever devised.

Despite my comment earlier that sales came quickly in television, my first few weeks, even months, as the head of TV network sales, were very difficult, frustrating, and at times confusing. I was dealing with a different sales culture, and I was dealing with a product that suffered several disadvantages, compared to NBC and CBS. Shorter station lineups, the constant pressure of time and the bottom line – having to make the sale at almost any cost, along with lower ratings, were disadvantages that affected prime time and every programming category the network had to sell.

Going into the 1963/64 season, starting in mid-September 1963, ABC had a basic affiliate lineup of 126 stations with a potential coverage of 92% of the homes in the United States. Some of the more popular ABC shows considerably increased their respective affiliate lineup by adding secondary affiliates, TV stations whose basic commitment was to NBC or CBS but who would choose to carry, mostly on a delayed basis, the better programs from ABC. By contrast, CBS and NBC had station lineups of nearly 200 affiliates with a potential coverage factor of 98% of US homes. Because of the disparity in distribution and the overall quality of programming, prime-time ratings on CBS and NBC were often 20% to 30% higher than those of the often called, third network.

I used to tell the sales staff that we had to be half again better and smarter than our competition just to stay even.

Being the third network also had its effect on the creative community. Top producers and writers were reluctant to bring their best efforts to ABC where the odds for failure were greater. Consequently, all of us at ABC had to be more innovative and aggressive in our programming and sales activities. History will show that the spirit of innovation played a major role in the company's eventual success.

The ABC TV Network in the nineteen-sixties was under a tremendous financial strain, having lost money from its beginnings as a network.

In the early years, it was said that the theater operations, with their profitable motion-picture business, carried the broadcast divisions. But gradually the television-owned stations, and to a lesser degree the radio-owned stations, came into solid financial positions as the broadcast advertising marketplace grew. Some television stations started to enjoy profit margins approaching an astounding fifty percent.

Despite the financial problems of the TV network, Leonard Goldenson had enormous faith and the vision to know that networks, especially his network, would bear great influence in the marketplace. Meanwhile, when I arrived in mid-1963, the burden of carrying the critical financial load on a day-by-day basis fell on the sagging shoulders of the sales department.

Ten

ABC with Class and Style

The medium of television exploded with its impact and reach during the nineteen-sixties. Because of TV's whirlwind growth, the advertising marketplace was always shifting, with sponsors and their agencies constantly seeking new, hopefully more effective, ways to use the medium. In the early and mid-sixties, a handful of high-budgeted, major advertisers, directed by powerful individuals at their respective agencies, dictated where the most popular prime-time programs would be placed on the three network schedules. Most importantly, these major advertisers' actions determined when the up-front selling season would begin.

The three companies that I remember being especially powerful were Proctor & Gamble, Philip Morris, and General Foods. These advertisers, working with dominant media buyers at their agencies, each bought sponsorship of four or five programs, mostly on CBS. Known as the "Tiffany" network, CBS had been the long-time leader in program ratings with shows like *I Love Lucy*, *Beverly Hillbillies*, *Green Acres*, *The Dick Van Dyke Show* and *Gunsmoke*, and attracted the big buyers. These advertisers, however, would dictate to the network where they wanted the shows placed: in what time periods and on what nights of the week. These purchases were usually made shortly before Washington's Birthday, February 22. CBS would then announce its fall prime--time schedule to the world, and the "up-front" sales season would begin. Other advertisers – well known companies like R. J. Reynolds Tobacco, Colgate, Lever Brothers, Brown and Williamson Tobacco, Chevrolet, Bristol Myers, and many others – would look to the best of the programs and advertising time slots on NBC; what was left on CBS; and finally, what was referred to as "the fourth horse in the three-network race," ABC.

This was also the era of the great program salesmen representing talent agencies like William Morris and International Creative

Management and also production studios like Universal Pictures, Warner Brothers, Paramount Pictures, Screen Gems for Columbia Pictures, United Artists and a handful of others. Representing specific programs or TV actors, these very slick and talented sales people would show up once a year in New York around the time of the program screening and scheduling sessions. They would often pre-sell their respective shows to national advertisers, subject to a choice time period on one of the networks. Those of us involved in the scheduling meetings would be bombarded with calls, day and night, with invitations to lunch, dinner, the theater, the fights at Madison Square Garden or a New York Knicks basketball game. The purpose, of course, was to better position their programs for the schedule and to find out any scrap of information about the schedule.

Probably the most colorful of these hucksters, despite the fact that he was rather subdued in his approach, was John Mitchell, the head of Screen Gems. We dubbed Mitchell "Big John," because he was about six foot two inches tall with broad shoulders and had the gait of a football player. In the spring of each year, Mitchell would show up at the networks with a proposition to place one of the Screen Gems shows in a prominent slot on the fall schedule. In his quiet way, Big John would announce that his particular "hit" show had a sponsor attached for one half of the program, and if it could be placed in a certain choice time period, that "hit" show could be ours with the right to sell the other half sponsorship.

After making his declaration and showing the pilot film, Mitchell would pause and paw at the rug with his foot, glance up and announce softly that we had one half hour to make up our minds since he had a meeting across the street – CBS – where they were ready to buy. It was all part of the dramatics of the season, but we had to listen and make a decision, even if it meant stalling for a few days since Big John often came up with hit shows and top sponsors. He brought us *Bewitched*, starring Elizabeth Montgomery, sponsored by Chevrolet. It became a long-running very popular program that helped ABC stay competitive in the mid- and late nineteen-sixties. The springtime locust-like visits of the super sellers gradually dwindled as the networks took more control of their programming.

Over the years, Mitchell became a close friend of mine and went on to become the president of the Academy of Television Arts and Sciences in Los Angeles before his death in 1985.

The networks had their own staffs of lawyers and business affairs people who dealt with the studios and the agents, especially after a deal had been consummated. Their responsibility was to get it down on paper, and untangle who said what to whom. ABC had the best in the business in Alan Morris, who went on to have a very successful career with his own company. Alan and I became very good friends and he has guided me through many business transactions for years.

When I arrived as the head of television network sales, the staff had just gone through a grueling up-front selling season where the majority of program buys for the whole year were made, and they were now trying to make the shorter-term opportunistic sales in the leftover, less desirable programs. The sales department's plight was made worse by the fact that network management in the late 1950's had given the company a bad reputation by not keeping their promises to several advertisers. ABC was simply not welcome at certain major companies and was not considered in their buying plans.

It was into this sense of crisis and confusion that I tried to infuse a different selling philosophy. By working together, I believed we could build an esprit de corps, reach our sales goals and prosper individually.

As you can imagine, it was very difficult trying to sort out and understand the different personalities in the department and determine who believed in the new mission and who didn't. Henry Hede, a veteran of many years in TV, was the vice president in charge of sales service, and, in his role as a general overseer of all sales contracts, he was extremely helpful to me. Henry would point out the considerable game playing among the sales people and kept me from making managerial miscues in the early weeks. Hede was not in great favor with many of the salesmen since he insisted that the business they brought in be according to the company guidelines. Often salesmen would permit special concessions to be written into an order and Henry would stop them in their tracks. The salesmen in turn would whine to sales management, and this would often result in screaming sessions, much like the one I experienced in my office.

After I arrived at ABC, Hede's position was backed without equivocation, since the rules the salesmen were bending were the new guidelines I had established. All Hede had wanted through his many years with the company was recognition of the contribution he made. I gave that to him and supported him completely.

Despite Henry Hede's watchful eye, I had to tolerate a lot of the New York "cunning" in the early days. Charley Ayres, who had been the head of the radio network and helped "save" the Realemon order during my radio sales days in Chicago, had become a television salesman and now reported to me. Ayres was a loner and would often get an order from one of his pals at an agency and then keep it in his desk drawer until it worked to his advantage to present it. You can imagine the responses from grumpy old Charley when he was challenged in a sales meeting.

"Charley, we need that Brown and Williamson order from Ted Bates. Do you have it?"

"Nope," mumbled Ayres. He then made grumbling noises with small intermittent coughs just as he used to do when he was in radio.

"Well, when do you expect to get it?"

"Don't know," Ayres would say glaring at you as if to say, you can't make me tell you.

I would finally cut through it by saying, "If we don't have the order by the close of business on Friday, I'm going to go through your desk and get it."

The rest of the sales force would crack up, as Ayres would just grunt. But he got the message, and he finally figured out at bonus time it was to his advantage to work with, not against, me.

As frustrating as some of the sales people were to deal with, management in the Eastern Division often made the situation more difficult. One incident involved our Eastern Division sales manager who, with the number two executive in the advertising department at General Foods, attempted to unseat the very well known General Foods advertising director with a sensational low-cost campaign on ABC-TV. The coup attempt included a zany, rather hilarious, although frustrating, explanation that their secret pact prevented our man from disclosing any information to me.

"I can't tell you anything," our man said with a straight face, "because we have an agreement. We have agreed to agree that we have not met until we agree to agree that we have."

I swear I thought I was in a Three Stooges movie. The sales manager and then Fred Pierce tried to justify their actions with, "We were just trying to get the order. Isn't that what we want?"

I let them know that being secretive and meddling in a sponsor's internal business was not the way I expected business to be conducted and they had better clean up their act or they would be gone.

Incidentally, a year later we got a nice piece of business from General Foods in the Monday through Friday daytime schedule as well as in prime time, appropriately from the advertising director who was going to be the victim of the coup.

While I had to sort out this kind of intrigue almost on a weekly basis, the sales staff had to endure my Boy Scout philosophy. In reliving it all, I can now understand why my bird story didn't fly. But I kept at it, and, gradually, order started to emerge from what I considered chaos. An organization started to come together. In the first year, seven or eight of the malcontents were dismissed or left, and some of them went on to be key executives in other departments at ABC or in the industry.

I hammered home the idea that we all had to learn to make focused and hard-hitting presentations on the value of our programs and on the fact that ABC was programming to the younger and more mobile audience who would be the advertisers' market of the future. Many CBS shows were getting tired and were skewing to a much older audience. There was an opportunity for both NBC and for us. I emphasized that we had to make our presentations at the highest levels in the companies, the chairman of the board, if possible, simply because television – and ABC Television – was becoming too important for them to ignore. And most importantly, we had to price and value our programs at realistic and obtainable levels – and stick to our prices. No more negotiating and no more giveaways. It was a sea change for most of the sales people, who previously depended almost solely on key contacts and carefully developed friends in agencies to give them business.

The hard and fast pricing philosophy didn't always work, since business was being written in millions of dollars and losing a large order was a major crisis. Television, unlike radio, counted the orders by the day, and Goldenson would call three and four times a week (on occasion three and four times a day) and run down the alphabet on sales prospects. I had to make some compromises and often it meant long and sleepless nights.

It was a very trying time for me. We often had late-night client meetings and dinners that got me home past midnight. I saw my children only in passing as they were getting dressed for school and I raced out the door to get back to my office and the sales frenzy. I remember one particular night when I had a client dinner and late-night entertainment at Mike Manuche's Restaurant on West 52nd Street. Tired from a long day and groggy from a few cocktails, I barely made the last train to Connecticut. To my dismay, the train broke down in the Grand Central Station tunnel and we sat in the dark for almost three hours. We lost electricity and the only lights I could see were the tips of lighted cigarettes as we sweltered in the smoke-filled car. I finally arrived at the Stamford, Connecticut depot at about 5:00 AM and took a taxi to Cos Cob. Instead of driving up to my home on Mimosa Drive, I had the driver let me off at the bottom of the hill near the Mianus River so I wouldn't wake up the neighborhood. Dawn was breaking and I could see the picturesque, old bridge that crossed the river a few yards down from where I was standing. I walked down to the bridge and watched the shadows from the night now turning into day shimmering on the river. Some ducks saw me and started to gracefully swim toward me in the hopes that I would feed them. A gust of wind started to rustle the trees. I thought I heard the voices whisper, "Go home. Go home." I knew they didn't mean down the street, but back to Illinois where I belonged.

I stayed at the bridge just looking and thinking for some time. I threw some pebbles in the water and watched the small circles get wider and wider and finally disappear.

"What am I doing?" I asked myself. "Is my TV sales job worth all of this? Maybe Cosell was right. Maybe I should pull the family together and go back to Chicago."

Just then, a milk truck drove over the bridge and the driver waved. "Just out for a morning stroll," I yelled and headed up the hill for home. I slept for an hour, took a shower, and caught a train back to New York.

Despite my misgivings, the sales department hung in there, and gradually, the level of sales lifted and the strategy of holding the line on rates and maintaining our pride started to appeal even to the skeptics.

After I had been on the job for about nine months and we had received a substantial order from the Motorola Company in Chicago, I got a call from Goldenson.

"Nice going, Jim," he said. "It took you a while to get your feet on the ground, but it looks like we're moving now." I knew I had been under close scrutiny.

About the same time, Tom Moore one day casually said to me in his Mississippi drawl, "Did you know that there were a lot of people in this business taking bets that you wouldn't last six months in this job?" Then he laughed.

"Oh, swell, Tom," I said. "Be sure and give me their names so I can take them off my Christmas card list."

In the spring of 1965, ABC moved into a new forty-story building on the southeast corner of 53rd Street and Sixth Avenue (later to be named Avenue of the Americas). Our prestigious address became 1330 Avenue of the Americas on Broadcast Row, just four blocks north of NBC in the RCA building, and just one block north of the handsome CBS building, known widely as Black Rock.

I had a large office on the southwest corner of the building, conveniently located near all of the sales personnel on the 35th and 36th floors. My office looked directly into the CBS Sales Department offices across 52nd Street. We would flash competitive or humorous messages back and forth on large hand-printed cards when unusual events happened in the industry or when we made or lost a big sale. On occasion, I would look over and see a large "EAT YOUR HEARTS OUT" sign posted in one of the CBS windows and know they had closed a big piece of business.

After we had moved into our attractive, but rather plain, new building a story appeared in the *New York Times* advertising section quoting Frank Smith, my counterpart at CBS. Smith apparently took the reporter over to his window, pointed at the ABC structure and said arrogantly, "That's the box that the CBS Building came in."

A breakthrough in my push to hold the line on our prices came in March of 1965 when we were selling prime time for the 1965-66 season. Allstate Insurance out of Chicago was interested in alternate-week half-hour sponsorships of three of our more male oriented shows: *Combat, Burke's Law,* and *Twelve O'clock High.* Allstate management had seen the shows and sent a contingent from Leo Burnett, their ad agency, to negotiate a deal. The Burnett contingent met with our sales proposal people to determine the package cost, looking for special pricing since Allstate would be a new client for ABC, and then came to my office to finalize the deal.

When I looked at the proposal, I saw that it was $750,000 lower, on a fifty-two-week basis, than the prices we had determined were the market value for these three shows. Obviously our salesmen and proposals management had decided to change it and were now looking for my approval.

I started very quietly and described the potential of the three shows and my confidence in their respective performances in the fall, especially in appealing to a young male audience, the audience that Allstate wanted to reach. I also told them how proud we would be to have Allstate Insurance as a member of the ABC family. Then I told them that the package as presented was under priced and was not acceptable.

There was stunned silence. Leo Burnett's VP in charge of programming grew red in the face and started to sputter. Fred Pierce, who had now replaced Ed Bleier as national sales manager, looked shocked and stared at me as if I were out of my mind. Bill Gillogly, our VP for sales in Chicago, and his salesman both turned pale.

"Wait a minute, Jim," one of the Burnett executives said sharply, "We didn't come all this way to be...."

"Please, I'm not finished," I said in as cordial a way as possible. And then I went on to describe why the shows were worth every cent of our asking price, and that I wanted them to consider, on behalf of their client, that they were dealing with a new ABC. I said that our intentions, on their behalf, were not for a short-range cut-rate deal, but for a partnership that would benefit both of us for a number of years. "I don't want this to be just another deal, but the beginning of a long-term relationship in which we can help you merchandise in every way possible."

"You're dead serious about this, aren't you?" The Burnett executive asked.

"Dead serious," I said smiling.

"We have to caucus," he said, and the four intense agency figures left the room.

"Well, there goes that goddamn piece of business," Pierce said bitterly. Gillogly and his salesman looked like they wanted to hit me with a chair. Henry Hede, who had been so helpful to me, had come into the office and sensed what was happening. He was smiling.

"Don't get excited," I said, "We haven't lost anything...yet."

Over the next three hours, the Burnett people came back four different times with twists or compromises. I held firm. Finally, they came back after more conversation with their client in Skokie, Illinois and said, "If we make this deal, will you cut a videotape with Bob Sheppard, Allstate's VP for sales, explaining the new campaign, that can be distributed around the country?"

"I would be very proud to," I said.

"Then you've got the order," the Burnett executive said, now with a big smile. I could feel the sighs of relief all around me. We all shook hands, and after the Burnett folks left, I called Tom Moore at home and told him we had the $5,500,000 Allstate business.

"Boy, that sure took a lot of guts," Pierce said shaking my hand.

I looked at him for a minute and said, "I think it took a lot more belief in what we want this place to be, rather than guts. But thanks."

The next morning one of our salesmen flashed a huge GOTCHA! sign at our friends at CBS.

From that point forward, our sales volume took a significant upward swing to the point that Leonard Goldenson and Tom Moore set a goal of $90 million for the department by May 1, 1965. If we reached it, the salesmen and staff would get bonuses and Fred Pierce, the national sales manager, and I could take a two-week trip anywhere in the world later in the summer, all expenses paid.

The sales department easily reached that goal, having billed over $120 million by the end of April. Fred and his wife, Marion, chose a two-week vacation through the Hawaiian Islands. I decided to take a tour through Europe and end up at the Russian-American track meet in Kiev. My marriage was really faltering at that time and since Betty had always had a fear of flying and was reluctant to travel, we agreed that this would be a wonderful experience for Jay, who was then fifteen years old. I don't think that Jay was quite as thrilled as I was. Since it was in fashion for boys to have longer hair, one of the conditions I stipulated was that he have his locks trimmed for our journey abroad. In retrospect, it was a rather foolish mandate since he felt it put him out of step with other young people we met on the trip. I remember one day, in particular, when we visited the Eiffel Tower in Paris, a group of giggling young Parisian girls followed him around. He was mortified that they might be laughing at his short hair. He also tried in every way possible to make it appear that he wasn't traveling with the older fellow, certainly not his father, when one of the girls started talking to him.

I was very excited about the vacation since it was my first trip to Europe and to Russia. Also, the trip was most important to me because it would give me valuable time alone with my son to reiterate some of the basic values that my grandfather had taught me when I was growing up. It would give Jay the benefit of seeing other cultures in some of the great cities in the world. Jay was in his greening years and was most susceptible to peer influences. This was at a time when many Americans, most especially young people, were confused by our mission in the Vietnam conflict, and, in many ways, a sense of rebellion was prevalent. Social drugs were quickly coming onto the American scene, and the seeds were being planted with many youngsters that would eventually destroy their lives and cripple our society.

Our trip consisted of three days each in London, Paris and Rome, a stopover in Vienna, two days in Moscow, and finally three days in Kiev for the track meet before we headed home. I will discuss the many exciting adventures we had in a later chapter. The trip was everything I had hoped and dreamed it would be and a great respite for me. One of the reasons that trip is so memorable to me is that I did grow very close to Jay. We maintained a good sharing relationship until his tragic death in 1994.

Refreshed from the journey abroad, I returned to our sales challenges and we continued to make significant progress. On our calls and in our conversations with clients, all of us in the sales department could feel a new sense of respect for the network. We redoubled our efforts and set our sights on certain industries where ABC had always lagged behind. One of these was the powerful automotive industry, including the big three – General Motors, Ford and Chrysler in Detroit. We also focused our efforts on the growing penetration by the overseas manufacturers in the United States. The sales results didn't always turn out the way we had planned.

There is the now famous story of the time two of our more aggressive sales people, who both happened to be Jewish, the eastern sales manager and the salesman assigned to Doyle, Dane and Bernbach, a hot New York advertising agency, took the pilot of *Twelve O'clock High* to show to some of DD & B's clients. As luck would have it, three executives from the Volkswagen Company in Germany, one of the agency's more distinguished clients, decided to sit in on the screening to get an idea about American television programming.

After a brief presentation, our lads started the screening. If you remember *Twelve O'clock High*, it is the story of the pilots flying B-17s, the famous Flying Fortresses, during World War II.

The picture opens with a squadron of B-17s flying through a bank of clouds under the opening credits. The camera moves to a closeup in a cockpit where the actor, Robert Lansing, with the fifty-mission crush in his cap, and a most serious look, speaks into his intercom.

"Yellow Jacket to Wing. Yellow Jacket to Wing. Target sighted. Target sighted."

The camera pulls back to a wide shot showing the bomb doors slowly opening as the planes soar through the darkening sky.

Again Lansing is shown in a closeup and says, "Bombs away, bombs away."

A long shot shows the bombs screeching down and exploding all over the landscape...POW—SMASH—CRASH!

When the noise died down, a small voice with a thick German accent in the back of the screening room said, "Vell, der goes our factory in Stuttgart."

There was total silence. One kind member of the agency team turned the lights up and the screening was over.

It took us several years to get any business from Volkswagen.

It was almost as bad as the sales genius who tried to sell the movie *Thirty Seconds Over Tokyo* to the Toyota Motor Car Company.

We did make some successful sales to the automotive industry, especially in Detroit, and worked with some of the legends in the business: Lee Iaccoca both at Ford and Chrysler; Gail Smith at General Motors; John Delorean and Bob Lund at Chevrolet; Pat Kane at United Delco; and Bob Benton and Don Peterson at Ford, among others.

Ford took a gigantic step forward in network television advertising in the fall of 1966, when it fully sponsored the movie, *The Bridge on the River Kwai*, to introduce Ford's 1967 models. It was the world television premiere for the movie and it got a record audience, over sixty million viewers, with a high percentage of young men as viewers, Ford's primary target audience. Moreover, Ford dealerships tied in with local promotions and contests weeks before the telecast, resulting in substantial increases in automobile and truck sales, and recognition for Ford all across the country. The movie was scheduled on Sunday evening from 8:00 to 11:00 P.M. EST in the heart of family viewing time. Kwai and Ford were the talk of America on Monday morning. Ford, indeed, "had a better idea."

McDonald's had a similar promotion with us in the fall of 1967 with a full evening's sponsorship of *The Sound of Music*. It was the first time the popular theatrical movie had been on network television. Again, it played on Sunday evening to an all-family audience and had promotional tie-ins at McDonald's franchises across the country. The results were extraordinary. In the thirty days after the movie played, it was reported that McDonald's sold some seventeen million more burgers than they had projected in their sales goals.

This was all part of the changing landscape in commercial television. Major companies that once dominated the network schedules with their own programs on a weekly basis could no longer risk or afford the escalating costs of producing network programming, especially in prime time. Except for the occasional one-time full sponsorships like *Kwai*, control of programming sponsorship availability moved more and more away from the advertisers and back to the networks. Full or partial program sponsorships gave way to minute sales in various programs and eventually thirty-second and, later on, even fifteen-second spots.

When the complete control of program content transferred to the networks and away from the direct scrutiny of the more conservative advertising companies and their agencies, it opened up new opportunities for the creative community. It brought about wider latitude in action-oriented story lines and in more suggestive movement and dialogue even in situation comedies. It was in this era that the voices started to build, including from Congress, about television's negative influence, especially on children.

As the shorter time availabilities in advertising evolved, there were loud cries from the industry, and even individuals, that the enormous commercial impact would be impaired. And the now-mighty medium of over-the-air television would lose its marketing power. The move away from clear sponsorship identification towards scattered, mixed advertising brought a tremendous concern about the possible effect of clutter on advertisers' messages.

I must confess that I shared those concerns, since the magic of TV's marketing and sales seemed to be most powerful in a one-on-one exclusive setting with viewers, and not in the clutter of many different messages. I do know that the new way of selling almost obliterated the art of the sale through the power of persuasion, and became a business of selling by the numbers and by the pound. It was especially disturbing to me because, as I have explained, I had found that the program ratings in television were suspect at best, grossly overused and even invalid. But the medium continued to be molded and shaped by supply and demand in the marketplace. All of television's advertising prices continued to spiral upward, as did the other costs of networking, including programming and the unions.

We had many humorous moments working with clients and the broadcasting personalities. Cosell was often in the lobby or in front of the building ad-libbing with, and performing for, passersby. I remember one day coming back from lunch when Howard was in front with Muhammad Ali, the heavyweight champion of the world at the time.

"Duffer, come here," Cosell yelled.

As I walked toward them, Howard said to Ali, "Champ, this is the guy I was telling you about. He hates niggers."

Ali's eyes grew very wide and he playfully started to box and lightly punch me while doing his famous Ali shuffle. A crowd started to gather, laughing and applauding.

Suddenly, Ali stopped and looked at Cosell. "Wait a minute," he said. "He ain't the one that hates niggers. You is." He started to swing lightly at Cosell, knocking ashes off of Howard's long cigar in all directions and even knocking his toupee slightly askew. The crowd applauded wildly. As tedious as the sales work was, we did have fun.

As for the weary band of overworked sales people that I inherited in 1963, most of them remained. Others joined them through the years. They were truly superb sales executives: Jim Shaw; Warren Boorom; H. Weller "Jake" Keever, who later became VP in charge of sales; George Newi, who became VP and general manager of the network and president of the network for a short time; Bill Breen, Ed Ryan, Helen Guy, Bill Koblenzer, Len Ringquist, Bill Firman, George Phillps, Vince Francis, Buzz Chapin, Bill Mullin, John Lazarus, Jack McCarthy, Bob Silberberg, Irv Cross, Ron Pollak, John Reed, Bob Cagelerio, Larry Freed, Gordon Link and Marvin Goldsmith, (these latter four went on to be leaders in the sales department), Bill Gillogly, Dick Wozniak, Ed Wollak, Mike Rubin, Jake Fendley, Ed Montanus, Ed Bishoff and the list goes on and on. I was also delighted when my prediction came true and some of my former colleagues from radio, like Rocco, Granath, Fountain, Bob Chambers, Bill Cummings and others, joined me in television sales.

The sales proposals people, led first by Fred Pierce, then later by Mark Cohen, Al Ruben and Tom Van Schaick, were and are an essential part of the sales operation. These are the talented people who put together the program packages to fit the advertiser's needs. The sales service people were outstanding, led first by Henry Hede and, later, by Charlie Allen, with a strong staff including Bob Wallen and Hal Geary. The department became acknowledged as the best sales force in the business. I'm sure that people who competed with us at NBC and CBS will not agree with that assessment, but we tried not to pay a lot of attention to what NBC or CBS thought anyway.

I would like to take credit for all of the accomplishments and kind words about that staff, but the truth is that we were helped mightily by the advent of the Prime Time Access rule in 1971 that restricted network prime-time programming to a total of 22 hours per week against the previous 25 hours a week. The three networks up to this point had been struggling in a two-and-a-half network economy – and ABC with its short lineups, was the one half. As some of the pundits of the day would say, ABC means, "The Always Behind Company." Or Milton Berle's famous line in the sixties, "If you want to end the Vietnam War, put it on ABC on Friday night, and it will be over in thirteen weeks."

With the cutback in network prime-time commercial availability, the marketplace tightened. All three networks were more in demand by advertisers, and it reflected on the bottom line. This helped us survive the loss of the tobacco business (some $225 million to the industry annually) that had many executives, including some at ABC, very leery of having anything to do with the sales area because its future looked so grim.

I do believe that we built a fierce spirit of pride in our accomplishments that even the hard-edged street fighters related to. I was proud of the fact that the network was billing $245 million in gross advertising sales in 1963, and became the first network to bill over $1billion a year; then $2 billion; and finally, when I was the president of the network, we stood alone in billing $3 billion in 1984, helped immensely by large sponsorships in the Sarajevo and Los Angeles Olympic Games.

My seven-year ride as the head of TV sales was a furious, rugged, crisis-filled, often stimulating adventure that taught me an enormous amount about the television business, mostly under very trying conditions. I have been asked many times if I would do it all over again. I have alternately characterized those years as my sentence in Hell, The Bataan Death March, and akin to being a jackhammer operator with a perpetual migraine.

On the personal side, those seven years saw many very happy times as our children were growing and adjusting to life in southern Connecticut. It had many difficult, and even sad, moments in my relationship with Betty. In the summer of 1967, after Betty and I had seen a counselor on many occasions, I decided that the best solution for all of us was to move out and, hopefully, give the kids a less troubled environment.

When I left my home on Mimosa Drive, I assured the children that I was not leaving them, that I would always be there for them, and that we would do things together, including seeing other parts of the country and the world...together. I visited almost every weekend, and we did take several trips that they enjoyed. The kids took it very well. They seemed to understand, even though they were really too young to fully understand; except Jay. He was sixteen years old at the time and he broke down and cried when I told him I was leaving. "Our family is breaking up, Dad," he said tearfully. I tried to reassure him, but he was right. It was disturbing and painful.

Would I do my seven years as the head of TV network sales over again? No, I don't believe that I would. Those seven years gave me some scars that still remain. They were instrumental in bringing about the breakup of my marriage and a heartbreaking longing for time at home with my children. It still haunts me to this day.

By the same token, I am very grateful for the opportunity at that time to have been in such a pivotal position in the growing years of network television. I thank God for every one of those loyal people who believed in what we were trying to accomplish and walked the rough road with me.

Then, in early February of 1970, a shot reverberated throughout the broadcasting industry that was to affect my career mightily.

Eleven

President of the Television Network

A *Variety* magazine headline in the winter of 1970 read: SI SIEGEL TO ELTON: YOU RULE.

When Elton Rule was named the president of the ABC Broadcast Division it marked the first time Leonard Goldenson, ABC's long-term, hands-on leader, had put a major executive between himself and his broadcast departments.

Rule would now be responsible for the audiences and bottom line performances for ALL of the company's broadcasting activities: ABC News, ABC Sports, the TV-owned stations, TV Spot Sales (a company-owned organization that sold advertising on the owned stations to national advertisers), the newly-formed four radio networks, the AM and FM owned radio stations, and the International Division, as well as the television network with its many departments.

The word was out that Rule was no longer a prince. He was now a king.

He had been the president of the television network since January of 1968 when Goldenson brought him in from Los Angeles. Rule had been the very successful manager of the company's West Coast flagship station, KABC-TV for a number of years. Goldenson and Siegel had been trying to get Elton to take a top management position in New York for some time because he presented the kind of clean-cut, straightforward image that they envisioned for the company. Rule was an extremely handsome, always tanned, native Californian who had a good business sense that went very well with his sharp personality and sense of fun.

I had been disappointed when Elton was brought into New York to head the TV network, since I had felt that I was next in line for the presidency based on my performance over a number of years. I learned later that I was Tom Moore's recommendation to

Goldenson, but Leonard saw this as the right opportunity for the company, and I respected Goldenson's view. I had much regard and admiration for Elton and was pleased when one of the first stops he made on his first day in his new office was to visit me.

"Jim, I know you must be disappointed in not getting the job as network president," he said. "I have a great deal of respect for you as a person and for the job that you do. We know each other [we had gone out to together several times on my trips to Los Angeles], and I think we will work well together. Hang in there. There are some good times ahead."

I found in working with him over the next two years that Elton, indeed, was a good executive and worked very well with Leonard and Si Siegel. He did not know a great deal about the operations of the network business, but he had the time to learn since he had experienced lieutenants all around him who could move the network ahead.

Two years later, when word of Rule's elevation to head all of broadcasting was rumored, I really wasn't surprised. He had not been comfortable with the line activities of the TV network, the constant affiliate squabbles and the stress and pressure of network sales, even though he had not been directly involved with them. He quite naturally migrated toward entertainment, primarily prime-time programming, since most of it was produced in his old California stomping grounds. Elton liked to be around celebrities, and they flocked around him – as long as he had a position of power that could benefit them.

Another reason I was not surprised was that the tobacco business had been forced off the air. Everyone thought this would have a considerable effect on ABC Television. The tobacco business, representing some $225 million, was expected to be especially tough to replace for the third place network. Rule was shrewd, if not brilliant. I suspect he worked on Goldenson for several months to be moved to the higher and strangely more protected plane of the Broadcast Division and let someone else be on the firing line for the potentially reduced sales and profit picture in network television. I figured that someone else was going to be me.

But Rule, calculatingly, played a waiting game in naming his successor to the network throne. After it was made known that he would become "Mr. Broadcasting," I went to see him on three or four occasions and discussed my own ambitions and the fact that I wanted the position as the head of the network, since every factor pointed to it, at least in my view. I had experience with all departments, success in the sales area, knowledge of the industry and the company, seniority, and the blessing of top management. Curiously this was the only time I had gone out of my way to seek a particular position in my twenty years with the company.

Rule merely answered, "I hear what you're saying. I haven't made up my mind yet."

The eerie feeling started to creep into my mind that Rule was a power player. He must have been holding off the announcement for this long period of time (six weeks) so that the broadcasting world, and certainly every employee of ABC, knew unmistakably who was in charge. Rumors started to fly all across the country. The broadcasting trade press printed speculative stories on who might become the new head of the TV network. Dick O'Leary, Elton's man from California, who was in charge of the TV stations? John Campbell, another Rule man from California, who had been in charge of the TV Spot Sales Division? Barnathan? Several names from TV stations and the other networks were all mentioned along with mine and John Gilbert's, who was then in charge of affiliate relations.

I was getting increasingly disturbed as the whispers came back from several quarters, "There must be something wrong with Duffy." Then one day Rule called me to his office and said simply, "I want you to be the president of the television network. You were my choice from the beginning."

I was relieved and obviously thrilled, but I did want to say to him, "If you knew it all the time, why didn't you say so and we could stop the rumors and get on with our business?" He continued with the terms of the appointment that left no question as to who was king.

"Who will you put in charge of sales to replace you?" Elton asked.

"I'd like to think about it before I give my final recommendation," I answered. "But the logical choice is Warren Booram. He is now second in command as the general manager of the department, and I believe he would do an outstanding job."

"Booram is okay," Rule said. He paused and gave me a hard smile and looked me directly in the eyes and said, "Part of the deal is that you name Jim Shaw as VP in charge of sales."

I was startled. Jim Shaw was a damned good man and would probably do an excellent job. He was currently VP in charge of the Central Division Sales Office, where I had sent him, but I couldn't quite figure out why that would be part of the deal.

Understand that in every promotion where I had been involved, the changes and appointments in a department became the responsibility of the new management. Of course, there would be suggestions and even recommendations to take a close look at someone, but that was mostly when the manager was placed into an unfamiliar situation. This was not the case. I had worked hand in hand with Booram and Shaw for a number of years.

"I'm not sure I understand, Elton. Are you telling me that I will only get this job if I appoint Shaw to replace me?"

"You figure it out," he said.

"Well, I want to think about it," I said. And I left.

I really wanted to tell Rule to shove it, because I knew by this time that Goldenson wanted me to take the job and would probably override him even if I refused to promote Shaw. But that would create an unworkable relationship with Rule. Jim Shaw was not the problem. The problem was that I recognized that if I took the job, I would be running the TV network on somebody else's terms, bad, good or indifferent. I was certain that would result in a relationship that was a time bomb.

I wrestled with the dilemma for a couple of days and decided I had little alternative other than to leave the company or stay in sales and be very frustrated.

I went to see Elton and told him that I was very concerned about taking the job in that, seemingly, I would not have the usual management autonomy. I told him that I didn't think it would work if I was told every step of the way how to run the network and who to hire or promote. I said that I had always been independent in my efforts, subject to the usual management overview and suggestions, including the past two years when I had worked for him.

"Trust me," Elton said.

And I said, "Okay, I will trust you. Let's go."

I went back to my office and told Booram of the decision without disclosing the source of it. He was devastated. He remained disheartened for a number of years, but he still stayed and did outstanding sales work. I called Jim Shaw in Chicago. A new era was born.

On Monday, March 23, 1970, I officially became the president of the ABC Television Network. This was by far the most significant promotion in my career to date. I was given a large corner office on the 38th floor of ABC's new building on Broadcast Row at 1330 Avenue of the Americas. My secretary, Alva Goodall, had a private office just outside. There was a huge reception room outside her office with a receptionist sitting at the far end, near the entrance off the elevator hallway.

The reception room was decorated with a subdued, off-white carpet and deep maroon couches and easy chairs. Its openness was very impressive to the casual visitor. There were just six executive offices on the 38th floor, including mine. The executive dining rooms and the boardroom were on the fortieth (top) floor. Goldenson, Siegel, Rule, Ev Erlick, the senior vice president and general counsel for the corporation, and Marty Pompadur, VP and Rule's assistant, had large offices on the 39th floor. Anyway you looked at it, my new quarters were in the clouds and a little intimidating.

The first morning, after moving into the new office, Alva came in with my coffee and said; "I guess we're in the big league now. It's so quiet. I feel like I should whisper when I answer your phones."

The solitude didn't last long. I was bombarded with phone calls and wires of congratulations. Friends and other staff people stopped by all day long to offer their support and best wishes. Predictably, I had many calls and notes and baskets of flowers from talent agents, producers and the heads of production studios. My new position had taken me into an expanded field of play – programming – and the players wanted to be certain that they registered with the new signal caller early on.

On the second day, I held a staff meeting in the large conference room that was next to my office and reintroduced my agenda and how I wanted the network to operate under my guidance. I wanted to make sure that we were all moving and thinking in the same direction. There were immediate and very important meetings coming up in the next few weeks: the National Association of Broadcasting's annual meeting along with a gathering with our affiliates in Chicago the following week; the program scheduling sessions in Los Angeles and New York in April; meetings with the programming department staff and key producers and studio heads while we were in Los Angeles; the announcement of the fall primetime schedule to the advertising community in New York and Chicago a few days after the schedule was finalized; and then the big annual affiliate gala and promotion managers' meeting in Los Angeles toward the end of May. This was not in the least daunting to me since I had attended and participated in all of these functions as the head of sales. Now, of course, I would be the host and leader of the meetings with Elton Rule looking over my shoulder.

I attended a large National Association of Broadcasting reception on Friday evening in Chicago and figured I would drive down to visit my parents in Princeton, Illinois before returning on Sunday morning in time to conduct my first affiliate meeting in the afternoon. I had seen many good friends and station people that I had known for years at the NAB reception. They were full of congratulations about my promotion. I was in especially good spirits when I left the Ambassador East Hotel early on Saturday morning because I knew both my parents were looking forward to seeing me. They, of course, were thrilled with my being named to the office of the president of the network. As a matter of fact, the local Princeton paper had run a story with the headline, LOCAL COUPLE'S SON IS TV NETWORK CHIEF.

I got a big kick out of it when I read the story because it was all about my folks, where they had come from, what they did, and where they lived in Princeton. The last paragraph had a brief mention with my name and new title. I teased them about stealing my thunder.

I also kidded Mom that I didn't know how she was going to explain my new title to her friends since she had told them all I was the president when I joined the company as a publicity writer twenty-one years ago.

My parents lived in a small white clapboard house on Chestnut Street in Princeton that my sister, Marge, and I had helped them buy after my father retired in the late fifties. It had a lovely, small yard with a beautiful flower garden that my mother tended meticulously. It was an ideal spot in a peaceful, little, Midwestern village for them to spend their later years. The house had a kitchen, pantry, dining room, living room, small sewing room and a bathroom on the first floor. There were three small bedrooms and a bath on the second floor. Typically, my mother had given all the bedrooms appropriate names; the Green Room and the Abraham Lincoln Room in the back, and the Martha Washington Room in the front where Mom and Dad slept.

When I arrived, and after a very warm greeting and a lot of hugs from Mom and Marge (she was living with our parents at the time) and hearty handshakes from Harold Francis (he didn't believe in men hugging) and a good talk for a couple of hours, I asked Mom if it was all right if I took a short nap, since I was tired from the reception the night before and the drive down to Princeton.

Mom took me upstairs to the Martha Washington Room and told me she would be honored if I would take my nap on her bed. I must have dozed off for a half an hour when I heard several voices mumbling and laughing in the front of the house. I could not figure out what was going on in my half-awake state. I finally got up and looked out the window.

There must have been eighteen or twenty people, neighbors in the area, milling around and talking with my mother. Mom was standing on the front steps to the porch and she suddenly hushed the crowd and I heard her say, "Be quiet. The president is sleeping."

I was so touched by her pride, and it was so funny, I didn't know whether to laugh or cry. I just gave her a big hug when I came downstairs and didn't say anything about it. As I hugged her, I was reminded of what a positive influence she had been on Marge and

me and how her unusual sense of humor had sustained us in difficult times. On this trip, she told us how she had been recently honored by the Princeton Women's Club and when she went up on
stage to receive her award, she slipped and did a feet-first slide right
into the podium. Trying to readjust her hat and hairdo, along with
her dignity, in front of Princeton's hushed gray-haired ladies, she
picked herself up, gave the familiar baseball umpire sign and said,
"Safe." Apparently, it brought down the house.

The problem with Mom when she told her funny stories is that
she would start laughing so hard she couldn't finish the story. Her
laugh was so infectious that we would all start laughing and end up
with our sides aching before she got to the punch line. I remember
a story she tells about a window washer who fell from the fifth-story
window just above our apartment when we lived near Sheridan
Avenue in Chicago. Mom saw the fellow hurtling past our window,
followed by his pail, sponges, water and the rest of his parapherna-
lia. She rushed to the window and found the poor man dangling
from his safety rope, pleading for someone to save him. She pulled
him up through our window, brushed him off, and when she saw he
was all right, sent him on his way. It could have been tragic, of
course, but, in retrospect, Mom thought it was the funniest thing
she had ever seen. Every time she told the story, she started laughing so hard she could not talk, and we would join in the hilarity.

On the drive back the next morning, I thought about those stories and started laughing to the point where I could barely drive.
And in between the laughs, I thought very seriously about what I
was going to say to the affiliates that afternoon. I rehearsed my
thoughts as I drove through the Illinois countryside that had been
so familiar to me in my youth. I rolled down the windows and listened to the wind as I headed east for Chicago.

That afternoon, I faced the affiliates with much enthusiasm. I
told them what big shoes I had to fill in replacing Elton Rule and
how I looked forward to the challenge of working with them to take
ABC and the affiliates to a new leadership position in the industry.
I also told them the story about my mother and how touched I was
with her intense pride and related the "president is sleeping" story.

It brought much laughter and applause. And after outlining our ideas on where I thought the network could go with their cooperation, I said, "I take great pride in the fact that if I really believe in something, I will work very hard to make it successful. I will never give up. And I deeply believe in this industry. I believe in ABC and our mission together. And I believe in you."

I felt it was a good beginning to a number of years where the affiliates, individually and collectively, and our network people did believe in each other and came to a leadership position. I was in high spirits with my new responsibility.

I was in great spirits, too, in my personal life. During my separation-from-Betty period, I met a remarkably bright and talented young woman from Orlando, Florida named Julie Marshall. She was extremely pretty and outgoing and seemed to be very giving and considerate of others. Julie had two children of her own from a previous marriage, a son, Jay, who was nine years old at the time, and a daughter, Jamie, age seven. Julie's children were staying with her parents in Orlando. As we spent more time together, I grew very fond of Julie. Whereas Betty had been totally disinterested in my job and rather disdainful of my promotions, Julie, a singer and actress herself, was very interested in broadcasting and seemed to enjoy meeting the various people in the business. She was very thoughtful and warm toward my children when they would visit me in New York and they, in turn, grew very fond of her.

After my divorce from Betty was final, Julie and I were married on May 24, 1969. The ceremony and reception were held at the home of Jack Harr, my old writing pal from Beloit College. Jack was my best man and his wife, Nancy, was Julie's maid of honor. My friend Duke Mortimer and his wife, Betty, were also in the wedding party. Most of the gang from ABC came to the reception along with friends from around the area. We had a grand time laughing and singing right up to the moment that we were whisked away by limousine from Harr's home to JFK airport in New York, well fortified by a magnum of Dom Perignon champagne to keep us refreshed on our journey. We spent our honeymoon in San Francisco, California where the affiliate meeting was held, and then we traveled through Big Sur country.

Julie and I bought a big rambling home at 201 Ridgewood Avenue in the quaint and quiet village of Glen Ridge, New Jersey, just four blocks from the Harr residence where we were married. My love of trees is what sold me on the place. It had large oaks and maples in the side and back yards. The home had just been remodeled with formal living and dining rooms and a spectacular circular staircase leading to the second-floor bedrooms. In all there were six bedrooms on the two top floors. Downstairs, in back of the kitchen, was an enormous family room with rollout windows that wrapped around the entire back of the house. And in the basement, there was a mother-in-law suite, including a living room, kitchen, bedroom and bath. The home was ideal for kids. I had a swimming pool and Jacuzzi put in the backyard, built a tree house, and even nailed up a backboard so I could play basketball with the boys. Julie's children came to live with us. I also spent a great deal of my non-working time with my own children, when I visited them in Cos Cob or when they came for long visits to Glen Ridge.

I guess we were the precursors of *The Brady Bunch* with our extended family. I do know that there were many happy and memorable moments.

The affiliate meeting in 1969 was memorable, too. It was here that Roone Arledge called in from New York and over the loudspeaker, while a red light flashed throughout the hall, told the assembled crowd that ABC Sports had obtained the rights to NFL *Monday Night Football*. The crowd stood and cheered with the great news. Even as loud as we all clapped and screamed, no one in that room had any idea of how that franchise would determine the fortunes of ABC Sports and all of professional football over the next twenty-five to thirty years.

Early in April, 1970, Marty Starger, the VP in charge of ABC-TV programming, and I, along with other staff members and his East Coast program staff, traveled to Los Angeles for the screening and scheduling sessions to determine the fall prime-time schedule. We were to meet with producers of the various programs that were on the air or that were in development hoping to make their way onto the fall schedule.

While we were there, Aaron Spelling, a former writer and producer for Four Star Pictures who had success with several programs for ABC, gave a cocktail reception for Julie and me at his palatial home in Beverly Hills. Candy Spelling, Aaron's wife, was a former dancer and a sleek, bejeweled woman who moved gracefully through the Hollywood show business crowd. Aaron and Candy must have had every major television performer and dignitary at the reception. Every time I turned around there was another recognizable face and a greeting from someone I had only previously seen in the movies or on television. I was especially delighted when Edward G. Robinson came over to me. I am not easily impressed with stars because I had been around them a great deal by this time, but it impressed me that "Little Caesar" and I were chatting.

We had several offers from actors and producers to go for a night cap after the party, but we declined because Hugh O'Brien, who had starred as Wyatt Earp on ABC and whom I had met in New York, had called that afternoon and said he was going to be at the party and wanted to take us to The Daisy, a local disco, following the party.

As president of the television network, I inherited Elton Rule's large, well-decorated network office on Sunset Boulevard and constantly had calls and invitations to attend functions of many varieties when I was in Los Angeles. Producers and agents would call with new ideas for programs. Actors and actresses would send letters and pictures asking for an audition for one of the situation comedies or dramatic shows. I, of course, sent them to the casting people. Some of the letters and calls from starlets were direct propositions in return for a role on television.

The attention that was showered on me was a practice that would continue for the next two years. It was further evidence, if I needed any, of the prestige and power that accompanied being the head of a television network. I had become someone who could make or break careers and destroy or build fortunes by deciding whether to place programs on or remove them from the network schedule. Producers and directors, studio heads and agents were very friendly, overly friendly, to me. It was apparent that the depth of their sincerity was gauged on how much I was doing or could do for them. It was a very heady and even uncomfortable place to be – one that I'm not sure I fully comprehended in those early years.

As you can imagine, the most exciting and demanding challenge for me as president of the TV network was in the area of programming. It was especially demanding because when I took over, ABC was in last place relative to most entertainment areas. At any network, programming is the most volatile of all the areas since the schedule changes every year (at least in prime time). Sometimes major changes are made three or four times in the course of a season. If the schedule changes or new programs don't appeal in large numbers to the viewing audience, then major eruptions ensue. One year's glowing success can be the next year's miserable failure.

Also, network programming in any form is tremendously expensive, with program production costs escalating ten to fifteen percent every year. In prime time, the costs for filmed entertainment programs, situation comedies, or hour-long action shows usually double in ten years. They actually tripled or quadrupled in my first ten years. That's why cost is a major factor in the advent of recent news-department-produced programs like *Dateline, 20/20, 48 Hours* or *Prime Time Live* in prime time. These shows can be produced in house at a much lower cost to the networks than the Hollywood-produced film shows. They are only viable, however, as long as they attract significant audiences.

I have often been asked where TV program ideas come from, how the programs are selected and who makes up the schedule.

Ideas come from people in varied occupations and from almost every corner of America. Mostly they come from the creative community in Los Angeles or New York, and from the professional writers or producers who are already in the television business. Occasionally, ideas come from a novel or a comedy sketch, or even from a series that had success in another country, such as *Till Death Do Us Part*, which aired in England. This series, adapted for Americans, became the astounding hit *All In The Family* for CBS in the United States.

In a given program development season for a network, there might be approximately 1,000 program ideas submitted. Roughly

100 of those ideas go to script, and only a few are commissioned by the network. Of the finished scripts, twenty or twenty-five might go to pilot (put on film or videotape as representative of what the series will look like). Of these, five or, at most, eight programs might make the schedule depending on the success of the previous season's performance (which determines how many programs will be carried over), the schedules of the other networks, and the strength of the advertising marketplace.

Since the late nineteen-sixties, a second programming season was developed and changes were made in midyear. Now new programs are introduced at various times of the year based on seasonal special-event programming, early failure of shows on the schedule, and canceling or moving shows by the other networks. Consequently, some shows that are developed for the fall schedule are held on the shelf for a better opportunity later in the year.

All programs don't have to go to pilot to get on the schedule. Often there will be spin-offs of characters from a successful series that will go on to become a series on their own, like *Laverne and Shirley* or *Mork and Mindy* from *Happy Days*; *Frazier* from *Cheers*; *Fantasy Island* from *The Love Boat* or *Melrose Place* from *Beverly Hills 90210*. And sometimes a program executive or writer/producer will get a brilliant idea, put it to a concept paper or script and get it on the air without a pilot, such as *The Bill Cosby Show*, or the Steven Boccho shows, *Cop Rock* and *NYPD Blue*.

I learned very quickly when I became president of the network that the pilot viewing sessions and the scheduling meetings for the prime-time schedule are always fascinating and loaded with controversy, interminable discussions and sharp, and sometimes loud, exchanges between the participants. All of the executives in the network looked forward to the meetings.

The research department's involvement was an essential part of the screening and scheduling sessions. Despite my skepticism of the accuracy of the Nielsen ratings, I marveled at the professionalism and dexterity of the researchers' ability to sift through all the numbers and present intelligent recommendations. The ABC-TV Research Department was especially noted for its efficiency, having bred a number of executives who started in research and went on to top positions in the industry. The list includes Fred Pierce, Julie Barnathan, Ollie Treyz, Leonard Goldberg, Gus Lucas, Gene Accas, Tom Werner, Marvin Mord, Allan Wertzel, Paul Sonkin, and George Keramidas.

In the 1970 screening meetings, Goldenson, Siegel, and Ev Erlick were usually in attendance along with Elton Rule, a number of department heads, and senior executives from the network, including myself.

The programming people would introduce a particular show, describe its development and name the production team. Then lights would go down in the screening room and the program would be shown. The screenings procedure for all the films and tapes usually lasted ten days to two weeks. Most of the time was spent in Los Angeles and the last few days in New York to finish up the screenings and to get set for the all-important scheduling meetings.

After about the third day, with three or four pictures being shown a day, it became really tough to stay fully awake, especially through a boring or badly produced picture. Many a screening room resounded with the ZZZZZZZzzzzzzz's of key executives, including corporate management, until a neighbor hopefully would nudge the snorer's knee or elbow him or her awake. When a picture was over and the lights would go up, there would generally be a long silence. Then, Leonard or Elton would be the first to make some remarks about the show. You could tell immediately if they really liked it just by the tone of voice. If they didn't like it, the opening line would be, "Well, it's kind of interesting, but what concerns me is...."

Then the comments from the rest of us would begin. "I think it's a piece of crap," one person would say, or "The damn thing doesn't have a story line," or "The blonde in the picture is sensational, but the rest of it stinks," and around and around it would go until someone would say, "How did it test? What does research have to say?"

One of the research people would take center stage and give an evaluation of the potential of the program, the audience testing results, and the recommendation on where it might go on the schedule. The research department's projected Nielsen rating for the program in a particular time period against certain competition might be hinted at, but the hard projections would be saved for the more definitive scheduling meetings. But once research had spoken, all of the yelling and arguing about the casting and quality of the picture would be forgotten because research – ratings – was the yardstick of success by which most programs were measured.

In earlier years, producers of programs would be invited to come into the screening room and present their wares and then watch with the assembled network executives. But it became embarrassing at the end of many screenings with interminable periods of silence or faked coughing or even giggles in the middle of intense dramatic scenes while the film was being shown. In later years, the producers were asked to wait outside, only to see the disapproving faces of the executives as they filed out or to get the bad news when they were called back into the screening room. It was rather inhumane treatment for people who had put their blood, sweat and tears, to say nothing of a huge chunk of money, into a pilot...even if some of them had the taste and morals of the characters in their programs. Later on, producers didn't even come near the screening sessions but found out the results by telephone post mortem.

I remember one screening in particular when Tom Moore was the president of the TV network. The producer of a proposed half-hour situation comedy about pirates introduced his picture to the group. When the lights went up, there was a long, long, long silence. There had not been one giggle, let alone a laugh, in the entire comedy. Finally, Moore turned to the producer and said, "Sid, do you think this picture is funny?" The producer turned beet red and stammered, "Of course, I think it's funny. I produced it. I think it's a howl." There was another long moment of silence. Moore turned to the rest of us, "Did any of you think this picture was funny? If so, speak up."

There was complete silence. It was so quiet in the room we could hear each other's breathing.

Finally, the producer stood up and yelled, "Well, fuck you guys. You wouldn't know a funny picture if it hit you in the ass." And he stormed out of the screening room.

It was also in the screening room that you got a sense of the priorities for programming the network wanted on the air, and the segments of the mass audience that programming was directed toward. At ABC, the shows were invariably aimed at younger viewers, 18 to 34 years of age, with a good core of 34- to 49-year old viewers. These were segments of the audience that were most desired by advertisers. This audience was more apt to try new products and was receptive to new television programming ideas. Incidentally, it is the very same viewing segment that the networks have coveted for the past several years.

Younger-oriented situation comedies or fast-paced action shows were very much sought after. It would be a rarity that the programming department would recommend, or a management executive would point out, a program because it was a good, wholesome, all-family show, or because a program has a message or sense of values. The only time the "softer" programs would come into serious discussion would be when there was an attempt to balance out the schedule against the more pointed permissive or violence-prone shows.

The attitude toward younger-oriented programs is what forced the highly popular *Lawrence Welk Show* off the ABC network in the fall of 1971. The Welk show had been a fixture for years on Saturday night on the ABC schedule, but it was finally determined that the constantly growing older audience attracted by Welk was affecting the entire evening schedule and the potential for broader audiences and higher revenues. After much discussion, the show was canceled. I received the full brunt of that decision. Not only did we receive tens of thousands of letters of protest, but also my own mother was highly upset. She called me two or three times to let me know of her disappointment, if not anger.

Al Schneider, the senior vice president of Standards and Practices, was the guardian of good taste in programming for the company. At one time, he was the chairman of the National Association of Broadcasters' Code Board, the guardian of standards and practices for the broadcasting industry. Schneider, "the good doctor," as I would call him, and his department were responsible in those earlier days for reviewing all material that went on the air, including commercials and program content for both radio and television. Materials had to adhere to a code of standards, established by the industry and the management of the broadcasting corporations and individual stations. Many of the program policies were standard in the industry, but with increasing competition, especially in television, the guidelines became more flexible. Ratings-conscious programmers pushed their ideas and shows with sex and/or violence right to the edge of if not over it. The good doctor was very tough in adhering to the guidelines, not just because it was policy, but also because he sincerely believed it was in the best interest of the company and the social mores of the country. I admired him for that and was a strong advocate of the very same principles. As far as program content is concerned, the industry in our country has always been entirely self-regulated and without government intervention, despite an occasional murmuring in Washington.

Schneider's presence called for some interesting moments in the screening sessions. I recall a meeting when an action-oriented Aaron Spelling picture was shown that had all of us on the edge of our seats. If I remember correctly, the program was a two-hour movie that was used as the pilot for a proposed one-hour series. The show had the usual Spelling formula, and a most successful one, of prolonged car chases and crashes, pretty ladies, fast action and jeopardy. The program opened in a restaurant where a crazed gunman with an automatic weapon suddenly appeared, leaped up onto a counter, and wheeling in circles, blew everyone in the restaurant away. Bullets and blood and bodies flying in all directions seemed interminable.

When the picture ended and Leonard and Elton had made their comments, I looked at Al Schneider and he was just shaking his head. I said, "We can't show that prolonged and obviously sensationalized opening. It is a very startling piece, but it is way overdone, in my opinion, to establish the fact that there is a maniacal killer on the loose. My God, he just keeps blasting away. That scene should be cut to one quarter of what it is."

You would have thought I had attacked someone's ancestry. People started to talk all at once, arguing that movies do that all the time, we can't sanitize this medium, we've got to have action to build audiences, and on and on. Others interrupted saying, "No, Jim's right, that scene was ridiculous." Finally, Goldenson stood up and said. "Let's be sensible about this. Jim has a point. The scene needs editing. We can't be blatant about these scenes of violence."

I appreciated Leonard's support. Still, as he said it, I thought to myself, 'Can't be blatant?' Is this a matter of what we can get away with, or a matter of what's right or wrong? Don't we have a conscience?"

I figured right then that television was in for a lot of trouble, and some well-deserved criticism if this trend was allowed to continue.

The scheduling sessions were also volatile. It was in these sessions that the group would create a prime-time schedule that would be the major gauge of the company's success, financially and otherwise, in the coming year.

In the early nineteen-seventies, the program scheduling meetings were held in a large conference room on the 38th floor near my office. In the first few days, the people who had been at the screenings would all assemble, with the exception of Goldenson, Siegel, Erlick and Rule. They would review all of the programs we had seen and the research materials about those shows, and have a complete review of programs from the current ABC schedule including those that might return. Potential new schedules for NBC and CBS were also analyzed. After four or five days of conversation and review on the art of the possible, the group would be reduced to just the department heads along with members of the programming department and myself. The scheduling debate would begin in earnest. Cards for the returning ABC programs and the shows that had been in development would be placed on a large six-by-eight stand-up magnetic board. The program cards would be moved around on the board in an attempt to come up with the most workable schedule. Later, cards with the various NBC and CBS programs, returning and new, would go up on the board as we wrestled with what a three-network schedule might look like in the fall.

These meetings, with much quiet reflection and much more loud debate and arguing, would go on for days, often late into the night. You could pick up verbal patterns that were often ridiculous in hindsight, such as the long-time veteran shows on the schedule, which were always "old and tired" when it came to the competition, but "proven and mature" when one referred to ABC. And the meetings would soon take on an informal air, with coats and ties removed, and people showing up in jeans, sweaters and sneakers on the weekends. And sometimes people would take strange positions for discussion.

I remember in 1970, Marvin Antonowsky, then the VP of audience research who would go on later to be the short-time program head for NBC, had a bad back and would often lie prone on the conference room floor during the course of the meetings. Marvin was a gaunt six-foot-six unusual type of fellow who looked as though he walked in sections anyway. And when he gave his research reports and comments from the carpet of the conference room, it was bizarre.

In our sessions, when the schedule was finally decided, Leonard and Elton would give the final approval, but the responsibility for its success would lie with the head of the television network and, of course, the VP in charge of programming.

There is a story about a scheduling meeting at ABC that has become somewhat of a legend. Ollie Treyz was president of the television network back in the late fifties and early sixties and he was a dynamo with his knowledge of research and his ability to speak swiftly and persuasively. One year Ollie was conducting the scheduling sessions, and after several tiring days of moving the ABC shows around on the board without much success, Ollie put up a schedule for everyone to take a quick look at and then discuss after a break for lunch. He carefully put up the cloth cover over the magnetic programming board with the cards all in place, and everyone left the room.

As the story goes, the cleaning man who came in on lunch breaks and evenings to clean up the trash inadvertently bumped into the big board with his cart, and the cards all came tumbling to the floor. In a panic, the poor man frantically replaced the cards helter skelter on the board, put the cloth back over it and left.

When Treyz and his group returned from lunch, Ollie stripped off the cover to once again look at his schedule. His eyes popped wide open with what he saw. He looked at the board from several angles and said, "I don't know who did this, but that's a hell of a schedule."

Along with the scheduling strategies, I had learned from my previous experience that one of television's great assets is its ability to innovate in its program forms. I found this to be especially true at ABC, because, as I experienced so painfully in sales, we were always behind in the ratings as fewer stations carried our programs and they were unable to reach as many homes as our competitors. The individuals who brought about such innovations were fascinating.

One example was the development of ABC's *Movies of the Week*. These programs were ninety minutes in length and scripted and produced especially for television on topical subject matters that brought a different genre of entertainment programming. The concept was the brainchild of Barry Diller, then a vice president in the programming department, who went on to become a leader in the television and motion picture industries and the founder of the Fox Television Network.

Brian's Song, one of the first of ABC's *Movies of the Week*, is a beautiful example of this form and demonstrates how television programming can be entertaining and still deliver an important social message, this one on human courage and loyalty. This program was important to me because I had an opportunity to view it in development form, long before it went on the TV network.

Elton Rule and I were in Los Angeles to visit the programming staff in the spring of 1971 to see how the shows that were in production were progressing and Barry Diller invited us to come to the studio to see, in rough-cut form, a *Movie of the Week*. Diller was very enthusiastic about this particular film. Elton and I were somewhat reluctant because we had a lot of bases to cover and not a great deal of time. We told Barry that we would at least watch a few minutes of it.

Brian's Song is the inspiring story of a Chicago Bears football player, a running back – Brian Piccolo – whose career was cut short at age twenty-six by cancer. The movie portrays the bond that was formed between Piccolo and Gale Sayers, also a Bears running back, who went on to be inducted into the NFL Hall of Fame. Piccolo was a white Southern boy from Wake Forest University and Sayers was an African-American from the University of Kansas. They were vying for the same position in their rookie year on the Bears' team, yet a deep-seated friendship was kindled that astounded the entire league. They became roommates and almost inseparable.

When Piccolo was struck with cancer and lay in his hospital bed for months, Sayers, along with Brian's wife, Joy, and his three little girls, would be at his side cajoling him, teasing him and praying for him. *Brian's Song* sensitively reflects Brian Piccolo's non-defeatist attitude and courage in the face of his battle with cancer and the devotion and attention of his wife and friends, especially Sayers, during his illness.

The movie was magnificently produced. It included several slow motion scenes of James Caan as Piccolo and Billy Dee Williams as Sayers running rhythmically stride for stride in training or gracefully sidestepping tacklers with the haunting strains of the *Brian's Song* musical theme as background. There were many emotional scenes.

One climactic sequence was when Piccolo had returned home from one of his many hospital stays for cobalt treatments on the same day that Sayers went to New York to accept the 1969 George S. Halas Award as the most courageous player in pro football. Sayers was awarded the trophy for coming back from knee surgery and rushing for over 1,000 yards in the season. When he accepted the award he startled the large audience of football writers and New York dignitaries by telling them that they had given the honor to the wrong man. He said, "The most courageous man in football is Brian Piccolo." He went on to say, "He has the heart of a giant and that rare form of courage that allows him to kid himself and his opponent – cancer. He has the mental attitude that makes me proud to have a friend who spells out the word courage twenty-four hours every day of his life. You flatter me by giving me this award, but I tell you that I accept it for Brian Piccolo. It is mine tonight, it is Brian Piccolo's tomorrow...I love Brian Piccolo, and I'd like all of you to love him too. Tonight, when you hit your knees, please ask God to love him."

Elton and I were mesmerized. We watched the entire movie from start to finish. Tears ran down my face several times during that screening. When it was over and the lights went up, we looked at each other. Elton had been a senior officer in the US Army and I wasn't overly given to crying about things. Both of us had tears in our eyes.

When Barry asked us what we thought, we both said it was a brilliant, beautiful and touching film, and if television could tell this kind of story, tastefully, with such a warm human message, and in a format that could accommodate the commercials gracefully, then we really had something.

When *Brian's Song* went on the air it got an enormous response. One of the criteria for success for any art form is how lasting it is. *Brian's Song* is still being aired almost thirty years later. It was a milestone for broadcasting. We recognized the fact that now television, which heretofore had copied other forms – radio, movies made for theatrical release, situation comedies, was really coming into its own with this longer form of movie, written and produced specifically for television. It constituted a major change in production and programming output for a television network. *Brian's Song* became the model that others tried to emulate. *Brian's Song* was also unusual in that it went on to play in the movie theaters. This was a reversal of the normal airing for movies.

Another creative young man in the programming department at that time was Michael Eisner. He was a tall, energetic fellow who came up with a constant flow of program ideas that kept Starger, Rule and the rest of us spinning. Michael developed the concept for *Happy Days*, among others, and was persistent in following its development through until it finally got on the schedule and became a smash hit. Most of us didn't take Eisner too seriously, aside from his obvious creative abilities, because he was so young and seemingly hyperactive. He, of course, went on to become the chairman of the Walt Disney Company and one of the most powerful men in show business. Eisner eventually became the big boss of Disney/ABC after the merger.

The ABC prime-time schedule in 1970/71 did very well, and on some weeks we were at parity with CBS and ahead of NBC. We knew that with comparable station lineups we could be in a leadership position. As a matter of fact, I was pleased that all elements of the network made substantial progress that year: ABC Sports continued its astounding progress under the aegis of Roone Arledge; ABC News under Elmer Lower's leadership made significant gains, especially with Harry Reasoner coming over from CBS as the evening news anchor; our Monday through Friday daytime schedule was finally coming into parity with some new serials, especially with young adult viewers; and late night, a longtime very difficult programming area, was showing some promise with a witty and bright new performer, Dick Cavett.

Few people outside of the industry realized it, but the Monday through Friday daytime schedule was far and away the largest profit maker for ABC. Our schedule of daytime serials including *One Life To Life*, *All My Children*, and *General Hospital* continued to grow in popularity, and with steady annual programming costs, brought in large advertising revenues. While the gross revenues were much smaller than prime time, the profit dollars were more than double the more illuminated prime-time area.

All of us with the network and with the company received enormous press coverage from this success. We were hailed as the "new ABC" and were described in various stories emanating from the annual press tour in Los Angeles, where writers from around the country would meet with the networks, as "the new network with class and style."

While, on the surface, it looked like a new day at ABC, I had many disturbing days. It became clear through several unpleasant episodes, as I had feared when I first took the job, that Elton Rule was not going to let go of the programming reins. As a matter of fact, Elton and Starger, VP for programming reporting to my office, teamed up and made some program purchases without my knowledge or consent on several occasions. Some of the programs that they purchased proved to be unappealing, unpopular and unprofitable. The problem was that as president of the network, I was held responsible for their success or failure.

One prominent example was when Rule and Starger met with the British producer Lew Grade and ordered twenty-six weeks of the hour-long musical shows, *The Tom Jones Show* and *The Englebert Humberdink Show*, and a thirteen-week order for a summer replacement musical show featuring a popular singer in Ireland named Val Donegan. I knew nothing of these negotiations and was only advised of them after they were completed. The Jones and Humperdink shows did fairly well for a few weeks and then faded badly. The *Val Donegan Show* was a disaster, as the American audiences didn't relate to his accent or singing. These three programs ended up with a bottom-line loss of some five million dollars for the network.

I immediately asked for a meeting with Elton and, in as diplomatic a way as possible, explained to him that his involvement with Lew Grade and other producers was important and welcomed, but that if I was being held responsible for the success or failure of the network, it was imperative that I be present at all meetings concerning decisions on programming purchases. He readily agreed and explained that he was doing what he felt what was best for the company.

I countered, with a smile that I, too, wanted to do what was right for the company, but having others making decisions on programs that were ultimately my responsibility was simply unfair and unworkable.

As unsettling as these episodes were, I was very pleased with the rapid success of the network. I was also very happy on the home front since on October 10, 1970, a beautiful blonde baby girl was born to Julie and me. We named her Corinne Frances after my mother and father.

With ABC's newfound stature, we had begun to know more celebrities. Danny Thomas, whom we had gotten to know through the *Danny Thomas Show*, sent us a twenty-one-year birthday candle for Corinne, to be taken out and burned down to the next level every year on her birthday. The great comedian and entertainer would call our home on occasion just to see how our new baby was doing.

Dealing with the major stars on a more personal level was somewhat of a new experience for me, although I had dealt with many as the vice president in charge of sales. Still, as the head of the network, I found dealing with celebrities was different and more demanding. Those dealings brought about some interesting friendships and situations.

At a reception on the Universal Pictures lot in Burbank in the fall of 1970, a handsome, rather rugged-looking young man came up and introduced himself. I recognized him immediately as the young adopted member of the Barbara Stanwyck family on the successful *Big Valley* show. He was Lee Majors. He introduced me to his girlfriend, an absolutely stunning young woman, who you knew at first glance was destined to be a superstar. Her name was Farrah Fawcett.

Julie and I met with Lee and Farrah on several occasions on our visits to Los Angeles and became very fond of them. I had the pleasure of sitting with Lee, Farrah and Farrah's parents at the Billy Jean King - Bobby Riggs tennis shoot-out at the Astrodome in Houston in the fall of 1970. Along with her sensational looks, Farrah, who comes from a fine Texan family, is a very down-to-earth, nice person who would be very difficult not to like even with your eyes closed. She is soft spoken, or at least seemed so in the early seventies, and highly intelligent. At first, she was cast as the "pretty blonde" in her television roles. In getting to know her, you could feel the intensity of a fine actress, which she certainly demonstrated later in her career, both in movies and on television.

Lee Majors, on the other hand, is more of an extrovert. He is from Kentucky, where he played football and other sports in college, and he liked the rough and tumble of physical activities in his younger years. I believe he did most of his own stunt work as *The Six Million Dollar Man*, one of ABC's bigger hit shows in the late seventies. I remember one evening at our suite at the Beverly Wilshire Hotel. Lee demonstrated a shoot-out scene from a western movie he was filming. The suite was a duplex and had a small balcony on the second level. Majors was squatting behind the balcony when he suddenly rose, drew an imaginary Smith & Wesson pistol and leaped over the balcony, landing on the coffee table and rolling off onto his feet, imaginary guns blazing. Not a hair was out of place, and the coffee table was still standing. He wanted me to try that scene, but I politely declined.

My meeting with Henry Fonda wasn't quite as pleasant. I had always admired Hank as an actor so I was particularly pleased to find that we were sitting across from each other at a dinner at Orsini's Restaurant on West 56th Street. It was one of the favorite Italian spots for celebrities in New York. Fonda was slated to star in a half-hour drama called *The Smith Family*, starting in the spring of 1971 on the network. Hank and his wife, Shirley, came into New York for a series of interviews and meetings, and we were asked to join them, along with the Rules and Goldensons and a few other executives and their spouses, at a reception in Elton's office. From there we went on to the dinner.

Fonda and I were having a fine conversation about his art and the new show and other casual comments. Toward the end of the dinner, and meaning it totally as a compliment, I said, "I have admired your work since the first time I saw *The Grapes of Wrath*." And I smiled and said, "So you're Tom Joad."

He bristled, "God damn it, I am not Tom Joad! You had better learn who I am if we're going to get along."

"Sorry," I said, as conversation at the entire table stopped. He didn't say much of anything for the rest of the evening, and I was relieved when the dinner was over. It once again reminded me that actors and actresses are human beings just like the rest of us, and that they, too, can have their tempers and quirks.

I flew from Los Angeles to New York on a couple of occasions with Henry Winkler when he was starring as "The Fonz" on *Happy Days*. I found him to be an exceptionally bright and interesting young man. We discussed everything from the state of show business to religion. Winkler would also call our home on occasion, not to talk to me, but to ask about the budding career of Julie's daughter, Jamie, as an actress.

I also came to know the since-deceased Jim Fanciscus quite well and spent some memorable moments at the crap tables at Caesar's Palace in Las Vegas with the handsome star of *Mr. Novak* and *Longstreet*. We almost broke the bank on one delightful evening as a room full of stars and starlets cheered us on. And Jim Brolin, then starring with Robert Young in *Marcus Welby, M.D.*, became a friend along with several others.

Part of the Hollywood and show business mystique has always been in its hotels, especially those in and around the very fashionable and upscale Beverly Hills and Bel Aire areas. The three most popular hotels among the stars, who then brought the movie and television executives and producers in their wake, were the old but always recognized pink and white Beverly Hills Hotel off Sunset Boulevard, the distinguished and red-awning-capped Beverly Wilshire in the heart of Beverly Hills, and the elegant hacienda, The Bel Aire Hotel, tucked away in the hills.

One of the marvelously phony bits at all the big show business hotels is the paging system, especially at the swimming pool, where the loudspeaker will blare out the names for an agent or star or "wannabe" for half of Beverly Hills to hear. Some swear that certain stars, sliding past their prime, slipped $50 or so to the telephone operators to keep paging them every fifteen minutes through the day. It was a known fact that certain agents made big payoffs for phony calls to impress talent or producers staying at the hotel and prime them for possible future business.

One of the first times I heard the paging system in action was in the early sixties when I was with the radio network and stayed at the Beverly Hills Hotel. We were down at the pool when the page came over loud and clear, "Paging Mr. Johnny Carson." A tall, skinny chap wearing a white dress shirt, rolled-up black pants, and black hose with wingtip shoes headed for the phone.

"Who the hell is that?" I asked Bob Pauley. The man was obviously out of place with his pasty face and small-town dress amidst the bikinis and briefs of the sun-tanned, beautiful people.

"That's Johnny Carson, the new replacement for Jack Paar on the *Tonight Show* on NBC," Pauley said. "ABC had him on a daytime show, *Who Do You Trust?* and it bombed."

"Well, he better get his act together or he'll sure as hell bomb in this town." I said, displaying my acumen in predicting long-range futures for television performers.

One of my most memorable occasions was at the Bel Aire Hotel ballroom when the programming people hosted a reception for the stars and producers of the highly successful *Movie of the Week* programs. The room was buzzing with excitement at the pre-dinner reception as the mingling celebrities chatted amidst the ice carvings (always the ABC signature in those days) and the beautifully arranged tapestries and fresh cut flowers. There were a number of stars from the movies who graced the programming people with their presence – Shirley Jones, Andy Griffith, Peter Strauss, Elizabeth Montgomery, and Jim Brolin.

When the time came to be seated for dinner, I went to the table where I had noticed earlier that I had been assigned to sit next to Elizabeth Montgomery, the star of *Bewitched*. She had done a brilliant job in the television movie about the axe murderer, Lizzy Borden. Much to my dismay, I noticed that another ABC corporate executive, who apparently fancied sitting next to the beauteous Ms. Montgomery, had displaced me.

Later, I found out that this executive had switched our cards when he found that his original seatmate was a notoriously difficult superstar. As I wheeled and walked over to my newly assigned table, I saw the familiar and alluring vision of a most familiar face, framed with a black silk turban, her dark eyes sparkling and the ruby red of her lips moist and appealing. She was also obviously an older woman. But it didn't matter. She was Gloria Swanson.

My three full glasses of Chardonnay had me ready for an introduction I normally would not have made. I took her left hand in mine, and whispered in a stage whisper that half of the room overheard, "I am delighted to be sitting next to the most beautiful and talented woman in the world."

I slid into my chair and looking straight into those deep dark eyes, said, "I am Jim Duffy with ABC. I want us to have fun, and I want us to be friends." I gave her my very best smile.

She turned in her chair and looked at me. At first, I thought she might haul off and slap me. Then she smiled and her eyes twinkled. "My, you are a charmer, aren't you? Let's do have some fun, and then we'll see about becoming close friends. Tell me again, about the most beautiful what…." she said and doubled up with laughter. So I did.

"Tell me about Norma Desmond," I said, referring to the remarkable and haunting character she played in her award-winning performance in *Sunset Boulevard*. "I could have saved her," I teased. "Couldn't I?"

She went into a deep-throated Norma Desmond dialogue that was enchanting and, even though she spoke very softly, people at other tables turned to see the performance. I noticed, with considerable satisfaction, that those at the Elizabeth Montgomery table were among the gawkers.

Gloria Swanson and I talked and laughed all through dinner. When the after-dinner remarks started, actor Darren McGavin, who was the talent host for the dinner, had to hush us so he could speak.

Even before coffee was finished, Ms. Swanson, said, "I must go. Will you escort me to my limousine?" I told her that I also was leaving. I rose and pulled back her chair and, arm in arm, we walked to the front door of the ballroom. At the door we turned and waved to scattered applause and much cheering.

I kissed Gloria Swanson on the cheek and put her into her limousine and waited for my own to pull up to the Bel Aire outer driveway. As my driver pulled onto Laucerne Drive, I was in a hazy state of "I don't believe all of this," when a limousine suddenly pulled across the road, blocking the roadway.

The driver got out of the long black limousine and opened the back door. Gloria Swanson (or Norma Desmond) stepped out in her flowing cape and all her majesty, and walked slowly toward my car. I got out and met her half way between the limousines on that darkened street in the middle of magic land. She handed me a long-stemmed white rose, kissed me on the cheek and said, "You were wonderful. Thank you for a lovely evening." She smiled that glorious smile, stepped back into her limousine and drove off.

I never saw her again. But I will always remember my evening with Gloria Swanson.

My mother, sister Marjorie Ann, age eight; and me, age seven, after we moved from Mendota to the farm in Moweaqua, Illinois

During the Depression (1933), this is the first grade class at the Little Red School House in Moweaqua. I am in the back row, third from the right.

Top - The Old Homestead, west of Moweaqua, Illinois, where I spent my early, happy years.

Bottom - John Wheeler Adams and Helen Jordan Adams with cousin Scotty, age eleven, outside of the west porch of The Old Homestead.

Whittier School (Oak Park, Illinois, graduating class, June 1940) I am top row, fourth from the left. Georgeane Bach is middle row, sixth from the left.

Oak Park River Forest High School Junior Varsity Basketball Team 1944. I am in the second row, number 14. My friend Billy Farber is number 22.

Graduation picture, Oak Park River Forest High School, Class of 1944.

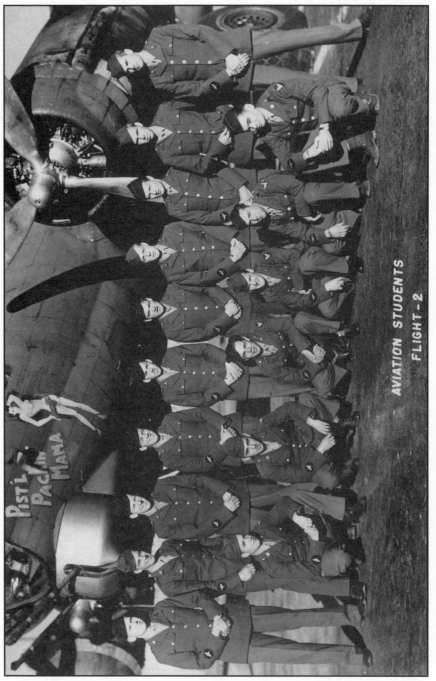

Aviation Students, Hobbs Air Corp Base, Hobbs, New Mexico, 1944. I am back row, third from left. Jack Drennan is back row, fifth from left.

My Air Corp Cadet portrait, 1944.

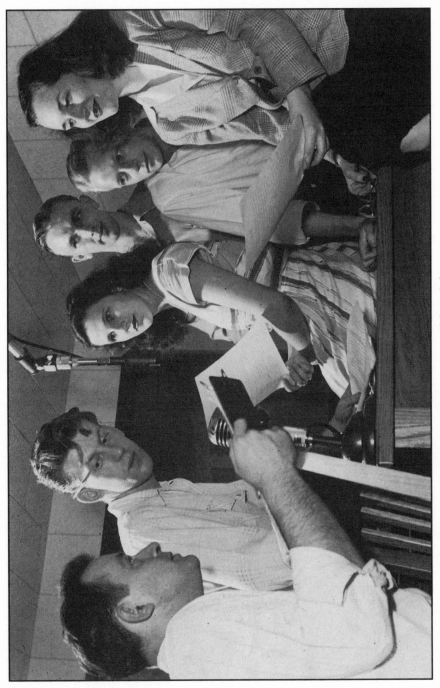

A Beloit College WBNB-FM drama rehersal in 1948. I am second from left.

On the air for WBNB-FM, the "Voice of Southern Wisconsin," 1948.

Jack Harr and I writing stories from the NAIB basketball tournament in Kansas City, Missouri in 1948. Beloit was nationally ranked among small colleges.

Clowning after graduation ceremonies from Beloit College in 1949. L to R - Howard Hagemann. Rich Peterson, me, Jack Harr.

Elliot W. Henry, Jr. with his wife Florence (Corky) at the NAB in Las Vegas in 1989. Ell hired me at ABC in 1949.

ABC Radio Network management with Don McNeill of *Don McNeill's Breakfast Club* in Chicago, 1962. L to R - me, Bob Pauley, McNeill, Bill Rafael.

The great newsman, Paul Harvey, with advertisers in Chicago in 1957.

My early days as VP of TV network sales, with the famed ship builder, Henry J. Kaiser (center) with Tom Moore, president of the TV network. Kaiser sponsored *The Greatest Show on Earth* on ABC on Sunday night.

Crooner Bing Crosby and actress Beverly Garland on the set of *The Bing Crosby Show* in 1964. On the right is ABC West Coast executive Herb Jellinek.

Lee Majors and the gorgeous Farrah Fawcett at a cocktail reception in Los Angeles in 1971.

Howard Cosell working the affiliate side in 1975, selling something to George Lyons, general manager of WZZM-TV, Grand Rapids, Michigan.

With Hall of Fame football player, Frank Gifford in 1972. Frank was the play-by-play announcer on ABC *Monday Night*

Actress Elizabeth Montgomery, who starred in *Bewitched* for ABC, at a cocktail reception at the Bel Aire Hotel in 1972.

Clarence Williams III of *Mod Squad* and Kate Jackson of *Charlie's Angels* at an affiliate reception in Los Angeles in 1971.

At a masquerade party at the Alan King Celbrity Tennis Tournament in Las Vegas, Nevada in 1974. L to R - Elton Rule, Betty Rule, tennis star Pancho Gonzales and his friend, Wally Schwartz, Fred Pierce, Marion Pierce, Julie Duffy as a Venetian fron outer space (she won first prize-a $500.00 gambling chip-in the costume contest), Howard Cosell, Ginny Schwartz, me as a World War I fighter pilot, Emmy Cosell.

Danny Thomas joins Marty Starger, ABC vice president for programming at an affiliate reception in Los Angeles in 1971.

Top - With beautiful actress Morgan Fairchild attending an ABC program reception in Los Angeles in 1986.

Bottom - Welcoming actress Raquel Welch to our meeting with affiliates at La Costa in 1981. Gary Pudney of ABC makes the introduction. To the right is Bob Bennett, chairman of the Affiliate Board. Deanna Lund Duffy is in front.

Beautiful actress/singer Shirley Jones has my attention at an ABC program
reception at the Bel Aire Hotel, Los Angeles, 1971.

With actor Tony Danza, star of *Who's The Boss*, at a promotional shoot in Los Angeles at the Century Plaza Hotel, Los Angeles, 1986.

On a trail ride during an ABC management meeting at Jackson Hole, Wyoming, June 1983. L. to R. Roone Arledge, president, ABC News & Sports; Fred Pierce, president, ABC; Dick Connelly, vice president of public relations; me.

The ABC Television Network "Flying Squad" that attend regional affiliate meetings in 1981. L. To R. Top Row: Milton Carney, VP, Confrence Planning; Dick Kozack, director, Affiliate Relations; Joel Cohen, VP Promotion and Planning; Mario Cucinotta, VP, Affiliate Services; Paul Sonkin, VP, Research. Bottom Row: George Newi, VP and general manager; Cindy Vanden Heuvel, secretary; me; Mary Jane Raphael, VP and assistant to the president; Bob Fountain, VP, Affiliate Relations.

Top - Bearded Robert Wagner, star of ABC's *Hart to Hart* at the Century Plaza Hotel in Los Angeles in 1986.

Bottom - Newsman Ted Koppel of *Nightline* at ABC Board of Governors meeting on the island of Hawaii in 1985. In the middle is David Burke, general manager of ABC News.

At a dinner honoring William Baker of Westinghouse Broadcasting at the Waldorf Astoria Hotel in New York, 1988. Clockwise from left: Tom Goodgame, president of Westinghouse Television; Bob Wussler, former president of CBS-TV; me; commentor Bill Moyer; Robin MacNeil of PBS; Gene Jankowski, former president of CBS; John Cannon, president of National Academy of Television Arts and Sciences.

On the deck of a yacht in the Mississippi River before the *Star Spangled Celebration of Literacy* telecast on July 4, 1988 in St. Louis. L to R - ABC executive Gary Pudney, actress Angie Dickinson, Barbara Bush, me, John James of ABC's *Dynasty*

Top - Leading the Fourth of July parade as Grand Marshall in St. Louis, 1988. Riding with me are ABC's Gary Pudney and Ellie Trueman

Bottom - Estel Sizemore, the first PLUS *Learner of the Month* with actor Dennis Weaver, star of the movie *Bluffing It*, at rehearsal for the *National Literacy Honors* dinner, November 1988.

Ringing the Liberty Bell to start the July Fourth celebration, 1988, with Joanna Kerns, star of *Growing Pains*.

Receiving the National Association of Broadcasters Distinguished Service Award in Las Vegas, April, 1989. Making the presentation are Eddie Fritts, president of NAB, left, and Wally Jorgenson, executive VP of NAB.

President Ronald Reagan presenting me with the President's Volunteer Action Award at a ceremony in the White House, 1986.

Greeting First Lady Nancy Reagan at a private reception at the White House following the President's second inauguration.

An interesting political picture. Governor Bill Clinton of Arkansas with Barbara Bush and me at a PLUS press conference in Washington, DC, 1987.

Top - With Governor John Ashcroft of Missouri in St. Louis, 1988. He is now the Attorney General of the United States.

Bottom - With Secretary of Labor Elizabeth Dole before a speech in Los Angeles, 1987.

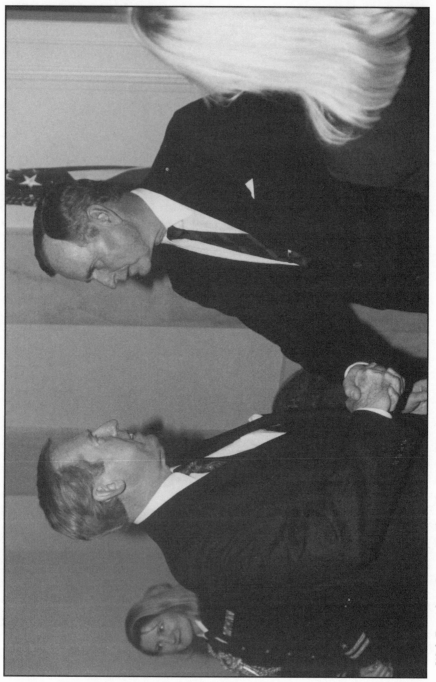

With President George Bush at the White House, 1992.

With General Colin Powell (center) and Sharon Darling, president of the National Center for Family Literacy at the Buisness Week Symposium dinner, Union Station, Washington, DC, 1994.

Twelve

Television Sports and News

As star-studded and magnetic as entertainment programming proved to be, it was almost matched by the growth and glamour of television sports and news. Both areas had tremendous upswings in the late sixties and the decade of the seventies. ABC Sports or ABC News did not report to me directly when I headed the network, but I worked very closely with them since we were responsible for the selling, promoting and clearing stations for the programming they produced. The growth of each was exciting for me and brought many adventures.

Sports and the medium of television were made for each other.

It is still inconceivable to me as I reflect through the decades, that the crackling accounts of the St. Louis Cardinals games that I listened to on the primitive radio set in the mid-nineteen thirties now have their modern-day baseball counterpart, live and in full color, for viewing (or taping) right in my living room on a fifty-inch TV screen. And it's almost amusing to remember how I would be a nervous wreck for days in anticipation of going to see a game, and how I would travel for a full day with my uncle and cousin and think nothing of it. Now, I can merely walk across the room (or sit on my sofa and push buttons on the remote), turn on the set and find almost any game or athletic event that I want to watch. It is said that we Americans are spoiled by an abundance of television programs, especially in the field of sports.

It was the advent of television that fueled the unprecedented growth of sports in America (and now across the world), not just with its reach and penetration, but also with its ability to pay huge rights fees – thanks to the underwriting from major sponsors – to sports promoters and organizers. These fees enabled the owners of the professional major sports to pay unprecedented, often outlandish, salaries to athletes. Many experts claim that this has been carried to excess and will eventually diminish the popularity of spectator sports in our country. I hope not, but the incidents of greed and overkill are growing.

Many of the stars in contemporary sports broadcasting are former athletes or coaches who stepped into the broadcast booth as color commentators and play-by-play announcers for their respective sports. John Madden and Pat Summerall with Fox and the NFL coverage have earned a distinct kind of fame from their TV comments. Dan Fouts followed Boomer Esiason, Frank Gifford and Dan Dierdorf on ABC's *Monday Night Football*. Other famous former athletes such as Dandy Don Meredith, O. J. Simpson, Fran Tarkenton, Fred Williamson and Alex Karras preceded all but Gifford on MNF. And Tim McCarver, the ex-St. Louis Cardinals catcher, Joe Morgan and pitcher Jim Palmer made it big in baseball coverage, as did Julius Irving, Pat Riley, Matt Gougas, Bob Cousy, Doug Collins, Huby Brown, Danny Ainge, Steve Jones, Bill Walton and several others in basketball commentary.

But much of the credit for the networks' success in covering sports must go to the professional, on-air sportscasters who worked their way up through local stations and have earned their positions and fame by experience and hard work. The list is headed by Jim McKay, Al Michaels, Keith Jackson, Vin Scully, Dick Enberg, Brent Musbruger, Bob Costas, Jim Nance, Chris Schenkel, Jack Whitaker, Jon Miller, Jim Lampley and goes on and on.

The individual who most stands out in this latter category is the inimitable Howard Cosell. During his working years, Cosell was the most revered and despised announcer in all of broadcasting. He stepped on many toes and angered many people with his "tell it like it is" style. It was interesting and fitting that the same people who criticized him, also eulogized this strange-looking, Jewish fellow with the irritating voice when he died in April of 1994. His critics were almost unanimous in citing Cosell as "the most significant single individual in influencing the evolution of broadcast sports."

Ironically, it was another individual who led ABC to positions of leadership in both sports and news and probably better deserves the accolade given to Cosell. His name is Roone Pinckney Arledge.

He was, and is, a controversial, highly talented and tenacious executive who sets his standards high, and then proceeds to build a team of talent and staff that will exceed his goals. He is controversial in some quarters because he has an unusual, sometimes disorganized management style and a penchant for not returning telephone calls.

Arledge was the creator of ABC's sports legacy with the introduction of *Wide World of Sports*, and its familiar "thrill of victory and agony of defeat" in 1961. He proceeded to creatively use the power and reach of TV to bring sporting events of all kinds, from log rolling to cliff diving to the major athletic events, into America's homes, hotels, hospitals, bars and social gathering arenas. He also discovered and promoted many of the sports announcers whom I have mentioned, and supported the controversial Cosell when others wanted him off the air.

It should be pointed out that while Arledge was the thrust behind the success of ABC Sports almost from the beginning, he did not start the ABC Sports Department. In the late nineteen-fifties when ABC was flailing in almost every program area, Tom Moore, soon to become the president of the network, saw sports on television as an avenue to lead ABC to prominence. Shortly after he became head of the network he hired a young advertising agency executive named Edgar Sherick, who had grown up in sports and had formed a company called Sports Programs, Inc. ABC bought the program from Sherick, and brought him into the company as an executive. (This is the same Sherick who eventually became VP of network sales and, later, VP of programming). A few months later, Moore appointed Arledge as the head of the network's sports operation. At the time, it had no real significance to me since I was heavily involved with the radio network and we did our own sports, including the broadcasts of the Floyd Patterson heavyweight championship fights.

I remember meeting the young man whom Arledge had tapped as host of *Wide World of Sports* shortly after I came to New York with the radio network in the early nineteen-sixties. I was having lunch with my new "best friend" Howard Cosell at Toots Shors' restaurant when a rather short, crew-cut, pleasant-looking fellow came over to our table.

"Duffer, this is the guy I was telling you about who hates Irishmen from Chicago," Howard said in his staccato style. "Shake hands with Jim McKay."

Jim McKay, of course, went on to win more Emmys and honors than any sportscaster in history and provided a different touch and sensitivity – a more human dimension – to the announcer's side of the video equation.

I will never forget McKay, "up close and personal" at the Summer Olympic Games in Munich, Germany in 1972. These games became the focus of a tragic news story, as well as an international sporting event. The Munich Olympics captured the imagination of the entire world as tiny Olga Korbut from Russia had seven perfect scores in winning three gold medals, swimmer Mark Spitz won an unheard-of seven Olympic medals, and Dave Woddle, with his floppy fatigue hat flying in the wind, came from back in the field to win the 800 meters and Olympic Gold.

But it wasn't in the swim hall, or the gymnasium, or on the track where the real drama came.

Arab terrorists made a sudden and shocking attack on Israeli athletes in the Olympic Village. The world, the Olympic Games, suddenly seemed to stand still.

It was in these stressful hours that Jim McKay really came into his own as a multi-talented broadcaster.

I still can feel the tension and sadness as a small group of executives from ABC sat in a client's booth watching McKay in the studio directly in front of us, reporting on the raid and the eleven Israeli athletes in jeopardy. After being on the air for almost fifteen hours, he reported that the terrorists had taken the hostages from the village and were headed for the airport. The four or five of us in the booth held hands and prayed as McKay, exhausted, sitting alone in the studio, related the situation, minute-by-minute, to a world-wide audience. Finally near dawn, he said, "This morning at ten o'clock, in a little more than six and a half hours, the athletes and people of Munich will gather in the great Olympic Stadium for a memorial service. They will pay tribute to the slain Israeli Olympians, then try to find some hope and solace for themselves and for this poor old world."

Then he said three words that none of us wanted to hear. "They're all gone." Eleven athletes had been massacred by the terrorists.

As the head of TV sales and, later, the president of the TV network, I had the opportunity to travel with clients and guests to most of the major sporting events covered by ABC sports: eight Olympic Games; three British Open golf tournaments as well as PGA and US Open tournaments; several baseball World Series; six Super Bowl games including the famous Joe Namath victory with his New York Jets in 1969 in Miami; The Kentucky Derby; the National Basketball Association and NCAA finals; tennis matches and on and on.

I had the opportunity to travel to many *Monday Night Football* games, with the crew, with clients, and simply as an intrigued football fan. It is an understatement to say *Monday Night Football* became a phenomenon in the history of television. And the truth is that while we cheered mightily back in 1969 when the announcement came that ABC had acquired the prime-time football rights, many of us wondered if football would have a broad enough audience base in the network prime time. CBS had tried pro football in prime time on two separate occasions without success, even with the attraction of Vince Lombardi and the Green Bay Packers.

A key questions was, would enough women watch prime-time football to make it financially viable?

The answer came rather quickly. Yes, women would watch football in the evening and so would kids, and whole families and many men who heretofore had been casual football viewers. *Monday Night Football* literally changed the habits and lifestyles of many Americans on Monday nights. Bowling leagues were cancelled, PTA meetings were rescheduled, restaurants did little business, and suddenly, saloons were jam-packed across the country every Monday night with fans cheering for their favorite team and often hurling epithets, even bricks, at the nasal-toned, opinionated Cosell on the television screen.

Howard, as an analyst, was one of the originals in the MNF booth. Arledge had considered many sportscasters to call the play-by-play on the games including Vince Scully, Chris Schenkel and Tom Harmon. Scully was tied to major league baseball, and Schenkel had an NCAA football contract. Arledge finally chose Keith Jackson, who had been doing the NCAA games for ABC. Jackson was and is a very talented individual who brings his own style and colloquialisms to every athletic event he announces. He provided a solid base for the first year of MNF. The selection of Cosell to provide color commentary was highly controversial. Many in and out of ABC thought Howard was too brash and "too Eastern seaboard" to be successful with a national audience. Some advertisers demanded that he be taken off of the air. Arledge stood firm. The third slot in the booth also became controversial since most experts thought three people announcing a game was overcrowding and cumbersome. Again, Arledge prevailed and finally selected a former quarterback from the Dallas Cowboys named Don Meredith, whom ABC Sports had used sparingly on replays in its NCAA football coverage. Actually, it was Frank Gifford, then under contract to CBS, who recommended Meredith to Arledge.

There is no question that the real stars of *Monday Night Football* were and are down on the field playing the game. But, make no mistake: Arledge put magic and mischief in the broadcast booth that was unprecedented. With Jackson, and later Gifford, as the peacemaker, fans looked forward to the verbal jousting between the good ol' boy, Dandy Don, and the "know-it-all New Yawker," Cosell.

In the initial years, Meredith and Cosell got along very well outside of the booth, even forming a friendship of sorts. No one would believe that, of course. After the very successful first year of *Monday Night Football*, Meredith did a great deal of traveling and public speaking around the country and was constantly asked about life with Howard.

In his book Cosell, written in 1974, Howard relates a funny story about Meredith's answer to the fans' questions about, "How do you live with that guy, Cosell? How do you really get along with him?"

Cosell wrote, "When Dandy honestly described our friendship, the reaction was always the same. He told me, 'They think we're enemies. It's amazing. They keep asking me what kind of a guy is Cosell? What's he really like?'"

"Well, I prodded, what did you finally tell them?"

"Don shrugged. 'I wind up telling them you're a son of a bitch. They won't believe the truth.'"

In its second year, Gifford was hired from CBS and became the play-by-play announcer, and *Monday Night Football* went on to become the most successful continuing sports franchise in television history. Incidentally, Keith Jackson went back to his NCAA assignments and has become a national figure and a broadcast Hall of Famer in the college football world.

Today, with the abundance of football on cable, and the rise of the Fox Network with its Sunday football telecasts, and the double headers on CBS and Fox, we tend to take *Monday Night Football* for granted and forget what the franchise did for the NFL and television sports in general. The fact is, the Monday franchise, with its long-time team of Al Michaels, Dan Dierdorf and Gifford, was among the prime-time rating leaders every fall and, currently with Michaels, Dan Fouts and Dennis Miller in the booth, remains among the most watched programs in all of television history. I got to know most of the aforementioned sportscasters on a personal basis and was always proud to be in their company on travels to the NFL cities around America, and always proud to represent them to sponsoring companies. The controversial Cosell was no exception.

Everyone who has ever been around Howard Cosell has his own stories. One of my favorites is the time we attended the Kentucky Derby in 1974 as the guests of then-Governor John Y. Brown, Jr. Cosell was always concerned about his popularity with the public, what people REALLY thought of him, and how much of a celebrity he had become. Howard and I, along with others, were sitting in the governor's box at Churchill Downs watching the preliminary races in the early afternoon. *Monday Night Football* had been on the air for three years and Howard had gained much notoriety.

With a glint in his eye, Cosell leaned over and said in a low, confidential whisper, "Did you see how many people recognized me when we came in here?"

"No, I didn't, Howard," I said. "I thought those people were probably looking at the governor."

"Heh, heh, heh," Cosell responded with his little guttural laugh. "Those people were watching me, Duffer. They love me." He paused and said softly, "I'm bigger than Frank Sinatra and Elvis Presley in this country."

"You're big, Howard," I laughed, "but not that big."

The smile left his face. "Come with me," he said.

Churchill Downs has a broad aisle way that runs the length of the grandstand in front near the track. As Cosell and I started to walk at one end of the grandstand, people started to stir and call out Howard's name.

"That's Howard Cosell," a man said. "Hey, Howard, how's Dandy Don?" others called out. As we walked on toward the center of the stands, the voices grew louder and a wave effect started with people rising from their chairs cheering and whistling. By the time we reached the far end of the grandstand, I swear half of the people at the races were on their feet cheering or booing the hunched-over figure with the nine-inch cigar from *Monday Night Football*.

Howard casually took a long pull on his stogie, then slowly turned around and waved to the crowd.

"I told you, kid," he said with a triumphant little smile on his face. "I'm bigger than Presley and Sinatra put together."

One of the truly great accomplishments of ABC Sports in the Arledge years was coverage of the Olympic Games. Of the twelve Olympic Games that ABC Sports has covered the one, to me, that best represented the marriage between television and sports was the Winter Olympic Games in Innsbruck, Austria in 1976.

These Games were significant because it was the first time that the Winter Games would be covered extensively in prime-time, with some twenty-six or twenty-seven hours being carried in the evening when the viewing audience is by far the largest, in addition to the daytime and weekend coverage. The Games were telecast in the month of February, when freezing weather in the northern half of the USA kept people at home in front of the television set. And Arledge and his superb team produced the games, really for the first time, for an all-family audience.

Some 160 million people throughout the USA watched at least part of the Innsbruck Olympic Games. Few of them probably gave much thought to what it took to bring those images from the ski slopes, bob sled runs and ice skating rinks thousands of miles away in the Austrian Alps, to the screens, large and small, in the living rooms, bedrooms, bar rooms, hospitals, clubs, schools and airport lounges. Transcending culture, race, socio-economic class and even language, television enabled everyone to share in the excitement and drama of international competition.

There seemed to be no distance separating the viewing public from the tiny twelve-year-old Russian figure skater who, apparently without a nerve in her body, charmed Innsbruck and the world with a childlike but elegant routine that outshone many more experienced performers. Or the 47-year-old Scandinavian speed skater who, wearing a pair of skates he had made himself, entered the most grueling long-distance race and bested many men less than half his age. The American audience watched spellbound when one of the world's finest women skiers broke a ski pole as she pushed out of the starting gate in the slalom and somehow managed to achieve the impossible, maneuvering three-fourths of the course in very good time before she hit a turn she couldn't handle. We watched in awe the men's cross-country ski relay, when the first Russian competitor built a huge lead before a binding on his ski broke two kilometers from the end of the course, compelling him to struggle home, uphill and down, on a single ski. His teammates went on to reward his persistence by recovering enough ground to win a bronze medal.

There is no way you could stage incidents like these. They occur, unrehearsed and spontaneous, at every Olympic Games. And they, as much as the winning performances and the pageantry, help make the Games an unparalled spectacle.

But in order to appreciate the entirety of the Games, the place to be was not Innsbruck, as enchanting and beautiful as it is, but in front of a television set. At Innsbruck, you could never have made it from place to place in time to see more than half of the action. Children in the United States who took naps during the afternoon so that they could watch the Games at night had a better feeling for what was happening than I did, standing on a hillside in the mountains at Siefeld, Austria.

The stars of the Olympics became household names throughout America. People would talk about the Games at work the next day or discuss the events over the phone. For their duration, watching the Olympic Games on TV supplanted many other routine activities. The nation – and the world – was watching thanks to ABC Sports.

The amount of equipment, the numbers of people and the sheer hard work that went into bringing the Games back to the United States was impressive. To cover the eight Olympic venues, ABC Sports mobilized 45 video cameras, six film camera teams for the human-interest stories of the Games, and a flash unit that rushed to the scene of any breaking news to provide instant coverage.

The cable for the cameras, some seventeen miles of it provided for the downhill runs alone, all had to be installed before the first snows in the Tyrol. All of it had to be located and put into service before the telecast could begin. The men's downhill, won by Franz Klammer, was covered by fourteen cameras from top to bottom. The women's downhill was covered by eleven cameras. Home viewers saw only a handful of the people – sportscasters, commentators – who made coverage of the Games possible. Some 300 other staffers backed the announcers and commentators, including producers, directors, cameramen, technicians and support personnel, not counting the 90 to 100 Austrians who were hired as chauffeurs, interpreters, spotters and stenographers. In the evening after a day's Games, we would watch the helicopters with special hoists carrying the video cameras over the Alps to move them into position for the next day's telecast.

Some claim that coverage of the Olympic Games is the most ambitious and difficult undertaking in all of sports. Having been there and seen it, I can believe it. Arledge and his staff, including long-time-behind-the-scenes sports executives like Jim Spence, Chuck Howard and Dennis Lewin, along with the technological genius of Julie Barnathan, the VP of broadcast operations and engineering, created absolute magic with their coverage.

I am sure that the production of all the succeeding Olympic Games including Lake Placid, even the unparalleled coverage of the 1984 Los Angeles Summer Games, or the Games in Liilehammer, Barcelona, and Atlanta, were just as fascinating, more complicated and far more advanced in the use of technology. But the Games at Innsbruck were the pivotal point for me and depicted a major change in sports broadcasting.

As I walked through the Hansel and Gretel wonderland of Innsbruck and later, when I returned to New York, I was truly impressed that the medium of television could mobilize this quality of resources, utilize technology, and gain the attention of so many individuals from all walks of life and social classes. I thought then and I believe now, surely we can use this medium to produce positive changes in our society as well.

When the Super Bowl or the World Series or the Olympic Games are on, the entire nation's schedule seems to change and pivot around the viewing time for these activities, which have a huge following worldwide. What this audience could at one time only read about or, at a later time, only hear about on radio, has, for years, been brought into the home with a full color, dramatic presentation. And the viewer has the additional luxury, through the cameras, of being down on the field, and can review the most dramatic moments in slow motion, instant replay, split screen or other wizardry of technology.

As I described earlier, my son Jay and I had the unique opportunity to be down on the field when we attended the Russian-American Track Meet in Kiev in 1965. It was unique because it was the first live sports telecast from behind the Iron Curtain and it set the precedent for future collaboration with the Soviet Union in television coverage.

For Jay and me, it was an adventure that transcended a sporting event, since the track meet was the culmination of a two-week trip through Europe before we joined the ABC Sports crew in Kiev. The journey to England, France and Italy, and finally Russia, was a whirlwind fascination to me and a fine educational experience for Jay.

We saw many of the sights of London and its surrounds, from Windsor Castle to Buckingham Palace and Westminster Abbey. We visited the Louvre, the Cathedral of Notre Dame and Versailles Palace among many other places in Paris. Rome was especially eventful for us. There is an aura about this capital city that we encountered as soon as we landed. I have traveled to Rome several times since and have always found the same sense of warmth and beauty. The summer breezes carried a rather exotic scent that one doesn't soon forget. I had hired a very attractive, raven-haired college student as a guide. Jay immediately fell in "teenage love" with her as she related the astounding history of the Vatican City, the Coliseum, the museums, and the surrounding Italian countryside.

One evening, Jay and I had dinner at an open-air restaurant at the top of a small hotel on the Via Vittorio Veneto. For some reason, on that night he had a particular interest in my childhood in Moweaqua and started asking me questions about life on the farm and my relationship with my grandfather. I told him about sitting around the fireplace in the West Room on the cold winter evenings and the stories Grandpa Adams told me about his life, and about the many things I learned from him. I told Jay, again, of the importance of being honest and the value of hard work. I was surprised at the end of the dinner when a stranger who had been sitting nearby came over to our table.

"I don't mean to interrupt," the man said. "I couldn't help but overhear your conversation. I just wanted to tell you that I wish I had a caring father like you when I was growing up." He patted Jay on the head and moved off. I was very appreciative of his comments, because in the fast-moving, time-consuming world of television, I was often concerned that a "caring father" was something my children might not be experiencing.

The highlight of our trip was being inside the Soviet Union. Moscow was everything I had envisioned – drab. Almost everything, including buildings, faces and clothing, were in shades of gray. It was cold, bleak, and, at least to me, unfriendly. Jay and I stayed in a small room with twin beds in a large hotel on Red Square. We were immediately struck by the shortness of the beds and the pull-chain shower system. The beds seemed to be about five and a half feet long with blankets encased in covers that seemed even shorter. And the shower spewed out very cold water if you had nerve enough to stand underneath and yank on the chain.

We had a guide assigned to us in Moscow. On our second day, we were told to be in front of the hotel at five o'clock the next morning to be taken to the Moscow domestic airport for our trip to Kiev. Our guide was a delightful young man who was studying at the university and seemed interested in the ways of the Western world, and especially Jay's views on his personal freedom.

At dawn the next morning, Jay and I were outside the hotel with my limited knowledge of the Russian language – consisting of my ability to say *nyet*. We looked for our guide. Two gruff-looking soldiers were the only signs of human life. Finally, a battered old gray automobile came wheeling up and the driver leaned over and motioned for us to get in the back. I attempted to ask about the whereabouts of our guide, but the fellow would have none of it, and again motioned for us to crawl in the back seat.

We drove to wherever we were going – and for a few anxious moments I thought it might be to a remote forest to disappear forever. The driver, who fell asleep twice while racing over some back roads, finally deposited us at the domestic airport.

Again, there was no guide to meet us, so Jay and I went into the terminal to find our plane to Kiev. While we were wandering around, several people started to follow us and made approving sounds about our clothing. I was wearing a checked tan sports coat that would not have raised an eyebrow on the streets of America, but here in the heart of the Soviet Union, I had suddenly become a reluctant fashion plate. Two or three men dressed in drab-looking coats circled us and finally touched the material and nodded approvingly.

Just when I was really becoming concerned about my inability to find the gate for our Kiev flight in the maze of the unfamiliar signs, I spotted an attractive, fashionably dressed woman walking past us.

"Excusez-moi, s'il vous plaît. Parlez-vous Français?" I said in the little French I knew.

"Yes, I do. But I think you probably are in need of some English," she said, laughing.

It turned out she was the wife of a *New York Times* correspondent who was covering the Games in Kiev. She not only spoke French, but she spoke and understood Russian and proceeded to guide two lost and confused Americans onto the plane and to the site of the international track and field event.

Kiev was much brighter and cleaner and seemed to be a happier place than Moscow. The people seemed to be much more jovial and friendly. The city was pretty with many green trees and flowering shrubs. It could be taken as a typical midsize town in America, except for the dress of its people. The clothing of the local folks seemed very crude, with burlap material for dresses and blouses. It reminded me of America's more rural dress before the turn of the nineteenth century.

Still, an ominous atmosphere remained with us even when we were at the stadium for the track and field events. Jay was hired by the ABC sports crew as a "go-for" and had a great time working with all of the announcers, including Jim McKay, and the production team. One time when he was scrambling up a ladder to a camera platform, he slipped and hit his head hard against a railing. He said later that he felt that one of the Russian guards had pushed him. I also had the feeling that our room and luggage were inspected every day by the way our belongings were moved around. After the second day, my camera would not function, and I was convinced the Russian police must have rigged it so I could no longer photograph the Russian way of life. I was somewhat chagrined when we got home to find I had inadvertently pushed an "off" button on the camera that I didn't know existed.

The track and field events were quite exciting and were transmitted back to the States with very few problems. If I recall correctly, the Russians soundly beat the Americans in most of the events, with the exception of the dashes, the mile run and the hurdles. The Russians were really dominant in the field competition, practically sweeping the discus, javelin and shot put events. The large crowds of Russians cheered lustily with every Soviet victory. We handful of Americans applauded and yelled when our athletes won or even performed well.

When the meet concluded, with a very picturesque closing ceremony in the Kiev stadium, Jay and I could not wait to get on the plane and head for home. It seemed like we had been away for months. We longed for the sight of our American friends and familiar surroundings.

In Moscow, just before we boarded our Aeroflot jet that would take us to New York's JFK International Airport, we had a chilling incident that promised to keep us in the Soviet Union for a few more days. On our departure, we had been asked to fill out papers listing our purchases during our visit and how much currency we were taking out of the country. As we stood in the long line to have our credentials checked, a tall, steely-eyed Russian soldier came up to us and motioned for us to step out of line and follow him to a room at the guard station. Two other military officials were in the room. They immediately started to shout terse sentences in Russian and kept pointing to a piece of paper. Meanwhile, our plane was being boarded to go back to the States. Finally, a Russian guide who spoke English rescued us.

The problem, it turned out, was that when Jay had filled out his customs declaration, he had put down $10.00 as his currency on leaving the country; however; he had forgotten to include the decimal point after the first zero and had inadvertently added an extra zero. It looked like the kid was skipping out with $10,000 or 100 thousand rubles, or whatever it was. We showed the guide and the guards Jay's crumbled up ten-dollar bill and they politely, but rather disgustedly, let us board our plane for home.

When we arrived at JFK Airport and had cleared customs, Jay knelt down and kissed the good old soil of the USA. The entire trip was an unforgettable experience for him. We both agreed that we were fortunate to live in the atmosphere of abundance and freedom of the United States of America. We had participated in and were witness to international television sports coverage in its earliest stages.

As compelling as the broadcasting of sports events can be, it is equally startling to me that the news Grandpa Adams would listen to every evening on the static-filled old receiver can now be heard with crystal clarity coming from the remotest parts of the world, or seen and heard with descriptive film clips and narration at almost any hour of the day. Of all of broadcasting's programming areas, the coverage and reporting of news, worldwide, nationally and in local communities, comes the closest to defining television's role of being the "Window to the World."

Thanks to the technology of satellite transmission and portable uplinks and lightweight and more mobile equipment as used in Olympic coverage, broadcasting has brought a new dimension to the Information Age with its worldwide news coverage. Because of the media's expansive, instantaneous stories, the American public has never been so well informed about a multiplicity of subjects: how governments work or don't work; issues of crime, health, education, and welfare; a crisis in the Middle East, Haiti or Bosnia; and issues that effect every one of us and our families, lifestyles and social consciousness.

The growth, reach and influence of radio and television news are breathtaking and even frightening. Broadcasting, and, especially television, is often bashed for its news coverage. "It's too liberal," "It's too conservative," "It's biased," "It's intrusive," and on and on. I respect people's right to have and voice opinions, but there can be no question about the media's ability to provide coverage of the extraordinary events of our time immediately from all corners of the world.

I often respond to skeptics who question the value and importance of broadcast news by asking them to consider the fact, that in the event of an international crisis, a news reporter sitting in a studio in our nation's Capital can get the heads of state concerned with that crisis on millions of television screens to discuss its significance in a matter of minutes. Further, the story is brought right to us in our homes or offices so that we can better understand it and make our own judgments on its merits.

Broadcast news has an impact on every sector and institution in our society, both here and around the world. Presidential election campaigns are strategized and "spun" around the coverage of media. So are the contests for statewide and local political positions, from governorships to the local school boards. Many will say that political campaigns are but media campaigns.

We are inundated every day by views and reviews. If we care to turn on our television or radios, we can later get more depth through newspaper stories and national magazine articles. And, of course, with the explosion of cyberspace and the Internet, we have the ability for even more depth and immediacy. It is a treasure of knowledge that many of us were not privileged to have when we were growing up.

I can't help but reflect on how it was all so uncomplicated and well intended when it started. I often think to my days in Milwaukee, watching a newscaster at WISN barking out the news of the world, reading most of it from the newspaper lying in front of him, or my own reporting days for WBNB, The Voice of Southern Wisconsin, when I would announce a late-breaking news story off the Associated Press wire about the Soviet Union or some European city.

I well remember the early days of television news in Chicago when my good friend Austin Kiplinger, later a neighbor in Maryland and famed for his business newsletters, would sit at a desk in a small studio, facing a single cumbersome camera, and deliver the evening news that he had written – and brilliantly, I might add.

Along with in-studio news reports, special events coverage brought all kinds of adventures in the early years.

I vividly recall the Democratic National Convention in Chicago in 1952, which I was assigned to cover as a publicity writer for the ABC Central Division. One evening I was at the Ambassador East Hotel with Ell Henry and some of the news crew after a long day at the convention hall, when I decided to visit the men's room on the subterranean level. As I approached the urinal, a pleasant looking, bespectacled gentleman was performing the same duties at the next urinal. He looked over and smiled at me and said in a flat Midwestern twang, "Evening, young man. How are you?"

I smiled back and said, "Just fine, Sir. Just fine. I spent a long, hard day at the convention."

I suddenly realized that this man looked very familiar – I knew him from somewhere.

He gave a short laugh as he finished his business and buttoned his fly.

"So did I," he said. "So did I."

When the gentleman left the room, another fellow who over-heard our conversation said rather excitedly,

"Do you know who that was?"

"I think so," I answered. "That was Harry Truman, wasn't it?"

"Yeah," he said. "Jeez, the President of the United States peeing alongside of you."

Don't ask me where the Secret Service men were. All I know is that if you have to relieve yourself, you might as well do it in the best of company.

It was at this same convention that a jack-of-all-trades named Vince Gerriaty, who had tremendous clout with the Chicago polit-ical machine and knew his way around the convention scene, was hired by ABC as a troubleshooter. At one critical juncture, the Texas delegation went into a closed-door caucus on the lower level of the Conrad Hilton Hotel, the official convention headquarters. Gerriaty, sniffing out a news exclusive, directed one of the large TV cameras (there were no minicams in those days) down the stairs to the wall of the caucus room, slammed his fist through the thin makeshift wall, and had the cameraman put the lens of the camera through the hole so that all of our viewers could see what was hap-pening in the secret conclave.

Suddenly, the door of the caucus room burst open and a huge, very angry Texas deputy sheriff stalked out and made a lunge for the cameraman. Gerriaty interceded and hit the man with a right cross, sending the Texas cowboy reeling against the wall. The enraged Texan charged the pugnacious Gerriaty, and the two of them put on a brawl in front of the live camera that went out across the nation. Muhammad Ali and Joe Frazier would have been envious.

It was one of the highlights of the convention, although it was not in keeping with the rest of ABC's convention coverage, anchored by the rather pompous John Charles Daly, who was the head of ABC News at the time but was better known for hosting *What's My Line* on CBS.

Chicago was also the site of the Democratic Convention in August of 1968, where rebellious hippies and flower children camped out on the grounds of the city's parks. One evening they stormed the front door of the Conrad Hilton Hotel. A riot ensued that created headlines across the nation about the Windy City being a "police state" because of the brutality used to quell the protest.

Elton Rule and I toured the city that night in an ABC News truck. It was not a sight that made one proud of the United States.

That was the convention, too, where ABC had hired two "experts" from opposite ends of the political spectrum – the very conservative William F. Buckley, Jr. and the most liberal Gore Vidal – to act as analysts for the convention proceedings. Rule and I were sitting in a client screening room with several other people one evening watching the telecast on TV monitors, when Buckley and Vidal got into a heated argument live on camera. Paul Newman, the actor, was sitting directly behind me and was getting equally heated over the on-screen confrontation.

As the altercation increased in its intensity, Buckley suddenly called Vidal something like a "sniveling little faggot," and Vidal leaped out of his chair, ostensibly to punch Buckley in the nose. The director cut to a commercial break and the two distinguished men of letters were restrained from scratching one another. Meanwhile, Newman, a known liberal, was incensed and walked out of the viewing room. We heard, later, that he had gone immediately to Buckley's dressing room trailer, had a few sharp words with the erudite commentator, then swiped a cold beer from the trailer refrigerator for good measure.

The nineteen-sixties were the developing years in news coverage and they were fascinating.

As part of our news sales operation during that time, Bill Firman, our director of ABC News Sales, would bring foreign correspondents in from around the world and tour five or six cities, giving news seminars for discussion with our advertisers and potential clients. Peter Jennings was then stationed in London, Barrie Dunsmore in Paris, John Scali covered the State Department in Washington, and Lou Cioffi was stationed in Rome. They, and others, gave dissertations on the state of the world. I attended many of these sessions and got to know many of the correspondents on a first-name basis. It was intriguing to see the youthful and handsome Peter Jennings, buzzing around the city on a motor bike while the rest of the newsmen involved themselves in Willie Firman's nightly poker games.

I had known Jennings since he was appointed anchor of the *ABC Evening News* in 1965. Peter, a Canadian, was 27 years old at the time. He had maintained some north-of-the-border pronunciations that did not sit well with the American viewing audience. ABC knew, and Peter realized, that he needed further seasoning. In 1967 he was sent to the European front as a roving reporter. Central Casting could not have come up with a better foreign correspondent than the dashing Peter Jennings, replete with trench coat and microphone in hand, standing in front of the Houses of Parliament or Buckingham Palace and relaying the latest news back to the States. He, of course, gained invaluable experience in the field throughout Europe and the Middle East and returned some ten years later to anchor ABC's *World News Tonight* and most of ABC's special events coverage.

The decade of the seventies was an unprecedented growth period for ABC News. Roone Arledge became president of ABC News as well as ABC Sports in the spring of 1977. It was a move that had the critics, television's and his own, howling. It was widely circulated that he would make a circus out of the news arena, including installing Cosell as an anchor on the evening news. But with a hefty budget and his usual tenacious determination, Arledge made steady and dignified progress. When Capital Cities bought ABC in 1986, his two-headed throne was eliminated and Roone was forced to choose between the two, with the strong suggestion from management that he choose the News Division.

Before Arledge's tenure, Harry Reasoner, in 1970, had come to ABC from CBS to co-anchor the evening news, first with Howard K. Smith, and later, in 1976, with a major star from NBC in a move that rattled the television world.

Barbara Walters had already become a giant (or is that giant-ess?) in the industry as the star of the *Today Show* and through her news interviews with leaders from around the world. Walters coming to ABC was a coup for the company, and it was also the start of the raiding wars that eventually threw the compensation system among network news personalities completely out of line. In fairness, Barbara was much more than a news personality. She also had a strong presence in the entertainment world. And when she came to ABC as the "Million Dollar Baby," half of her unprecedented $1-million annual salary was paid by ABC News and the other half by ABC Entertainment, for whom she would do a series of entertainment specials.

Nonetheless, it was really the start of the star system among news personalities, later perpetuated by Arledge. The practice of building undue celebrity is questionable, in my judgment, in a field as serious and impactful as the reporting of news. Many others in the industry share that feeling. Hollywood, the glamour capital of the world, has countless stories about so-called stars who became disruptive with their demands, people who get the idea that they are bigger than the studio they work for and the industry that has afforded them the celebrity status. There are several occasions when I have been personally involved with the prima-donna attitudes of news, sports and entertainment celebrities.

One such incident involved Barbara Walters shortly after she had joined ABC. I might say at the outset that Barbara is a person for whom I have a great deal of respect and one who has done an exceptional job for ABC.

In the fall of 1976, the National Asthma Center in Denver, Colorado, along with some of my co-workers at ABC, had arranged a large reception and dinner in my honor at the New York Hilton Hotel. It was saluting the work that I had done for the center after a family tragedy, which I relate later in this book.

I vowed that I would dedicate myself, in whatever way I could, to help others avoid the same kind of tragedy. In the following months, I worked closely with the National Asthma Center. I made several visits to the hospital and research center and learned all I could about the very insidious, life-crippling, and, as my family discovered, fatal disease. I filmed some public service announcements for the Center, made speeches around the country, and was involved in several fundraisers that brought in tens of thousands of dollars for the Center.

For our efforts, the National Asthma Center arranged a dinner in New York where I was to be honored with the first annual Golden Sammy Award. A host of dignitaries had agreed to attend the dinner and Don Johnston, the personable president of J. Walter Thompson, a leading New York advertising agency, had agreed to chair the event.

The dinner committee apparently had agreed not to have the traditional dais in the ballroom, but instead had a head table in the center of the room for my family, special guests and me. The dignitaries would be recognized from their tables. After a lovely reception, I was sitting at our table with my family and friends when a waiter came over, tapped me on the shoulder and told me that a very irate woman was looking for me in the foyer.

When I arrived at the edge of the ballroom I spotted Barbara Walters, and she appeared to be very unhappy.

"Hello, Barbara," I greeted her. "I had no idea you would...."

"How dare you leave me standing alone," she said heatedly. "I have been waiting in that lobby for fifteen minutes and I have better things to do than be treated like this."

I studied her as she spewed out her unhappiness. Her face was taught and her lips tight and pursed as she spoke.

I tried to explain to her that I had no idea that she was going to be at the dinner or that she was supposed to be met. I apologized for her inconvenience and tried to explain that I was at the dinner as a guest of honor and not as one of the organizers. She would have none of it. The room had turned to ice. "Well, do something," she snapped.

Have you ever considered what the exact right moment might be to tell someone to "shove it where the sun don't shine?" I came very close. But I didn't. Instead, I went back to the table and told one of the program organizers that "Godzilla is at the gate," and "please take care of her."

As it turned out, Barbara was the guest speaker and, I must say, she was out of keeping with the purpose of the evening. Maybe she was still angry, but as a professional she should have risen above that. She didn't say two sentences about me, about asthma or the National Asthma Center. She spent about twenty minutes talking about the crisis in the Middle East, and while it might have been a rave at the National Press Club, at this dinner, to me at least, it was a dull thud.

By contrast, Dick Clark, a celebrity and a multi-million-dollar baby in his own right, was in New York at that time and apparently, at the last minute, had been asked to fill in as master of ceremony for David Hartman, who was on assignment. I had met Dick Clark on several occasions and had always been impressed with his work ethic. He was not just a performer. He was always a hands-on worker, making the call, helping the crew, whatever it took to get the job done. He had been a giant for ABC, both in radio and television with many programs and especially the classic, *American Bandstand* to his credit. And he was simply extraordinary at the Golden Sammy Awards dinner. He was warm and gracious and immediately caught the sensitivity of the event and made it an evening for me to remember always.

In accepting the award, I told the audience of my feelings about the dangers and deceptiveness of asthma and the heartbreaking story of the tragedy in my family. I accepted the award on behalf of every member of our family and received a long standing ovation. Dick told me later, "I admire a person who can speak from his heart."

If I recall, Ms. Walters was long gone by the time I spoke. I don't know what her problem really was that night. Maybe she had a bad day in the newsroom, or maybe Harry Reasoner, whom she could not get along with, stepped on her shoe. And maybe she hadn't been fully filled in on the purpose of the dinner. All I know is that a prima-donna attitude damn near ruined a very special evening for me. And I don't mean to judge anyone on a bad day or night's performance. We all have our moments. I met Barbara on several occasions afterward, even traveled on speaking engagements with her a few times. Neither of us ever mentioned that evening. I guess it was better left that way.

Arledge and ABC News presented Barbara Walters with a new, long-term $10 million-a-year contract in the mid-nineties. That contract started a domino effect among the news superstars. Agents of the prominent news personalities immediately descended on every network. The fact is Ms. Walters has done some extraordinary things for ABC. She was and is a tireless worker, has unprecedented contacts with leaders and prominent figures across the world, and I am told she will travel on a moment's notice anywhere in the world to get a story. Her specials with high-profile personalities have rated extremely well and she has hosted many well-received news and entertainment specials. She also hosted ABC's long-running *20/20* program with Hugh Downs and developed and produced a popular daytime talk show for women, *The View*, on ABC.

It is my opinion that in today's economic environment and in the financial framework of the network business, no TV news personality, or semi-news on-air talent, should be compensated at $10 million-a-year as a contract employee. The escalation in scale is the result of building a star system in news that is out of proportion to the financial delivery to the corporation and the stockholders of any communications company. It was not many years ago that the news divisions were large money losers. The only reason such skyscraper salaries are justified by the news divisions, is that news became more involved in prime-time programming with several weekly "infotainment" shows that have followed the lead of CBS's *60 Minutes*. These programs, less expensive to produce than filmed entertainment programs, can and often do return big profit dollars.

I have always believed that there are thousands of young, very talented actors and actresses or news reporters or sportscasters at local stations all across the country who have every potential, if the industry will just provide the opportunity for them to get the exposure, the promotion and the experience that the aforementioned superstars have been afforded. There is no dearth of talent. I believe that a performer does not make television great. Television gives the performer the opportunity to be great. Besides, as all of the superstars must know, fame is such a fleeting thing.

All of that having been said, I have the utmost admiration for the continuing progress in news coverage by radio and television. Broadcasting is the true catalyst in bringing our nation together in times of great crises or triumphs or tragedies. We were all touched by the coverage, coming right into our homes minute by minute, of the assassinations of President John F. Kennedy and Dr. Martin Luther King, Jr.; by the thrilling "Do you believe in miracles?" victory of the US hockey team in Lake Placid in 1984; the astronauts' walk on the moon; the Presidential debates and on and on.

I believe that the growth of broadcast news, reaching out to report on more and more dimensions in our society, paved the way for a greater awareness of the industry's responsibility for public service. For me, it opened up entirely new avenues to pursue.

Thirteen

Children's Programming

In 1970, early in my tenure as president of the TV network, my assistant, Jack Ansell, and I would sit for hours assessing the areas in the television landscape where we could make positive changes. Four areas were most prominent – the ratings system, public service projects, the glaring disadvantage in the number and quality of affiliated stations and, last but not least, children's programming. That doesn't mean to say that all the other elements of the network under me were in great shape – they weren't. Many areas needed direction and nurturing, including prime-time entertainment programming, since ABC was widely regarded as being "fourth in the three-network race."

The children's programming area was obviously neglected and needed immediate attention. It was the only entertainment arena that did not have its own programming staff, a creative force to design, execute and purchase programs. This was also true of NBC and CBS in the early seventies. I simply could not believe that none of the television networks had a department whose purpose was to design shows for children. So, early in 1971, we created a Children's Program Department and named the famous cartoonist and artist Charles "Chuck" Jones as the vice president for children's programming. The very affable and talented Mr. Jones, originator of the *Road Runner* cartoons, had worked with Walt Disney among others, and his appointment in television management created quite a stir in the industry. Jones and a small staff immediately began to design concepts and programs that blended entertainment with education, and upheld values for young people.

I immensely enjoyed working with Jones and his staff. They were exceptionally creative and seemed to be in touch with the sensitivities and the needs of children. We spent long hours in the evenings, often at my home in Glen Ridge, New Jersey, talking about what was needed for high-quality children's programming, why the industry had failed so miserably in this important area, and how we could circumvent the ratings system that we were convinced was an obstacle to more enlightened children's programming.

In the winter of 1971, I received a call from the Action for Children's Television (ACT) group in Boston, who wanted to come to New York to see me. They had just started the organization because they were fed up with the negative influence of TV on children. I was delighted to meet with them, and I told them of my own concerns and what we at ABC were doing about it. One of the ACT members was Peggy Charren, the long-time president of the organization. She seemed surprised that network executives were really concerned about the welfare of children.

With all of this activity and concern, Jones, Ansell and I decided that an industry-wide Children's Television Programming Workshop was very much in order. It would be beneficial to ABC and to the entire industry. I announced it at our annual affiliate meeting in June 1971 in Los Angeles as follows:

> *I would like to talk to you today about a subject that I feel is of paramount importance to all of us. It is the area of children's programming....*
>
> *You have been hearing for many weeks about the Children's TV Programming Workshop, which ABC has been planning.*
>
> *This is a full-scale seminar to which we have invited representatives from advertisers and advertising agencies and our producers, as well as the other networks, concerned citizens groups and industry-oriented organizations and, of course, your representatives, for an exchange of ideas and views through which together we might bring about a healthier, commercial television for children; a television for children that we can all be truly proud of. ...I sincerely have never been more encouraged or stimulated about any project in all of my broadcasting career.*

I went on to enumerate some of the questions that would be raised at the workshop, with an emphasis on one of my pet peeves – the Nielsen Rating System.

> *Ratings, themselves, are not the problem; it is what we do with them that creates the problem. In this particular, extremely sensitive area of programming to children, it is not just the networks or the stations, but the advertisers and the buyers, all too often thinking solely in terms of circulation, who must step forward and be counted. These are not merely numbers that we are talking about in this area. These are not just millions of little cereal-eaters; these are children – yours and mine!*
>
> *These children are our nation's tomorrow, and we had better face that right now.*

The response was immediate and very gratifying. I received a sustained standing ovation, and the idea of doing something meaningful for children was the talk of the reception and dinner that followed, especially among the affiliates. Several members of ABC management were skeptical and suggested that I was opening a can of worms. Perhaps I was, but as I saw it, high-quality children's programming was a responsibility of every network.

In late June of 1971, we convened the workshop at the Sheraton Hotel on 7th Avenue in New York, bringing together people from all across the country to discuss television programming for children. I had been the president of the ABC Television Network for a little over a year and the Children's Programming TV Workshop was the culmination of months and months of work intended to bring about positive and substantive changes in this severely neglected area of television.

The workshop accomplished everything that I wanted. It also brought harsh criticism from an advertiser's representative and a few others who felt threatened. Over 250 people, including producers, writers, Federal Communications Commission representatives, advertising agency executives, advertisers, educators, network and station executives and even some entertainers, met and debated for two-and-a-half days. I opened the session with remarks on why we were meeting and what we hoped to accomplish. Then Fred Pierce, later to become president of ABC, Inc., took over as moderator for the sessions.

There were brief presentations from representatives of each children's group involving the effects of TV programming. Breakout sessions followed in which small groups met to discuss problems and possible solutions. The effect of commercials and how they were crafted was discussed. There was a long conversation, often heated, on the ratings system and its effect on high-quality children's programs. Writers and producers introduced some new ideas for more educational programming that would help keep the content entertaining and fun. Proposals were discussed for shorter musical and cartoon segments of an informative nature that could be inserted around the traditional cartoon shows. Chuck Jones and Jack Ansell were right in the front row of all of these sessions, as was I. Our every intention was to take a consensus from the meetings and implement the ideas as part of our new ABC children's programming strategy.

Danny Kaye was the luncheon speaker on the last day. He brought an entertainer's perspective and a different kind of endorsement to our efforts. The young senator from Massachusetts, Ted Kennedy, had hoped to join us at the meetings but sent a most supportive wire instead, which I read to those assembled.

At the end of the last session, I held a press conference to wrap up what I thought we had accomplished. One reporter asked, "Mr. Duffy, specifically what do you think the long-range effect will be on the television industry from this conference?"

I responded, "I can't give you the specific differences it will make. But I will tell you that what was discussed here these last few days and the programming that will result from it, will make a fundamental difference in children's television programming for years to come."

A few days after the workshop, I was sitting in my office on the thirty-eighth floor and reflecting on its success. It had been our idea and I had helped to oversee it. I was pleased with what had transpired and the solid positive ideas that came from the meetings. I knew we had made significant advances in changing attitudes toward the importance of children's programming. Looking through the papers and mail in my in-tray, a headline in the radio-television section of *Variety* magazine, the bible of show business, caught my eye with good reason: it began with my name!

DUFFY SHOWBOATS AT CHILDREN'S CONFERENCE.

SHOWBOATS! The headline hit me right between the eyes. What are they talking about? There wasn't any area of broadcasting I felt more concerned about than children's programming, and I had been sticking my neck out on the subject for some time now, even though I could see that the general feeling within the industry, even within my own company and among my peers, was "just let sleeping dogs lie." I grabbed the magazine and started reading. The article left me stunned, hurt, angry and more than a little bewildered.

Les Brown, who later became the editor of *Variety* and, even later, gained some fame as the television critic for the *New York Times*, had written the article. I had known Les when he was a reporter for *Variety* and I was in charge of the ABC radio office in Chicago. He knew my strong feelings concerning the influence of radio and television on young people, and the importance I placed on the public service responsibilities of the media. Why was he making this unfounded insinuation?

I was bewildered because showboating didn't occur to me in organizing the conference. In my mind, such a meeting was long overdue. It was not my purpose to gain attention for the company, or myself, but simply to assemble leaders who could bring action and positive change in a neglected area of the growing and influential medium.

At the same time, there was a very different response to the same conference from Nicholas Johnson of the FCC (Federal Communications Commission). It was reported in *The Philadelphia Evening Bulletin* of 14 December 1971 by Rex Polier, the *Bulletin's* TV critic:

It's very seldom that Nicholas Johnson, the FCC's self-appointed watchdog of TV, has a nice word for a broadcasting executive, especially the president of a commercial TV network. But Johnson has lauded James E. Duffy, president, the ABC Television Network, in a letter that he, Johnson, made public, not Duffy.

The FCC Commissioner applauded Duffy for calling on his fellow broadcasters to cut down the commercial time in their non prime-time children's programming by something like six minutes an hour.

'Whatever you end up doing, whether this is a wise proposal or enough, the fact that you have made it is a heartening sign indeed,' Johnson wrote. 'For starters, you have made a tremendous number of friends among parents – and Washington officials – which is itself kind of novel and newsworthy in these days for the broadcasting industry.

More important, you've positioned yourself so that you are now participating in change – instead of simply waiting for it to happen to you... I trust that the long range impact upon the industry's interests from their following of your leadership will prove to be much more favorable than the present posture of intransigence and obstructionism.'

Duffy...did not mention Johnson's letter in an interview last week in his New York office. But he did say emphatically "in spite of all the pressures and criticism we are subject to today, I still believe we ought to regulate ourselves. We're in the best position to do so."

Whether his fellow broadcasters will heed Duffy's plea remains to be seen. Traditionally, the broadcasting industry does not take kindly to self-appointed crusaders who allow their suggestions to reach the press and public too. Such things apparently do not bother Duffy, a rugged Midwesterner who sees his job first to make ABC commercially successful yet to shape up to what is expected totally of TV in the seventies.

"It was simpler being a network president twenty years ago," commented Duffy, who became ABC's president in 1970. "The emphasis was almost entirely on entertainment value and the necessity of getting it on the screen.

The seventies brought new realities, responsibilities, and a certain amount of self-criticism. We are concerned whether the medium is really achieving its potentialities – culturally as well as commercially.

The general criticism in the press and government is said to have caused us to upgrade children's programming. We started to do it a long time ago.

TV today – ABC and the others – have the responsibility not only of making 'em laugh, but to make 'em think...."

Those words are a philosophy that I have believed in throughout my career in broadcasting. The common misconception within the industry was, and probably still is, that culturally responsible programming and commercially successful TV were mutually exclusive. And that social service and financial success were, like oil and water, unmixable. The interesting fact is that both these firmly held beliefs are fallacious and have been proven to be again and again. I never was confused about these issues.

So why did Les Brown come out with his accusation of insincerity? In talking to him later, I gained insight into why he characterized my efforts the way he did. It was based on the same reason that many key executives at ABC shied away when the conference was first announced.

Children's programming was a topic that was loaded with dynamite for the industry. It was under constant review by members of Congress and a growing number of citizens' action groups, including Action for Children's Television. It was an area where viewership was measured, like all other areas of network television, by an inaccurate rating system that became even more ridiculous when applied toward ill-conceived programs for youngsters.

Children's programming was, and remains, an area of television that is quite profitable. Cereal advertisers or toy manufacturers, who bought their own shows and placed them on the networks, paying handsomely for the privilege, scheduled most Saturday morning shows. The networks did not have the expense of creating programs of their own, with a few exceptions such as old cartoons and serial films like *Flying Aces*.

The networks wanted to disguise the fact that the children's area was a profit maker since so much heat was being generated on the influence of television on children. The heat was justified. In some cases, it was almost impossible to tell where the program ended and where the commercial began, because the same characters who were in the movie or cartoon were selling the kids, transfixed by the action, sound and color, on the benefits of their particular brand of breakfast food or toys during the commercial.

During the course of that Children's TV Programming Workshop, I had heard criticism leveled at me similar to the *Variety* story. One advertising executive who handled children's advertising clients, James Harvey, from San Francisco, was one of the principal speakers at the conference. He declared that I was painting an unfair picture of children's programming and that I was a "pontificating, insincere perpetrator" in an area that I knew little about and where I did not belong.

As I stared at the *Variety* headline, it became clear to me that I was accused of showboating because I was spotlighting problems that the broadcasting industry (and the advertisers who benefited from existing practices) didn't want to illuminate and were not willing to change. People in many quarters felt uncomfortable under this spotlight, preferring their activities to remain in the shadows, out of public view and scrutiny.

The Children's Television Programming Workshop came about because I had been frustrated for years by the inadequacies and negligence of children's programming. I had vowed, when I was vice president in charge of ABC's TV Network Sales, that if I were ever in a position to do something about children's television, I would.

I sincerely believe that because of the Children's Workshop a new attitude was implanted among most of those in the business about the need and importance of high-quality programming for children. As a result of that conference, *Curiosity Shop*, a weekly, hour-long educational/entertainment program for children, was conceived and produced. Other programs that can be traced to the workshop are the *ABC After School Specials*, *Rainbow Sunday* on NBC, the three-minute musical *Scholastic Rock* jingles (remember *Conjunction Junction?*), the Saturday morning Movie Classics for Children and several other programs that presented social values in a manner that could be enjoyed and understood by younger viewers.

I announced that I hoped to convene the Children's Workshop every two years so that we as an industry could assess the progress made in the spirit of working together for the young people of our country. Unfortunately, that promise was never fulfilled since the programming area was later removed from my responsibilities. Despite my continued recommendations, the ABC Children's Workshop was never convened again. However, I did stay involved with children's programming throughout my fifteen-year tenure. In 1974, I proposed to the Code Board of the National Association of Broadcasters that "bumpers" be placed between commercials and program content in all kids' programs so that children could differentiate between the two. It was accepted as an industry standard.

In an industry speech prior to the NAB board proposal, I recommended that children's programming be eliminated from the Nielsen Rating Index and a new form of measurement be developed that would show not only the numbers of viewers but, more importantly, *who* was watching, and the effect of the program and commercial content on the young viewers. I called this psychographics. When I proposed this concept, you would have thought I had burned the American flag or attacked motherhood. The best reaction I could get was a mumbled, "Yeah, we oughta look into it," from a couple of television executives who couldn't get away from me fast enough. I did not give up on this idea, as you will read later.

It is curious that, seemingly, the only time the industry, including ABC, dresses up its children's programming is when the heat is on from Congress or alarmed citizens' groups or when public relations points are needed. An example is a two-page advertisement in the February 1, 1978 issue of *Variety*. It was in conjunction with the company's twenty-fifth anniversary celebration. The headline reads: "ENRICHING CHILDREN'S PROGRAMMING...AND THERE'S NO END IN SIGHT ON ABC." The main body of the ad reads in part,

> *ABC has made a serious commitment to quality pro-*
> *gramming for children which has been recognized not*
> *only by the industry leaders, but also by critics and groups*
> *of concerned citizens from coast to coast.*

The advertisement goes on to describe specific *After School Specials* dealing with subjects of interest to young people, and mentioned other important developments in children's programming – *ABC Weekend Specials: Schoolhouse Rock; ABC Nutrition Commercials; Animals, Animals, Animals*, and several others. The article ends by stating, "Whether it's afternoon, prime time, Saturday or Sunday morning, ABC is committed to quality television for young people."

I was pleased to see the ad. It was almost seven years after the Children's Television Workshop and the ad featured many of the shows that were born as a result of the workshop meetings.

I still believe that commitment to children from the television networks should be in force every day and not just dressed up and trumpeted for special occasions.

I have also noted with mixed satisfaction that every time a Congressional hearing has been held in Washington on children's TV programming, the ABC folks invariably take the Children's Television Programming Workshop of 1971 files out of mothballs and solemnly tell the committee about the "wonderful things we have done for America's children." It is interesting to note that through the years several others at ABC, including Michael Eisner, Brandon Stoddard and Squire Rushnell, have been given credit for convening the workshop. They are all fine broadcasters, but they had absolutely nothing to do with that first workshop. I might add that Rushnell, in later years as VP of children's programming for ABC, did some outstanding work for youngsters.

My involvement in children's programming was most gratifying and provided a defining time in my career. I think our efforts did make a difference, but they were not enough. The fact is, the same problems that led us to convene the workshop in 1971 still exist in children's programming on commercial TV today at both the network and local station levels. In commercial television, the ratings still rule. The fact that PBS, not dependent on ratings or advertising dollars, has had extraordinarily good programming for children for many years illustrates the point.

Television, with all of its reach and impact and power, has initiated many changes in our attitudes and our lifestyles over the years, but it has failed in providing high-quality programming for children. There is an urgent challenge for the new leaders in the industry, including cable and the Internet.

The positive reactions from the Children's Workshop and the approving letters from advertisers and station managers reinforced my belief that we were on the right track as we looked to the 1971-72 fall season. Jack Ansell, who had done yeoman-like work on the conference, was especially pleased because he, too, had come under fire from his ABC colleagues before and during the meetings.

"You can't lead blind horses," Jack said. "And these folks are blinded by the ratings."

At least Elton Rule and his assistant, Marty Pompadur, were both complimentary about the children's meetings and agreed we were setting a sensible tone for the industry. It was encouraging after the early skepticism.

Speaking of children, my own youngsters were growing and on the move. Jay had graduated from high school and had opted to travel west and attend college in Arizona. We had many discussions about the possibilities of Arizona University in Tucson and Arizona State in Tempe. Instead, since his grade points were low, he chose Pima Junior College in Phoenix with the intention of transferring to a four-year school in a year or two. I should have known that, without supervision, Jay's adventures into higher education were to be short lived. Jay, always popular and outgoing, moved into a house on the outskirts of Tempe with some friends. I later learned, that there was far more activity "smokin' weed, drinking beer, entertaining coeds and raisin' hell" than cracking the books and attending classes. It is no excuse, but this was at a time when the younger generation had just waded through the rebellious sixties and the infamous drug culture. Jay and Terry were no exceptions. Both were musicians of sorts, Jay a talented drummer and Terry a rock singer. Both loved music and were close followers of the emerging superstars of rock & roll and, I know, were impressed with the anti-society, anti-institution messages and attitudes. It made life very difficult for a father raised on the strict principles of Grandpa and Grandma Adams.

Jay dropped out of school after a year and, after traveling free style with some of his friends, avowed some interest in the entertainment business. A good friend of mine and a fine broadcaster, Dale Moore of Missoula, Montana, offered Jay a job as a production assistant at one of his stations in Montana. Jay would have none of it. He assumed he was being isolated where, he figured, there were few women, fewer parties, and no fun.

I finally asked Dick Clark, who visited me often when he was in New York, if he would consider interviewing Jay for a position with his growing production company in Los Angeles. He did and was impressed with Jay and offered him a job as a general assistant. Jay, fortunately or unfortunately, took to the LA lifestyle immediately and was consumed by his responsibilities with the production company. One of the highlights that he would excitedly tell me about, in our frequent telephone conversations or when I visited him on the West Coast, was working with the rock bands that came to the studios. He reached a real high when he sat in on a gig with one of the groups after they recognized his talents on the drums. Unfortunately, it wasn't the only "high" he reached.

One day, Dick Clark asked to see me in my office in New York. After exchanging pleasantries, he looked me straight in the eyes and said softly, "This is a real tough thing to do, but I have to tell a father that his son has a serious drug problem. It is getting worse, Jim, and I can't keep him on like this. I really like Jay, and I hope you can do something about it for your sake and his."

They were, of course, words that I didn't want to hear, but I was very grateful to Dick Clark for his forthrightness and courage. I flew out to California and brought Jay back to Glen Ridge and got him into a drug rehabilitation center in Summit, New Jersey. It was to be the first of many. Poignantly, some years later at a drug rehab center when residents were asked to "fantasize" about their life's accomplishments, Jay wrote of the many shows he had produced for Dick Clark Productions.

Meanwhile, Terry, who was sixteen years old, came to live with us in Glen Ridge and immediately made too many friends at the Glen Ridge High School, which was directly across the street from our home on Ridgewood Avenue. He became kind of a cult figure with his soft good looks and long hair and offbeat sense of humor. Like Jay, there was far too much fun and too little time for the books. We finally sent him to finish school at the Pine Ridge School in Burlington, Vermont. Diane and Marcia were still living with Betty but were spending more and more time with Julie and me in New Jersey. I could sense that the girls were restless and that things were not going well with Betty on the Connecticut front. Baby Corinne was just a toddler and described by Chuck Jones as "the most perfect angel on earth." Cori observed some years later that with all the comings and goings of the older kids at our Glen Ridge home, "I grew up in a forest of kneecaps."

In reflection, some of the happiest moments of my life were when I was with my boys, playing and laughing and enjoying one another. That does not exclude Diane or Marcia or Corinne. I loved them very much, but in a different, sweeter way. There is just something very special, I learned with a broken heart, about a father and his sons.

All of entertainment programming, including the children's area, was a major responsibility in my new position including dealing with actors and their agents, producers, writers and studio heads. As the head of the network, I also learned that one of the most important dimensions in the commercial over-the-air network business, both television and radio, is the working partnership between a network and its affiliated stations across the country. The combination of local stations, or affiliates, actually is the network, since without them the so-called programming networks would have no place for the programs to be seen or heard.

Along with Dick Beesemyer, vice president for the ABC Affiliate Relations Department and his staff, I was ultimately responsible for the world of our network's affiliated stations. It was a difficult responsibility because, again, ABC had fewer stations than the other networks and it was always a struggle to keep the stations happy and get maximum exposure for our network programs.

The annual ABC Affiliate Meetings were an important element in building the partnership. Part of the strategy was to make the annual affiliate meetings colorful and inspiring events. These conventions were usually held in Los Angeles where the majority of television programs are produced and where station managers, their spouses and key staff members would come in droves from all across America. From the first annual convention that I hosted in 1970, these gatherings became very important to the growth of the network and also for my career.

One of the most effective early measures in partnering with the affiliates during my presidency was a series of regional meetings in strategically located cities around the country. For these sessions a handful of key executives from the network would travel to designated locations to meet with station managers face to face. It was the reverse of the traditional procedure where affiliates would go to the annual meetings once a year or visit the network headquarters in New York to discuss how the network plans related to their own stations. The regional meetings were somewhat akin to the strategy I had learned and adopted in my selling experience: travel to meet advertisers on their turf. Elton Rule started the regionals concept in 1968, and I expanded on the meetings when I became the head of the network.

In my first year, I designated a "flying squad" of department heads of all of the program departments – news, entertainment and sports – as well as research, sales, standards and practices and appropriate people from affiliate relations to be the network team. Over a two-week period we would travel to five or six cities in different parts of the country: Boston, Atlanta, St. Louis, Dallas, Denver and San Francisco.

The meetings were strictly informal, with a reception to get acquainted or renew old friendships the night before, and then a full day of meetings. The sessions were usually held around a large square table where all the participants could be part of the process, shirtsleeve style. We would present our plans to the affiliates for the upcoming months and ask for their comments and suggestions. We held an open forum in the afternoon where any station manager could discuss his concern about program content, compensation, competition, long-range planning, management style or any number of potential problems. We did it "Donahue style." I would roam around the room with a hand mike, taking questions and exchanging ideas on the issues. My announcing experience came in very handy on these occasions.

The network mission, of course, was to alleviate as many problems as possible and come away with maximum cooperation for all of its programs. The message was very clear and straightforward. "Look, you need the best possible programming from us throughout your broadcast day. We, in turn, need maximum clearance for ALL of our programming. If we can build that kind of a working agreement and make it happen both ways, we will be the strongest and most successful group of stations and television network in this business. And we will take great pride in being ABC stations and the ABC Television Network. Can you believe in that?"

At first, some stations were skeptical since they had been burned with false promises in the past. A distinct distrust of the New York "suits" from the network had been ingrained from the earlier years. There was a perceptible "them and us" syndrome. But little by little, as the network got stronger in its programming effort and we kept an open line and a listening ear to the stations, a real trust started to emerge. Some strong personal friendships were established with station managers and personnel.

Among my more difficult assignments with the affiliates was the annual Affiliate Board of Governors Meeting, where a select group of station managers appointed by the ABC Television Network affiliate body would meet with corporate and network executives and department heads to discuss the policies and plans for the upcoming year or years. These meetings were usually held in some exotic resort setting and would last for five or six days. The meetings were difficult to plan and conduct because they were more personalized with groups of twelve or fifteen station managers and their spouses, even more in later years, all looking for attention and acknowledgment. The ABC personnel, most of whom looked for sufficient recognition to satisfy their own sense of importance, were also included. On top of that, special guests, including performers or stars of current series were flown in for the social side of the meetings, adding substantially to the burden of balancing egos.

The Board of Governors Meetings were assuredly not just fun in the sun with a host of friendly and compassionate cohorts. It was here in the two-and-a-half-day business sessions that the problems and frustrations of the affiliated stations and the network were hammered out, hopefully arriving at resolutions that would carry the partnership atmosphere on through the following year.

My most difficult Board of Governors Meeting was my first as president of the network. It was held at the Carleton Estates Hotel in Christiansted, St. Croix, US Virgin Islands in November of 1970. The island had a shoot-out and a killing near the hotel a couple of weeks before our meeting. There was a distinct tenseness in the air as I conducted my first board meeting with a roomful of equally nervous and rather hostile station managers, only for different reasons. In late 1969, AT&T had increased its line charges to the networks by some six to ten percent.

Both NBC and CBS had decided and announced that they would absorb those charges, while ABC management, in a poorer financial position, decided to pass along a percentage of the increase to the affiliates. What that meant was each station would get less compensation from the network based on a complicated mathematical formula depending on the individual station's market size. This management decision was made just prior to my appointment as the head of the network. I inherited the charge of convincing the affiliates that this was in their best interest in the long run. My mission was somewhat akin to Pickett's Charge at Gettysburg.

Elton Rule opened the meeting with a few welcoming remarks to an audience of hard-eyed and unsmiling affiliates. Elton then quickly turned the meeting over to me.

I told those assembled how pleased I was to be the head of the television network after working with many of them in my previous capacity in network sales. I started to outline the agenda for the meeting when George Kohler, the chairman of the Affiliate Board from Philadelphia, interrupted.

"That's all well and good, Jim, but we have something to put on the table right at the top of this meeting. What I want to address head on is your disgraceful decision regarding cutting compensation to your affiliates. At a time when local competition is increasing, and cigarette business leaving the industry, you...."

Kohler, an intelligent and extremely articulate man, continued for the next twelve minutes. He laced the network up one side and down the other, and most of it was directed at me as the new head of the network delegation.

Finally, Rule stepped in, "Now wait a minute, George. There is a very practical reason for our decision, and we want the opportunity to discuss it before you or any one else comes to harsh conclusions."

We did discuss it over the course of the next two days with each of the board members having his or her say, candid and to the point. The result, as so often happens, was that the affiliates assigned a task force to come into New York and review the compensation formula.

Legend has it that the opening session got so heated I had to rush outside and throw up in the bushes. That is not true, but it did make for a very uncomfortable three or four days. At the reception for the final banquet, the station managers gathered at one end of the hall and the network and corporate people stayed at the other. It was so ludicrous that finally Bob King, the Capital Cities station manager from Buffalo, and I simulated a gunfight that broke the tension. We finally mixed and had a fine evening.

I think that the St. Croix Board of Governors Meeting, for all of its difficulties, broke the tension not just at that particular session, but also in the relationship between the network and its affiliates. It established a different and deeper respect by ABC management, especially in the entertainment, news and sports areas, for the power and influence of the affiliate body. It served all of us well, including the programmers, toward building a stronger network and industry.

The affiliate meetings helped establish an esprit de corps among the departments at the network. The sharing of ideas and hopeful solutions to common problems brought a closer bond among most ABC people who were involved. The meetings also provided a sense of importance and pride to the people who worked in the ABC Affiliate Relations Department.

The spring and summer of 1971 were extremely active for all of us at the network. We had been through the rough and tumble of the screening and scheduling sessions and the annual affiliate and promotion managers' meetings, prior to the Children's Television Programming Workshop. It was especially important that we were all pointing in the same direction as we headed for the fall season.

Despite the *Variety* story on the children's meeting, the good press on the success and progress of the ABC TV Network continued to grow. Elton and I were selected as the outstanding executives in broadcasting by the Gallagher Report and received national press including stories in *Business Week* and *Newsweek* magazines:

> *Business Week* May 16, 1971:
> *Two men – Elton H. Rule, president of ABC, and James E. Duffy, president of the company's TV network – are the cornerstones of the "young aggressive team the affiliates are banking on."*
>
> *The network's millstone over the years has been that it has only about 155 affiliated stations in the country's primary markets, while each rival has about fifty more. To make up for this disparity, the network has gone after the under-fifty audience. "We have six out of the top ten programs if you just count the 18-49-year olds," says Duffy.*

> *Newsweek* Jan 10 1972:
> *Among TV-industry wags, ABC used to stand for the*

'Almost Broadcasting Company.' ...Not even the most gag-starved comic, however, is laughing at ABC these days. In as sudden and improbable a turnabout as any of Alfred Hitchcock's, ABC has achieved parity with its two rival networks in virtually all arenas of combat.

Another reporter wrote:

On the Nielsen charts last week, ABC for the sixth time since Jan 1, [1971] led the three networks in total audience; fifteen of the top forty programs were ABC's...So formidable has ABC become as a competitor that the massive overhauls in television programming for next fall are at CBS and NBC while ABC is making the fewest changes of all.

The screenings and scheduling sessions were complicated in the early spring of 1971 by the fact that Rule came down with a severe case of hepatitis and was bedridden at his home in Scarsdale, New York for two months. I kept in constant touch by telephone, as did all other executives of the company who reported to him. But it was extremely difficult to relay all of the factors in the long scheduling sessions, as they were loaded with different points of view from the various department heads. Elton was sent scripts and films and had seen most of the programs proposed for the schedule, but trying to communicate all the research data and recommendations was a real challenge. I really felt for him. It was obvious he was physically weak and I could tell by his tone he was concerned that his command, especially over programming, might be slipping away in his absence.

These particular program meetings were further complicated by the fact that the economy had weakened, affecting all of advertising including broadcasting sponsorships. While our TV network sales were still strong, other divisions of the company were in trouble. We were under orders to keep the cost of the prime-time schedule down as much as possible. Despite the fact that for the first time in its history, the ABC Television Network showed a profit during the 1971/72 season, retrenchment (later it became known as "downsizing") became a reality along Broadcast Row. Rumors had circulated that a number of ABC's employees in other areas of the company were to be fired.

But the American Broadcasting Company, Inc. had far more pressing concerns than the economy, or the prime-time schedule or even children's programming, during the latter part of 1971 and the beginning of 1972.

Leonard Goldenson had a severe heart attack in late May of 1971 which kept him hospitalized and out of action for a number of months. It brought into immediate focus the question of who the next leader or leaders of the company might be, since the number two in command, Si Siegel, was nearing his 65th birthday and was about to retire.

The decision reached in January of 1972 had an impact on the entire broadcasting industry and represented a turning point for me.

Fourteen

Diminished Authority; New Opportunities

Mid-afternoon on Monday, July 9, 1972, I got a message that Elton Rule wanted to see me in his office on the thirty-ninth floor at 5:00 PM. I didn't think too much about it since Elton would call us to his office on various occasions, but less so now that he had been promoted to his new exalted position as president and chief operating officer of the American Broadcasting Companies, Inc. If Rule had been the prince before, he had now had the coronation to be the king.

Leonard Goldenson, back at work after the first of the year, had accepted Si Siegel's decision to retire in January at age 65, and Goldenson and Siegel, along with the board of directors, had promoted Rule. Leonard became chairman of the board, which left a vacancy in the position of the president of the broadcasting division. The position had just been established in the previous two years to accommodate Elton Rule.

It crossed my mind as I went up the back stairway to Rule's office that, perhaps, after months without word on the Broadcasting Division post, and despite our differences, he might be calling me up to offer me the overall broadcasting position. In my mind, the job that I had done with the television network certainly warranted consideration. The network had moved ahead on all fronts, and on certain weeks in prime time, it was at a virtual tie with CBS. Daytime had moved into the lead; sales were up despite a recessionary economy; and we had just completed a highly successful affiliate meeting and a sensational press critics' meeting. The network had just turned a profit for the first time in its history. Other divisions looked on the television network as the shining light in the American Broadcasting Company.

Marty Pompadur, who had been promoted as Rule's vice president and special assistant, was in Rule's office when Mary Blaney, Elton's secretary, ushered me in.

Marty was seated to Rule's left and Elton remained seated behind his large, marble-topped desk. His tanned face seemed friendly enough, but he seemed a tiny bit nervous as he put his hands behind his head, leaned back in his chair and started talking.

"Jim, you've probably heard some of this. We're making some major changes in the company, and I wanted to go over them with you." He paused and looked at me.

"I haven't heard about the changes, Elton. Nobody has spoken to me."

Rule looked over at Pompadur, as much as to say, "Haven't you hinted to him?" Marty just stared at his shoes.

"We're breaking up the Broadcasting Division. All of radio will now report to Hal Neal (who had been president of the Radio Owned Stations Division) and all of television, except for news, will report to Wally Schwartz. We're bringing Wally over as part of the TV team." He paused again.

I was shocked with what I had heard. I had known Wally Schwartz for a number of years and he had done a great job as president of the four radio networks, but he had absolutely no experience in television.

"What are you telling me, Elton?" I said rather sharply. "Where does that leave me and the television network?"

"I want you to stay on as president of the TV network," he said. "But we're realigning your responsibilities. We are spinning off the programming department and calling it the ABC Entertainment Division. Marty Starger will run it, and in time, we hope to be in production beyond television programming and get into Broadway and movies for theaters. We may even want to do some international productions."

He paused again. I sat with my hands together, touching my mouth, watching him. I could feel the blood pressure start to rise in my temples and my eyes were growing hard and cold.

"Is that all?" I said.

"We're also splitting off the Strategic Planning Division and Fred Pierce will run that," Elton said in a tone that said, "Let's get this over with." "He'll report to Wally along with Starger. You will still have responsibility for sales, affiliate relations, publicity and promotion...." He hesitated and said, "Look, Jim, I can see that you're not pleased with this, and I can understand. I want you to know that you have done a tremendous job for the company and we, especially Leonard, want you to stay. Your job as it is now is a ball breaker. This will give you time to concentrate on your strengths and have some fun."

I looked at him for a long time. Finally, I said, "What do you expect me to do, Elton? Say thank you?" I turned to Pompadur. I respected Marty very much. We had worked closely when he was a lawyer for the sales department.

"Why the hell, are you sitting there watching your shoelaces, Marty? Are you here to witness the guillotining? From here on, I would prefer that this meeting be between Elton and me."

Pompadur nodded, looked at Elton and got up and left.

Elton was no longer leaning comfortably back in his chair. From the expression in his eyes, I think he thought I was going to take a swing at him or do something violent.

"How would you feel, Elton, after thirty-one years in the company, if you had to sit here and listen to this barrel of shit?" I said with my voice and Irish starting to rise. "We have worked too hard and accomplished too much for the company and the television network to be sideswiped by one of your cockamamie schemes. Your plan might be a good one for the long run, Elton, but it will fall flat on its ass in the next few years and the company and all of us in this company will suffer."

Elton didn't say a word. He just continued to look at me. I felt betrayed, like I was standing alone on the edge of a precipice. I reached back through the years and brought forth the word that I had used for the grade school principal in Moweaqua.

"You are a son of a bitch, Elton. You didn't have the decency to discuss the possible changes before they were finalized with me or any of the network people, obviously, other than Starger. You have done the same thing here that you did with the sneaky program buys and I resent it. After the fact, you call me in and stick the knife in. The network has made enormous progress, and you and Leonard know it. We don't deserve this. Why don't you just fire me, and get it over with, you son of a bitch?"

Believe it or not, I was rather calm. I did not rant and rave. But I did get off my chest the tremendous sense of unfairness that had been steadily building for a long time. If I had been Rule, I probably would have fired me on the spot from the personal things that I said. But he didn't, and one of the reasons he didn't was that Goldenson wouldn't allow him to, I was sure. I found out later that Leonard was very skeptical about the new management scheme, especially how I might be affected. I was confident that if Si Siegel had still been with the company, the disruptions would never have happened.

Elton finally said, "Jim, just think about it. I understand how you feel."

I did think about it. I thought about it so long and hard that my body and head ached. I still had a position in the industry, but it had been greatly diminished. The press, which had been so complimentary less than a month before, came out with the slant that I had undoubtedly failed behind the scenes, despite Leonard and Elton praising my work in the many interviews that took place. Several in the industry voiced the opinion that I had gotten too close to the throne, and the king had decided to rein in the prince's power. These sentiments were echoed in a *Newsweek* article that appeared shortly after the announcement of the changes.

Given all of our success at the network, I simply could not understand Elton's reasoning. I wondered if a problem that was developing on the home front with my wife, Julie, had played a part in his decision. I had started to realize in the past few months, much to my dismay, that Julie had a problem with alcohol.

One evening I was at the dais at a banquet in the Grand Ballroom at the Waldorf Astoria Hotel in New York for an industry function honoring Johnny Carson of *The Tonight Show*. Most of the broadcast industry leaders and many major celebrities were there. Just before dinner, Jane Morgan, the beautiful singing star who was and is married to Jerry Weintraub, the producer, came up and sat next to me at the head table.

"I just wanted to say hello," She said. "Here you are one of the most powerful people in America, and you looked so lonely sitting up here."

What I didn't tell Jane Morgan, or anyone else at the time was that I wasn't lonely – I was petrified. I had just seen my pretty wife, Julie, consume too many cocktails at the assigned ABC spouses' table in the audience and stagger over to butt in on Isabel Goldenson's conversation.

Isabel had the reputation of being a tigress. I noticed the very disapproving reaction to Julie, so I exited the dais at an appropriate moment and got my inebriated wife out of there. I know Elton observed that episode. I was told that Julie had previously called Elton on the telephone, unbeknown to me, when she was inebriated. Her drinking was a problem that I had not recognized before we were married. Lovely and gifted in many ways as she was, her alcohol addiction became a problem that gave my family and me many heartbreaking moments. It almost ruined her life and eventually ended our marriage.

Whatever Elton's reasons for making the changes, I thought seriously about resigning. Herb Schlosser, the president of NBC, called and talked about my coming to work for NBC. There were three or four other "Let's talk" propositions and an offer from my friend, Charles "Duke" Mortimer, to join him in his New York company, Westfall Productions. Mortimer was a fine, creative executive who had given ABC and me millions of advertising dollars when he was the senior vice president for programming at the William Esty Advertising Agency. I considered Mortimer's offer very seriously, but deep in my heart I knew I did not want to leave ABC. It had been my life's work, and I loved the company and I loved its people – well, most of them.

I traveled to Miami for the Republican National Convention in August 1972 to be with some corporate sponsors. I was still smarting from Elton's sword and trying to decide what to do.

Bill Sheehan, a senior vice president in ABC News, who in a couple of years would head the News Division, pulled me aside and gave me a solid piece of advice.

"Don't resign," he said. "You have too much talent to let this force you out. I know a dozen guys who left companies when they felt they'd been screwed, and they were never the same. Play it cool. Make it work for you."

Ev Erlick, the senior counsel for ABC, was also very supportive and encouraged me to stay. A highly respected executive who many thought should have been Goldenson's successor, Ev advised me to stay positive and let my record with the company speak for me.

The words from Dick Hemingsen in the high-school locker room came back to me, "Jeez, Duff, you've been screwed."

And then I thought about my grandfather's advice that had helped me so often, "Don't quit. Never give up."

As I began to analyze the situation, I saw glimmers of the positive side of what might be accomplished in my new role. I could still keep my hand in sales; I could help – even lead – in the all-out drive for more and higher-quality affiliates; and I would have more time to become a company – or even industry – spokesman on the issues I deeply believed in, including my feelings that television was not fulfilling its potential. I also determined that if I still had a role at the company's executive table, as both Rule and later Goldenson assured me I would, I could be a strong and challenging voice in the programming sessions, representing the sales department's, the affiliates' and the viewers' points of view.

I turned it over and over in my mind. I began to realize that the new role could perhaps give me the time and freedom to dedicate myself to what I had envisioned for some time: using the enormous reach and power of television in helping find solutions to a growing number of problems in our country. Up to this point in time, public service in broadcasting was, almost out of necessity, without real compassion. I was confident that there was a more meaningful and effective way to use the medium for social benefit.

I went back to see Rule. I told him that if I stayed, I did not want to be stuck in the office, that I would want to travel more on the sales, affiliates and public-relations fronts. I also told him I wanted an administrative assistant to handle the inside work. And I told him I wanted an automobile and a driver to take me to my meetings in the New York area and back and forth to my home. And I told him that I still wanted to have a meaningful voice and vote in the program sessions. Rule quickly agreed to all of it and seemed genuinely pleased that I was going to stay. I know he was greatly relieved because Goldenson was most concerned that I would leave.

"You won't be sorry," Elton said. "You'll make a lot of money and find some real satisfaction." To show his good will, he gave me the only contract I've ever had in my life, for one year. As it turned out, it actually worked against me, because at year-end, contract employees were excluded from receiving bonuses.

A cocktail reception honoring the people who were promoted was held at New York's 21 Club on 52nd Street. Jim Hagerty, President Eisenhower's former press secretary, who had joined us to run ABC News and now had a corporate assignment, raised his glass and gave a toast: "Congratulations to all of you," he said. "And our special best wishes to Jim Duffy. He is a real pro." It was an acknowledgement that I appreciated very much.

I immediately hired my new administrative assistant, an attractive and bright young woman named Mary Jane Raphael from the network sales department. Mary Jane proved to be invaluable in the coming years, a real asset to me and to ABC. I was determined to get into my responsibilities with a renewed enthusiasm and positive outlook. And the first place I wanted to look was at the affiliate world.

Earlier I described the importance of the network/affiliate partnership. For years that relationship was the only way to distribute network programs into the American home. Direct-broadcast satellite transmission has changed that dynamic in the past few years, but transmission to the home dish, and even cable, lacked the one dimension that the over-the-air system developed and made operative over the years: television and radio stations are in the heart of a respective community, large or small, and reflect the news, views, and people of that community. The local station has its roots in the soil of that community and provides the hometown flavor around the multi-million-dollar programming (especially in television) – be it entertainment, news, sports or public service – that the network feeds to the local stations around the country.

Many people outside of the broadcasting industry may not really understand the relationship between the network and the affiliated station. Most don't fully realize which programs come from the network, which are produced by the local station, and which are syndicated programs that the station buys from independent, non-affiliated distributors. Furthermore, many people really don't care. They want their favorite programs aired wherever and however they are produced.

Yet the synergy of the system, developed over the past fifty years, has created a national, even international, framework that can bring unparalleled and unreachable entertainment programming, sporting events and the news from around the nation and the whole world to local communities *instantaneously*. The local station surrounds that national programming with its own originated shows, with its own flavor and its own commercials, sold by its own sales staff or a representatives' group, which represents the station to regional or national advertisers.

The latter factor – commercials, selling the advertising spots within programs, both network and local – is what fuels the engine to keep the networks and stations not only using better technology to produce better-quality programs, but keeps them prosperous and growing.

The fact is that, as predicted, the broadcasting industry, especially television, has become the greatest marketing tool for the selling of goods and services ever devised. According to the McCann Erickson Advertising Agency, in 1950, the radio industry had a total advertising billing, network, national spot and local, of approximately $610 million. In 1994, it was just shy of $10 billion. In 2000, the total radio advertising expenditures were over $19.8 billion.

In 1950, the fledgling television industry had gross billings of $170 million. In 1994, the over-the-air total commercial television industry (network and local) revenue was almost $29.5 billion. In 2000, total television advertising revenues were over $41 billion, with network advertising revenues representing over $20 billion.

If programming is the cargo that fills the train, and advertising is the fuel that drives the engine, then the affiliated stations are the rails and depots and stations that make distribution possible to homes all across America. And, strangely, many people within the industry don't really understand and appreciate the dynamics of the affiliated station's role and how useless the triangle would be without it.

One person who understood and respected the significance of the affiliate relationship was Leonard Goldenson, especially in the growth period of the ABC Television Network, the early fifties to the mid-eighties. Leonard not only knew the power of the stations, but he knew the station managers and group owners on a first-name basis. He studied the performance and signal power of every station on the network *and* stations that might be a potential to join the network.

I have mentioned on several occasions this disparity in the number and quality of affiliated stations between ABC and NBC and CBS. It was a personal nemesis throughout my career. In my new role I was determined to do something about it.

I assigned Dick Beesemyer, "Beese" as I often called him, to the role of VP of the new ABC-TV Affiliate Acquisitions Department. He and Bob Fountain, the newly appointed VP of the Affiliate Relations Department, became the point men to prowl the nation and make raids on our competitors' markets. This was not done as a whim. A strategy was very carefully thought out and charted. A game plan was devised over a five- and a ten-year period. We assessed the strengths and weaknesses of all affiliated and independent stations, the clearance record of each station, their position in their respective markets, management of the stations, and the strength of local programming, especially news.

The Affiliate Relations Department executives reporting to Fountain were especially helpful in giving Beese insights into the strengths and weaknesses of ABC affiliates and competitive stations in respective markets. The district managers responsible for servicing ABC affiliates were necessarily loyal to their stations and would not divulge confidential inside information. But they knew the television landscape and brought valuable insights to the table. During our station acquisition drive, Peter Zobel, Bob Hinkel, Dorothy Botts, Tim Kearney, Warren Denker, Buzz Mathesius, Tom Day and Joe Neidzwicki served as district managers. Dick Kozak was the general manager of the department under Beesemyer and, later, Fountain. Two veteran, professional affiliate relations executives, Joe Giaquinto, VP for strategic planning, and Mario Cuccinotta, VP for station operations, were also key to the success of the department.

Our affiliate acquisition team (later in the early eighties, Dick Savage joined us) and I would target the cities where we wanted to make a change and then pursue our mission, often under bizarre circumstances. Our trips to competitive stations would be on a confidential basis. Beese or Savage would meet with the NBC or CBS station managers and staff in strange places: on ski slopes, in the back room of restaurants, or as Beese once related, "This guy wanted to meet me under the downtown bridge so nobody would know I was in town."

One of the most productive meeting places with station personnel was at the Plaza Hotel in New York. In 1977, I made a trade deal with the hotel, which was one of the great arrangements of all time. In exchange for a handful of unsold advertising spots on *Good Morning, America* ($250,000 worth annually) the TV network received the fulltime use of a four-bedroom penthouse suite on the 58th Street side of the Plaza. The hotel shared the redecorating costs with us and the result was a showplace that turned our competition and other division managers at ABC green with envy.

We used the suite for a broad range of business purposes: advertiser receptions, visiting network personnel, Christmas parties, sales meetings, corporate receptions and meetings, and special events (closed-circuit screenings of championship fights, etc.). The suite actually saved the company substantial money since it was used to tape news and sports interviews and other programming that otherwise would have run up large studio costs. I was criticized by many who didn't have a clue about our network strategy because the suite was too "ostentatious."

What they didn't know was that we used the suite consistently for affiliate acquisition purposes. We would invite a station group owner and his wife or an important station manager and his wife or girlfriend for a weekend at the Plaza suite. During the course of their stay, which included some glittering New York entertainment, we would make our proposal on why the station should switch its affiliation to ABC. These "pitches" were very akin to the sales presentations that I learned in radio and TV sales. Interestingly, Beesemyer, Fountain and Savage had all worked in sales. The effort paid enormous dividends, as I will describe later.

But whether our meetings were in the Plaza suite or an airport coffee shop at midnight, whatever we did, we sought Leonard Goldenson's counsel. We reported our plans to Pierce and Rule, but we listened carefully to Leonard. Much to our amazement, he would know all the facts about the station we were seeking, point out its programming or signal weaknesses, and offer to help in any way he could, including traveling to the station city with us.

And Leonard shared our pride when we did convert a station to ABC. An example is when we enticed the Hubbard station, KSTP-TV, in Minneapolis-St. Paul to join us after some thirty years as a basic NBC affiliate. Leonard was so excited that he invited us to the corporation's Board of Directors meeting and eloquently praised us for our major contribution to the growth of the ABC Television Network.

Getting the Hubbard station to switch from NBC was a difficult but most gratifying experience. Bob Fountain had gotten to know Stanley S. Hubbard, the owner's son, quite well and had called on him on several occasions, laying the groundwork to get the station to switch. Stanley was becoming quite an important figure in his own right, as his father, Stanley E. Hubbard, the pioneer, grew older. I had seen Stan on a few occasions at industry meetings and suggested that we would like to talk seriously to him and his father. One day Fountain got a call from Stan, inviting us to visit the station. They were willing to talk.

When we walked into the elder Hubbard's office, he remained seated behind his desk and just stared at me. He was a pleasant-looking man, balding and rather stout, with sharp blue eyes. After we introduced ourselves, he cleared his throat and said, "I'm disappointed."

"Why are you disappointed, Mr. Hubbard?" I asked.

"I was expecting an older man," he mumbled.

I was a little taken aback and somewhat flattered, since I was fifty years old at the time.

"Well, I'm not exactly a spring chicken, despite my youthful figure," I laughed.

"And I don't like New York city slickers," he said without a smile.

I could see that the meeting was going to be difficult. Bob and I looked over at young Stanley and he just winked.

"Do you know where Moweaqua, Illinois is, Mr. Hubbard?" I asked.

"My weak what?" the old fellow said.

"Moweaqua. M-O-W-E-A-Q-U-A. It's a little town in central Illinois. That's where I grew up." I answered.

Hubbard smiled and said, "Sit down. We can talk."

We had learned that both of the Hubbards had grown increasingly disturbed with the NBC network performance, especially the ratings falloff in prime time and news. After a most pleasant and to-the-point meeting, Mr. Hubbard took us all to dinner, but first, he drove us out to the fairgrounds to see the KSTP radio and television booth at the county fair. He drove in an older-model car and as we pulled out of the station parking lot, he reached out the window and put a flashing blue light on the roof. As he drove, careening through the traffic, he kept up a continuous conversation, and kept looking over at me sitting in the front seat while he talked. I know Fountain and young Stan sitting in the back could see my shoulders tense up because I was positive we were going to crash into any number of cars as we snaked our way through the traffic. I immediately thought of my childhood days driving with Grandpa Adams.

Later that evening, we went back to the station and Mr. Hubbard, with great pride, showed us his new acoustically perfect television studio. He made us sit in some extendible bleachers at one end of the studio, and as he backed farther and farther away, he would cup his hand to his mouth and whisper, "Can you hear me now?"

When he got all the way out in the hallway and out of sight, we heard a very faint, "Can you hear me now?"

Fountain and I were ready to crack up. He was a marvelous old gentleman and a real pioneer and visionary in the broadcasting business. The elder Hubbard and his son and the entire Hubbard family were a class act and people with whom I wanted to do business.

The station had been the second affiliate to join NBC back in the fifties, so it was a difficult decision for them.

We shook hands warmly as we left. Young Stan smiled at us and said, "We'll give you a call."

The next week we got the good news. KSTP became a full-fledged ABC affiliate.

The latter years of the seventies were a bonanza for us in terms of affiliate switches and acquisitions, but it became much more difficult in the early eighties, when ABC's prime-time performance started to diminish. One of the last stations that we switched (from NBC) was KOMU-TV in Columbia, Missouri, owned by the University of Missouri. Dick Savage, at the time in charge of affiliate acquisitions, had been working on the station for some time since we had a weaker station in St. Joseph, Missouri and the area was dominated by KOMU's strong news operation coming out of the university's journalism school.

Savage and I made a couple of trips to Columbia and met with the station personnel, and were advised that our real obstacle was the new vice chancellor of administrative services for the university. We were told that she was a strong-willed German woman who was opposed to change and had asked for a meeting with us.

From the moment I heard her coming down the hall, I knew we were in for a hard time. The woman had a steel-edged air about her that entered the room before she did. She had a stern pageboy haircut and hard, piercing, blue eyes that intently scrutinized every line in your face. On this day she wore a long, sack-like, brown dress that came to the floor. I could swear she was wearing steel boots, hidden by the dress. I expected her to click her heals together when she entered the room. We immediately identified her as "the Iron Maiden."

We made our presentation on why KOMU-TV should be with ABC. The vice chancellor nodded, thanked us, and left the room. Two days later we received a call from Tom Gray, the station manager, advising us that the vice chancellor liked us and what we had to say. Much to my surprise, we had a deal.

Shortly after the contracts had been signed and we notified the St. Joseph station of the disaffiliation, Savage rushed into my office one morning and said, "Tom Gray is in a panic. The Iron Maiden has changed her mind. They're staying with NBC."

"They can't do that, Dick," I said with no little irritation. "We have a contract. We've already notified St. Joe. We're getting promotion announcements ready. Are they crazy?"

"Maybe," Savage answered. "But Tom Gray says she's adamant. He wants us to fly out right away."

The next morning we flew to Columbia and were met at the airport by the ashen-faced station manager.

"The vice chancellor is really serious," Tom nervously told us as we headed for the station. "Somebody told her that the ABC ratings are in a nose dive and NBC is on the way back. It's a mess. We had our local switchover promos ready to go. Jim, she's expecting a call from you this morning."

When the vice chancellor came on the phone, I could, once again, feel the steely aura precede her voice. I pulled together all the charm I could muster, and, in a quiet tone, outlined the problems that revoking our agreement would create, legally and otherwise. I told her that we had already notified our current affiliate of the switch and had made a public announcement of our new affiliation with the university and its extraordinary television station.

There was a long pause. Finally, in her thick German accent, she responded calmly but in a very firm voice. "Let me zee, if I hear you correctly, you are telling me, zat zis means you no longer have a televizion station in zis area if ve don't join you. Vell, Mr. Duffy, it zeems to me zat is your pwoblem. Good day." And she hung up.

It took two more phone calls and a Caesar salad at a local Columbia restaurant, but we got her to change her mind, and we got the affiliation.

In our drive to upgrade the network through affiliate acquisitions, we had some detractors inside of the company who didn't understand the long-range significance of what we were doing. But the fact is that the affiliate initiative in the seven-year period from 1975 to 1982 saw some 77 affiliate additions or changes to the ABC

Network bringing the network to equal status with the other two networks. For the first time, ABC was a dominant force with its upgraded lineup of over 200 stations.

Beesemyer has often reminded me that when he assumed the responsibility of affiliate acquisitions in 1975, ABC had a total of 152 primary affiliated stations. When he left in 1982, the total had grown to 202 primary affiliated stations. The major market switches from NBC or CBS where ABC already had an affiliated station are not reflected in those numbers.

The large city station switches from another network were unprecedented and startled the industry and really got a momentum going for us. Among those markets were Atlanta, San Diego, Charlotte, Indianapolis, Knoxville, Dayton and Jacksonville, as well as a host of mid-sized cities.

One of the most influential switches was Station WBRZ-TV, Channel 3 in Baton Rouge in 1977. Doug Manship and his sons owned the Baton Rouge newspaper as well as the radio and TV stations. The elder Manship had become a most influential senior member of the NBC network counseling board. The station's switch sent a message to all NBC affiliates that ABC might be the place to be.

The all-out affiliate acquisition drive started in 1975, but Beesemyer had made many calls and some switches prior to that time in his role as the head of affiliate relations. It was also clear to us that in order to build our lineup we would have to be a full-service network, meaning having a full slate of programming throughout the broadcast day. At that time ABC did not have early morning programming to compete with NBC's very popular *Today* show and that was an obvious weak spot in our conversations with key NBC stations.

Few people in the industry realized this, and fewer still have ever acknowledged it, but the birth of *Good Morning, America* came about because of the persistence of Beesemyer and me in our quest to upgrade our stations. We made several requests to management to consider a programming slot in the morning hours (7:00 to 9:00 AM, Eastern Time) where we could share commercial time with stations and compete with the dominating *Today* show. The economy was very shaky at that time and the network was doing badly in prime time under Starger and the new Entertainment Division. Management was very reluctant to make an expenditure that would take several years to realize a profit.

"We'll lose $8 million the first year," Fred Pierce, the strategist, said. "Leonard won't do that."

"Yeah, but in ten years you'll make tens of millions of dollars with longer and stronger station lineups," we countered. "And we need that morning show to get it done."

Finally, Pierce, who replaced Schwartz as president of the Television Division in 1974, led the way, and a new morning show entitled *AM America* was launched in 1975. The program got a very poor reception from both audiences and stations. It was replaced after nine months by *Good Morning, America* with David Hartman and a series of women as co-hosts, until Joan Lunden came along as a permanent fixture. *GMA*, of course, is now a broadcasting institution and has made many significant contributions to the country with insights and reports on issues that concern us all. It has earned millions of profit dollars for the company.

And it was a centerpiece for our affiliate raiding strategy.

I honestly believe that upgrading our station lineup was one of the key factors that brought the ABC Television Network to a position of undisputed leadership in later years. Leonard Goldenson has stated this on many occasions, but some in ABC management, especially when Capital Cities took over ABC, criticized us for having reputedly paid too much compensation to bring stations over from NBC or CBS.

It is a known fact that, in the mid-eighties, all three chairmen of the purchasing companies of the three major networks – Larry Tisch at CBS, Jack Welch at GE and NBC, and Tom Murphy at Capital Cities/ABC – were displeased with the amount of compensation paid to stations, running into the hundreds of millions. They each quickly tried to cut back on the compensation payments. They soon found that local stations have a very effective tool at their command – pre-emption of network programs. This is when the local station simply decides to air its own programming and its locally sold commercials instead of the network's program in a given time slot. Preemptions have caused the loss of millions of dollars for the networks and eventual cancellation of programs because of lack of clearance.

It is curious that some ten years after the new owners of the three major networks announced their immediate intentions to cut station compensation, they are each reportedly paying *twice as much* compensation for their affiliate station lineups – an overall increase of hundreds of millions of dollars for each of them.

The network/affiliate relationship is a delicate and sensitive balance that must have mutual benefits. The most important ones are financial, of course; but mutual trust and respect are also essential.

Incidentally, it gave me no sense of satisfaction to see Elton Rule's revised management structure fail miserably in its first couple of years. After the 1972 fall season, the prime-time schedule had a sharp decline as the programming area, with the blessings of the new Entertainment Division management, tried to broaden its audience and moved away from the young-adult-oriented programming that had been a principal factor in ABC's growing success.

The ratings for prime time in the 1973-74 season fell even more drastically and started to affect sales and the performance of the ABC-owned television stations and the company's profits. There was a period in 1974 when there was great anxiety in the management ranks and the possibility of changes that could affect the very top of the company, Goldenson excluded.

Variety had a headline concerning ABC that read, THE NEW SEASON RATING DISASTER IS SHAKING THE CORPORATE SYSTEM TO ITS NERVE ENDS.

It was then that Schwartz, a terrific broadcaster who had been put into an impossible position coming from radio to become the head of television, was transferred to another non-broadcasting division, and Fred Pierce, my former sales sidekick, was given responsibility for the Television Division. Starger came to the end of his contract on the entertainment side and was given a substantial buy-out deal from Rule to start a production company in Los Angeles.

Fred Pierce, always the strategist, convinced an unhappy Fred Silverman, the CBS programming wunderkind, to join ABC in May of 1975. The next three years, thanks to the programming touch of the two Freds, and to a strengthened affiliate lineup, were the most successful in ABC's history, bringing the network to an indisputable leadership position in the industry.

If there was emotion and stress from my perceived loss of power at work during the early and mid-seventies, it was infinitesimal compared to what my family and I endured during late 1973 and 1974. My father, Harold Francis, had been ill for some time with emphysema, having been a smoker most of his adult life. He was hospitalized on two separate occasions in the summer of 1973 when he couldn't breathe properly. Displaying his indomitable Irish spirit, both times he crawled out of his hospital bed, dressed himself, and walked home in the middle of the night.

Finally, Mom called me in early October and said he had wasted away to some ninety pounds. I flew out to Princeton, Illinois immediately, but by the time I arrived, he was dead. My dad was a rare individual, often misunderstood and belittled. He died as he had lived, fighting every inch of the way. My mother, who had had such problems with his drinking while he was alive, had mellowed in her later years, and was devastated when he died.

On December 22 of that same year, I received a telephone call in the late afternoon from the New York Police Department. They informed me that my daughter, Diane, then sixteen, had collapsed outside of Grand Central Station and had been taken along with Marcia to Bellevue Hospital. She and Marcia (then fifteen years old) were coming to visit us in Glen Ridge for Christmas and had taken the train from Cos Cob to New York. During the ride, Diane apparently had an asthma seizure and used her inhaler. When she walked out of the train station, holding hands with Marcia, she suddenly called out to her sister, and then her heart stopped. The police took her to Bellevue Hospital and she was pronounced dead on arrival. Julie, Terry and I jumped in the car and raced into Manhattan. At the hospital, we were told she was dead, and I was asked to identify the body. A Catholic priest gave her the last rites and steadied me as I looked at the body of my lifeless child. I cannot describe to you how I felt. It was so unreal. It was a tragedy of monumental proportions that shook me to my very foundations. There was no preparation for it, there was no reason for it – it was simply inexplicable. Every member of our family was utterly devastated.

With all of us in a state of numbness and absolute shock, the priest followed us out to the car and offered his blessings to Marcia, whom we had retrieved at the hospital. We somehow drove to my former home on Mimosa Drive in Cos Cob, and informed Betty. She, of course, was beside herself. We all just sat in stunned silence for the longest time. In the late afternoon, several neighbors came by and tried to console us.

After a few days, and a lovely, but very emotional, service for Diane at the First Congregational Church in Old Greenwich, Betty, Julie and I agreed that it might be easier for Marcia if she came to live with Julie, Terry and me in Glen Ridge. Jay was still living at the Cos Cob house with Betty, so she wouldn't be left alone. Marcia did come to live with us and thrived on her experiences in Glen Ridge. She met a host of new friends and did very well at Glen Ridge High School. Diane's death had to be a severe shock to her, but Marcia had always been in Diane's shadow and eventually her new sense of being brought out a new personality in her.

The final blow in that most unhappy period came in June of 1974 when my mother died suddenly from a heart attack at home in Princeton. Mom had always been independent and had taken care of Harold Francis in his later years. She had remained in good spirits after his death and had even traveled east with my sister, Marge, for Diane's funeral. But later, her friends told me, she seemed to miss Dad so much, that she didn't maintain that great humorous spirit and her heart gave out. I flew out to Princeton immediately. Marge and I arranged a special and beautiful service for our wonderful mother. I was really struck by the love and affection that Mom had earned from her neighbors, friends and members of various clubs, including the Princeton Women's Club where she had slid into home plate so gracefully.

I was weary and stunned from attending so many funerals. Through all of this period of grief, the people at ABC were extremely gracious to the family and me. Beautiful baskets of flowers were sent to all of the services and Elton Rule called me each time and offered his personal condolences. After my mother passed way, he called me in Princeton and said. "You have really had it, Jim. My heart goes out to you. Thank God you are strong."

We were strong. All of us. We pulled ourselves up by our bootstraps and walked forward. Life does go on.

Fifteen

Roots and New Program Forms

A cyclone of unprecedented proportions swept across the American landscape in the last week of January 1977. It was not an atmospheric storm but a blitz across the nation's television screens that heretofore had never been experienced. Tens of millions of television viewers sat transfixed for eight solid nights from January 23 to January 30 watching the most monumental event in the annals of television programming. They were witnessing television history.

The program was Alex Haley's *Roots*. The opening scenes on the first night showed a lithe, strong, young African warrior, Kunta Kinte, frantically racing through the jungles and villages of his native land, pursued by rough-looking American white slave traders. Eventually, the young warrior is captured and bound in chains and brutally thrown into the hold of a schooner – a slave ship – along with hundreds of other African men and women. Half starved and under hideous circumstances, they were being taken to America to be sold into slavery, commodities in a growing industry. Thus began the saga of an African American who traced his family's heritage from their beginnings in Africa to the present day.

As I watched the program in my own family room, I was deeply concerned about the reactions it might bring from the American viewing audience. Some months before, after production was underway, I had seen some of the early footage, including one of the most riveting scenes, when a slave master brutally whipped the defiant Kunta Kinte because he had supposedly been disobedient. As I sat in the screening room, I cringed at the lash of the whip and wanted to turn away at the sight of the bleeding welts which appeared across the warrior's shoulders as other slaves stood by in fear and bewilderment.

I thought to myself, "I don't know if a general viewing audience is ready for this." I learned later in the scheduling meetings that others at ABC shared that view. But the more I watched the superbly produced program, the more enthralled I became with the story and the people. So did most of America.

Roots, unexpectedly and almost inexplicably, captured the imagination of an entire nation and became a television phenomenon. It scored the highest ratings in TV history for an entertainment program, but also became a landmark for the medium in popularizing its form and subject matter. The 12-hour miniseries was a shared experience for the nation that brought unprecedented reactions from the American viewing public. During those historic eight days, bowling alleys were closed, church services changed, restaurants were empty, civic meetings were canceled and motion picture theaters lost considerable attendance as millions stayed home to view a saga that few white Americans could watch without feeling some sense of compassion and even guilt.

The impact was so profound that 250 colleges and universities proposed courses based on the series and the book. Some thirty mayors in cities around the country proclaimed the last week in January 1977, *Roots* Week. The scripts and films from *Roots* were used in hundreds of elementary and secondary schools as study materials. Later, when *Roots, The Next Generation* was presented, over twenty million students were involved in the program through classroom assignments. These two shows were the foundation of the education/television connection that years later became part of my work with Project Literacy US and other educational initiatives.

Approximately 143 million – or 85% of all television homes – watched all or part of the twelve hours of *Roots*. According to Nielsen, an estimated eighty million viewers watched the final episode. The eight episodes of *Roots* averaged a phenomenal 44.9 rating and a 66 share of audience over the eight days, far surpassing any previous program or series of programs. The final telecast had an unheard-of 51.1 rating (meaning over 50% of all American homes were tuned in) and a 71 share of audience (over 70% of all homes tuned to television), making it the all-time leader with over 36 million homes for that final night.

The program was so successful that an industry wag suggested that NBC was going to take *Seventh Avenue*, a series it was airing about New York's garment district, and rename it *Suits*. He also joked that one of the networks was considering a series about an Irish family and would title it *Spuds*.

But, unusual as the audience numbers and reactions were, a drama of equal proportions was played behind the scenes for many months before the show was telecast. The entire process of purchasing, producing, writing and finally telecasting this *Novel for Television* was an enormous risk for ABC. It was bought by the network as an idea, before Alex Haley had written a word, two years before the book's publication. It was inordinately expensive for its day, eventually reaching $8 million to produce. No one knew, or wanted to guess, what the novel and program's eventual acceptance and popularity might be. As I have described, the subject matter was extremely controversial, dealing with the sensitive racial issue of a Black family tracing its roots back through slavery to Africa. The featured players were predominantly African American, most of the villains were white, and it was to be presented to the entire nation, including, of course, the Deep South, where sensitivities about the War Between the States still smoldered. And there were some disturbing questions concerning how it would play in regard to the basics of our network system. How would advertisers react to *Roots*? Would the controversial subject matter drive sponsors away and prices down? Would the affiliates even air the show, especially in the South?

Because I was responsible for advertising sales and the affiliate relations for the network, I personally had major concerns. We had heard so much about the program as it was being developed that I feared backlash might develop. Press stories had gone so far as to suggest that the program could spark riots in parts of the country.

When the press announcement was made that we were going to telecast the program in January, threats were made to a few Southern affiliates. Our station in Little Rock, Arkansas, received threatening telephone calls with a message that said in essence, "If you carry that program, we will blow up your transmitter." For several nights, the station had special police and snipers protecting their property. There was obvious anxiety among many station managers.

Several major advertisers expressed their concern. One in particular said to me, "I question your wisdom in showing this program on the network. You're touching a very sensitive nerve in our country."

It wasn't an unexpected opinion, and I was quite prepared to hear him out.

"Less than a decade ago we had race riots. The show can stir up all of these emotions again," he continued. "On the commercial side, you would like me to sponsor part of this program, yet over 80% of the people who buy my products are white. Does that make sense to you?"

I could have said to him, "Well good, that means you'll be introducing your products to a lot of new potential buyers." But I didn't. Instead I said, "Whether you sponsor the show or not has to be your call. But I would urge you to see some tapes of the program before you make harsh judgments about how it will affect race relations in this country. *Roots* is written very sensitively and is beautifully produced. Because of its impact, it will perhaps help heal some of the wounds that have divided this country. And it may be important and serious enough that a company like yours will be remiss in not being associated with it." He just shook his head.

Because of the concerns from many different quarters, including from corporate management and the Board of Directors, the scheduling of *Roots* became part of the dilemma. Would it be most productive for the network if it were played in hour-long segments stretched out over a number of weeks, much like other miniseries (such as *Rich Man, Poor Man*) that had preceded *Roots*? Or, because of its intense subject matter, would it play better over consecutive nights?

The answer was fairly simple. Silverman (who came to ABC after the show was purchased), Pierce and most of the programmers, in truth, didn't have confidence in the audience appeal of the show. They felt it could well turn a lot of viewers off, and if it were played over a series of weeks, could badly damage the prime-time schedule in which ABC held a dominant position at that time. And they did not want to risk playing a major part of the program in the important February "sweeps" period where, for a four-week period, the ratings of local stations established their local and national spot sales rates for the following months. Further, it was determined that the program was "safest" at the end of the evening since, if it did "bomb," it wouldn't affect the regular series comedy and dramatic shows that would otherwise follow it. If affiliate station managers had been present in those scheduling meetings, they would have been furious with that logic since playing it at the end of the evening meant if it "bombed," it could severely damage the audience for their local news programs that followed.

"We'll schedule it at the end of January, just before the sweeps," said Silverman. "We'll divide it in one-hour and two-hour segments and play it at the end of each evening over the eight nights."

If I recall those scheduling meetings correctly, nobody, including all of the programming and research executives, disputed that decision. These same people were absolutely astounded at the program's success.

To my mind, the greatest contribution *Roots* made was that it brought the entire industry to a new level. It exemplified how this often-criticized, far-reaching medium could be a catalyst and a unifying force for the country, even through an entertainment program.

Roots was the high point in the mid- and late seventies when ABC, with its lengthened and strengthened station lineup, finally moved into a position of parity with NBC and CBS. Along with that equity, improved programming finally resulted in a sudden burst into a position of leadership for ABC. Many of the program concepts developed by Starger, Eisner and Diller, like *Happy Days, Laverne & Shirley, Starsky & Hutch, Baretta, Barney Miller and Charlie's Angels,* came into full bloom during Silverman's tenure. Silverman and his team came up with some hits of their own during the mid-seventies such as *The Six Million Dollar Man, The Bionic Woman, Captain & Tenille, Three's Company, Soap, Eight Is Enough, Family,* and *The Love Boat.* It was a splendid run for the once-third network.

With the heightened competition from ABC – long the industry doormat – the network television industry was forced to work harder, and to innovate by producing different and higher-quality programs. In essence, ABC's sudden and unexpected rise to leadership brought to the whole industry a greater sense of responsibility to the viewing public and a most welcomed and growing maturity.

New and dynamic programming forms were created that were distinctly television's own, not to be replicated by other entertainment media. One of the new forms was a concept called *Novels for Television*, adaptations of fiction books for the TV screen. These programs represented a dangerous gamble. Production costs were very high, with filming generally taking place in several different locations. Telecasting time of the programs could range anywhere from four to eighteen hours. Still, the philosophy was, What better place to graphically tell the story of great novels than through the sight, sound, and color of television in the personalized setting of people's homes?

Many in the industry, including several critics, were highly skeptical of the idea of a program stretched over several nights.

"The public will never sit still for it," one renowned critic wailed. "People have too much to do. They'll have to skip some episodes and they're not going to remember one night to the next what the story line is." This skeptic forgot the age-old concept of the daytime serials, where a brief synopsis at the top of the show brings the viewer up to speed on the program's story to that point.

It was acknowledged, however, that the stakes were very high, and it was with courage that ABC's Entertainment Division, with Goldenson's support, moved full steam ahead and purchased several novels to be considered as miniseries, one of which was *Roots*.

ABC's first *Novel for Television* was *QB VII* based on the book by Leon Uris.

QB VII is a powerful story and deals with a difficult subject, especially for television – the Holocaust – including castration. This program was followed by Irwin Shaw's novel *Rich Man, Poor Man* in 1976, featuring Nick Nolte, Peter Strauss and Ed Asner, which was immensely popular.

In addition to these and *Roots*, and *Roots, The Next Generation*, ABC presented several other *Novels for Television*, including *Washington Behind Closed Doors*, *The Thorn Birds*, *Masada*, *North and South*, *Love and War*, *Hollywood Wives*, *The Kennedys of Massachusetts* and the monumental Herman Wouk novels *Winds of War* and *War and Remembrance*.

Later in the eighties, CBS and NBC carried miniseries of their own with some success, but it was the presentations by the ABC programmers, especially Brandon Stoddard, who later became president of ABC Entertainment, that brought the real plaudits. Stoddard was responsible for the acclaimed and widely discussed *The Day After*, starring Jason Robards, Jr.

Strangely enough, despite the enormous popularity and success of most of these *Novels for Television*, few of the programmers really believed in them or felt that the astounding response to them was genuine. With some exceptions, most programmers – Silverman included – seemed to feel that they were aberrations from the mainline programming avenues. They kept waiting for the next one in line to fail.

Shortly after the success of *Roots* and long before the John Jakes' Civil War story *North and South* was purchased and telecast, I had a conversation with one of the program executives about the possibility of a miniseries built around Michael Ansara's book *The Killer Angels* and the story of the battle of Gettysburg.

"Period pieces just don't work," he said. "History just doesn't seem to appeal to viewers."

"What the hell do you think *Roots* is?" I asked. "People are extremely interested in their heritage and the history of this country. There is no greater drama than in the people and events that have shaped the world and helped make us what we are. You guys think if a picture doesn't have a car chase and four bimbos in bikinis nobody will watch it."

The programmer just grunted and went back to his script of a new movie made for TV called *Little Ladies of the Night*, a hard-hitting insight on pimps and prostitutes in Los Angeles.

The philosophy that high-quality programming, period pieces or otherwise, can't deliver a large enough audience on a sustained basis to satisfy management and the financial demands of the system is still prevalent at all the networks. Take a look at the Fox network prime-time schedule as it jiggles and giggles and sensationalizes to get the attention of the younger audience. And watch the programming on the two new networks, United Paramount Network (UPN) and the

Warner Brothers Television Network (WB) that debuted in January of 1995. The idea that there has to be shoot-outs and car chases and lots of "tits and ass" for a show to be successful is still prominent.

Along with the *Novels for Television*, in the mid-seventies ABC also presented some outstanding special dramatic programs, some under the title of *ABC Theater*, that won high acclaim and respectable audience ratings. My good friend Ed Vane, a senior vice president in programming and a very creative and classy guy, was responsible for many of them. Among the offerings were *Eleanor and Franklin*, a five-part series on the relationship of Eleanor and Franklin D. Roosevelt through various stages of their lives; *The Glass Menagerie*, the TV adaptation of Tennessee Williams' play starring Katharine Hepburn in one of her rare appearances in the medium; *Long Day's Journey into Night*, a brilliant adaptation of the Eugene O'Neill classic; and *Love Among the Ruins* with Sir Laurence Olivier. Along with ABC's regular prime-time series programming, both drama and comedy, these programs brought the network to new heights in critical and popular acclaim.

It was a high time for ABC Television. By the year 1978, the network was the leader in most programming areas, and it was considered almost a miracle that ABC had such a commanding lead in prime time after the precipitous fall-off in the 1973-74 and 1974-75 seasons after Rule's restructuring of the Entertainment Division. Fred Silverman's transfer to ABC from CBS had a great deal to do with the success from a programming standpoint. Silverman and Fred Pierce seemed to click from the first day, Pierce as the strategist in planning and scheduling and Silverman, the "wunderkind," as the show tinkerer and fixer.

To my mind, Silverman was not a great creator. He was truly a child of television having grown up with the medium. He would sit and watch his shows hour after hour. He would take tapes with him to the affiliate and board of governors meetings and he would stay in his room and watch them over and over. And, finally, he would make a declaration that Fonzie should be featured more on *Happy Days*, or *Laverne and Shirley* should be less giddy and more compassionate and on and on. The changes were made and they worked every time. It was astounding.

Pierce's experience in research and sales made him a master strategist. He could smell what show belonged where on the schedule. He was an average programmer, but Silverman was there to fill that side of the equation and together they made an exceptional team. I'm not sure how much they liked one another, but I know they had great admiration for their respective talents.

After the extraordinary success of *Roots* and the 1976-77 schedule, Goldenson and Rule threw a celebration party at the 21 Club. After dinner, Elton made a toast and said, "Congratulations to every single one of us at ABC. This is probably the highlight of our careers. We will probably never see a triumph like this again."

Many of us were too filled with glory to believe that. But he was right. From a programming point at least, no other single network has reached those heights or probably ever will.

All of this worked very well for me as the president of the television network, since it put me quite naturally in the role of spokesman for all of the network's activities. I received invitations from advertising associations and individual ad clubs, state broadcasting associations, citizens' groups, and even individual stations, in conjunction with their local promotion activities, asking me to speak and appear on local radio and television shows to talk about the progress of the network and the issues of the day.

Often my dialogue with viewers could get very amusing because, try as I might, I could not convince some viewers that as president of the network, I had not actually produced *Roots* or some other program where the viewer had high praise or a critical point of view. The more I would patiently try to explain who the producer was and the network's rationale on a particular program, the more heated the viewer would become on my bad taste, or my poor judgment, or on the good side, "my utter genius." I would be cursed for the more controversial programs like *Little Ladies of the Night*, and praised for the triumphs, like the coverage of the Olympic Games.

I remember one trip in particular when I traveled to my birthplace of Decatur, Illinois, to give the keynote address for the kickoff of the local United Way Campaign on behalf of our affiliate, WAND-TV, Channel 17. It was in the late summer of 1976 and we had announced that a new situation comedy called *Soap* would be on the fall schedule. The program, written and produced by Susan Harris, was absolutely hilarious, somewhat off-color, and featured Billy Crystal as an out-of-the-closet homosexual. Television had not portrayed gay characters in such an outlandish manner, and it brought loud protests from many quarters even before anyone had seen the program.

A few days before my trip to Decatur, Barry Geghegan, the general manager of the station, called me and warned me about a meeting that was likely to take place.

"You better be prepared when you arrive," Barry said. "Some of the church groups got wind of the fact that you'll be here. They are really up in arms about *Soap*. They insist on having a meeting with you. What do you want to do?"

"I'll meet with them, Barry," I answered. "That's my home country. I understand those people."

After Geghegan met me at the airport, and we drove to the station, I was astonished to find the lobby filled with chattering white-haired (with a blueish tint), elderly women waiting to see me.

Barry invited them all (there must have been thirty-five) into the conference room. I sat at the end of the table and the women sat and stood in every available space in the room. As I smiled and looked around the room, I could not help but think that every single one of those women looked like my Grandmother Adams, especially when she was angry and searching for a hickory switch.

The spokesperson for the group wasted little time with introductions. She ripped into the network for putting that kind of "lascivious smut into the living rooms of God-fearing Christian homes." After a few more women had chirped in and had their say, I explained to them that the press had overplayed the contents of the show without even seeing the pilot. I told them that I shared some of their concerns (which I did) and that we were still in conversations with the editors about further changes in some of the story lines. I asked them to please hold their criticisms until they had at least seen the program.

They seemed to be somewhat mollified, but just before they left, one of the women said, "We are very disappointed that a fine man like you, a native son of Moweaqua, would be mixed up in this kind of trash."

I swear at the United Way banquet that evening, I saw two or three of those ladies sternly shaking their fingers at me.

My direct contact with the viewing public was difficult at times, but it was also great experience because it gave me a first-hand insight on the man (or woman) on the street's perspective about the medium and its program offerings. I brought the messages from my meetings and appearances back to the network and discussed them thoroughly with management and in the programming sessions. I became a strong voice from the affiliate world and from the general viewing public. I was an ombudsman of sorts, and while it didn't make me especially popular in the management meetings, I think it served the company well.

It was important to me in my speeches and appearances that I not excuse the network or the industry for its excesses in violence or permissiveness in programming. If I thought our network or another network had gone beyond the line on a respective program, I would say so, but still defend the medium in its ability to inform and entertain. Because I had built a strong constituency through my relationships with the affiliates and through my years of experience, nobody in management really questioned my judgment in responding to criticism. A couple of times Fred Pierce called me in when I had been particularly critical of obvious salacious remarks or situations in a particular program.

"Hey, Jim, we all have to talk with one voice," he said.

"Hey, Fred, let's all be governed by the same goals, and we'll be one voice," I answered.

The trips and speeches also gave me a chance to reach for higher ground and encourage a sense of responsibility within the industry. The following short excerpt from one of my speeches at an ABC affiliate annual convention is fairly representative of the message I was attempting to get across to others within our industry:

It falls to us at this time to take the lead in defending certain basic American values — freedom of expression, artistic and creative freedom, freedom of choice, individual responsibility for behavior — those values that the would-be censors of television are attacking. This is a challenge that we must meet head on.

We have another responsibility – to give something back to this medium, to further enrich it for the benefit of the public. It has served our own interests well, just as we believe it has served the American public well. We are long past the 'give me' and well into the 'give something back' stage. This calls for renewed dedication to public service in the largest sense of that term, well beyond public service announcements, to enhanced service and quality in everything we do.

It was a combined message: on one hand, I felt that we in the industry had to be constantly vigilant to ensure that we were maintaining our responsibility to the public; on the other, I felt we also had to defend ourselves from unwarranted attacks stemming from prejudice or other questionable motives.

I spent a great deal of time traveling and came to really appreciate the power of a close relationship between the network and its affiliated stations. KATV, Channel 7 in Little Rock, Arkansas, was a good example. In 1976, Bob Doubleday, the president and general manager of KATV, invited me to speak before the Little Rock Chamber of Commerce and be a guest speaker at the station's fall promotion gala for advertisers. Our Little Rock station had always been among the leaders in its market and had benefited greatly from the network's success, as had most of our affiliates around the country.

Riding on the crest of the network's preeminence, the local affiliates were able to gain in popularity within their own markets. The more success the local station enjoyed, the higher its ratings with a consequent increase in the value of its advertising time. This in turn increased revenues and made it possible for the station to buy and produce better programs. And it all spiraled upwards.

KATV, along with our affiliate in Tulsa, Oklahoma, KTUL-TV, was owned by Jimmy Leake, a marvelous gentleman from Muskogee, Oklahoma, who also happened to be one of the country's foremost antique car collectors.

When I arrived at the Little Rock airport, I was met by a limousine driver in full uniform and escorted to a beautiful antique touring Queen Anne limousine that had once been the official

Buckingham Palace automobile for the Queen of England. With the official royalty flags fluttering from the two front fenders, Jimmy Leake, Doubleday and I sat in the back on the high cushioned velvet seats and toured the city with the townsfolk waving and honking as we drove around Arkansas' capital city.

Doubleday hosted a reception for me at the Little Rock Country Club, where I met the governor, the mayor and most of the town's civic leaders, including Frank Broyles, the University of Arkansas' Director of Athletics. Broyles invited me to join him in the famous Razorback "Soooowie, Pig" yell which brought down the house. It was quite clear from the number of prominent Little Rock citizens present that broadcasting was considered an important part of the community.

Doubleday also held a late-afternoon reception and dinner at a resort hotel in nearby Hot Springs for advertisers and their agencies. The entire affair was a massive celebration of the network's stellar performance and the equal success of the local station. Clips from network programs that would be in the 1976-77 prime-time schedule were shown as well as a snappy presentation on the Channel 7 shows. When Doubleday introduced me, representing the network, he praised me so lavishly that I received a standing ovation before I had even spoken a word. I felt like Bob Hope must when he is introduced. People just automatically start to laugh before he has said anything at all.

On the way back to the airport riding in our elegant Queen Anne limousine after a fun-filled two days, I said to Doubleday, "My God, man, you treat me like the President of the United States."

"Pard (Arkansas talk for partner), you have no idea how the success of the network reflects on us," Doubleday answered. "It really is, in my eyes, a two-way street. The stronger the network is, the better we can perform and serve our community."

This was a far cry from conversations he and I had had as little as five years before when he would tease, but not entirely in jest, about how "the high-powered network folks from the big city didn't care about what happened with us farm boys at the local station."

But now that had all changed. We were a team, and he could see that we did care a great deal about the affiliates and their importance to the network. Doubleday was not alone in his sentiments. I ran into similar feelings with most of our affiliates. These scenes would come back to me later in the mid-eighties when, under totally new management, the entire network television industry was mistakenly trying to economize at the expense of one of the most critical elements of the business: the affiliates.

If the mid-to-late-seventies was a time for celebration in Little Rock and other ABC cities around the nation, it was most certainly a time of joy back at the ABC headquarters in New York. The year 1978 marked the modern-day ABC's 25th anniversary. The company's progress in those twenty-five short years from the shallow, shaky days in the riding arena back in 1953, had captured the attention and the admiration of the entire broadcasting industry, many leaders in the nation's capital and even the general viewing public. It was, indeed, a time for celebration.

In honor of those twenty-five years, the company planned a glittering gala *Silver Anniversary Celebration* TV program to be aired on Sunday, February 5th, 1978 between 7:00 and 11:00 PM, Eastern Time. It was produced by Dick Clark and Dick Clark Productions and was styled to be a "Tribute to the vitality of ABC through a fond and fun-filled look at its past, starring the personalities who were...are...and always will be...part of the very special family of ABC."

The program was taped on January 8, 1978, at the ABC Television Center in Los Angeles, one month before the actual on-air telecast. A gala reception preceded the taping. It seemed that every star of every show that had ever been on the network appeared in formal dress for that celebration. I was driven from the Century Plaza Hotel to the studio, and as I stepped out of the limousine with searchlights scanning the sky and music blaring, the flash bulbs practically blinded me. Television cameras and photographers were everywhere. They would shoot at anything or anybody that stepped out of a limousine, hoping to catch a prominent star. More than once, I have been photographed at that kind of gala, only to have the photographer mutter, "Ah, he ain't nobody," in true Hollywood paparazzi style.

A large studio adjacent to the one in which the taping was to be done was used as the reception area. It was suitably decorated with banners, ribbons and huge posters and pictures of past and present stars and programs. A giant anniversary cake sat high up on a large round table in the center of the room surrounded by ice sculptures of the ABC logo. At floor level around the edge of the enormous circle was food and hors d'oeuvres of every variety. Bars were at each corner of the room.

Vincent Price, who had a fine sense of humor, came over to me and said, "That's a huge mound you've got in the middle of the room. What do you suppose is buried under there?"

"All of our failed television shows," I answered. He laughed and went over to tell other performers that their canceled programs were buried in the middle of the room under the anniversary cake.

Along with so many of the past series stars like Chuck Connors, Barbara Eden, Vince Edwards, Fred MacMurray, Robert Stack, Robert Young, Harriet, Ricky and David Nelson, Cheryl Ladd, John Forsythe, Suzanne Sommers, John Travolta, and Billy Dee Williams, there were many performers who appeared in special programs. Barry Manilow, Cliff Robertson, Patti Page, Leslie Uggams, Ben Vereen, Rudy Valley and the "Duke" himself, John Wayne, were all there.

It was a thrill to meet the All-American westerner in the flesh. "Howdy, pilgrim," Wayne said as he ambled over with that unforgettable gait, "Pleased ta meet cha." He had been featured on a special about western programs and seemed very pleased to be in attendance. He had a great time towering over most of the guests. "This is some kind of a party," he said and then laughed: "You throw these every night?"

All the assembled were in such high spirits that the taping proceeded for the full four hours with barely a hitch. At the end of the show, all the performers and members of the audience were invited up on the stage for the finale. Long after the cameras were off, the crowd remained on stage, stars and executives and stagehands alike, dancing and singing the ABC promotion theme song, *"We're still the one and we're still having fun."* I remember one of the female stars whispering to me, "This really is a family affair." And she was right. It was something of a Golden Age for the ABC family.

I still have the large group picture that was taken on the stage and look at it from time to time with mixed feelings of fondness and personal sadness. On the personal side, that photo, which includes my wife, Julie, and myself, was one of the last in which we would appear together. After some very happy years in Glen Ridge, Julie, for some reason wanted to move to Connecticut where she stated she thought I would be happier. She found a magnificent California ranch home deep in the woods on Delafield Island Road in stylish Darien, Connecticut. We moved in the summer of 1975. Despite some great times with all of our kids, our marriage continued to flounder, mainly because of Julie's drinking. A few months after the anniversary gala, we agreed to separate. Julie moved to New York and eventually to her home state of Florida. We were divorced in 1979 and Corinne, who was then nine years old, stayed with me to be raised in our home in Darien.

Another reason that picture is so significant concerns events that were soon to follow which would shake up ABC and the whole industry. Fred Silverman, then president of the Entertainment Division and a major contributing factor in ABC's success at the time, is kneeling in the front row alongside Goldenson and Rule. All three of the executives are smiling blissfully, seemingly in total harmony. But things were not as they appeared. Goldenson and Rule might have worn an entirely different expression had they known what was to come. Remember the picture was taken some weeks before the actual February 5 telecast celebrating ABC's 25th Anniversary.

Silverman's contract was coming up for renewal in June of 1978, and apparently just before the 1977 Christmas holidays, he had assured Pierce and Goldenson that he wanted to stay at ABC. On many occasions he reportedly had told Pierce, Rule and Goldenson that if he ever did leave ABC, he would not leave to go to another network. (Silverman apparently denies this. He claims he said he would never leave to be a programmer at another network.)

After the holidays and the Silver Anniversary taping, on Thursday morning, January 19, I received a call from Pierce asking me to meet him in his office. When I arrived, Mark Cohen, a senior vice president for the Broadcast Division and a long-time Pierce confidant, was there along with Tony Thomopoulos, another long-time Pierce pal and then special assistant. Pierce's face was ashen. He was so angry he was almost shaking.

"Silverman is leaving," he said bitterly. "The son of a bitch is leaving and he lied to me."

I frankly wasn't that surprised. There had been rumors for some time that the programming genius was restless. Skeptics had it that he was jealous of Roone Arledge's prominence at ABC and in the industry and was even envious of Pierce's power as president of all of broadcasting. Silverman had hinted about the possibility of taking over ABC news or forming his own production company or even going into politics.

"Where is he going?" I asked.

Pierce, the great stone face, stared hard at me. His jawbones tightened. He finally said, "He's going to NBC. The prick is going to run NBC, not just the Television Division, but all of it, the whole works – radio, news, sports, the station divisions. He went back on his word to all of us."

That news did surprise me. In my opinion, Silverman was not qualified to run the entire company. Fred was a magnificent series programmer. As I stated earlier, he was a child of the television medium. He understood the needs of the mass television audience. He was a master at adjusting situations to make a program funnier or more appealing. And he was a superb promoter. But, as history would bear out, I knew he was not a well-rounded broadcasting executive.

Corporate management at RCA, the owner of NBC, made a classic error in selecting a prominent program executive to run their entire operation. Fred Silverman had earned an extraordinary reputation as a programmer during his days at CBS and ABC. The non-broadcast management at RCA must have determined if he could do that in programming, he could do it in all the rest of the operation. It was the same kind of logic that Elton Rule used, but for different reasons, in bringing Wally Schwartz from radio to run the Television Division without a day's experience in TV. Broadcasting is not a simplistic business. It is a very complicated and intricate industry that deals basically with people – listeners and viewers and their actions and reactions – not products. And experience in many phases of the industry and especially in understanding and dealing with people of many different cultures and beliefs, is an essential part of a skilled, versatile broadcasting executive. Corporate leaders who are responsible for multi-billion-dollar companies simply can't make, or should not be allowed to make, those rather obvious bad judgments of appointing people with narrow experience to head key divisions.

As I watched Pierce struggling with what he had just painfully told us, I could not help but feel sorry for him. He had been responsible for bringing Silverman to ABC in 1975 by promising him full authority on the program front. The fact is that despite his substantial success at CBS, the Tiffany mind set of the people at Black Rock reportedly never fully accepted Silverman, a rumpled and rotund Jewish boy, into their inner circle. Pierce appealed to Silverman's pride in inviting him to join the ABC Family where he would be warmly welcomed. Besides, Pierce offered him a contract for $300 thousand a year, plus homes on both coasts, a chauffeured limousine and a million-dollar insurance policy.

The two Freds worked extremely well together for two and a half years. Now, with Silverman leaving, some of the silver was gone from ABC's 25th Anniversary celebration.

"Elton is in with Leonard now," Pierce said. "They don't know." He grimaced. "I have to get Elton out of there and tell him. Then we'll tell Goldenson. Leonard will be furious."

Goldenson was furious. Just a few days before, he had assured his friends and associates that Silverman would be with ABC for some time. After they got the news, Goldenson and Rule went back with Pierce to his office. They called Silverman to join them. It was a short and unpleasant meeting. Goldenson told Silverman that he would have to fulfill the terms of his contract before going to NBC. Goldenson immediately spread the word among his Board of Directors and through the press that in the post-Silverman era, the ABC Television Network would be as strong as ever. He lavished praise on the team of young programmers that had been developed and especially on Fred Pierce, who had worked so closely with Silverman to bring ABC to its position of leadership. Early in February, Pierce appointed Tony Thomopoulos to replace Silverman as president of the Entertainment Division and ordered all troops full speed ahead on all fronts. Privately, Goldenson was concerned with the appointment of Thomopoulos and he questioned the network's ability to prosper after the loss of Silverman.

The next few years proved that Leonard's concerns were justified. After riding on the Silverman/Pierce schedule for about a year and a half, ABC prime time fell off badly. To those of us on the inside, it became reminiscent of the pre-parity days when ABC-TV was the joke of the industry. If there was any satisfaction, it was in the fact that NBC fared even worse. Silverman's tenure as the president of NBC was a disaster that eventually almost undermined the entire foundation of that company's broadcasting divisions. CBS profited from the failure of both networks and eventually became the leader, once again, in prime-time programming. Silverman was dismissed by RCA in mid-1981. Grant Tinker became the president of NBC, and immediately started to rebuild the network in the very cyclical television industry.

Sixteen

Partnering with Local TV Stations

Affiliate station managers and owners really looked forward to the annual affiliate meetings. It was a meeting of the clan, and the one time in the year when the network and company executives mixed with the affiliates in formal and informal sessions to show our programs and discuss plans for the coming year. It was also an opportunity for the station people to visit the sets of daytime or prime-time programs in production. The stars and producers would come to the receptions or final banquet to shake hands with the people who made it possible for their shows to be seen in towns and cities, large and small, across America.

And the stars came out in galaxies, rolling up in their limousines to the circular driveway at the Los Angeles Century Plaza Hotel. Banks of photographers, reporters and screaming fans would greet them as they stepped out for a lavish evening (dreaded by many of these stars) that became an annual ritual for those performers whose shows were on the schedule or would be debuting the following fall. John Forsythe, Linda Evans, David Janssen, Robert Young, Jacqlyn Smith, Farrah Fawcett, Lee Majors, Vince Edwards, Ryan O'Neal, Shirley Jones, Robin Williams, Billy Crystal, Carol Burnett, Darryl Hannah, Tom Hanks, Leslie Nielson, James Arness and hundreds more all attended the annual affiliate meetings at one time or another.

Headline talent from the TV shows often performed as part of the final banquet's entertainment, where some two thousand affiliates and friends packed the Century Plaza Ballroom to be entertained and became immersed in the spirit of ABC.

The most outlandish performance was probably that of Robin Williams, the zany, sharp-witted and most unpredictable star of *Mork and Mindy*. In 1976, Robin was well known even then for his very funny but often off-color monologues. He had been warned before the show that this distinguished crowd was important to our business. Many of the affiliates were from the Bible belt and would be offended by "blue" material.

Robin just grinned and said in his false Russian accent. "Don't vorry none, boyz. I handle it real goot."

During his opening monologue, Williams handled it "real goot." In his Russian peasant garb and after a few wild and funny jokes about the affiliates in attendance, he went into his Russian dialect and said, "I understand there are some nayze ladies from Iowa sitting in the first row of tables. Could you move back a leetle because I have to take a pee pee." And he unzipped his fly as he moved toward the front of the stage.

"Whadda a thrill," he screamed as he reached in his pants. There was a collective gasp as the "nayze" little old ladies from Iowa ducked for cover.

He never did expose himself, but I was convinced, as was most of the audience, that he would. And somehow, after a brief silence, it got an enormous laugh and then Robin went on with the rest of a hilarious performance.

I met Robin in the lobby of the hotel after the banquet and told him I was about to strangle him. He had scared me to death.

He immediately dropped to his knees in front of a gathering crowd, started to shine my shoes with his cap and said, "Forgive me, King of Kings," and proceeded to go through an encore zany performance in the hotel lobby that had all of us aching with laughter.

Seeing the stars gathering at those annual affiliate meetings reminded me of the days when television was still a child and the Hollywood movie industry absolutely refused to have anything to do with the world of television. Now TV develops many personalities who go on to successful motion picture careers. Robin Williams, of course, is a prime example. There are many others including Tom Hanks, winner of several Oscars, who started his television career in an ABC situation comedy called *Bosom Buddies*; Bruce Willis from *Moonlighting*; Billy Crystal from *Soap*; John Travolta from *Welcome Back Kotter*; Woody Harrelson from *Cheers*; and Tom Selleck from *Magnum P.I.*

There were many thrilling and memorable moments at these affiliate meetings. One was in 1984 when Roone Arledge had many of the Olympic medal winners from past Olympic Games, including Muhammad Ali and George Foreman, take the stage as the University of Southern California Marching Band paraded triumphantly up and down the aisles. This was all a build-up to the Los Angeles Olympic Games, to be telecast around the world by ABC Sports in August of that year.

And there was the time, as a wrap-up to a lavish sports presentation, the great Ray Charles was to sing his famous rendition of *America, The Beautiful* and invite the entire audience to join in as a sensational finale. I was sitting in the front row, since I emceed the affiliate meetings.

A hush fell over the very hyped-up crowd as the spotlight fell on the piano, just to the left down from the stage. Ray Charles was not to be seen. Several uneasy minutes passed, and I was about to go backstage, when the flashy Charles appeared, decked in a bright yellow checked sport coat and a black tie, with his usual dark sunglasses. He flashed a huge smile and bobbed and weaved and finally sat down and played and sang his inimitable version of the stirring patriotic song. The audience went absolutely nuts, cheering and whistling long after the session was over.

The crowd was so taken with his performance that they were stomping their feet asking for more. Many in the audience started to sing, *"America, America, God shed His grace on thee..."* and the clapping and cheering and singing made the ballroom a cauldron of excitement.

I learned later that the reason for the delay was that Mr. Charles apparently had had a few nips before he went on and made it known that, unless he received an additional $10,000, he was not going to perform. After some squabbling, our ABC people, with little choice, agreed. His performance was costly, but truly sensational.

ABC News provided some outstanding moments by occasionally providing a live satellite feed to the White House, where President Reagan would give a live, personalized message to the assembled and then take questions from the audience on issues of the day. At several meetings, ABC News presented its first team of Jennings, Walters, Donaldson, Koppel and Brinkley for a panel discussion regarding the state of the nation or the events of the world. These panels made for some lively moments.

The affiliate meetings were far from all flash and dash and show business. We very carefully constructed our presentations to the affiliates to get maximum clearance cooperation and build a strong spirit of pride in our partnership. At every convention, we hosted a business meeting where affiliate members could voice any concerns with the network. The effect of the more personalized regional meetings came into play here, because I knew most of the managers and their staff members. In conducting the meeting, I could call on individuals from the floor on a first-name basis. People were often astounded that I could remember so many people by their first names. It wasn't difficult when you had as much contact as we did.

A real sense of family was created from all of this, and it paid enormous dividends as ABC ascended to a position of leadership in the television industry. This was recognized at the 1980 affiliate meeting in Los Angeles when I accepted a handsome, specially designed Steuben crystal statue from the ABC Affiliate Association. The call letters of all of the stations were printed on the base and there was a beautiful inscription on the elegant crystal surface. I don't know who wrote the inscription, but it was someone who understood the value of the network/affiliate relationship.

> *The Winds and the Waves are always on the side of the ablest navigator.*
>
> *In a world of increasingly competitive forces, Jim Duffy has elevated respect for the words integrity and tact. In his thirty years at ABC, he has kept the open eye, the quick ear, the judging taste, the keen smell of both trouble and success, and the lively maestro's touch for unity. He has helped us to interpret the riddles in this business and to surmount its inevitable obstacles.*
>
> *He is the statesman among us all. He always sensed and did what had to be done – now, not tomorrow.*

His is the road to progress. He speaks and lives by the words, "Here is a way we can go together."

In my acceptance speech, I referred to what I had told the affiliates when I first addressed them as president of the network: that I believed in them and all of the people who worked so hard to make our partnership possible and productive. Our television leadership was a symbol of our collective success.

The affiliates might have wanted to temper all of their flattering words after the affiliate meeting in New York City five years later. The 1985 meeting was the last convention that I presided over, and, while successful for the most part, it was probably the most disappointing to me. For years, the television network had two major presentations in the spring. The first such event was usually held early in the spring for the advertising community. The prime-time schedule was featured, with film clips of the shows for the new fall schedule and appearances by the stars in the programs. A month or so later, the presentation would be made at the Annual Affiliate Meeting. Because the announcement of the schedule to advertisers kept moving later in the spring, within weeks of the affiliate sessions, I decided to break the mold of tradition and bring the entire ABC family – advertisers, affiliates, producers, talent and employees – all together in one gigantic event at New York's Radio City Music Hall for the presentation of the schedule in late May.

It seemed like a brilliant idea at the time since we had been looking for a new venue for the affiliate meetings for a long time. We had been going to the same site, the Century Plaza Hotel in Los Angeles for many years. Also, I figured having one meeting would save the company substantial dollars since two meetings doubled production costs, overhead and travel expenses. But, most of all, the merger with Capital Cites and ABC had been announced, but not ratified, and this was an ideal opportunity to put ABC's best business and show business foot forward for the new owners. Besides, it was my last year as the president of the TV network.

The affiliate meetings, including a successful, informal business session, were held for three days in the Hilton Hotel directly across the street from the former ABC headquarters at 1330 Avenue of the Americas. For the final evening, we arranged for the affiliates to stroll five blocks down the avenue to Radio City Music Hall where they would be joined by advertisers and their representatives from around the country, ABC talent and employees, and special guests. We arranged for a star-studded entertainment show, including the famous Radio City Rockettes, along with a carefully crafted presentation of the fall ABC schedule that we had hoped would bring the entire audience to a standing ovation.

The program was to be ninety minutes long, no more, no less. At the conclusion of the show, everyone in the audience was invited for a stylish reception and dinner at the Hilton Hotel Ballroom. We had arranged for the police (no easy task) to block off the Avenue of Americas from 49th Street to 54th Street for an hour following the presentation so that our guests could walk on a red carpet down the middle of the avenue from the theater to the hotel reception.

I had spent a good portion of the afternoon with the producers from ABC's Entertainment Division at the theater to make sure the show would be on schedule and timed to perfection. I was assured that everything was in order and that we would have a spectacular evening.

Spotlights from in front of the theater flashed all over the New York sky on the evening of the program. Hundreds, if not thousands, of onlookers stood behind the police barricades cheering as guests and celebrities entered the famous Radio City Music Hall.

About 4,000 guests were in the auditorium when I stepped to the podium to greet them and introduce the governor, Mario Cuomo, who in turn would welcome everyone to New York and Manhattan. I saw all of ABC management in the audience, many celebrities from ABC's news, sports and entertainment programs, and importantly, our soon-to-be-new employers from Capital Cities/ABC, Tom Murphy, Dan Burke, Joe Dougherty and several others. There was a rare aura of excitement in the theater that evening as our program got underway with a stirring medley of the ABC program theme songs as rendered by the Radio Music Hall Orchestra.

On looking back on that evening – which I have many, many times – it was a very special celebration with many memorable performances, but the problem was that the show was too long. It went on and on and on to the point that I was backstage pleading with the executive producer to cut some acts and let us get to the reception. The program ran for almost three hours – twice as long as we had scheduled. By the end, many guests had left the hall and had gone to the reception and by the time the more patient guests got to the hotel, the food was cold and the party was almost over.

To this day, I don't know if the program overrun was deliberate. The West Coast-based producers had always resisted having the show in New York and were lukewarm with their cooperation. Or perhaps it was just a lack of control in handling the egos and timing of the many entertainers who performed that evening. I, probably more than anyone, was very disappointed because I wanted the evening to be memorable for the right reasons. We had accomplished a great deal. We had come a long way and we had much to be proud of.

One of the highlights of the affair for me was to meet with Governor Cuomo. Before the show, the producers put me in a small dressing room on the second floor backstage, where I was to meet the governor. When he arrived, accompanied by two police officers, he was immediately friendly, charming and unassuming. He said that he knew who I was and complimented me for the work we were doing with the *American Television and You* campaign. We chatted for a few minutes about television and its positive and negative influences and I described the audience that we both would address. Finally, there was a knock on the door and someone yelled, "Show time."

As I opened the door of the dressing room, I could see that the small hallway was packed with photographers. Flashbulbs started lighting up the hall as the governor and I walked toward the elevators. Governor Cuomo put his arm around my shoulders and whispered, "Everyone's asking, 'Who's the guy with Duffy?'"

Every family has its share of unique characters, and ABC was no exception. One of the more distinctive personalities was a fellow who was in charge of putting the affiliate functions together, be they the smaller regional meetings, the complex and huge Annual Affiliate Meetings or the more personalized Affiliate Board of Governors Meetings.

Milton Carney was appointed director of Conference Planning in 1968 for the ABC Television Network. He took command immediately. His large ambling presence, often dressed in sweat suits or colorful outfits, even at more formal functions, was always felt. He had a strong flair for the dramatic, having been a student of Shakespeare, and he often acted out his parts as he proceeded to line up and "terrorize" a hotel staff at five o'clock in the morning, preparing them for the day's activities. One of the several features that brought Milton notoriety was his glass eye. On occasion, he was known to remove it and absolutely shock whoever his audience might be.

For all of his idiosyncrasies, Carney was exceptionally bright and able. Anyone attending a meeting where he was in command could expect a professionally organized, high-styled and exciting conclave, along with some unexpected and memorable happenings.

At one Board of Governors Meeting in Hawaii, Milton had a huge *ABC* cut into the thick, lush grass in front of the Maui Surf Hotel so that all of us could see it from our balconies as we looked down at the lawn and onto the beautiful blue Hawaii surf. Not all the guests were pleased with the message, especially many of the CBS group who were vacationing at the hotel.

I remember starting a Board of Governors business meeting with a warm welcome to our affiliate guests and some well-rehearsed words setting a family tone for the meeting, only to hear a loud BEEP, BEEP, BEEP in the back of the meeting room. My monologue would be lost as everyone turned to see Milton in his sweat suit scurrying across the room with his command beeper blaring away.

"Morning, Milton," I said.

"Garp, mornnnnning," Milton mumbled and out the door he charged to face another crisis.

Station managers attending the board meetings, for the most part, were exceptional broadcasters who had grown up in the business. Along with a keen sense of their own respective markets, they had insights and progressive views about television's evolution. They were very cognizant of the importance of the network as a business entity and the affiliates' role in maximizing television's potential. The station managers not only represented affiliated stations, but in reality, they were the voice and mind of the American television viewing public. The concerns regarding violence and permissiveness in prime-time programming were often introduced by station managers.

One of Milton's most crushing moments at an affiliate board meeting came at the Kauai Surf Hotel in Kauai, Hawaii in the mid-eighties. At each board meeting, we would plan an elaborate opening reception to get the group in a receptive frame of mind prior to the sometimes-difficult business sessions. On this particular evening, as the sun was setting and darkness was beginning to fall, the ABC affiliate family, assembled on an outdoor patio, suddenly stopped their chattering and put down their cocktails to watch a ship sail across the harbor. On its twin masts was a large banner with bright lights that spelled out WELCOME ABC AFFILIATES.

The crowd started to whistle and applaud, when the banner started to very slowly sag as though the ship were sinking. When the sky was totally dark, the banner limply floated down to the ship's deck, the lights blinked off, and it appeared that the boat had sunk.

Milton immediately rolled up the pant legs of his white Polynesian royalty outfit and wadded out into the surf. With his arms raised to the heavens, he cried out in his best Shakespearian tones, "It's the Kona winds. Beware of the Kona winds."

It wasn't our most spectacular welcome, but the affiliates talked about it for years.

The most unusual and zany board meeting was on the island of Martinique in November of 1971. It was memorable because the entire trip was loaded with obedience to Murphy's Law: that which can go wrong did go wrong.

The Berlitz Travelers' Guide describes Martinique as the scent of frangipani with a trace of Gauloise smoke; an haute couture gown accented with hibiscus bloom. To those of us who arrived on the beautiful Caribbean island, it had more of a scent of disaster waiting to trap the pasty-faced folks from up north.

Actually, the affiliates were in good spirits since the compensation cutback from the previous year had been postponed. The ABC network had made significant ratings progress in all day parts and was building its reputation as the place to be. But from the time we arrived at the Pointe du Bout at the Le Bakoua Hotel across the bay from the capital city of Fort-de-France, we were hexed. Our meetings were scheduled for five days with a farewell reception and dinner on the last night, Thursday.

Shortly after her arrival on Sunday afternoon, Isabel Goldenson, the strong-minded wife of the ABC chairman, and Elizabeth Warren, wife of the Affiliate Board Chairman, and two or three other wives, strolled eastward from the hotel down the beach to view the beauty of the lovely French island. They had not strolled too far when they discovered they were smack dab in the middle of a young, swinging nudist beach run by Club Med. Shocked and shaken (and probably thrilled) they ran back to the hotel and announced the discovery. Isabel in the same breath demanded to know why we would have a meeting in such a scandalous place.

I asked Milton the same question without getting a coherent response. And it was soon forgotten when the Club Med promised to move the bathers further down the beach. Of course, some of the most curious of our group felt it necessary to travel down the beach to see how bad the situation was. As a matter of fact, I, myself, had to make that trek just to ensure that our members weren't getting involved in the display.

At the same time, on the other side of the hotel on the curving beach, Beesemyer had discovered a rather weatherbeaten sailboat anchored offshore that had two young, very tanned Australian lads as its captains. They were traveling around the world with four nubile, bikini-clad young women as crewmembers. Being most hospitable, Beese invited the young people to attend an informal reception that we were having that afternoon for Reeve and Meg Owens from Chattanooga, Tennessee, who were celebrating their 25th wedding anniversary.

Not only did the sailors come to the party, but the curvaceous young women came in their string bikinis (appropriate enough for a beach party) and the two Aussie lads brought along a keg of the most powerful rum you can imagine. The rum mixed with the French wine provided by the hotel, coupled with the tropical sun, put everyone in a fun-loving and rather boisterous mood. It was about this time that Isabel Goldenson and her party arrived back at the hotel from their nude beach adventure and observed a party in full swing, decorated by the nearly-nude sailboat crew. There was more hell to pay! And this was only the beginning.

At the opening dinner on Monday evening, everyone was having a wonderful time enjoying the fine French wine and gourmet food, when a loud gasp erupted from Elton Rule's table. Elton apparently swallowed a spicy island pepper. He gagged, his eyes rolled back in his head as he turned absolutely white, and his head dropped to the table.

"My God, he's dying," someone yelled. We all leaped to our feet. Beesemyer raced over to the bar, wrapped ice cubes in a towel and put it around Elton's neck.

After a few scary moments, Elton stirred and sat up. He shook his head and said, "It's okay. I'm fine." The dinner then continued.

Betty Rule asked the hotel manager why they served such potentially dangerous peppers. The hotel manager replied, "That's a good question, because we've had that happen a couple of times before."

That same evening, one of our affluent affiliate guests visited the fancy men's room near the outdoor restaurant. Le Bakoua provided young French lads to polish the guests shoes on the way from the rest room. This special gentleman, full of island warmth and spirits, decided to tip one young boy with a ten-dollar bill. The lad, babbling in his local French dialect, ran to the hotel gendarme claiming the man was propositioning him. It took considerable negotiating in broken French to convince the policeman and the boy that our distinguished gentleman had only generous and honorable intentions.

The next day Michael and Jane Eisner decided to go for a sail in a small Sunfish that the hotel provided. No one had bothered to advise them that some of the boats had had their rudders removed. Had one of the staff members not noticed the frantic waving of the Eisners as they sailed on and on toward the great beyond, Michael and Jane might have ended up in Africa or wherever the island winds and current might direct them. After some scurrying around, motorboats were put into service and the Eisners were rescued.

That evening some of us went to Fort-de-France for dinner, returned to the hotel and headed for our rooms when we caught sight of the pretty wife of one of the ABC executives sitting in the shadows on a low, white, wooden fence in front of a row of bushes. She sat motionless and alone, almost stonelike.

Suddenly, the young woman's wine glass flew up in the air as if it were in slow motion, turning over and over. Slowly, she fell backwards and passed out in the row of bougainvillea bushes.

It was all so comically bizarre that we didn't quite know how to react. On seeing the poor girl spread-eagle among the beautiful flowers we became very concerned, not only for her health, but also for anyone who might see her in that condition.

Beesemyer said to Marty Pompadur, "Let's get her to her room."

Someone whispered. "I think they're in room 321."

As Beesemyer tells the story, when they got to room 321, he and Pompadur softly knocked on the door, praying it was the right room and her husband was there. A light went on and the door opened. There, sleepy-eyed and in his pajamas stood William Warren, the chairman of the Affiliate Board, the oldest and the most dignified of all the board members. Mr. Warren, a highly religious and moral gentleman, wore a hearing aid, which he turned off to sleep. He gazed out into the darkness and saw Beese and Marty carrying the attractive young blonde. He wasn't entirely sure what was happening.

"Sorry, Bill," Beesemyer stuttered. "I think we have the wrong room."

"How's that?" asked Mr. Warren. He turned up his hearing aid, surveyed the situation and said rather sternly, "You have the wrong room," and he slammed the door.

The following afternoon, two ABC executives, Dick O'Leary and Dick Savage, unaware of the Eisner's trauma, sailed a Sunfish to the shore of the mainland directly into a group of children in the middle of their swimming lessons. Savage jumped overboard to stop the boat and landed on several sea urchins. After having the very painful spines removed from his feet, Dick returned to the hotel rather displeased with our island paradise.

But the best, or worst, remained for last. Despite several mishaps, we had successful and productive meetings with the affiliate members. We discussed and came to resolution on contentious issues such as the station's compensation, early morning network programming, and problems with late-night ratings. Leonard and Elton seemed very pleased, as did the station executives. We all went into the final reception and banquet in elevated spirits.

The reception was noisy and filled with laughter as the attendees reflected on the past few days and the experiences they'd had. The dinner was served in magnificent style out on the verandah. Couples danced to romantic island music. A clear sky and warm tropical breezes made for a perfect setting. A squall had passed through in late afternoon so the air was fresh and very clear.

After dinner, Milton ambled over to me and whispered, "Wait till you see this. You'll love it."

I wheeled to grab him, because "this" meant a surprise – a Milton Carney special, and God knows what that might bring. Suddenly, the loud noise of gunfire started and tracers of light shot back and forth across the concrete verandah floor. People scrambled to their feet screaming and started to run for the adjoining buildings. One woman started sobbing and dove for cover under the table. The island locals, who were standing next to the fence watching, became hysterical, thinking they were being attacked by gunmen.

People were shouting, "What the hell is going on?" I ran over to Milton and grabbed him by the shirt. He stood in the center of the floor with his head down, motionless and totally despondent.

"The rain shorted out my fireworks," he said almost sobbing.

"Well, for God's sake stop it," I bellowed.

The intended spectacular display sputtered out and people started to relax and even giggle nervously in relief. A humbled Milton announced what had happened. The music started to play again, but the evening was over. And thus ended our adventures in

Martinique, the mysterious island described as *flirtatious and subtle as perfume in the evening breeze.* It is not a description that the attendees at the ABC Affiliates Meeting would necessarily endorse.

The Board of Governors Meetings, with the exotic settings and unusual adventures, proved to be a strong platform for the network/affiliate relationship. In the early days, the regional and annual affiliate meetings were instrumental in framing our issues, introducing new programs and generating corporate spirit and loyalty. But the Board of Governors Meeting was the genesis of policy and direction for the network. Many broadcasters who would later be recognized and honored by the broadcasting industry attended these meetings. John Conomikes (Pittsburgh) and the late Mickey Hooten (Milwaukee), Hearst Broadcasting; Tom Cookerly (Washington, D.C.), Albritton Broadcasting; Bill Turner (Cedar Rapids) and Bob Rice (Peoria), Dudley Broadcasting; Martin Unmansky (Wichita), Bob Doubleday (Little Rock) and Tom Goodgame (Tulsa), Leake Broadcasting; Burt LaDow (Phoenix), KTVK; Joe Drilling (Fresno), Retlaw Broadcasting; Joe Hladky (Cedar Rapids), KCRG; Jeff Davidson (Atlanta), Combined Communications; Mike Shapiro, Ward Huey and the late David Lane (Dallas), Belo Broadcasting; Mort Cohen (Asheville), WLOS; George Lyons (Grand Rapids), WZZM-TV; Fred Barber (Atlanta), Cox Broadcasting; Tom Chisman (Norfolk), Corinthian Broadcasting; the late Clayton Brace (San Diego), McGraw-Hill Broadcasting; and the very popular Bob Bennett of WCVB (Boston), among several other former board chairmen who are mentioned elsewhere in this book, are examples of leaders who distinguished themselves in the industry.

All of the Board of Governors Meetings were memorable in different ways. Many business decisions were discussed and made, including a brand new programming effort for the morning that became *Good Morning, America*; a sharing of costs for the Olympic Games absent station compensation but providing the ability to sell more local spots around the Games; the discussion of growing concerns about violence in movies on TV; and a new compensation plan for all affiliates.

We were also fortunate to have some exceptional professional athletes at our board meetings to help our affiliates and their wives, and, as a matter of fact, all of us, with golf and tennis. These activities were especially important for the non-business hours. It turned out the pros had as much fun as anybody and were considered members of the ABC family. Dave Marr and Bob Rosberg, who worked with ABC Sports on golf coverage, alternated each year with duffers on the links and set up golf tournaments for the attendees.

On the tennis side, we also had a champion. Nancy Chafee Kiner joined us in Maui in 1969 and she attended every ABC Board of Governors Meeting until the time I left the presidency. Nancy, who played center court, Wimbledon, with Gussie Moran in the mid-fifties, was not only a great tennis player but also a vivacious, fun-loving personality. No tennis tournament was ever without plenty of laughs and shenanigans. Nancy and her attractive daughter, K.C., who assisted her mother on occasion, kept our spirits soaring on and off the courts.

One of my favorite Nancy Kiner stories was from Acapulco, Mexico in 1982. The board meeting was at the Princess Marquis Hotel, just down the beach from the larger Acapulco Princess. One evening when Kiner strolled down the beach at dusk, she noticed a strange-looking man standing off in the distance next to a sand mound. As she looked closer, she saw that he was naked and waving frantically to her with one arm while he entertained himself with the other. When she told us the story at the evening cocktail reception, we all said in unison, "What did you do, Nance?"

"What do you mean, what did I do?" She laughingly said. "I told Security to arrest him and bring him to my room.... Naw," she said laughing even harder. "I didn't do anything, but I felt like telling him he'd have better luck if he quit jumping around so we could see what he was offering."

Nancy was married for a number of years to Ralph Kiner, the famous home-run king with the Pittsburgh Pirates who later became a sportscaster for the New York Mets. Nancy later married Jack Whitaker, one of broadcasting's all-time outstanding sports announcers.

The board meetings also had some memorable moments involving programming talent.

The *Love Boat* sailed into Acapulco Harbor in 1982 replete with the entire cast from the show, for an opening reception with the stations. The cast of the award-winning *Winds of War* miniseries visited the board meeting on the last night in Acapulco. Raquel Welch visited, and The Gatlin Brothers entertained in Palm Springs. The venerable star R. J. Wagner, then of *Hart to Hart* fame, was with us in Maui in 1984. All who were at La Costa in 1980 will remember being entertained by a very funny young Black comic who was just starting out. His name was Arsenio Hall.

One of the most meaningful of all the board meetings, at least to me, was the meeting in Wailea, Maui in 1983, where my friend Ward Huey of WFAA-TV, Dallas, the chairman of the board that year, would coin the phrase, "the spirit of Maui," which signified the matured relationship between the network and its affiliates. A handful of skeptics ridiculed it, but for most of us, that spirit represented what so many of us had worked so hard to attain over a long period: an effective distribution framework, without which our best programming efforts would be moot.

The relationship with our stations and many station managers laid the foundation for the growth of ABC Television in many directions, including public service, of particular interest and importance to me.

Seventeen

American Television and You

*We are all here this evening to address a common
concern: the problem of alcohol abuse – and especially
teenage drinking and driving. Last year, more than 10
million adults were classified as problem drinkers.
According to the Presidential Commission on Drunk
Driving, between 1973 and 1983, more than 250,000
Americans were killed in alcohol related accidents.*

I was standing at a podium in the 36th floor screening room at
ABC's headquarters in New York. It was evening and we had invited
some sixty representatives from organizations concerned with alcohol
abuse, plus educators and youth group leaders, to join us for a screening of a program on teenage drunk driving. As I looked down, I
could see the interest and the concern on the faces in the audience.

*Three and a half million young people between the
ages of 14 and 17 are considered problem drinkers, I
continued. And it is reported that more than 93 percent
of all high school seniors try alcohol before they reach the
legal drinking age.*

We had called this group together, just as we had a month earlier with members of Congress and their staffs in Washington, to
show them a hard-hitting program called *One Too Many*. It warned
against the effects of teen drinking by portraying a young man inebriated from drinking beer, who entices his girlfriend into his car
and has an accident in which they are both killed.

*If the story is powerful – and I think you will agree
that it is – this program should serve as a warning for*

> *teenagers,* I said. *We believe that media can have a central role in dealing with these issues. We are taking the initiative. This is a preventative measure – it's part of broadcasting's responsibility to the public to make sure that issues like drinking and driving are not inadvertently glamorized or made to look socially acceptable or without consequences.*

This important evening on May 1, 1985, was all part of a strategically planned public service initiative that grew out of a change in television programming in the late seventies when movies made for television used social issues as core themes. It was a pivotal move. It began to connect the power and reach of broadcasting with national and local organizations that were coping with and seeking solutions for the country's growing social problems. It was the beginning of a dynamic partnership that held great promise.

Social issues as subjects for television movies started out as a logical concept for new and interesting materials that fit quite naturally with the immediacy of the medium. Little thought was given at first to how the subjects and issues being depicted on the screen could be tied to local communities and organizations that were grappling with those very issues. The subject matter was often controversial and created a stir among image-conscious advertisers and even some affiliates who were reluctant to carry certain programs for fear of offending their viewers. This, of course, provided fuel for television's detractors and critics.

ABC presented an issue-oriented, controversial show in early 1971. Entitled *That Certain Summer,* it was one of the first TV programs to deal with homosexuality. On first hearing about the show, advertisers and some affiliated stations were leery of being associated with it, but after special screenings and its subsequent national airing, the program became one of the most talked about of the year. The very sensitively written and produced movie, featuring Hal Holbrook and Martin Sheehan, won an Emmy from the Academy of Television Arts and Sciences as the best film of that year.

Another controversy came when NBC aired a made-for-TV-movie entitled *Born Innocent* in the early seventies. It contained a violent sexual scene in which inmates in a juvenile detention home rape a fourteen-year-old girl with a broom handle. The movie was unwisely aired at 8:00 PM Eastern Time and had a large audience of young viewers. A few weeks later, other children sexually molested a young girl in California in a similar manner. The child's parents sued the NBC network. It was then that three Congressional committees demanded that the Federal Communications Commission take action to protect children from excessive sex and violence on television. This was the genesis of the industry's adoption of family viewing time in 1975. It was an industry-wide policy that the first two hours of prime time (7:00 - 9:00 PM Eastern Time) would contain only programs suitable for all age groups. The policy, which became part of the television code for all broadcasters, was later declared illegal by a US District Court judge. Nevertheless, networks of their own choice made the commitment to keep the early evening hours free of excessive sex and violence.

I had long contended, and said so in many speeches to industry groups and in private conversations, that all of prime time, and indeed all of television, should not have "excessive" sex and violence. While I did believe in the family-viewing concept as a step in the right direction, what it said to me was that this would permit programs to possibly increase excessive sex and violence *after* the early evening hours. Family viewing time is a neat package that lets the TV industry say to the world, "Look what we are doing about this!" But the fact is that there are many young people watching television after 9:00 PM, and even more after 8:00 PM in the Central and Mountain Time Zones where the later shows are aired.

Again, the questions perplexed and alarmed me, as they do to this day. Where is the conscience of this industry? What is its moral code? What does broadcasting genuinely believe is its responsibility to its audience?

The following season, NBC reran *Born Innocent* at a later hour, and had edited the more graphic parts of the rape scene. It also added an advisory for parental guidance at the start of the movie. If these steps had been taken to begin with, much of the outcry and possible copycat crimes would have been avoided. The movie's original showing appeared to be another case where the quest for high audience ratings won out over responsible judgment.

Many lessons were learned from those earlier movies that dealt with sensitive yet very meaningful subjects – lessons that served us well in later years. Toward the end of the seventies, all three networks produced important movies that were instrumental in raising awareness on many illnesses and destructive excesses that were affecting the well-being of many people. NBC produced a sensitive program on missing children entitled *Adam*, and an outstanding production on domestic abuse, *The Burning Bed*, starring Farrah Fawcett. CBS presented a hard-hitting movie entitled *License To Kill* about teenage crime. At ABC we produced many movies concerning topical issues, including the one on teenage suicide, *Survival*, along with stories on drug addiction, child abuse, domestic abuse, anorexia, the hearing impaired, illiteracy, homelessness, alcoholism and many others. At one point, one of the industry quipsters claimed we were producing "the disease of the week."

These programs had their effect. We found that thousands of people would write to the network after a given telecast and relate how the dramatic portrayal of the subject had helped their own family in coping with the problem. As the public began to respond more and more to these types of programs, two important dimensions were added.

First, the performers in certain movies were asked to step out of character at the end of the movie and advise viewers that if they were involved with the problem the movie portrayed, they could get help or more information by calling a national hotline number that appeared on the screen. An outstanding example of this was when ABC aired the made-for-television movie *Something About Amelia*, a dramatic presentation on incest starring Ted Danson. Another example about child abuse was entitled *When She Was Bad*, featuring Robert Urich and Cheryl Ladd. At the end of the movie, Ms. Ladd, a long-time worker toward solutions for the abuse of children, came on the screen and made an announcement to this effect:

"This program was the dramatization of the almost inhuman abuse of a child. The problem of child abuse is widespread and growing in America. If you are or have been the victim of child abuse, or know others who are, there is help available. Please call this number."

Thousands of calls were received and child abuse clinics across the country were inundated with requests for information and assistance. Once again, a national disgrace was brought into the open and assistance offered.

At a reception in Hollywood for the cast of the hit show *Charlie's Angels*, Cheryl Ladd told me that performing in that movie and knowing the reactions it received was one of her most gratifying experiences in show business.

Cheryl, a beautiful young woman, said with a very intent look on her face, "We don't all realize the impact of television. I thought it was extraordinary from being on *Charlie's Angels*, and the number of people who would recognize me, but it is awesome when you can play a role that actually helps people positively change their lives."

The second new dimension was really the major step that tied the impact of the message on the TV screen to every community in America – where people are affected by these illnesses and problems.

In 1977, we formed a Community Relations Department at ABC. Its purpose was to increase communications, working relationships and understanding among broadcasters, educators, parents and the public in general. We hired Dr. Pamela Warford, a mother and a former teacher, to head the department. Community Relations' principal responsibilities, as outlined in its manual, were to provide informational materials for classroom use, expand the opportunities for public dialogue, and encourage the use of the television medium to facilitate formal and informal learning for educators, students, and parents.

Later, the department produced special half-hour programs entitled *ABC Notebook*, which were designed to help answer some of the tough questions that young people were asking and shed light on issues related to their lives. These programs were created and produced by Jane Paley, who had become the director of the

Community Relations Department. *ABC Notebook* played four times a year and was aired at 4:00 PM Eastern Time immediately following *General Hospital,* daytime television's highest-rated show. These programs, on occasion, would tie in to one of the movies of the week with a look at the background of the issues.

To me, the most important use of Community Relations was more simplistic and direct. I saw the department as the catalyst and communications source for all parties involved on a particular issue in a program that was to be aired on the network. For instance, if we had a TV movie or a news documentary or a series on *Good Morning, America* on the subject of alcoholism, the department would prepare materials (brochures) that illustrated what the show was about, who would be on it and even viewer tips on what to look for and suggestions for watching it with other members of the family. If it were appropriate for classroom discussion, these materials would be sent to thousands of teachers in schools around the country.

Our community relations people would immediately be in touch with those national agencies and institutions dealing with alcoholism (e.g. the National Council on Alcoholism, Alcoholics Anonymous, Mothers Against Drunk Driving) and advise them that the program was going to be aired on the network with a given time and date. They would then suggest that the agency or organization inform all of its own local organizations and partner organizations around the country that this important program on alcoholism was going to be telecast in their respective communities, and they could contact the local ABC station for local tie-ins.

Meanwhile, the network community relations people would contact their counterparts at ABC affiliates, inform them of the program and the fact that agencies and organizations had been contacted in their communities, and send them brochures. All of the organizations and stations would be advised that at the end of the movie or during the program, a message would be aired that help was available and a national hotline number for referrals to local numbers would be shown. That, of course, was the signal for all parties involved to be fully prepared for an avalanche of calls and activity.

This, to me, was the concept that tied national to local and became the center pole of the broadcast partnerships. It was action oriented and tied all the players together, top down and bottom up to not only achieve acknowledgement of the problems but also to facilitate change and action.

It was the procedure that was employed for *One Too Many* when we invited the groups to the screening, as well as for many different programs on a variety of subjects. *One Too Many* was very special to me. It was originally produced as an *Afterschool Special* to be played in the afternoon hours. It was so powerful we decided to run it in an early prime-time hour, to bring maximum exposure to young people just prior to graduation ceremonies and parties in late May of 1985.

Along with our special screenings, videotapes of *One Too Many* were sent to individual members of Congress as well as to state governors. And we tied it into a specially produced *Don't Drink and Drive* public service announcement campaign using our TV stars for brief five-second messages at the end of prime-time and daytime programs. It was a massive campaign and brought a positive reaction from all around the nation. Most of all, I think it undoubtedly helped to save many lives.

Two other ABC programs about alcoholism were *Shattered Spirits*, featuring Martin Sheehan, about the affects of the disease on the family, and *From This Day Forward*, starring Elizabeth Taylor in a story where a wife and mother comes to terms with her alcoholism.

The community relations efforts in developing active partnerships brought extraordinary results. The respective agencies and organizations were astounded at the penetration and power of the medium. It was exhilarating and gratifying to all of us who viewed broadcasting's potential as being more than a light-hearted entertainment tool. This process was the gateway, established the foundation and planted the seeds for the sustained and unprecedented Project Literacy US campaign.

Two other forces of change were at work in the broadcasting arena at this time: increased concern among broadcasters about the burgeoning competition from cable telecasting, and the growing and loud dissent among the citizens' groups about television program content.

Most of the executives at all three networks, affiliate group owners and managers were becoming alarmed that cable would severely diminish the broadcast viewing audience and networks' dominance would be lost forever. In the late seventies and early eighties, respected columnists and industry prognosticators on Wall Street and main streets everywhere were predicting that the broadcast system, especially TV, was a "dying breed" and by the end of the eighties could well be extinct. One story in *TV Guide* illustrated the demise of commercial television by depicting the three networks in cartoon form as dinosaurs.

The prognosticators who really don't understand the commercial system were way off the mark. The fact is that the early cable gold rush era was mostly hype. The infant cable industry, with its multi-station operators and newcomers to the business, was struggling to get a foothold. Cable operators made some of the same fundamental errors that broadcasters had made in the earliest days, such as insulting the intelligence of their audience with poor-quality programming. Still, many on the edges of the communications business kept announcing cable's potential. In reality, many cable channels that had come on stream were presenting mostly rerun programming and included uncut movies with violence and sex that made the networks look like the *Hour of Faith*. The would-be saviors in Congress and a new citizens' group called the Moral Majority lumped all of the programming together as "television" and came after the networks with bared fangs.

Triggered by cable's uncensored movies and pointing to the increase in the number of permissive situation comedies and action-prone dramatic shows along with the subject matter in the issue-oriented made-for-TV movies, war plans against the television networks were devised.

Headlines that carried the Moral Majority's war cry started to appear, especially in newspapers in the south.

TV TEARING DOWN MORAL FIBER OF NATION.

The Reverend Donald Wildmon of Tupelo, Mississippi, long a squeaky wheel on program content issues, had formed his Coalition for Better Television with the Reverend Jerry Falwell's Moral Majority as its main component. In the summer of 1981, the Coalition announced a three-month monitoring project, assessing the content of all network shows for what it considered to be excessive sex, violence and profanity. The coalition then threatened a one-year national boycott of all advertisers associated with the offending programs.

An article in an issue of *Variety*, entitled "Television: Who's in Charge?" summed up the problem.

> *Organized criticism of television itself has become a growth industry. Never before have we experienced the kind of sophisticated, professional public relations and political tactics used by these groups.... All of these groups may be wide apart on their goals, but they are agreed on one thing: They want to do something about television.*

The main result of the Reverend Wildmon activity was that he got himself a lot of national notoriety (which many are convinced was his principal mission), and it created some unhealthy perceptions about television. His proposed advertiser boycott fizzled like a wet firecracker.

Goldenson, Rule and Pierce all grew more concerned about the increased heat on program content and the effect that cable and multi-cable systems, video cassettes, and the emerging plans for direct broadcast satellites would have on the networks and commercial broadcasting in general.

Pierce, in his remarks to the ABC-TV network affiliate body in 1979, exhorted local stations to speak out about the value of free, over-the-air television and the meanings of community service. He stated that the local community relations efforts were growing in importance because, "they are based on a very important principle – taking positive initiative instead of merely reacting or being defensive.... [We] cannot succeed in improving the climate of opinion about television without a strong grassroots effort."

There was no question in my mind about the assured future of the networks. I was quite vocal about the free advertiser-supported system and the threat from the approaching cable systems. I told those attending the Association of National Advertisers workshop at the Plaza Hotel in New York in the early eighties:

> *There is a lesson that has come home in the case of cable and the fading of the gold rush psychology of a year or two ago. A new technology – a new means of distribution – is important, but it is only the beginning. Some cable systems obviously are going to succeed and claim a share of the market, but it is going to require a slow, patient process of moving ahead on all four of these fronts (distribution, product, acceptance and underwriting) more or less simultaneously, just as it did for free advertiser-supported television. Again, some perspective – five years from now network will still claim about nine percent of the total national advertising dollar. Cable will have risen to one percent. And in the years beyond that, the growth of the pie – the increase in households using television – and the ability of network television to adapt and improve is going to keep the basic pattern much the way it is now.*

Another group with whom I shared my views about the threat from cable was the Kansas City (Missouri) Advertising Club:

> *The outstanding characteristic of television has been its ability to grow, to change, to adapt, to improve. I can assure you that the networks are not sleeping giants. Fundamentally, we are in the business of providing news, information, and entertainment programming. The development of cable will expand the need for precisely those services. All three networks have begun to make arrangements to provide various types of cable services, and many local television stations are doing the same.*

You will see more of this when some of these regulatory restrictions I referred to are lifted. No one is in a better position to provide news, information, and entertainment services to a local community, whatever the form of distribution, than the local television station. It is in place, it has an identity, capital, talented staff, and a tradition of community service.

Does all of this suggest that we are preparing for some significant movement away from the free advertiser-supported system? Certainly not. We believe that system, much as we know it today, will remain the dominant force. The new technologies will broaden, diversify, supplement – but not displace.

One afternoon in the spring of 1984, Pierce came into my office, closed the door and sat down in front of my desk. With that great stone, sphinx-like face, he just stared at me for a few minutes.

"Well, howdy, Fred," I finally said. "What's happening?"

"The American people really don't understand the commercial television business, do they?" Fred said almost matter-of-factly. "They read all this garbage from the Moral Majority and the do-gooders from the far right. You travel all over the country. Is that true? Do people really understand how this system works? Do they understand what TV means to their lives? We get painted as the bad guys no matter what we do, yet we're doing such great things and don't seem to get credit for it. If we ever shut television down for a month, I mean have all of television go black, this country would be set back fifty years."

"That's true," I said. "No, I don't think the average American – the viewer – really understands commercial television and the effect it has on his or her family's life. And I'm not sure if he or his family really cares. They sure as hell would if television ceased to exist."

Pierce was deep in thought and just nodded.

"I'll tell you who really doesn't understand it," I continued. "The Congress of the United States. People on the Hill are sometime television viewers for the most part, except for the news. They see the medium as a whipping boy to help them with their constituencies. But I don't believe they really know what's on the air on any consistent basis, how broadcasting works as a system, or how powerful it really can be, aside from election time."

Fred continued with his silent thoughts while he stared at me. Finally, he said, "Can you come up with a campaign that in graphic and simple terms will help people – including congressmen and business leaders and Joe Citizen – understand television and how it works and how important it really is to them?"

I had already been working on that goal through my speeches and local radio and television appearances. The idea of a full-blown campaign appealed to me.

"I think so, Fred," I replied. "Let me work on it."

Pierce smiled. "It's a real challenge," he said. "Let me know what you need." And he left.

I had formed a new department called the Office of Communications, headed by Jack Harr with Matt Zucker as his assistant and Karen Maser from ABC Radio as a writer/producer. Later, a personable and smart young woman named Nancy Nielsen would join them. The department's purpose was to create and administer public service and special project initiatives for the network. Over the next few days I discussed Fred's request with Harr and his staff and we designed the outline of a plan that would have national scope but would also have the strength of grassroots support through our affiliated stations. It was the national and local – top down, bottom up – kind of structure that worked so well with the movies and programs dealing with social issues.

The plan had three main facets: (1) on-air information spots on the television network; (2) a series of print editorial ads to be seen in newspapers and special publications in seven to ten major markets and (3) a series of in-depth market visits around the country.

Approximately a month after our initial meeting, I went in to see Pierce and presented the plan. I recommended a full-scale multimedia campaign of at least two years' duration that would be aimed at the general public, but would have elements that would also be focused toward corporate and civic leaders, especially political leaders in Washington as well as around the country. The purpose was to explain and illustrate the fundamentals of the television business in a simple but compelling manner. The idea was to involve the thinking and emotions of people – the viewers – as much as possible. I proposed that the program be called *American Television and You!*

After I had finished describing all the particulars of the campaign, Fred just nodded.

He liked the plan. I think he really liked the plan, but was concerned about the proposed budget, which was well over $1 million a year.

He read over the proposal a couple of times after I stopped talking.

"Let me talk to Leonard," he said. "I'll get back to you."

Two days later he called and said, *"American Television and You!* is a go. Let's do it."

Two months later I found myself on top of a remote television truck parked at the corner of 52nd and Madison Avenue in the heart of New York City. Buses, taxis and automobiles darted by us, honking horns and adding to all the noise and confusion that only a midtown street in Manhattan can create. I was standing at the back end of the truck; a remote camera, facing me, was perched on the top of the cab and a floor director was kneeling down on the side. The producer and director were down inside the truck with their remote board and monitors. Looming up on each side of me were the towers of commerce – the skyscrapers that are so much a part of the landscape of New York. I took a deep breath to get ready for my taping and almost choked from the exhaust fumes that permeate America's largest city.

"All right, let's roll one," the director said over the inter-communications system. The floor manager said, "Take One – Advertising spot – Duffy, AT&Y." He counted me down, the red light lit up on the front of the camera, and I started talking.

"This is Madison Avenue," I said turning slightly to my right and gesturing toward the street behind me. "This is the famous street where most of the major advertising decisions are made that determine the commercials you will see on television. Advertising is what makes it possible...." Just then a bus rolled by and left a huge cloud of exhaust in its wake, settling right over the spot where I was talking.

"Cut! God damn it, Ricky," the director yelled at the floor manager from the truck. "Didn't you see that bus coming? We can't shoot with all that shit going on around us."

"Sorry, coach," Ricky said. "I'll watch it. Hold it for a minute. Here comes another one."

When we were in the second take and I was almost finished with what I thought was a good read, I heard a voice at the side of the truck yelling, "Hey, Duffy. What the hell are you doing up there?" The director yelled, "Cut!" and I looked down to see the face of a neighbor from Darien.

"Are you trying to become a TV star?" the guy giggled.

"No, Charley," I said with some amusement. "Just trying to make a living."

After a dozen or so takes, including other interruptions from people waving and honking, we had two or three spots that the director thought would be effective after editing, scoring and all of the amazing things technicians can do to enhance a television spot. It wasn't one of the better spots since it was one of the first that we did, but it was fairly effective. Later, we filmed another spot in a studio while a commercial was being filmed in the background underscoring the importance of advertising.

One of the recommendations in the communications plan to present television to the American public was to use a national spokesperson for the campaign. The marketing concept was to have a credible person from within the industry who could explain the workings of the television industry and its programming to the viewers. Because of my announcing experience and background in the industry, I was selected. I became the national spokesperson, on-air and otherwise, for *American Television and You!*

Taping and later filming the spots was fun and gave me a first-hand understanding of what it takes to appear on TV and deliver messages effectively so that they connect with viewers. It's not easy. I enjoyed the experience of being in different locations and striking different moods and inflections depending on the subject of the spots. I presented the first few tapings as though I was delivering a newcast, with far too much voice projection and a solemn and almost preachy tone. It had shades of my first football game announcing for WBNB in Beloit. Gradually, I got into the rhythm of it and the message on the air was much softer and more believable. When we started filming instead of taping, the announcements had more quality and depth. The taping process is done with regular television cameras and can be processed and edited immediately, while filming a spot was done with 35-millimeter cameras and needed more sophisticated lighting and setup time. One of the members of the film production company tutored me on timing and mood preparation for being in front of the camera. She was a wonderful, petite woman named Camille, and she would take me off to the side of the set and softly talk with me about the subject. She told me to relax and deliver the lines in a quieter manner and directly to the camera, as though I were speaking to just one person. The coaching helped immensely, with the result that even some actors and news people congratulated me on the delivery.

As much as I enjoyed making the spots, it was never my ambition to be a television personality. I was convinced that having a spokesperson as the centerpiece of the campaign was essential to give it cohesion, continuity, and credibility. I did hope that my personal conviction about what I was saying would come through and would appeal to the viewers.

After the campaign was underway and the spots appeared on the air, we had many detractors, both within and outside the company, which we fully expected. Some thought it was self-serving; others thought it inappropriate to use our own airtime to discuss the medium. And there were those who thought I was featured on the air to promote my own self-interest.

I ran into Robert Wagner, the star of *Hart to Hart* at the time, on a set in Los Angeles and he expressed some good-natured envy: "You son of a bitch," he said, "I've been on shows in television for over twenty years, and in one week you get more exposure then I've had in my whole career."

"R. J.," I retorted, "You have to know the right people."

Wagner was right about the amount of exposure. The spots ran twelve to fourteen times per week in programming throughout the day. For the first time in the industry's history, the spots were placed in weekly fixed positions, within programs and not subject to pre-emption or the whims of program schedulers, as were all public service announcements in the past. In the subsequent weeks the time slots would eventually change to be in every program on our schedule, resulting in the maximum cumulative audience.

During the following months, serving as the host, I introduced some twenty different segments about commercial television. We started with an introductory announcement laying out the purpose of the campaign and then mixed in other spots explaining how programs are selected, how ratings work and are used, Broadcast Standards and Practices and censorship, news and the free press, sports programming, closed captioning for the hearing impaired, what is a network, the role of an affiliated station and its relationship to the network, public service, the importance of advertising, the use of new technology, and even letters from viewers.

When the campaign premiered, the introductory spot ran for approximately two and a half weeks in all the time slots on the network. In the third week, we mixed in a new spot that would run for approximately ten days with the intro spot. When the initial announcement phased out, the second spot was featured alone for three weeks until another announcement shared the positions for a period of time. The new spot would then go it alone, and the cycle would continue. The on-air schedule had all the spread and mix and impact of a major product advertising campaign. If it had been in commercial time, the airtime would have been valued at approximately $25 million a year.

To accompany the on-air campaign, we produced a series of op-ed newspaper and magazine pieces to be run in five to ten large cities, including Washington, New York, Chicago and Los Angeles. The articles, authored by Jack Harr, were in-depth thought pieces on broadcasting, designed as quarter-page advertisements that would run approximately twice a month and serve as companion pieces to the briefer, but more frequent, on-air announcements.

Typical of these op-ed pieces was one about program content:

WHAT YOU WON'T SEE ON TELEVISION

One role of American television is to present careful and intelligent explorations of sensitive issues. Usually those are issues we don't want to confront, but we know we shouldn't ignore. ABC's Consenting Adult, which dealt with the effects of a son's homosexuality on an American family, and NBC's The Burning Bed, about domestic violence, are recent examples.

In developing these dramas, broadcasters must be extraordinarily sensitive to the balance between the public's freedom to be informed on an important subject and the sensitivity of the topic. The issue is: how do you prevent information from becoming sensational?

There's no better example of this delicate balance than a 1984 ABC made-for-television movie about the psychological and emotional effects of incest. Editors for ABC's Broadcast Standards and Practices Department were involved in all stages of production for Something About Amelia, from script writing through final post-production review.

Editors reviewed every word, scene and image to appear in the movie. Their goal was not to interfere with the artistic or dramatic content of the program, but to ensure that material to appear on the air in viewers' homes would be suitable for a wide audience. In the end, Something About Amelia drew public approval and generated interest nationwide in examining the problem of incest.

Programs dealing with sensitive themes require special scrutiny, but all network entertainment and commercial material is given special attention. As for commercials, at ABC alone editors review more than 50,000 submissions each year. In fact, of all new commercials received by ABC in 1984, more than one third were rejected outright or returned for modification according to network commercial review standards.

Broadcast Standards are constantly reevaluated to keep pace with current interests and needs. We study viewer letters and meet with community leaders.

We commission research studies on all areas of broadcasting. On programs of special significance, like Amelia, we consult with prominent experts to assess the social impact of material.

Of course, it's not an easy task to determine the suitability of particular subjects or words. In a nation as diverse in habits, lifestyles and composition as ours, a single standard is impossible to come by. But the responsibility of America's broadcasters to be sensitive to the viewing public is balanced by your freedom to turn the channel if you don't like what you see.

The op-ed articles were well crafted and very well received. We got an impressive reaction from leaders in business and government that showed us that interest had been stirred, and a dialogue was underway.

"Is that stuff about 'reviewing every word and scene and image' true?" one Congressman asked. "If so, why don't we know about it?"

"Thanks for your kind thoughts, Congressman," we wrote back. "It is precisely why we're doing the *American Television and You!* campaign." I wanted to tell him that I wished every programmer had the same sensitivity and conscience that the article suggested, but, unfortunately, that would not have been the truth. Most programmers dance to a different drum – ratings.

Getting to the grass roots was the heart of the *American Television and You!* program. We proposed trips to local markets as one of the basics of the campaign. The plan was to cover four or five different parts of the country during the course of the year, with three or four cities in a given region being visited over a week or ten-day period.

Our first regional trip was in the spring of 1985 to the beautiful Northwest. John Behnke, who was president of the Fisher Broadcasting Stations in Seattle and Portland, invited us to come out for a week's visit and tell our story in these two great American cities and the surrounding areas.

Behnke is a good friend and superb broadcaster who believes in the medium's use for public service. Through the years he, and Bill Warren, who preceded him as president, had built stations KOMO-TV in Seattle and KATU-TV in Portland to be among the finest in the country. Both men had been chairmen of the ABC Affiliate Board of Governors and had the utmost respect of their fellow broadcasters.

One of the highlights of our trip to the Northwest (and others that followed) was getting to know the culture and history of the cities, as well as many prominent people. In both Seattle and Portland, the news helicopter crews took us on sightseeing flights to acquaint us with each city. Both cities are spectacular, but we were especially thrilled when the helicopter took us beyond Portland into the canyons of Mount St. Helens. It was just a few weeks after this famous volcano had erupted. We could see the smoldering patches of lava and miles of parched and twisted bare trees as we zoomed in and out of the valleys.

Incidentally, the station manager in Portland was a fellow named Tom Dargen, who became a strong supporter of our information campaign and, later, of Project Literacy US. He battled fiercely for us with the ABC affiliates even while he was dying of cancer.

On the business side, I introduced *American Television and You!* as a guest of honor at receptions in both Portland and Seattle, made several speeches to influential groups, appeared on radio and television programs and in the local press, and in Seattle, conducted an on-air town meeting, which was telecast, live from 6:00 to 7:00 PM on Sunday. I was seated in a chair in the middle of the stage while the host of the show, Ken Schram, roamed through the audience with a hand microphone to field questions about television.

One of these questions – one that we would often hear in our travels to local markets – came from a very articulate member of the audience, who introduced himself as a doctor of internal medicine. It concerned news bias.

"My friends and I have become increasingly concerned about the very Eastern Seaboard liberal bias that is evidenced in your news coverage. It would appear that there are few, if any, checks and balances levied against your news reporters to protect the viewer from distortions and personal opinions."

"Doctor, this isn't the first time I have heard that comment," I answered. "Only, in my travels, and depending on what part of the country I am in, the comment about news bias has been posed differently. I have been asked why there is such an overt conservative slant to our news. I have been told that our news is racially prejudiced. It has been suggested that our news is anti-feminist. One woman suggested that was the case since Harry Reasoner didn't get along with Barbara Walters...."

"But you do agree that there is a bias?" the man interrupted.

"No, I really don't," I said, after considering his question carefully. I wasn't interested in rolling out some glib answer and wanted to make sure that I sincerely believed what I was saying. "I think all of us can assign bias depending upon our own point of view and how we regard a particular news reporter or personality. But after having been in and around a number of television and radio news rooms, both network and local, for a number of years, I am convinced that broadcast news stories are as balanced, if not more so, than in any other media."

"I simply don't agree," the doctor said. The audience was now sitting straight up starting to get involved in the debate.

"Well, think about it," I continued. "A television news story is scrutinized for accuracy and fairness more than any other communications system I am aware of. First it is the responsibility of the reporter and the crew on location when covering a story to see that it is done factually and fairly. A unit editor for the program that will air it then checks the story. A line producer and the executive producer of the program then approve it. If there is any question as to either its accuracy or its balance, it is checked by the executives of the news department and even the president of the news department. I don't know of any other news-gathering source that has that many check points."

"It sounds good," the doctor said, "But I still don't like the way Sam Donaldson treats President Reagan." That brought loud applause.

In Portland, I was also featured on an audience participation show and answered similar questions, except in the Rose City, the concerns centered on children's programs.

"I simply won't let my children watch TV," one woman said. "The cartoons on Saturday morning are loaded with violence."

This gave me the opportunity to discuss my feelings about children's programming and to discuss the children's workshop and the several elements we had proposed for children's programming, including the sharp curtailment of the action-oriented cartoons. That particular segment also got applause from the audience.

During the trip, I taped some local announcements for *American Television and You!* working with news personalities from the two stations. I met with the mayors and newspaper editors in both cities and I had meetings with Senator Bob Packwood in Oregon and Congressman Al Swift in Seattle, both of whom applauded our efforts.

The grassroots aspect of the campaign in the Northwest, and subsequently in other regions of the country, really built the momentum. People are interested in a national campaign mostly when it relates directly to where they work and live.

From its inception, the *American Television and You!* campaign in all of its phases received an enormous response, which continued for more than two years of activity. We had many supporters. Our efforts were featured on the Charles Kuralt *Sunday Morning Show* on CBS and other TV shows and in several magazine and newspaper stories as well as in the broadcasting trade press. I was even parodied on a cable comedy show with a lisping delivery of my *American Television and You!* closing line from the TV spots.

We, every member of the AT&Y staff, regarded all of the criticisms and the wisecracks and the praise as part of the price one pays or the rewards one enjoys when undertaking an activity as controversial and as visible as *American Television and You!* It won several media awards and we all knew that our work was a genuine and sincere effort that had a beneficial effect for ABC and for the television industry.

An independent national probability sample by the R.H. Brushkin Research Company showed the following results to the survey after 32 weeks of the AT&Y campaign:

* Of all respondents, 53% were aware of the television spots.

* 89% of those aware of the spots said it was an excellent, very good or good idea that a network present informational messages about television to viewers.

* Among national newspaper readers, 23% were aware of the AT&Y newspaper stories.

* Of those, 87% said it was excellent, very good, or good that a network present these messages in a newspaper.

* 25% of those aware of either the on-air spots or newspaper pieces said they had a more positive feeling toward television than they did before seeing the message.

The survey also showed that having a believable industry spokesperson was an important part of the campaign.

We were very encouraged since these figures represented significant increases over earlier research studies. I was as surprised as everyone else when the New York State Broadcasters recognized the value and effectiveness of the *American Television and You!* campaign by naming me the "Outstanding Communicator of the Year" for 1986. I interpreted this recognition as an acknowledgment from the industry that providing information on TV and programming was of value.

American Television and You! ran until the spring of 1987 when we decided to concentrate on other public service campaigns that we had begun to develop.

The early and mid-eighties were a good time for me personally to be involved in all of the activity of the media campaigns. Along with my continuing work as the head of the television network, these activities kept me extremely busy traveling and speaking in different cities. The fact that I was so busy helped to take my thoughts and concerns off of some problems on the home front that eventually became very troubling in one case and finally tragic in the other.

My daughter, Marcia, had done very well in her schoolwork, having spent two years at Glen Ridge High School and then two years at Darien High, where she graduated in 1977. She attended Endicott College in Beverly, Massachusetts, where she tried very hard to study and fit in socially, but grew increasingly unhappy. She left Endicott in the spring of her first year. After working at a couple of jobs in the Darien area, she decided to drive to Orlando, Florida where she got a job at Disney World. After a few weeks, she couldn't perform her work and started to complain that she heard voices giving her potentially destructive commands.

Marcia resigned from her job. I arranged to get her home immediately and had her evaluated at Stamford Hospital. The initial examinations were inconclusive and Marcia got a job in Stamford with a vacuum cleaning company, when the voices returned and became severe. On the doctor's recommendation, Marcia was placed in the Elmcrest Medical Center in Middletown, Connecticut, for a few months. After a visit to another institution in the summer of 1980, she was diagnosed as having developed a form of schizophrenia. It is an insidious illness that haunts her to this day. She is much better now, thanks to the miracle drugs Clozaril and Zyprexa and some steady care and counseling at the Devereux Foundation in Devon, Pennsylvania. But, the fact is Marcia has gone through periods of mental torture for the past twenty years. Through it all she has retained her great sense of humor (probably inherited from my mother) and is grateful for the blessings life has given her. She is a very courageous person.

The following year, I had another personal tragedy. On March 21, 1981, I was at a meeting in the conference room next to my office when my assistant, Cindy Van den Heuvel, came in, ashen-faced, with the message that my ex-wife, Betty, was on the phone and it was urgent that she speak with me.

"Steel yourself," Betty said, sobbing. "I just got the word from the Colorado State Police that Terry is dead."

I was shattered. Tears started to cascade down my face as I just sat there holding the phone motionless, unable to speak. After moving in with us in Glen Ridge in 1973, Terry had attended Glen Ridge High School and then finished at Pine Ridge School near Burlington, Vermont. He wanted to work for a couple of years before attending college, so he got a job in production with an audio-visual company in New York and traveled around the country helping to set up large presentation extravaganzas, including some for ABC Television.

Terry had always wanted to live in the West, so in 1978, my friend, Al Flanagan, the vice president and general manager of Channel 9, the ABC affiliate in Denver, interviewed Terry and hired him to work as a floor manager with the station's news team. On my trips to Los Angeles, I would stop in Denver and have dinner with Terry and his girlfriend, Jane. The three of us talked very seriously about drugs and the effects of alcohol. Terry admitted that he imbibed too heavily on occasion and he had started to see a counselor. He most of all wanted to go to college and study creative writing. He had written several essays and he was convinced that he could be a good and successful writer. He enrolled at the Denver Campus of the University of Colorado in the fall of 1980. Terry was a very handsome kid, tall with blue eyes and long sandy hair in keeping with the "flower children" of the sixties. He was quiet and rather pensive, and the girls all seem to want to mother him. It was inconceivable to me that Terry was dead.

Betty, sobbing on the phone, explained that Terry, who was 26 years old, and his roommate had been drinking and apparently played a game of Russian roulette with a Magnum 350 handgun. The Aurora, Colorado, police later explained that the cylinder in the gun rotated counter-clockwise instead of clockwise and the single bullet clicked into the chamber when Terry pulled the trigger.

Betty wasn't up to the journey west, so Jay and I flew to Denver and went to the apartment in Aurora where Terry had been living. We met with his roommate and friends as well as a funeral director, a minister and the police. We were assured that it was a tragic accident, and that there was no evidence of suicide or foul play. Jay and I were in a state of immense shock and grief.

The most devastating experience for me was identifying Terry's body at the coroner's office just as I had identified my daughter Diane's body some eight years before. I am sure that the tragedies I experienced with my own children spurred me on to help other children when I could through my position at ABC and the power of television. But that was no particular comfort to me as I saw that the dead body on the slab was indeed that of my own son. Jay waited outside in the car, sobbing. He did not want to see the body of his dead brother and I understood.

We arranged for a lovely service at a small church in Aurora, where most of Terry's friends lived. We all sat holding hands during the entire service. On the way home in the plane I started writing, trying to get rid of some of the grief: "Grandpa..." I began, "You never told me it would be this way!!"

Along with the trauma of Terry's death, my personal life had changed just prior to that time. After my divorce from Julie was finalized, I became reacquainted with a beautiful actress named Deanna Lund, whom I had met casually several years before when she was featured in an ABC show entitled *Land of the Giants*. Deanna had been in the school of young actresses slated for stardom at the Twentieth Century Fox Studios in the late sixties. Others in the group included Connie Stevens, Dianne Carroll and Janie Wald, all of whom did very well with their respective careers. Along with her television appearances, Deanna appeared in many theatrical releases, including *Tony Rome* with Frank Sinatra and features with Burt Reynolds and Jerry Lewis.

When I met Deanna in the late seventies, she was in the process of a divorce and proved to be a wonderful companion on my trips to the coast. She had two grown children, Randy and Kimberly and a daughter Michelle, then eight years old, a year younger than my daughter Corinne. In later years, Michelle had a brief but successful career of her own in network television under her given name, Michelle Matheson.

After spending considerable time together in New York and Los Angeles, Deanna and I were married in late August 1980. She and Michelle moved east and, with Corinne, we lived in our home in Darien, Connecticut. Michelle and Cori got along very well for the most part, but Deanna hovered over Michelle. I often felt that Cori got short shrift when I wasn't at home. We joined the renowned Ox Ridge Riding Club and Deanna and the girls had their own horses and were involved in hunter-jumper competition. Despite the fact that we had some wonderful times during the initial three years of our marriage, Deanna was simply not happy in the East.

After three years, she moved back to California, where she seemed to be happiest surrounded by her network of show business friends. We bought a house in Century City but because of my job and my children, I spent most of my time on the East Coast. As with other bi-coastal marriages I have seen, the back-and-forth travel became too much. We gradually drifted apart and our marriage came to an end in 1986. It was a very difficult time for me with the death of Terry and now a third failed marriage.

As Deanna and I began more and more to lead our own separate lives, I dedicated a good deal of my time to the ABC media campaign and the rigors of traveling around the country. It was a tremendous experience for me, examining all of the aspects of television and broadcasting in general so as to present them to the general public. I came to have a greater understanding and respect for the system and its enormous effect on our society. I was particularly struck with how effective broadcasting was through public service programs. The medium had grown beyond seeing public service as a reluctant obligation and began to blend issues and messages into the content of programs. The seeds were planted from which the Project Literacy US idea would sprout.

Through my appearances for *American Television and You!*, I also gained an insight into what life must be like for celebrities. People would stop me on the street or at airports and say, "Hey, American Television and You," and, on occasion, even ask for my autograph. I found I was recognized more in the news centers in the country like Washington and New York, and especially in Los Angeles where everyone who is on television is treated as a celebrity.

It was ironic that in certain New York restaurants where, even as the head of a TV network, I might previously have had to wait in line, I was now instantly recognized and taken to a table. The 21 Club on 52nd Street in New York is famous for its policy of seating important people on the left-hand side of the room in the downstairs restaurant; semi-important people (whatever that means) are seated in the middle section; if you are not important according to their standards, you are taken to the far right-hand side of the room or seated in no man's land. I didn't frequent the 21 Club that regularly and had to identify myself if I was meeting someone. I never cared where I sat in the room. But a couple of months after being on TV, I went to meet someone at the restaurant and as I came to the Maitre d's station, I was met with a sugarcoated greeting.

"Ooow, Mr. Duffy. How nice to see you. What a brilliant news program you have. Just in from your Washington studios?"

I smiled and walked past him and joined my friend sitting in the right-hand part of the room.

In the winter of 1985, rumors were rampant about another company possibly merging with or buying ABC. One of the most prominent names being whispered was Capital Cities Communications, a medium-sized, but very successful, media company that had several television and radio stations affiliated with ABC. Because of my dealings with the affiliates, I had come to know the people from Capital Cities – Tom Murphy, the chairman; Dan Burke, the president; and Joe Dougherty, the executive vice president; and a number of the station managers – and I had great respect for them.

The negotiations between Murphy and Goldenson had been going on for some time but had been complicated by ABC's continuing ratings slide in prime time. It resulted in constant revisions of the financial projections. ABC's financial position became so uncertain that Murphy, a long-time leader in broadcasting, almost called off the entire deal.

NBC, after its Silverman disaster, climbed into a dominant number-one position in the evening hours under the leadership of Grant Tinker and a Silverman programming protégée, Brandon Tartikoff. CBS was struggling and about to be purchased by Loews Theaters but still stayed well ahead of ABC.

Goldenson was furious with his network's continuing decline. Elton Rule had retired in 1983 and Leonard had appointed Fred Pierce as the president of ABC. Shortly thereafter, Pierce named Tony Thomopoulos president of the Broadcasting Division despite Goldenson's strong reservations. Thomopoulos, in turn, brought in John Severino as president of the Television Division and appointed Lew Erlick to run the Entertainment Division in hopes of stopping the downward slide in prime time and other entertainment program areas. The game of musical chairs didn't work, and ABC was starting to get a reputation reminiscent of the early sixties. I was relieved not to be on the inside of that circle but frustrated that much of the network's reputation and success that we had helped build, was swiftly disappearing.

We were all surprised when the announcement was made on Monday, March 18, 1985, that the American Broadcasting Companies, Inc. was being sold to Capital Cities for $3.5 billion. The financial package alone illustrated the phenomenal growth of ABC as orchestrated by Goldenson. He had purchased the company for 25 million dollars in 1953. Thirty-two years later, the sale price was almost 150 times greater.

Late one spring afternoon in 1985, shortly after the announcement, Thomopoulos, in his new role as the head of broadcasting, stopped in my office.

"Fred and I have been talking, Jim," he said. "We want to get our house in order before the merger kicks in next January. Would you consider being the president of Communications for the Broadcast Division instead of continuing as president of the television network?"

"What does that mean, Tony?" I asked, being very skeptical of the kind of the maneuvering management might be scheming in view of the Cap Cities purchase.

"It simply means you could devote full time to the activities that you have been doing so well for the past couple of years. You will keep the same office, the same benefits, same salary and everything else. You'll have responsibility for all public service activity and public relations, and you'll be the official spokesperson for the entire Broadcasting Division. I think the title will give you even added prestige. And it will let us rearrange the TV network and do some downsizing."

"Let me think about it, Tony," I said. "I'll get back to you in a couple of days."

I knew as soon as he had left my office that I would accept the new position, not for his reasons, but for my own. The network would be left in good hands since I had appointed George Newi as VP and general manager of the network some years before and key executives were in place in all of the departments. I was concerned about his "downsizing" reference that might affect some of the good people I had hired or worked with for so many years. Yet, I had been president of the television network for fifteen years, eight years longer than any other network president in the history of the television industry. I was excited about the *American Television and You!* campaign and the new challenge of Project Literacy US and other public service activities I knew would come. I felt I was getting stale with the sales and stations activities that were both in excellent shape. I was intrigued about the opportunity to spend more time in Washington and work with government agencies to bring changes to some pressing issues. I was chomping at the bit to utilize my years of experience in broadcasting to accomplish something more meaningful.

Project Literacy US gave me that opportunity.

Eighteen

Project Literacy US

I could feel the electricity in the air. There was a sense of excitement and anticipation that I personally had not felt in some time. I was standing – pacing is a better word – in a small anteroom next to the Whittall Pavilion in the Jefferson Building at the Library of Congress. It was approximately 9:30 in the morning on Tuesday, December 10, 1985.

This was the morning that ABC would officially announce an unprecedented alliance between two major networks, the ABC Television Network and the Public Broadcasting System (PBS), in an all-out war against the hidden and debilitating problem of illiteracy in America. Project Literacy US (PLUS) would become a magnetizing force in the coming years in America's literacy movement.

I am usually nervous before most of my speeches or appearances, but never with the feeling I had on this particular morning. As I looked out at the reporters, service providers, educators, Congressional staff members and others filing in for the press conference, it was more a feeling of underlying excitement, a tingling of anticipation because I, like every other person who was working on the campaign, really wanted it to be accepted and be effective. My department knew from our experience with previous broadcast public service campaigns that we had a dynamic partnership strategy if only the various organizations would put aside their turf issues and work with us. We were confident that PLUS could set a standard for helping to find solutions for social issues in the future.

Al Schneider, ABC's vice president for Standards and Practices, was standing off to one side of the waiting room talking to my long-time associate Dr. John Harr, a vice president and co-founder of PLUS. When I spotted him, Schneider said, "You guys are doing a terrific service. I'm not sure everyone appreciates and understands what your literacy project can accomplish."

"That's what we want to tell them this morning, Doctor," I said. "They will sure know by the time we are finished." Harr nodded his assent.

"I hope so, Jim," Schneider answered. "You know you still have a lot of skeptics about why we're doing it. Bennett [William Bennett, Secretary of Education] came in a few minutes ago and had a couple of comments. He's going to make a few remarks and read a message from the President."

"Yeah, so?" I said, anxious to know why Bill Bennett was skeptical.

"I heard him tell one of his aides, 'If these television people were really serious about this, they'd put an hour-long show on the network to teach reading just before *Monday Night Football.* That would sure get attention.'"

"That shows how little the Secretary really knows about television." I answered. "It might get attention every Monday night, but it sure as hell wouldn't teach many people how to read. We're going to bring an enormous awareness to this problem through all of our TV and radio shows, and we're going to show non-readers and people with low skills where they can go to get some help. The experts, the service providers, some of whom are sitting out in that room now, will teach them how to read and how to keep on learning."

Secretary Bennett's lack of understanding of what we were attempting to do was not surprising. In the many months building up to this announcement we had run into many skeptics who thought we were doing PLUS as a promotion for the network or as a marketing scheme for a new show that would be coming on the air.

At one meeting with a cross-section of educators – elementary school principals, high school teachers, university professors – a woman who was an executive with one of the teachers' unions stood up and said, "Why are you doing this? You people are not educators, you are television people. Why don't you just produce your comedies and leave education to us?" I could have answered: "Well, we've tried that, and now there are tens of millions of illiterates in the country. Why didn't you educate them?" But I didn't. We were determined to change what we recognized as an insulated, short-sighted, fear-stricken view.

Dr. Daniel Boorstin, the distinguished Librarian of Congress, walked to the podium in the jam-packed room. This was the signal for the four of us who would speak to take our positions at a table in the center of the oblong room. Joining me at the dais were Bruce Christensen, president of PBS; Lloyd Kaiser, president of Station WQED in Pittsburgh, PBS' flagship station for the literacy project; and Joe Jerkins, president of KVUE-TV, Austin, Texas, and chairman of the ABC Affiliates Association, representing all of ABC's affiliated stations.

"Here goes the start of a long and productive journey," Christensen whispered as we walked to the front of the room.

A hush fell over the crowd and Dr. Boorstin welcomed the audience, congratulated ABC and PBS for breaking new ground, briefly outlined the scale and nature of the illiteracy problem and introduced Bill Bennett. Secretary Bennett delivered his remarks, which were reservedly supportive, and read a very warm and complimentary message from President Reagan. Senator Paul Simon of Illinois was also introduced and had glowing praise for the potential of the literacy alliance. Dr. Boorstin then introduced the panel members.

When I was introduced, my remarks expanded on Dr. Boorstin's opening with some shocking statistics on the extent of illiteracy in America:

> *We are the least literate nation in the free world.*
> *Twenty-three million adults, 18 years of age and over,*
> *cannot read or write beyond a fourth grade level.*
> *Another 35 to 40 million adults can't read or write*
> *beyond an eighth grade level.*

As I spoke and looked out over the audience of intense faces, some not quite believing and others rather shocked, I found it hard to fathom what those statistics really mean. Almost one quarter of the adult population is at some level of illiteracy. Think about it. Almost one out of every four adults in our country can't read or write or function to a degree adequate to cope with everyday living, let alone hold a job, raise a family, and enjoy so many of life's treasures.

I continued, *More than 72 million adult Americans have never earned a high school diploma.*

Approximately one million young people drop out of school every year [actually, it is 700,000 dropouts and 300,000 chronic truants].

Seventy percent of our prison population is functionally illiterate.

Seventy percent of those inmates will be released within three years, and a minimum two thirds of those individuals will be back in prison within the first year because they can't cope in the outside world.

That was enough of the hard statistics. The audience was starting to get nervous.

We have a plan to help do something about illiteracy through Project Literacy US, I said. It can involve every person in this room and can affect every person in our country.

I explained that PLUS would be divided into two broad time phases – the outreach phase and the awareness-raising phase. It was our plan to build task forces in every major community in America working with our ABC and PBS stations over the first eight or nine months of the campaign. Then, starting in the fall of 1986, the awareness-raising activities would begin with on-air programming by ABC and PBS, supplemented by local programming by ABC and PBS stations throughout the 1986-87 broadcast season.

PLUS's mission was to raise awareness of the illiteracy problem and serve as an all-out call to action against illiteracy and weak basic skills in the United States. It would employ (1) community outreach, (2) visibility through on-air programming and public service announcements nationally and locally, (3) partnerships with affiliated member TV stations and national and local literacy and education organizations, and (4) continuity of the message over a long period of time.

"This is a very deliberate strategy and it is important to understand why," I explained. "Everything we have learned about the illiteracy problem so far tells us that it is absolutely essential that community resources be mobilized, organized and in place before awareness raising with on-air programming begins in earnest. This is so that people who respond to that programming – those who need and want help and those who are able to help – will have somewhere to turn to in every sizable community in the United States. In other words, we will be ready on the local level where the problem really exists for what we hope and believe will become a major national, all-out assault on illiteracy."

I ended by saying,

> *"We're starting something and we hope it will grow into a national movement. The best thing that could happen would be if individuals and organizations of every kind see this as an opportunity to join the fight against illiteracy – other broadcasters, the print media, business, labor, farm groups, religious leaders and church groups, service agencies... everyone. If we can blend all of those resources, if we can all work together, then we will really make a difference."*

The press conference brought a very positive reaction from the traditionally cynical press corps. There was still a let's wait and see attitude, but the response to our plans was exceptional.

But not one of those on the panel who spoke, nor anyone in the audience listening, could really envision at that time the extent of what PLUS would accomplish.

That press conference at which PLUS was launched was the culmination of events which had really begun years before. ABC's possible involvement in this kind of wide-reaching public service activity was first mentioned at an affiliate Board of Governors meeting in Maui, Hawaii, in November of 1983. The Department of Education had just released the shocking *A Nation at Risk* report that showed how our educational system was badly failing in preparing young people for the future. President Reagan had issued a call for a national literacy initiative in that same year and stressed the need for private involvement, public-private cooperation, and community action. It was Martin Umansky, the president of KAKE-TV, Wichita, Kansas, who originally approached me with the idea when I was the president of the television network.

"You know, you fellows ought to do a public service campaign on education," he said. "Young people in this country are simply not being taught the basics. They don't know how to read and they don't know how to learn. Tens of thousands of them graduate from high school and can't read or write or communicate. It's a tragedy and a network campaign could bring awareness to the need." The seed was sown.

In our 1984 affiliate meetings, we found a growing number of station managers who were interested in collaborating in a public service campaign that could be beneficial for the industry, for their communities, and for our country.

When the ABC Office of Communications was formed in 1984, I discussed the pros and cons of a long-range public service campaign with the staff. The more we talked, the more obvious it became that if we, through a national-local campaign, illustrated why an educational reform was needed, then we could create a spark that would ignite all across the country. Many respected leaders and organizations had publicly acknowledged that the US education system was in dire need of reform and attention. The levels of basic skills that were acceptable during the agricultural era and later during the manufacturing revolution after World War II had simply become inadequate in the fast-paced service era with its exploding technological advances.

In investigating the possibilities of an education public service campaign, we discovered quickly that the subject is a firecracker, probably too controversial to get the needed cooperation for a national campaign.

During the course of our look at education, we discovered the shocking figures on the extent of illiteracy. Once we carefully examined statistics on literacy in the United States, we knew something must be done. We felt compelled to make the effort to change this hidden and often silent affliction.

There was a literacy mission that preceded us. The National Literacy Coalition, organizations from around the country concerned with literacy, was formed in 1981 and aired a short-lived campaign with the Advertising Council in 1983. They had an on-air spot portraying a father struggling to try to read a story to his daughter who was seated on his lap.

We discovered that the Public Broadcasting Service (PBS) shared our desire to do something to help with the problems of illiteracy. In early 1985, Margo Woodwell, the vice president and general manager of Station WQED-TV in Pittsburgh, one of PBS's leading stations, had urged the Corporation for Public Broadcasting (CPB) and PBS to undertake a significant initiative on literacy. We met with Margo and her staff and later with Bruce Christensen and the CPB board, and our alliance for PLUS was born.

It was the first time that public broadcasting and commercial television had collaborated in any major fashion. And it gave the campaign a real substance and legitimized it in the eyes of many skeptics – some of whom were present at the press conference – and were wary that PLUS might be some kind of program exploitation.

At the press conference to announce PLUS, Harold J. McGraw, then Chairman of McGraw-Hill Publications and the founder of the Business Council for Effective Literacy, said it best:

"We have needed some real power in the literacy movement for a long time. When I see these two big television battleships coming over the horizon, I know we are in the battle."

It was very significant to our eventual success that Barbara Bush, the wife of the then Vice President of the United States, was active in the cause of literacy.

Following the press conference, even before the Christmas holidays, all of us involved with PLUS, both at ABC and PBS, were feverishly at work. PBS, again mainly through Margo Woodwell and WQED, had the expertise in coalition and task force building and they immediately went to work to reinforce or start task forces around the country.

The base of the literacy task forces, depending on the size and character of a respective community, were built around a representative from the mayor's office, educators, religious leaders and prominent citizens. This was reinforced by the local literacy service providers and volunteer organizations. The ABC and PBS stations were asked to play a key role as catalysts for the task forces in their communities. In truth, some stations came forth wholeheartedly and some lagged behind, still not convinced that literacy was an issue of urgency. But, little by little, the task forces grew and so did the number of stations and citizens who became involved.

The original goal was that 150 task forces would be in place by the time the on-air campaign started in September. When we went on the air in the fall of 1986, there were 220 PLUS Task Forces. The number eventually grew to over 550.

Meanwhile, the PLUS folks at ABC were getting as much information as possible from all of the different constituencies involved in literacy on what materials and ideas would be most effective in our upcoming on-air blitzkrieg about illiteracy.

On three separate occasions the PLUS staff and I met with a cross-section of the country's educational leaders including Mary Futrell, president of the National Education Association; Albert Shanker, president of the American Federation of Teachers; Sam Sava, executive director of Elementary School Principals; and Gordon Ambach, executive director of the Chief State School Officers, among several others. The reaction was mostly supportive, but there were a few who asserted that we should stick with broadcasting and let the teachers teach. A month after the first meeting, the leaders of educator organizations such as the American Federation of Teachers and the National Education Association asked for another one where they pledged their complete support.

One distinguished educator who championed our cause from the beginning was Dr. Frank Newman, president of the Education Commission of the States. He later went for an important research project at Brown University, became a good friend and joined me on the executive committee of the National Mentoring Partnership.

We also met with labor leaders and some of the nation's foremost economists to get their slant on how to approach our broadcasting mission for a more literate America.

Church groups and the leaders of various religions were especially important to us. We knew that their support and encouragement from the pulpit would be a powerful ally. On April 23, 1986, we met with a distinguished group of religious leaders for a think tank luncheon at the Jefferson Hotel in Washington, D.C. Among the sixteen to eighteen guests present were Father Theodore Hesburgh, C.S.C., president of the University of Notre Dame; His Eminence Joseph Cardinal Bernadin, Archbishop of Chicago; Rabbi Joshua O. Haberman, Senior Rabbi, Washington Hebrew Congregation; Bishop James Haskell Mayo, Congress of National Black Churches; and Dr. Ray H. Hughes, president, National Association of Evangelicals. Our guest speaker at the luncheon on the subject of a more literate America was Bill Brock, the Secretary of Labor.

The reason Bill Brock was at the luncheon was that, in his powerful position as the Secretary of Labor, he had become a strong supporter of Project Literacy US. On March 3rd, a good month and a half before the religious leaders' session, our office had asked for a meeting with the Secretary and key members of his staff because illiteracy is a major problem in the American work force (it was widely reported that over 15% of America's work force is functionally illiterate). After we explained PLUS and what we intended to do in the coming months and years, Bill Brock came right out of his chair.

"Wow. That's really powerful," he said. "You are certainly to be commended. We'll be supportive in every way we can." Then he laughed. "I guess I'll have to change all those nasty things I've been saying about television."

It was a remarkable luncheon. The clergymen in attendance were open and thoughtful and posed very insightful questions on broadcasting's role in this kind of initiative.

"I must say, I am surprised that television would undertake this kind of a mission," Cardinal Bernadin said. "So often we are led to believe that media can be destructive. What you are proposing here can be a salvation."

In the following weeks, I received letters from all but two religious leaders who had attended the luncheon. Father Hesburgh sent an especially encouraging letter pledging his support.

We also had several meetings with Secretary Brock, including sharing the podium with him at summit meetings with educators and state political leaders.

Hand in hand with our meetings with a broad spectrum of external organizations, we met with all the divisions inside of ABC. The purpose was to solicit support, cooperation and most of all, interested involvement in PLUS. It wasn't always easy. But despite several skeptics, we prevailed and kept moving forward.

By the fall of 1986, we were ready for the on-air campaign. We had produced a number of thirty- and sixty-second public service announcements all tagged with the line, "It is never too late to learn to read." We had arranged with the National Hotline Center in Lincoln, Nebraska, to have a telephone number follow all of the network spots for people who wanted assistance.

Since I had on-air experience, I assumed the role of host for PLUS and introduced the spots for the opening months of the campaign.

We sent copies of the PLUS announcements along with promotion materials to our ABC-TV affiliates and to the ABC Radio networks and their affiliated stations. PBS sent some of the same materials to their 314 member stations along with their own programming flyers. And we also sent kits and supplementary information to our partner national and local public and private organizations, which had grown to a powerful 138 in number. It was a community relations model at work on a grand scale.

All areas of ABC's programming departments finally cooperated and scheduled programs or announcements for PLUS, led by ABC News. The trumpets of war against illiteracy had sounded and we were ready to lead the charge.

After thirty-six years in the broadcasting business, the last fifteen as a president of a major network, I found myself on the doorstep of one of the most inspiring and rewarding adventures of my life.

One of the meetings in the introductory period of PLUS was especially fascinating and certainly memorable. It was with Secretary of Labor Brock and a famous ex-Hollywood actor. As the president of Communications for Capital Cities/ABC following my tenure as the head of the TV network, I was appointed to President Ronald

Reagan's Private Sector Initiative Board. At this particular meeting, the more human, personal side of the man came through. Secretary Brock asked me to make a presentation on Project Literacy US to the President and the employees of the U. S. Department of Labor. As a matter of fact, it was unprecedented for a representative from the private sector, and especially the media, to be a presenter at such a meeting. The large assembly hall was jam-packed with over 2,000 Department of Labor employees. I sat at the end of a long, slightly curved conference table on a platform at one end of the room with the President, Secretary Brock, and two high-ranking Department of Labor officers, Dennis Whitfield and Roger Semerad, who later became a very close friend. President Reagan sat at the center of the table. I studied him as the meeting got underway. He struck me as a most handsome and charming man, with an attractive smile, even though he was in his late-seventies at that time. When you looked at him and saw the darkened hair, he looked much younger than he was. There were stories that he used to nod off, but I didn't see it, although he repeated the same joke in a couple of meetings I attended and apparently didn't remember that he had already told it.

I was the last speaker introduced and as I delivered my presentation directed mainly to the President, he nodded and followed my eyes very closely. He knew who I was because I was on his board. I'm not sure that he really was focused on everything I was saying, but he nodded and seemed to approve of broadcasting's involvement and leadership in the literacy and work force movement.

After the presentation, the panel members were chatting in a long hall outside of the assembly room when Secretary Brock and the President came by to talk with us. I shook hands with the President and the Secretary and thanked them for their kind words. As Bill Brock was finishing his words about the presentation, I felt a strange tug on my coat sleeve. It was President Reagan. He said very softly, "I have a bone to pick with you."

I became immediately concerned. I looked at his face and there wasn't a stern look; he had a soft expression, almost a small smile, but an intensity that indicated we have a problem here. My first thought was that Sam Donaldson had called him something awful or somebody from ABC had really ripped one of his decisions.

I just said, "Well, Mr. President, what is it?"

"You've lost my son!"

Here was the President of the United States telling me we had misplaced his son, Ron, whom I had met, and who was working as a reporter for *Good Morning, America.* "I beg your pardon. What do you mean?" was all I could say.

"He's working for *Good Morning, America* and you sent him over to Russia for a story," the President said. "He hasn't been heard from in three days. His mother is trying to reach him. We're a bit worried."

And I said, "Well, ah..., gee, ah, Mr. President, Ron really does an outstanding job on the program. Ah...let me look into it right away." So, I ran over to a telephone and called the *Good Morning, America* office. I can't remember who was in charge, but I said, "Hey, we have to get to the news bureau and find out where Ron Reagan is and have him call home!"

And they said, "Yeah, we're very much aware of the situation. This is not the first we've heard of it. We spoke to him this morning and told him to call."

As it turned out, young Ron was engrossed in his assignment and finally did call the First Lady.

As I walked out of the Labor Building on Independence Avenue, I looked up at our nation's Capitol in all its splendor and I remembered how I had gotten into this business back in Beloit as a reporter. Here I was, an executive for a major TV network, and I was being asked by the President of our nation to check up on his son, who worked as a reporter for the same network. Is this a great country, or what? It could only happen in America.

PLUS started its awareness-raising phase on Wednesday, September 3, 1986.

As I mentioned earlier, it was not easy getting to that point. We had many skeptics both outside and inside of our company prior to the merger of Capital Cities and ABC. We were now working for a new company and we really didn't know what the attitude toward the campaign would be.

The merger between Capital Cities and ABC became effective in January of 1986. The first place I went was to the management of the newly merged company, Tom Murphy, the chairman, and Dan Burke, the president. I had informal meetings with Murphy and Burke prior to the finalizing of the merger and they seemed supportive of our PLUS plans. I did not know how genuine that support would be once they were in full command.

Burke, as the chief operating officer, was the person responsible for overall activities of the corporation, including my activities and the Office of Communications.

When I went in to see Dan, I realized that the timing in asking for the new company's support, financially and otherwise, was just about as bad as it could get. ABC had fallen off badly in its ratings and earnings in 1985 and had given Murphy and Burke some sleepless nights and second thoughts about the wisdom of finalizing the merger. Capital Cities had the reputation of being lean and mean, of being a well-managed company but without any frills and commitments that didn't fall in direct line of its businesses.

I had considerable trepidation as I walked into Burke's office on the 39th floor of the ABC building. In shirtsleeves and totally relaxed, Dan was extremely friendly and gracious.

"Hey, kid, it's nice to see you," he greeted me. (I always enjoyed Dan's "kid" since I am a couple of years older than he is.) "I hear you are doing some wonderful things."

I thanked him and brought him up to date on all of our activities, including Project Literacy US and the recently held press conference at the Library of Congress. And then I asked for the company's continuing all-out support in our mission.

Dan dispelled all of my fears in one sentence. "What you are doing is too important to this company and our country not to continue." And then he added, "You have my complete support. Take it as far as it will go. I believe literacy is a key to this country's future."

I later learned that Dan had a personal interest in literacy since he and his wife, Bunny, had quietly tutored a young person with weak skills for a number of years. He also was on the boards of directors and was a driving force behind other literacy and education initiatives such as *Reading is Fundamental* and *Cities in Schools*. Dan Burke became our catalyst for PLUS, encouraging us to reach out to new audiences and new partners. He urged us to measure our progress at appropriate steps along the way.

His words were especially encouraging to me, even if they were somewhat in jest. "You're doing God's work, kid. You're going to get all of us through the pearly gates."

Another Burke was also extremely helpful to us. His name was David Burke and he was at the time a vice president and assistant to the president of ABC News, Roone Arledge. He would later become the president of CBS News. While the legendary Arledge was often inaccessible, David Burke was available and willing to listen. He immediately understood the significance of the literacy campaign and became the connecting link to the different news departments and programs during the months leading up to the fall of 1986.

Cooperation within the company depended on whether a particular performer, producer or program head really believed that the literacy project was beneficial not just to the company and the country, but to his or her particular program. There was no way we could "force feed" literacy into a program on ABC.

Jack Harr and I visited with David Hartman, the long-time host of *Good Morning, America*, along with the program's producers. They were very interested and supportive since their program deals with a broad range of topics. The people at ABC Sports were also quite cooperative, as were the executives and producers for the Monday through Friday daytime program schedule.

The most resistance came from the ABC Television Entertainment Division and the people responsible for the prime-time schedule, and from certain executives within the TV network itself.

The prime-time programming people in Los Angeles were cordial in our meetings and very congratulatory, promised their support, but none was forthcoming. We finally fixed that by working directly with the studios and producers of shows who had an interest in PLUS.

Inside the ABC network we experienced a similar lack of cooperation but with fewer false promises. John Sias, the president of the Network Division, was most cooperative and said privately that he thought we were doing a great service for our country. But the operating heads of the departments, which I had previously been responsible for as the president of the TV network, showed little interest. The fellow who replaced me as the head of the network was heard to say on several occasions, "He [meaning me] is using valuable air time with the same kind of crap as the information campaign."

The lack of interest from the network departments didn't slow us down in the least since we had many contacts in the advertising community and with the affiliates. The disinterest and anxiety was a sign of the times at ABC, an attitude based on the descending profits and ratings position in the mid-eighties and a far cry from the spirit of the "ABC family" of just five years earlier.

The ABC Radio Division became a great ally from the first moment we met with the key network and station executives. The radio network people immediately caught the spirit of the campaign and were writing lines for PLUS announcements practically before we left the meeting room. The reach and frequency of the radio announcements and programs over their several networks added a strong reinforcement to the television messages. Later, National Public Radio added its considerable support. I was well aware from my own experience that radio put TV in business.

The PLUS on-air campaign opened with a startling piece on *Good Morning, America* on the dimensions of illiteracy and its effects on people's lives. David Hartman interviewed several leaders in the literacy field and talked about the new, unprecedented broadcasting campaign.

We ran our PLUS public service spots all through the day. On *World News Tonight*, Peter Jennings made an announcement about the national literacy initiative along with a suggestion for viewers to watch special news programs about illiteracy later in the evening.

The centerpiece of the kick-off for the campaign was an hour-long documentary entitled *At a Loss for Words, Illiterate in America*. The program was hosted by Jennings and produced by Tom

Lennon, who produced ABC's Emmy and Peabody Award-winning documentary, *To Save our Schools, To Save our Children*. The literacy program was brilliant. It outlined the problems of illiteracy and showed the debilitating constraints on people's lives.

One scene was set in a small town in the Rust Belt of the United States. Jennings, in his narration said, "The inability of the work force to read written instructions or do basic math has plagued the factories here."

A carpet factory executive explained that thousands of dollars were being wasted every week because many employees didn't know how to read a ruler. One of the workmen, a young man wearing a baseball cap and a tee shirt, was interviewed.

"I ain't comfortable at all with fractions," he said. "I don't even know anything about fractions," he shrugged and said with a smile. "If half and half makes a whole that's as close as I can get."

Jennings, in his narration, explained that about half of America's workers read or compute at about an eighth grade level or below. "A generation ago that didn't matter so much," he said. "But now work is more complex, competition more fierce."

The workman was asked that if a document were put into his hands did he feel he could read it.

"I don't even know what a 'document' means," the man said with uncertainty. "I wouldn't...ah.... Would it be a book? I...I really wouldn't know...."

The announcer explained to the man that document means a piece of paper with information on it.

The man grinned a bit sheepishly, "As long as it wasn't over five letters long, I could probably handle it."

In another segment, Jennings interviewed a middle-aged woman from Pittsburgh who was just beginning to learn to read.

Casual in shirtsleeves, Peter sat at a table across from the woman who was pictured slightly in shadows.

He asked gently, "What would you like to read most?"

The woman brought her hands up to her face and started to cry. She paused and finally said, "The Bible."

"It is incredibly courageous, Loberta, to be learning to read at fifty-one," Peter said. "Is it also exciting?"

Fighting back her tears, she nodded her head and said, "Yes."

"What's the best thing?" Peter asked.

"By getting new words," Loberta struggled and almost sobbed, "words I could never read before, I ca...I can read now."

Jennings paused to let her get her composure. "Like what?" he asked.

Loberta slowly took her hands away from her mouth. "Like 'bird' and 'wing.'"

On the screen, a picture of two birds gracefully winging their way through the sky appeared while soft music came up underneath.

That scene with Loberta is so moving that every time I see it – and I have seen it at least fifty times – tears come to my eyes.

At a screening for newspaper critics and columnists a few days before the campaign premiered, I showed the Loberta clip. Several ABC executives, including Leonard Goldenson, were in attendance as well as Jennings, whom I had asked to say a few words. When the lights came up after the scene with Loberta and Peter, all those in the room, without exception, had tears in their eyes – including Peter Jennings.

One of the reasons that the subject of illiteracy is powerful on television is that it is so touching and human. Jennings, who has been all over the world and has witnessed the effects of hideous crimes and the devastation of war, told me that he has never been as moved as in his discussion with Loberta.

At a Loss for Words, Illiterate in America brought a widespread reaction from viewers and unusual critical acclaim. One critic wrote, "It was hard hitting and touching at the same time, the kind of programming that TV needs." And for those whose interests were concerned with ratings, the program won its time period (10:00 –11:00 PM EDT) against entertainment programming on NBC and CBS. It was the highest-rated documentary of the season.

Wrapping up the literacy premiere day, Ted Koppel devoted his full *Nightline* program to the extent of illiteracy with a special look at what brought about the problem and a discussion on how a lack of understanding of words can threaten personal freedom.

On Friday of that same week, the news-produced program *20/20* did a special piece that featured Hugh Downs in a grocery store in Finland, where the labels and symbols on cans and boxes were unrecognizable and unreadable to those who could not read or understand the Nordic language. It graphically brought home the plight of millions of illiterate Americans who struggle every day in a similar fashion in their own country.

On Saturday afternoon, September 5, ABC Sports did a special live cut-in from the National Literacy Hotline Center at half time of the Oklahoma-Nebraska football game, and showed the PLUS volunteers busily at work on the phones.

The following morning, *This Week with David Brinkley* devoted the entire program to the subject. Sam Donaldson, Brinkley and other reporters delved into the problems of the lack of reading and writing skills in the country and what it might portend for the future. They interviewed leaders in the literacy movement, including Harold McGraw, who had been so forceful at our press conference; David Harmon, professor of education at Columbia; author Sidney Shelton and others.

In their usual hard-hitting fashion, Brinkley and company, with some skepticism, hammered at the reported statistics on the extent of illiteracy. Frankly, it was a little embarrassing for McGraw, because it was obvious that the reporters didn't believe in the importance of the literacy movement and it came through in the questioning. I was told later that Brinkley and his staff resented the idea of being asked to do a program on the subject, feeling it was not that significant. I was also told that they later admitted their "miscalculation" after the literacy effort reached the top of the nation's agenda.

In the following week, PBS presented its documentary entitled *A Chance To Learn*, which also received positive reviews and was used in many schools as part of classroom assignments. Two weeks later, PBS presented *Project Second Chance: Drop Outs in America*, hosted by Robin MacNeil. It examined the reasons students drop out of school and the results of their actions. PBS also featured literacy spots and segments in other programs, including their highly recognized children's shows.

During these opening weeks, many ABC and PBS stations had tailored their own local PLUS programs to supplement the network offerings and ABC Radio had started its campaign, which was also augmented by local radio stations around the country.

Later, story lines involving illiteracy appeared in prime-time dramatic and comedy shows, including *Growing Pains, Webster, Hotel, Sidekicks, Jack and Mike, Hooperman* and *Who's the Boss*. Continuing story lines were developed in the daytime serials Loving and *Ryan's Hope* and the network featured an *ABC Afterschool Special* for younger viewers entitled *Daddy Can't Read*.

Project Literacy US was like a barrage of missiles in an all-out broadcasting blitz – a coordinated effort on a single issue that media had never attempted before. Within a month after we started our on-air campaign, we knew we had hit a national nerve.

The national hotline number, which had been getting two or three thousand calls a month prior to PLUS, suddenly was getting twenty to twenty-five thousand calls a month. Local literacy hotlines experienced similar escalation in the number of calls for information and help. At the literacy coalition in Charlotte, North Carolina, there were more calls in the month of September than in the previous ten years. The ABC affiliate in Boston, WCVB-TV, in conjunction with the Boston PBS affiliate, produced a literacy resource guide for Massachusetts residents. In the two months after PLUS debuted, the Massachusetts hotline received more calls than it did in all of 1985.

The national service provider organizations, Literacy Volunteers of America and Laubach Literacy, doubled and even tripled the number of new learners, and out of necessity put on local drives to increase the number of tutors to accommodate the increased number of learners. We received reports from many local coalitions that their numbers were increasing as many as tenfold. Typical of the many letters I received was one from a Betty Gall-Vaughn in Anchorage, Alaska:

> *Mr. Duffy,*
> *Since TV awareness of the problem last fall, our American born adult student count has increased 160%*

in one year. We hear the story over and over: the
American born illiterates thought they were the "only
one." They also believe they are stupid and there is no
help.... Our thanks and undying gratitude for your part
in literacy awareness. Both you and PBS have made vast
differences in the number of prospective adult students
and tutors responding to our program, the Anchorage
Literacy Project.

The problem of illiteracy, affecting some sixty million Americans – young and old, from farms and cities, and from every ethnic group and culture – started to emerge from the shadows. What had been a humiliating and embarrassing deficiency to so many of our citizens was now coming into open light where people could see that there were others with the same problem and, most importantly, that there was help available and an opportunity to find new meaning in their lives.

A national literacy movement had truly begun. The impact of the national awareness had reached the local providers, and now the importance of "learning" had evolved into action all across our nation. It was exciting to see how the power and reach of broadcasting, along with the efforts of national leaders and literacy service organizations, had helped trigger a literacy reformation movement.

We were aware that we were only at the beginning. But we indeed had begun. Our original commitment for PLUS was eighteen months, from December 1985 through June 1987. In the spring of 1987, we held a press conference to announce that we would continue the campaign. Mrs. Bush had videotaped a special message for the conference saluting PLUS for its progress. Governor Bill Clinton of Arkansas, Senator Ted Kennedy, and Mayor Wilson Goode of Philadelphia joined us at the conference. They were effusive with praise for PLUS and eloquent in their appeal to keep the literacy mission in high gear.

Tom Murphy, chairman of Capital Cities/ABC, was at the press conference and said a few words on our behalf. Before the meeting started, I introduced him to Governor Clinton. I said to him, "This is my man. He's going places." Murphy has reminded me several times how I introduced him to the next President of the United States.

I announced that we would continue the ABC/PBS campaign for at least another year. Privately we hoped it would be for much longer. Publicly, I said in several speeches that we hoped to continue as long as we are needed.

As I left the Mayflower Hotel ballroom where the press conference was held, Governor Clinton stopped me and patted me on the back.

"This is really powerful, Jim," he said. "You're making a difference in this country. Keep it up."

I felt motivated and excited. I found those early days of PLUS to be among the most rewarding and stimulating experiences of my career. All of us involved in PLUS knew that in less than one year on the air, the campaign was working and that we were making a difference. Yet we also knew that we had just started. We knew that we had to keep our messages and programming fresh and vital in the coming months and keep adding partners who could help in our battle for a more literate America.

There were many more exciting days to come, many involving a series of what I called PLUS tent pole events – major programming occasions around which the rest of our literacy activities could rally. Some of these events would involve the gracious woman who was soon to become America's First Lady.

Nineteen

Barbara Bush

Barbara Bush was destined to be a leader in America's, indeed the world's, literacy movement. Her husband's visibility and position at various levels of government gave her the platform from which to inspire and lead. But, more importantly, Barbara Bush did not just choose literacy as a cause; it was a fundamental belief. She loves children and always loved to read to children, her own and others, long before the problem of illiteracy was spotlighted.

Despite the fact that we had worked closely with Mrs. Bush's Chief of Staff, Susan Porter Rose, in preparing for PLUS, I had not personally met Mrs. Bush until after the PLUS on-air campaign was underway.

On Wednesday, September 10, 1986, Jack Harr, Nancy Nielsen, Anderson Clark and I were invited to the Vice President's house at 10:00 AM for a meeting with Mrs. Bush and her staff to discuss our literacy plans. As we drove through the gates of the seventy-seven-acre estate on Massachusetts Avenue, I was excited about meeting the person who had received positive reactions from almost every quarter in the tough and often cruel political world of Washington, D.C.

The residence is a large frame house that sits on a long carpet of immaculately maintained grass. Two large ship anchors flank the entrance near the security gate, testimony to the fact that the house was originally built for an admiral on the Naval Observatory grounds in 1883. It officially became the home of the Vice President in 1974 and was made somewhat famous by Nelson Rockefeller, who used the house to entertain, although he did not live there.

We were ushered into the house and taken past a dining room and into a small sitting room. We were chatting amiably with Susan Porter Rose and a member of her staff, when Mrs. Bush entered. The entire room came alive.

I had always envisioned Mrs. Bush in bright blue, probably because I had seen so many pictures of her wearing blue dresses that accented her blue eyes and white hair. On this morning, she wore a gray skirt and a subtle gray and green cardigan, and a very warm welcoming smile. After the formality of the introductions, we told Mrs. Bush and the others of our progress with PLUS and how pleased we were with the reaction to the press conference which had been held the previous week. I thanked her for the very supportive tape that she had narrated for the press conference, and emphasized how we looked forward to working with her in the future.

"I will do whatever I can to be helpful," she said. "You are doing a wonderful service for our country, and George and I cannot thank you enough for all that you are doing and will do."

Mrs. Bush told us how she came to embrace literacy as a cause. "When George first got into politics," she said, "I figured that I should really have a cause that we could rally around which would help other people. I figured if people could learn to read and write they could do just about anything. I love books and I thought if I could help others get interested in reading, it would be a worthwhile service."

This meeting was the beginning of a wonderful relationship that would have many unusual and meaningful moments in the following five years.

Because of my connection with literacy and education I not only had access to civic and business groups and literacy service providers, but I visited resource and remedial training centers and met many students involved in the learning process. On one visit in early 1987, I went to the IBM training program in the Silver Oaks Center near Cincinnati, Ohio, where I toured the facility and met a number of new students. One student was a fifty-year-old man named Estel Sizemore.

After I watched Mr. Sizemore work at his computer training station, I asked him how he was doing in the program.

"I couldn't read hardly at all when I first come here." He said. "Now after three years, I got so's I can read pretty good. You know a lot of people learn to read so that they can read to their children. I never got to do that. Now, I've got a great-granddaughter... tears started to well up in his eyes. ...and I'm going to read to her."

"We've got to get this on tape," I thought as I listened to Estel. He would be an inspiration to other people who were unable to read. Before I left, Estel took me out and proudly showed me his pick-up truck. On a banner across the back was a sign that said, "IT'S NEVER TOO LATE TO LEARN TO READ. AND IT'S FREE. CALL THIS NUMBER...."

"I tell everybody I can," Estel said. "This has changed my life."

When I got back to New York I discussed my Estel Sizemore experience with the PLUS staff.

"There has to be a way we can get people like him on the public service spots. It would really be powerful," I said.

Jack Harr suggested that we do a series call the *PLUS Learners of the Month* where every month a public service announcement would feature a new student who exemplified progress in a literacy program. Estel Sizemore became the first *PLUS Learner of the Month*. It was a series that lasted two years and brought an astounding reaction from a broad spectrum of the television audience. Non-readers and folks with low basic skills in the audience related to the people on the screen, and they reacted and responded. The hotline calls would escalate every time a *Learner of the Month* spot aired. We could track the trends in the monthly call reports.

On a trip to Asheville, North Carolina, where I was invited to make a speech on behalf of our affiliated station to the Asheville Area Chamber of Commerce, I encountered another powerful story.

Following my speech, the local station showed a documentary on literacy that they had taped in western and southern North Carolina. Toward the end of the program, they told the story of J. T. Pace, a sixty-four-year-old Black man and the son of a sharecropper. Pace had failed to learn to read because, from the time he was very young, he worked long hours every day in the fields. He told his own story in the program. He had always wanted to read the Bible, and finally, after joining a literacy program, he was able to read. One glorious day he stood up in front of his rural church congregation and with tears streaming down his face, read passages from the Holy book. In the closing frames of the program, there was a closeup of Mr. Pace's face as he said, with his eyes filled with tears: "When I broke out and said, 'Hey, I can't read, I've never been to school,' that freed me. It's something that I can't explain. I'm so free. All the feelings of guilt for so many years in my life now have turned into joy."

J. T. Pace became another *Learner of the Month* who helped motivate others to do something about their inability to read.

I found out that illiteracy is not relegated to certain social classes or income brackets. In San Diego, California, I was invited to give the keynote luncheon address to the city's Chamber of Commerce. When I arrived at the hotel ballroom, I saw a tall, good-looking blond fellow standing near the dais talking with a group of people. As I approached him, I thought he must be the president of the Chamber or the mayor or a civic leader. He introduced himself as John Corcoran and told me that he was also one of the speakers on the program. He told me that he was very nervous because he had never read a speech in front of a group. Despite getting through college and having been a teacher, he had never learned to read until recent months. He had bluffed and faked his way through forty-eight years of his life with a secret that he had shared only with his wife. Amazingly, he was a self-made millionaire in the construction business.

Mr. Corcoran spoke just before I did (following the luncheon) and, frankly, I should have stayed home. Haltingly at first, Corcoran read his story in public for the first time. As he got toward the end his voice gained in strength coming to a very powerful finish. The audience gave him a sustained standing ovation. It underscored to me how very human the entire matter of literacy is. John Corcoran also became a *PLUS Learner of the Month*, and was featured on an episode of *20/20* on ABC-TV and in several national magazines. John Corcoran has gone forward to become a champion for literacy, recognized as one of the top speakers on the subject. And he has authored a book on the extraordinary story of his struggle with illiteracy. Corcoran was later appointed to the Board of Directors of the National Institute for Literacy.

At that luncheon in San Diego, Helen Copley, the publisher of the *Copley Newspapers*, invited me to speak at the annual Copley convention of newspaper editors the following January at their ranch, Borrego Springs, in Palm Desert, California. It was an opportunity to tell the PLUS story to Copley editors from around the country. It also provided the opportunity to meet with former President Richard Nixon, who was invited to speak at the conference.

President Nixon has been criticized for many things, but one of them surely cannot be his ability to speak off the cuff. One afternoon, in the oblong conference room, with an enormous circular table for the guests, Mr. Nixon stood in the center of the room and talked for almost an hour. Without a note of any kind, he predicted the demise of Communism in the Soviet Union and the rising power of the Republic of China. He told of his travels to both of these world powers and the people he met. Nixon detailed those who would come to prominence and those who would fail. I was mesmerized.

When he finished, I heard one of the editors seated near me whisper, "He's one of the smartest sons a bitches that ever walked."

Later at a reception, I introduced myself to President Nixon. I told him how much I enjoyed his insights. I also told him briefly how we were using the power of broadcasting to help in the literacy movement.

He stared at me and then awkwardly reached out and patted me on the shoulder a couple of times. "Good boy," he said. "Good boy." I don't think he really listened to what I had said.

As for the tent pole events, those extraordinary programs that rise above usual television programs, we tried for months to get the attention and the cooperation of the ABC West Coast program people. Prime time is where the largest viewership exists and the programmers don't let you forget it. One of the elements we had talked about with executives in the ABC Entertainment Division early on was the possibility of an *ABC Movie of the Week* concerned with the problems of illiteracy. We were encouraged by the entertainment division president's assurance that it might be possible, but also desirable. When we met with the executive in charge of the *Movies of the Week*, it was a different story.

"Look, there is no drama in illiteracy," he said. "It is frightening and boring to the audience."

I fought to keep my composure, "No, you look, you nitwit," I wanted to say. "You are wrong..." Instead, I said, "Hey, Lou, you're way off base. You should travel with us and meet some of the new learners. You can feel the emotion and the drama of how their lives have changed. There are hundreds of very human and compelling stories. Many classic programs that have done well in the theater and on television have had an undercurrent of have and have not, of illiteracy in essence, and they have done extremely well. What do you think *Pygmalion* is about?"

He didn't want to listen. He just smiled and went back to his script of *Hookers and Hype on Sunset Boulevard* or some equally shallow relevant ratings generator.

Finally I said, "Well if you won't do it, somebody else will."

Ultimately, we got the entertainment division to agree to a gigantic Fourth of July Special from the waterfront in St. Louis, Missouri.

The St. Louis fireworks celebration was known as the best in the nation, and over a three-day weekend, it attracted as many as four million people. The programmers were interested since this was in the middle of the summer in a low-rating period. The show could possibly attract new viewers with an all-star cast, especially if we could deliver Oprah Winfrey as master of ceremonies and Barbara Bush as a special guest.

We could and we did. On June 5th, the sponsoring group for the Fourth of July Celebration, Veiled Prophet Fair, had a special luncheon and reception at the Adam's Mark Hotel in St. Louis where Oprah and Mrs. Bush, along with Missouri Governor John Ashcroft, were guests of honor. I remember it well because it was the first time Barbara and Oprah had met and the contrast was striking and delightful. I had the privilege of introducing Mrs. Bush to the audience of civic leaders and later of acting as her escort at the reception.

One rather crass reporter approached Mrs. Bush as she spoke with a crowd of admirers and asked bluntly, "How do you feel about the rumors going around about your husband's affair with a secretary?"

Everyone stopped talking and stared incredulously at the reporter and then back at Mrs. Bush. This was at a time when an unnamed government official had suggested the Vice President had been dallying with one of his staff members The rumor was later found to be totally false.

Mrs. Bush looked back at the reporter with her large and warm blue eyes and with a slight smile said, "Oh, I don't pay any attention to those kind of things." Then she looked at me and said, "You know Jim Duffy and I have been having an affair for some time."

I blushed and said, "You promised you wouldn't tell."

The crowd laughed and the tension was broken. The reporter, chagrined, crawled off to look for other dirt.

The Fourth of July program was a three-hour entertainment magazine extravaganza that originated on a stage under the Gateway Arch on the Mississippi River waterfront. Entitled *A Star-Spangled Celebration*, it was advertised as a benefit for the National Coalition for Literacy.

Robert Urich co-hosted with Oprah and introduced the various program segments. These included many entertainers, brief statistics, and taped pieces about the effects of illiteracy and the literacy movement. Marty Pasetta, in conjunction with Gary Pudney and Don Colhour of ABC, produced the program and blended the elements into a fast-moving, entertaining evening. Among the stars performing on stage were Tony Bennett, Jennifer Holiday, Suzanne Somers, Peter Allen and the Radio City Music Hall Rockettes, Bernadette Peters, Chubby Checker, Dwight Yoakum, and Phil Driscoll. Appearing on cut-ins from locations around the country were Barbara Mandrell, Alabama, Ben Vereen and Loretta Lynn. Speaking for literacy were Secretary of Labor Brock and former Chief Justice Earl Warren along with Mrs. Bush.

The highlight of the show was when Mrs. Bush appeared on stage in front of an audience of 800,000 people under the Gateway Arch, and read the Preamble to the Constitution with our friend J.T. Pace, the sharecropper's son from North Carolina. From my vantage point behind the scene, I had observed J.T. Pace enjoying the refreshments with the entertainers and I became concerned about a possible embarrassing situation. When J.T. was called on stage, he had a huge smile and was glowing and not entirely articulate. Mrs. Bush calmly took charge of the situation and with her arm around his waist, asked everyone to join them in reading the Preamble. It was one of many magic moments that Barbara Bush brought to the PLUS campaign.

My prophecy to the ABC Entertainment Division that someone else would produce a movie for television on literacy came true.
We got a call from the J. Walter Thompson Advertising Agency
advising us that their client, Nabisco, was interested in sponsoring a
movie on the effects of illiteracy and wanted to possibly coordinate
with PLUS.

Of course, this was music to our ears. The agency had already
contacted a fine producer, Don Ohlmeyer (later president of NBC
West Coast), whom we knew well from his days as a producer at
ABC Sports. We met with Ohlmeyer and his staff in Los Angeles
and were very excited because they immediately understood the
drama and emotions of the illiteracy problem.

The movie that was produced was *Bluffing It*, which became a
benchmark in the literacy movement. It starred Dennis Weaver as
Jack Dugan, a family man who has reached middle age with no one
except his wife knowing his secret. He is functionally illiterate.
Dugan is a factory foreman who has faked his way through life by
developing a collection of tricks and excuses that have kept everyone
around him from recognizing his problem. He is also a natural leader
and well liked by all of his fellow workers. One day word comes
down that the plant will be computerized. Dugan must face a
moment of truth. In a very compelling scene, Dugan is with his boss
on the assembly line in front of his co-workers, while the boss rather
excitedly shows Dugan the new technology that is being installed.

"Let's have some fun," the boss says. "Let me show you how it
works." He types in a command on the large keyboard and then
looks over at Dugan.

"Just punch in 'ENTER', Jack."

Dugan is panic-stricken. He looks down at the foreign keys and
words and doesn't know what to do. He starts to stammer and perspiration breaks out on his face.

"Press 'ENTER,' Jack. Right in front of you."

"I can't," Dugan almost sobs. "I can't do it."

"You mean you won't do it," the boss says accusingly.

"No, I mean I can't," Dugan screams frantically. "I can't." And
he turns and walks away and then turns back and as he throws his
clipboard to the ground he yells, "I quit."

The trauma of losing his job, and the near-fatal accident he causes because he couldn't read the road signs, finally force him to do something about his illiteracy. Fighting his feeling of shame and inferiority, he enrolls in a literacy program through the local library.

The response from the audience was overwhelming. Tens of thousands of people related to the plight of Jack Dugan. In my conversations with non-readers who had joined literacy programs after seeing the movie, almost every one said, "That person on the television screen was me."

I don't believe there has ever been a TV program on a social issue that generated anywhere near the response of *Bluffing It*. At the end of the movie, the tag line of the PLUS campaign was read, "...It is never too late to learn to read. If you need help, call this number."

By the next morning, over 20,000 calls had been received at the National Literacy Hotline Center in Lincoln, Nebraska. The Center could not get enough phones or volunteers to handle the flood of calls that day and it continued through the week. When the movie was repeated on the network on a Sunday night in June of 1988, the response was the same: 20,000 calls to the National Hotline by the next day.

People still talk about *Bluffing It* whenever I attend literacy and education meetings and conferences.

Another tent pole event, smaller, but still very important to PLUS, was an *Afterschool Special* that played in June of 1987, entitled *Read Between The Lines*. It was significant because it starred the Broadway actor Philip Bosco, along with the Harlem Globetrotters, in a story about a toy maker who had never admitted he couldn't read and faced the loss of the rights to his greatest creation. This program also solicited a large response, and, importantly, much of it was from the teenage audience.

While we were involved in the show business aspect of PLUS, ABC and the television network continued to struggle with its entertainment prime-time programming. Grant Tinker had put NBC in a strong leadership position that was somewhat reflective of the ABC glory days in the mid-seventies. Cable and other technologies on the horizon continued to pose a threat to commercial broadcasters. Most of the cable networks were more promise than performance at this point, but ABC, wisely, had major equity positions in two cable operations that showed unusual potential: ESPN and Arts & Entertainment. At Fred Pierce's urging in the seventies, Leonard Goldenson had made a major investment in the two cable entities. It created some confusion with ABC's strong campaign promoting over-the-air television against cable and the constant assurances to stations and advertisers that commercial broadcasting was ABC's primary business. Goldenson's investment later paid enormous dividends. ESPN, which has become a definitive center of the sports world, has made substantial profits.

As the president of Communications, I found myself in an increasingly comfortable position with organizations and institutions in the world beyond broadcasting. In Washington, and especially on the Hill, I was no longer perceived as "one of those greedy network guys." As president of the network, I had been viewed, as were most other network executives, as only visiting Washington when I wanted something from the government that would benefit my company. In the communications position, and especially because of the growing visibility of PLUS, I was looked on as being in a position to help members of Congress in public service pursuits.

"You're on the side of the angels," one Congressional staff aide told me. "What you're doing with literacy helps my senator in his state. He wants to rub shoulders with Project Literacy."

Consequently, I was able to meet with many senators including Paul Simon of Illinois, Howard Metzenbaum of Ohio and Orrin Hatch of Utah, and congressmen such as Tom Sawyer of Ohio and Gus Hawkins of California – all of whom had a working, genuine interest in literacy. I also met with several cabinet members in the Reagan and Bush administrations including Jack Kemp of Housing and Welfare, and Elizabeth Dole.

I became acquainted with Secretary Dole when she called out of the blue and asked me to have breakfast with Senator Metzenbaum and her in her office. She was interested in the role television could play in the literacy movement, especially as it applied to the American work force. She became a strong supporter of

PLUS. We developed a great friendship and I became a genuine Elizabeth Dole fan. She is a very intelligent, articulate, dynamic woman. I had the privilege of introducing Secretary Dole from the podium on several occasions when she addressed literacy and education groups. As I listened to her speak, I thought to myself, This person is destined to be a national leader.

One of our greatest supporters through the PLUS campaign was Roberts Jones, an undersecretary in the Department of Labor. Bob spoke on PLUS's behalf at many important meetings with business, education and labor leaders. He quickly recognized the synergy of the broadcast project with the Work Force 2000 campaign that the Department of Labor initiated. Later, he became the president of the National Alliance of Business (NAB) and a close personal friend.

As the intensity of the PLUS campaign grew, my activities and travels expanded as well. I made major addresses to annual gatherings of civic, political, educational, business and broadcasting groups about Project Literacy US and our quest for a more literate America. At each session, I would show tapes of PLUS featuring on-air spots and clips from various ABC or PBS shows. I made the point that we are all touched by illiteracy in our nation and we would welcome their involvement in PLUS. The presentation never failed to bring a strong emotional response, often sustained standing ovations. Among the groups that I addressed were The National Governors Association, The US Council of Mayors, The Advertising Council, The Parent Teachers Association, The National Education Association, The National Alliance of Business, The National Association of Broadcasting, The Educational Correctional Association, The State Governors' Wives Association, The American Bar Association and the White House Staff.

I was invited to join the boards of directors of several prominent organizations because of my involvement in literacy and education. I had been a member of the Advertising Council board since 1975, so I had a broad purview of what was happening in public service across the nation and that served me well. In 1986, President Reagan appointed me to his Private Sector Initiative Board, which worked with volunteer initiatives in the country and proved to be a strong connection for our PLUS activities. One of the highlights of my experiences on the Private Sector Initiative Board was a trip to London in early May of 1988 where I, along with other board members, made a presentation to business leaders at the British-American Conference on Private Sector Initiatives. It was fascinating because Prime Minister Margaret Thatcher spoke at the meeting, as did Prince Charles, the Duke of Wales. I had the opportunity to meet and chat informally with both of them.

Mrs. Thatcher had recently visited with Barbara Bush and asked me to extend her best regards and appreciation. The Prime Minister is a most impressive woman and a spellbinding speaker.

I also joined several other boards including the National Association of Partners in Education (NAPE) and The Action Volunteer Group chaired by Governor George Romney, The Foundation for the Improvement of Education (NFIE), and the National Alliance of Business. The latter organization consists of a group of business leaders who work with several departments in the government, predominantly the Department of Labor, on work force and education issues. I was pleased for several reasons to join this distinguished board that included several corporation chairmen and presidents. And, I had the opportunity to meet some new and fascinating people.

One summer evening prior to a New York board meeting, the NAB staff took us on a boat trip around Manhattan, a rare adventure especially on a clear night. Following dinner, John Ong, the personable chairman of the Goodrich Tire Company and the chairman of NAB, toasted the good health of those assembled and started to lead us in singing. With my love of singing, I, of course, was in the forefront of the group. In the middle of one of our most robust tunes, I noticed Coretta Scott King, a member of the NAB board, sitting quietly on the side listening to our songs. I went over to her, took her by the hand and asked her if she would join me in a song.

"I haven't sung in a very long time," she said. But she got up, and standing in the middle of the group, tightly clutching my hand, she started to sing. As her voice grew stronger, an absolute hush fell over the crowd. As we sailed past the Statue of Liberty, skyscrapers and skyline of New York, we heard the compelling and emotional

"Amazing Grace," sung by one of America's most celebrated women. It was an unforgettable evening.

At breakfast the next morning, Mrs. King thanked me for a wonderful evening. She told me it was the first time she had sung in public since Dr. King's assassination.

Another reason I wanted to join NAB was that it gave me an opportunity to emphasize the importance of literacy and our work with PLUS to the NAB board as well as to the membership of NAB. Finally, it was through this organization that I met the woman whom I would eventually marry.

Pierce Quinlan, the executive VP of NAB, who would become one of my closest friends, came to visit me in my office in New York and brought with him the newly hired director of Marketing – a beautiful younger woman named Ellie Trueman. Ellie directed economic development and job training programs for New Hampshire Governor John Sununu. After receiving national recognition for New Hampshire's innovative and successful economic development programs directly tied to work force issues, Ellie was recruited by NAB to head their marketing and communications department in Washington, D.C. John Sununu would later become the controversial, but effective, Chief of Staff to President George Bush.

Since I had just joined the NAB board, Quinlan had come to New York to ask me to be the chairman of the Marketing Committee working with Ms. Trueman. Being a bachelor at the time, and a believer in the work force issue that was growing stronger by the moment, I told them I would consider it, and that, perhaps, on one of my trips to Washington, Ms. Trueman and I could discuss it over dinner. Ellie, a Wroxton scholar at Oxford with a master's degree in communications from Boston College, quickly proved that she was most adept at promotion and marketing and created several campaigns that won national awards for NAB. Eventually, Ellie and I were married on June 2, 1990 in a beautiful ceremony at St. John's Church across from the White House.

Project Literacy US grew with every passing day. New coalitions were formed and expanded and partnered with additional literacy organizations every week. More and more national and local clubs and organizations adopted literacy as their cause, including the American Bar Association, the American Legion, The Newspaper Publishers Association, SER, Jobs For Progress, The Junior League and Rotary Clubs, advertising clubs, women's clubs, and communications and community organizations of all kinds in cities large and small across the nation.

We started our PLUS on-air campaign focusing on the problems of adult illiteracy. As the program grew and expanded, keeping our word to ABC corporate executives, we tried to keep it vital and fresh for the programmers at the network and the stations. In the summer of 1987, we briefly featured Civic Literacy and tied in with a massive three-hour presentation by ABC News on the bicentennial of the Constitution, entitled *The Blessings of Liberty*. The PLUS connection to this program was acknowledging that almost one-fourth of the US adult population is unable to read or understand the fundamental documents of our nation.

In the spring of 1988 at a press conference announcing our third year of PLUS, we introduced our theme for the coming year, Literacy and Youth. Many studies made it clear that illiteracy and weak basic skills have a direct link to five major problems rampant in America's youth: drug and alcohol abuse, teenage pregnancy, crime, unemployment and school drop out rates. Statistics from this period clearly depict that illiteracy is a common denominator to some of youth's most troubling issues:

* Every year, almost one million youngsters drop out of school.

* Eighty-five percent of young people who appear before juvenile courts are functionally illiterate.

* Female teenagers who are illiterate are five times more apt to have a child out of wedlock.

Our on-air spots and inserts in programming zeroed-in on the youth problems. Our *PLUS Learners of the Month* series featured young new readers. We started a new feature called *Unsung Americans* that honored those people behind the scenes: tutors and mentors who gave so much of themselves in helping young people. The following year, we launched a campaign on Literacy and the Work Force tying in the Department of Labor's Work Force 2000 initiative. The combination of the different campaign themes brought tens of thousands of new learners, new tutors and coalitions and organizations to the literacy movement.

I had a wonderful experience in St. Louis at the second *ABC Star-Spangled Celebration* over the Fourth of July holiday in 1988. Governor Ashcroft, whom I had gotten to know quite well, asked me to be the Grand Marshal in the annual St. Louis Fourth of July parade and be a guest of honor at the official ceremonies along with actress Joanna Kerns of the situation comedy *Growing Pains*. In the parade I rode on the back of an open convertible accompanied by Ellie Trueman, directly behind the governor's car. The streets were mobbed with people cheering and waving as we slowly drove through the long parade route and to the reviewing stand in the heart of downtown St. Louis. As we happily drove along, waving and smiling, I heard a woman scream, "Hey, I know you." I puffed up knowing that she had undoubtedly seen me on one of my television spots, and I gave her a big wave back. "Not you," she yelled. "Hey, Ellie. Ellie Trueman." It turned out she had worked for Ellie in New Hampshire. Again, so much for our own perception of importance.

Later that summer, I was invited to speak at a luncheon honoring Barbara Bush at the Republican National Convention in New Orleans. The other speakers were Senator Nancy Kassenbaum of Kansas; Congresswoman Lynn Martin of Illinois, who would later become the Secretary of Labor; Lee Atwater; and Dr. Billy Graham.

I spoke for three minutes, attempting in this brief period to adequately describe the genuineness of Mrs. Bush's efforts for literacy and her tireless work with children that I had witnessed first hand. I wished her Godspeed in her upcoming new adventure. Dr. Graham, whom I had met several times before, sat next to me at the dais and offered his assistance in what he termed our "most meaningful mission."

Earlier in the summer, Mrs. Bush at my request came to the ABC annual affiliates meeting. She was going to be in California at the time of the meeting, and I suggested that perhaps the network would be interested in having her as a surprise guest at one of the sessions where prominent figures are presented. To my astonishment, I got a cool reaction within the ABC network.

"What the hell is she going to do for us?" the man who had replaced me as president of the network said. "Why would we want her?"

"Because she is most likely going to be in the White House in November and one of the most prominent women in the world. She is the leader of the literacy movement. I think our affiliates would be honored."

He wanted none of it. Instead, I invited Mrs. Bush to the annual affiliates promotion managers' meeting that was held the day before the station managers' gala began.

In the middle of the meeting, we came through a back door of the ballroom and entered the stage from the rear. I went on stage first and told the crowd that we had a surprise guest – Barbara Bush. The place went nuts. The audience of mostly young people – working their way up the ladder in promotion departments – stomped and cheered for five minutes. Mrs. Bush was totally sincere, gracious and warm as always. After the meeting, Dick Connelly, one of ABC's co-hosts for the meeting, couldn't get over it. "That was wonderful," he said. "She was a home run."

The chairman of the affiliate board approached me later at the managers' meeting and said, "I understand Barbara Bush appeared at the promotion meeting. Why couldn't we get her to come to our meeting?"

I just smiled and pointed at the head of the network. "We could have. Go ask him," I said.

During the course of her stay in Los Angeles, I also introduced Mrs. Bush at a special ceremony for literacy at the First Congregational Church of Los Angeles, where Dr. John Killinger was the pastor. Dr. Killinger, as the co-chairman of the Clergy for Literacy, had been one of the participants in our PLUS think tank session the previous year.

A few days after our California meetings I received the following handwritten note from Mrs. Bush:

*Dear Jim – A million thanks for two very nice introduc-
tions and for letting me share in two very nice programs.
I am your biggest fan as you know and although I had
high hopes for PLUS, I didn't hope high enough. You
have far surpassed anything I ever expected – and I don't
think it's hurt ABC one bit in the polls! Many thanks.
Most warmly – Barbara*

On November 8, 1988, Project Literacy US reached an apex.
We held the first annual *National Literacy Honors* in Washington,
D.C., as I described at the opening chapter of this book. The morn-
ing after the *National Literacy Honors* dinner, PLUS and Barbara
Bush had feature stories all across the country and the literacy move-
ment was at the top of the national agenda.

Twenty

The Power of PLUS

After the 1988 Christmas holidays, Dan Burke gave me a call and asked if I could come to his office. I was puzzled, since I had seen Dan shortly before the holidays and he had been in great spirits, especially with the reactions he had heard from numerous sources to the *National Literacy Honors*. He showed me a note that Barbara Bush had sent to him that was glowing, thanking him for all that Capital Cities/ABC was doing for literacy. One line was especially prophetic: "I think we will feel the ramifications of the effects of that wonderful evening for many years to come."

"You said something to me recently that I really didn't fully grasp," Dan said in his usual friendly manner, "You said that one day soon you might want to step back from what you are doing and even take a semi-retirement. I was thinking about it over the holidays, and if that's what you want to do, I want to be helpful in every way I can."

"Thanks, Dan," I answered. "I have thought a great deal about it. I would like to step back from the administrative chores of the Office of Communications and have more freedom. I have been in New York now for twenty-eight years and I would like to smell some fresh air, I think."

After my divorce from Deanna, I sold my home in Darien and bought a stunning two-bedroom apartment at the United Nations Plaza in New York City. I say stunning because the views were overpowering with the ceiling-to-floor windows in all the main rooms of the apartment offering a panorama of the city: the East River and its many bridges to the left; the United Nations Park with its spectacular trees and the United Nations Building, hemmed by multi-colored flags, in the middle; and New York City and its East Side to the right. Corinne was finishing her schooling at Purnell, a prep school in Pottersville, New Jersey, and would bring her friends home to the apartment on weekends. Cori was born in New York and grew up with a love for the dynamism and electricity of the city that she holds to this day.

A year later, in 1987, as an investment I, with Ellie as a partner, had bought a beautiful thirty-acre farm in Maryland, twenty-four miles west of our nation's Capital, with the idea that it might be a possible place to smell the roses when I retired. The house on the property was a pre-Civil War home that cried out for some paint and some loving care. Ellie and I became engaged shortly after I bought the place and she did a spectacular job in restoring the main house, a carriage house, an ancient smoke house and a stone-bank barn on the property, to the point where it became a show place on the Maryland State Historic Registry. The more I saw and spent time at Eminence Farm on my weekend trips, the more I yearned to leave Manhattan full time.

Besides, the place reminded me very much of The Old Homestead in Moweaqua: the sounds of the wind in the black walnut trees; the whirring buzz of distant tractors; the same engulfing yet dark silence at night.

Frankly, there was another reason that I wanted to leave New York and the Capital Cities/ABC headquarters. In my position as president of Communications, I felt somewhat isolated when I was in the Manhattan office, despite all of our successes with public service campaigns. As president of the TV network, I had many people reporting to me and I interacted with different people every day. As I have stated, the old ABC had a tremendous esprit de corps. Working with Capital Cities was different and more rigid despite the fact that I had total freedom in my job.

Many of the people I had grown up with at ABC had moved on – Rocco, Fountain, Beesemyer, Savage and even Elton Rule, among several others. Elton retired from ABC and returned to his native California before the Capital Cities merger, and he was sorely missed. I heard, in the late nineteen-eighties, that he was struggling with lymphatic cancer. I visited him a few times in his California office and we replayed the glory days. I admired Elton very much, despite our off-again on-again relationship in earlier years. He was a mentor to me, and I was extremely saddened when he died in the spring of 1989.

To show you his style, at his Celebration of Life Memorial Service, Cindy, Elton's and Betty's oldest daughter, stood up and simply said, "My dad is very pleased that you would come here today. He wants you to enjoy and remember this day. He said he'll see you later."

The time seemed right to move from New York. Marcia was settled at The Country Place in Litchfield, Connecticut, and while still struggling with the voices, was able to visit on regular occasions. I felt the farm was an ideal environment for Marcia for meaningful long visits and a place where Corinne could spend time with Ellie and me during the summer before going off to college.

"Whatever I do, I don't want to stop working on PLUS, Dan," I continued. "Even if it is on a volunteer basis. We all have too much at stake to walk away now. But I was and am serious about making a change if it works out for the company."

"Why don't we make it work for both of us," Dan said. "Why don't we work out an informal arrangement for you to be a consultant to the company and continue as the spokesperson for PLUS. This could give you the freedom to travel and work closer with the government and other agencies in Washington."

"Would you believe a young fellow like me will have been with ABC for forty years on July nineteenth of this year," I said with a laugh. "Can we make it effective August first?"

"You've got it, kid. Let me work out the details," Dan answered. He paused and then said, "We'll make it effective for as long as it works for both of us."

We shook hands and I felt elated as I left his office. Dan Burke was one of the smartest, most sensitive and capable executives with whom I had ever been associated and I will always be grateful for the way he supported me. Good to his word, Dan came through with a handsome financial arrangement for me as a consultant and in the summer of 1989 I became a gentleman – I'm sure some of my pals would question that – farmer.

Our work with PLUS escalated both before and after I left the New York headquarters. YOUTH/PLUS was in full swing in the first nine months of 1989, and I traveled extensively to hammer home this newest phase of our campaign.

In May of that year, I also had an enjoyable and exciting trip to Paris, where I was invited to be the chairman of a colloquium for news and media executives as part of the International Task Force on Literacy. Jack Harr was also invited and it was a learning experience for both of us. Representatives from twenty-four different nations spoke and discussed the problems of illiteracy in their respective countries. The International Task Force was a program of the United Nations and UNESCO and a buildup to the World Conference on Education for All to be held in Jomtien, Thailand in March 1990. I was privileged to be appointed by President Bush to attend the latter conference as the private sector representative for America.

The Paris conference was an unusual experience for me because some seven different languages were spoken and I had my first extensive participation in working through interpreters. I chaired the meeting and tried to keep the dialogue moving and intelligible in any language, despite the different voices in my headset.

During one session, I got into quite an exchange, again through an interpreter, with Professor Vilioner Yegorov of the USSR Committee for Television and Radio. I talked about the extent of illiteracy in the United States and its effect on our young people. Professor Yegorov kept shaking his head and saying in Russian, "What a shame, what a shame."

During a coffee break, I cornered the Professor and told him through his interpreter I had noticed him shaking his head and I wondered if he would tell me the extent of illiteracy in the Soviet Union. The professor was a jolly sort with a huge beard and twinkling eyes. "Nyet. Nyet. We got none," he said through his interpreter. He laughed and then looked first to the right and then to the left. He motioned me to come closer. "We got plenty, just like you," he said in English as plain as day. The walls of Communism were tumbling down.

Before I officially left Capital Cities/ABC in August, I was honored on several occasions – most gratifying after my many years. The company gave a lavish farewell party for me at New York's Tavern on the Green; and the affiliates had a reception in my honor and later, in front of the entire affiliate body, presented me with a silver tray and three large leather-bound books with personalized letters from the general managers of each of the stations. I mention these occasions to show the extent of the appreciation we all received – that includes the entire staff – for our work in public service.

I was especially thrilled in the spring of 1989 when The National Association of Broadcasters presented me with their Distinguished Service Award, the broadcasting industry's highest honor, at the annual meeting in Las Vegas, Nevada. This recognition came because of my long career in the industry but also because of the distinction that Project Literacy US brought to broadcasters. My award acceptance speech to 2,500 of my peers gave me the opportunity to tell them how passionately I felt about the enormous power of our medium and the responsibility we have to use it wisely.

Here is a quote from the speech:

> *Broadcasting has flourished because this is a free and open country. Within limits, people are going to get the programming they want on radio and television. I fervently hope that the current trend toward sensationalism will peak and then wane and will be more than counterbalanced by a willingness to hear responsible critics and by a dedication to quality programming.*
>
> *As you are aware, our industry and especially television, has recently come under criticism for the effect of its programming on young people. Among the critics is Cardinal O'Connor, the Archbishop of New York, who said, "Television is one of the most difficult elements of the American culture that we must deal with. He pointed to the "incredible emphasis on materialism."*
>
> *I have spent much of my career, as many of you have, defending the positive values of our media. I sincerely believe we have made and do make a positive impact on our society. But we are a powerful messenger. We do por-*

tray role models and attitudes. Our country and its peo-
ple have some rough times ahead. We must listen very
carefully. We must constantly examine our portrayal of
the fundamental values of our society.

As thrilled as I was receiving the NAB Award, I think the most touching and meaningful recognition to me personally came during one of my station visits.

One day, in the fall of 1986, a call came into my New York office from a Sister Caroline of the Order of the Sisters of Nazareth in Eastern Kentucky who was involved with a literacy effort. She had seen me on our network public service announcements and was interested in the PLUS project. Sister Caroline heard that I was going to be in Louisville, Kentucky to make a speech and wondered if there would be an opportunity to see me during my visit. I told my assistant, Cindy Vanden Heuvel, that it was fine with me if we could fit it in. Then I forgot all about it.

A few weeks later, I was at our affiliate in Louisville doing a public affairs show taping when, during one of the breaks, the receptionist came in and handed me a note. It said, "Mr. Duffy, there is a woman named Sister Caroline out in the lobby waiting to see you."

I suddenly remembered the call to the New York office. After the taping I went out into the lobby. The sun was filtering through the ceiling-to-floor windows. Aside from the receptionist, the only person in the lobby was what at first appeared to be a little old lady, sitting on a chair. I approached her and she slowly stood up and said, softly, "Mr. Duffy, I am Sister Caroline." I saw then that she was actually younger, maybe in her early forties, and she was wearing a very plain dress, not a nun's habit as I had expected. Her hair was short and she had intense blue eyes.

She said, "I drove over from Frankfort, Kentucky to see you. I just wanted to say thank you for all that you are doing for those of us who are working in the field of literacy."

"Well, thank you for coming to see me," I said rather surprised that she didn't have a request of some kind. "Is there anything I can do for you?"

"No, all I wanted to do was just touch your hand and say 'God bless you,' and now I must go." She turned and started to walk out.

"No, no, wait a minute," I said. "Please, you drove all the way over here. Come in and let's talk for a minute."

We went into a conference room that was around the corner. It was rather awkward because it was a large conference room and there were just the two of us seated at a long table. Cindy, who had traveled to Louisville with me, came in and I introduced her to Sister Caroline.

"Tell us about the work you do and how Project Literacy can be helpful," I said.

She explained, "We work through the Sisters of Nazareth in a program that attempts to help people in the hills and the hollows who can't read and write. We have a severe literacy problem here, especially in Eastern Kentucky. We are attempting to get people into our literacy program. It was very difficult before your program started. I have seen and heard your commercials on radio and television [she called them commercials, although they were public service spots]. So have many of the people who live here in the hills because all of them, you know, have television sets and antennas. Many of them don't have telephones or toilets, but they do have television sets. Your message that it is never too late to learn to read is reaching them. It is astounding that in the past few months, our attendance has quadrupled."

She paused and looked at me with a slight smile. Before I could respond, she continued, "You're doing God's work, you know. I wanted you to know how important it is, the work that you're doing, and how you're touching people's lives."

I started to get chills. I hardly knew what to say. I thanked her profusely and said, "Sister Caroline, I can't tell you how much I appreciate your coming to see us and for your kind words. We intend to stay with our literacy program, as long as there is a need. Please stay in touch with us and let us know how we can be helpful."

And she said, "God bless you," got up and left.

This incident made a deep impression on me. I was highly gratified but a bit humbled by the whole affair. I was embarrassed because she was singling me out as the one who was responsible for her literacy program's progress. There were many people and many organizations that were working in the literacy movement. I did understand Sister Caroline's message, however, because I was visible from the radio and TV spots. I have always felt that an important factor in the program was having a spokesperson – an executive in the company, a common man, not an actor, not a celebrity – who believed in the importance of the literacy movement. It was equally important that people in the field could relate to, and even trust the spokesperson.

I was really moved by Sister Caroline's visit and her words because it reinforced my feelings that the medium was reaching out, not just with situation comedies, soap operas, sporting events and news reports but with messages of social significance that were making a difference.

The meeting with Sister Caroline was one of innumerable incidents which have brought home to me time and time again the power of broadcasting and the tremendous responsibility of the broadcasting industry – those who create and choose the material that goes out on the airwaves.

It also underscored the often forgotten responsibility of the viewing public, that enormous mass of individuals whose "average" viewing tastes ultimately dictate the type of programs that come out of that inconspicuous box.

After I left New York, our Project Literacy work continued in full swing. A dynamic *Making the Grade* initiative was held in conjunction with YOUTH/PLUS where cities around the country were asked to assess and grade the problems of youth in their own communities. Again, the ABC stations played a central role in planning the meetings and the proposed follow-up sessions. Part of the mission of *Making the Grade* was to have communities create plans to work toward solutions to their youth problems and then assess their progress in following years. A tent pole event, an ABC News documentary on *Youth in Crisis* played on the network around the time of the town meetings in September of 1989 and helped once again to make the national/local connection.

Although the national spokesperson's role on the air was eventually dropped, the public service announcements on literacy and youth were very effective and brought awareness to statistics that were unknown to most Americans:

* One in four young Black males have never held a job.

* One child in five in the United States lives in poverty.

* Forty percent of Black and Hispanic four- and five-year-olds live in poverty.

* One of every four children will become a problem drinker in high school.

* Less than 50 percent of teen mothers graduate from high school.

* 18-25 percent of teen mothers will be pregnant again one year after delivery.

* On any given night over 100,000 youngsters are homeless.

If you read these startling statistics again and think about them long enough it might make you want to forget about the golf game this weekend or luncheon at the club tomorrow and do something about it. We think literacy is the key to these problems. Jonathan Kozal said, "Literacy is the foundation of our nation," and I agree with him.

One of the major themes of YOUTH/PLUS was to promote reading by children. The theme began in the spring of 1988 via a series of programs conceived by Anderson Clark, our consulting associate since the early days of PLUS. The programs included *The Celebration of Family Reading*, which focused on family reading and early childhood; *Read America, Win America,* a promotion through America's libraries and theme parks; and *The Summer of the Readasaurus.* The latter program featured two mythical dinosaur twins named Rex and Rita, whose species have survived because they have the capacity to read. Rex and Rita encouraged millions of kids to read during the summer months when children tend to regress in their reading and writing skills. Our on-air announcements were geared toward reading to children. Some featured Rex and Rita and others included ABC television celebrities who were popular with kids.

PBS joined in with two powerful documentaries that focused on young people. One was entitled *First Things First*, regarding families at risk and programs that are working to break the cycle of intergenerational illiteracy. And the other was *One to One*, an insightful look at mentoring and the opportunity we have to help underprivileged children.

While all of the programming activities were underway, I, in my new breath of freedom, expanded my horizons by working with many organizations and agencies on literacy and youth issues, including activities with the federal government.

I was appointed to President George Bush's Education Policy Advisory Committee (PEPAC) in September 1990, because of my work with Project Literacy US and other educational committees and literacy organizations. It was during my work on this committee that I observed the President in a crisis situation that impressed me greatly.

PEPAC was a very high-level operation, chaired by Paul O'Neill, Chairman of the Board of Alcoa, and had among its members Lamar Alexander, Secretary of Education; Keith Geiger, president of the National Education Association; Al Shanker, president of the American Federation of Teachers; Senator Bill Brock; John Akers, then chairman of IBM; Roger Porter, Deputy Assistant to the President; and several other distinguished leaders. The committee would meet quarterly and lay out policies and ideas to guide the President in his mission to restructure the failing public school system, mainly through the National Education Goals, which had just been announced. It was significant that at the end of our committee meetings, we would always meet with the President for a few minutes in the Cabinet Room in the White House to review our recommendations.

In the first quarter of 1991, the PEPAC meeting was scheduled and then rescheduled several times because a conflict with Saddam

Hussein seemed imminent and had the President and his cabinet in constant meetings.

Finally the word came that we would meet on Thursday, January 17, in the Old Executive Office Building, but it was very doubtful that we would meet with the President because of the Persian Gulf crisis.

One hour into our meeting, we were told to reconvene in the Cabinet Room in the White House and that we would indeed give our education briefing to President Bush. In the initial meeting, I had proposed a marketing plan to make parents aware of and get involved in the National Educational Goals through a mailing of the goals to all elementary schools. The youngsters would then be charged with taking home copies of the goals and discussing them with their parents. Lamar Alexander thought it was a lousy idea that would involve too much of his department's time. But Paul O'Neill suggested I might want to review it for the President.

As we entered the West Gate of the White House, we saw hundreds of camera people and reporters on the lawn waiting for the announcement that the bombing of Iraq had begun. There were still whispers among our group that the President would not make the meeting. As we took our seats in the historic Cabinet Room, I could not help but think about the many mighty decisions that had been made in that very room, including several declarations of war. When we took our seats, I was in a chair at the far end of the oblong polished walnut table and the closest one to the door to a hall that led to the Oval Office. We had waited for a few minutes when the door opened and President Bush walked in, followed by his chief of staff, John Sununu. The President was all smiles as he shook hands with each one of us. I was nearest to him so he warmly greeted me first.

President Bush went around the room and welcomed every member of the committee. He finally sat down at his usual middle seat at the table near the windows and asked the chairman to begin the meeting.

An assistant interrupted and said, "Excuse me, Mr. President, you did tell the press members that they could have a few minutes at this time."

"Oh, all right. Let them in for pictures. But just for five minutes," the President said.

When the doors at each end of the room opened, a mob scene ensued. Flash bulbs were popping and reporters were yelling questions one after the other.

"Mr. President, when will the war start?" "When will the bombing begin?" "Have you talked to General Schwarzkopf?" "Give us a statement," and the voices grew in volume.

The President good-naturedly put up his hands and signaled for quiet. "I'm not going to answer any questions about the Persian Gulf," he said. "There are other important issues we must deal with here at home. One of them is education. This is a meeting of the Education Policy Advisory Committee. If you have questions about education please ask, and I or any one of these distinguished people can answer it."

The press, hungry for the hot story, backed off and we resumed our meeting. I watched the President carefully as he listened to the recommendations of the various members. I knew his mind must be filled with the anxiety about what was happening in the Persian Gulf. I had enormous respect for his attentiveness to what was being said.

Paul O'Neill suggested that I give a brief capsule of my idea for parental involvement in the National Education Goals. I directed my remarks right at the President and when I was through, he said, "Sounds like some pretty good thinking. What do you think, Lamar?"

"I think Duffy ought to answer all the mail my department is going to get," the Secretary answered. And the room broke up with laughter.

The President, on what turned out to be an historic day, stayed with us for a full forty-five minutes. He finally pushed back his chair, smiled, and said, "Well, I have some important phone calls to make," and went back to the Oval Office.

When I got home later that afternoon, I turned on *World News Tonight* with Peter Jennings. Five minutes into the newscast it was reported that the first bombs had fallen on Bagdad at 6:35 PM, Eastern Time. Jennings cut to a live telephone report from ABC's Gary Shepard in Iraq.

ABC was the first to report the start of the Persian Gulf War. Marlin Fitzwater, the White House Press Secretary, officially made the announcement at 6:55 PM. The best and most comprehensive coverage of any military conflict in history was underway by all three networks and especially CNN.

All of us in the PEPAC meeting that day had to be impressed by the President's cool under crisis. He calmly and attentively addressed another important issue, the education of our children, a few hours before the Persian Gulf War began. I doubt many people have seen that side of George Bush.

Following the PEPAC appointment, I was asked to join the board of the prestigious Carnegie Foundation for the Advancement of Teaching and had the opportunity to work with Dr. Ernest Boyer. My experience with PLUS melded nicely with the Carnegie priorities since activism on children's issues was ongoing, thanks to Dr. Boyer's leadership, until his death in 1995. Ernie Boyer was an inspiration to many, including me. He was an extraordinary educator and visionary.

I also joined the board of the Keenan Foundation's National Center for Family Literacy, the One to One Mentoring Foundation, YouthEnternet of America, Educate America, and the Civil War Trust, so my time was well spent when I wasn't traveling on behalf of PLUS.

Project Literacy US reached its apex when Capital Cities/ABC, in conjunction with the White House, hosted *National Literacy Honors* programs in 1990 and 1992. These programs were significant and gained national attention because they were produced in the East Room of the White House in a studio setting with a packed audience of dignitaries. Each program was later televised in prime time on the ABC Television Network. The programs represented the culmination of many national and local literacy activities and honored individuals who had made unusual progress in their reading and tutoring skills.

The PLUS staff worked for months in preparation for each of the programs. Susan Porter Rose, Mrs. Bush's Chief of Staff, was especially helpful in getting approval to stage such events in the

White House. It was a long and tedious process but well worth the effort when the programs were presented. Gary Smith, an award-winning television producer and director, was the executive producer for both telecasts.

President and Mrs. Bush acted as hosts for the programs and made presentations to the new learners and literacy volunteers who were being honored. Patrick Swayze, Jamie Lee Curtis, Shannon Dougherty, Anita Baker, Morgan Freeman, Barbara Mandrel and Winona Judd provided dramatic readings and entertainment for the shows.

As the spokesperson for PLUS, I introduced each of the *National Literacy Honors* programs from the stage especially constructed in the East Room. It is an unusual, intimidating feeling to stand on a platform in that historic room and look down into the faces of a room full of dignitaries like Vice President and Mrs. Quayle, Supreme Court Justice Sandra Day O'Connor, baseball star Cal Ripken, Jr., and a number of senators and congressmen and their wives. I welcomed them on behalf of the President (to the White House). I was honored to be with President and Mrs. Bush before and after the shows. Before the first program, I remember pacing nervously, rehearsing my lines, in the famous Hall of Presidents that leads to the East Room. Several Secret Servicemen eyed me suspiciously until the President and Mrs. Bush entered and greeted me with their usual warmth. The thought occurred to me more than once, "What is a small-town boy from Moweaqua doing in the home of the President and First Lady of the United States?"

The *National Literacy Honors* telecasts were well received by critics and the television audience. Each program brought prestige and further visibility to the literacy movement. Unfortunately, the second *National Literacy Honors* program, *To Be Free*, represented the last great national thrust for literacy via Project Literacy US.

The program was taped just prior to the November Presidential Election in 1992. There was great concern that if President Bush was not reelected the new administration might not give the same priority to literacy. In the world of politics, national or otherwise, history confirms that a new administration – especially the opposition party – does not continue private sector programs of the previous administration. That is what happened when Bill Clinton became President in January 1993. The 'L' word became verboten in the Clinton White House.

The Office of Communication, which became the Office of Corporate Initiatives at Capital Cities/ABC under the aegis of Charley Keller, a long-time and very able company executive, also made a major change that would affect the national intensity of the literacy movement. In reviewing the PLUS campaign in 1991, Keller and his staff decided to continue the effort in a revised format. The decision was to broaden PLUS in line with the growing education reform movement in the country. In 1992 it was announced that PLUS would continue but with a broader mission. Project Literacy became Project Learning US. The campaign continued but the slogan in the network PSA's changed from, "It's never too late to learn to read," to "Never stop learning." In staff 'think tank' meetings, I expressed my concerns that the literacy movement might lose its momentum owing to the PLUS program shift and wondered if learning and literacy couldn't both be employed. I soon learned that my voice did not have the same authority now that I was a consultant.

The new campaign centered on the importance of life-long learning. The idea was generated by the changes taking place in technology and the workplace wherein it is crucial to every person, no matter their age or occupation, to upgrade their skills and keep on learning.

Initially, the learning campaign was well accepted by the affiliated stations. In the campaign, the local stations received especially tailored local materials that they could sell to appropriate advertisers in their markets. This added to a station's revenue and immediately caught the station's sales department's attention. The packaging of PLUS material for local sales did increase the stations' participation, but it also gave the highly recognized campaign a questionable commercial identity.

The Office of Corporate Initiatives' long-range view was that the materials for local stations would become important enough so that the network could *sell* the materials at a profit, thus making PLUS a profit center for the company. This, of course, was the antithesis of the original vision for our literacy initiative. I was very vocal in my objections to it. Part of the magic of PLUS was its non-profit status in serving the public. As it turned out, the station sales brochures became an additional expenditure for Capital Cities/ABC, were not offered to the stations for a fee, and the idea was quickly dropped.

In the following months, PLUS, now Project Learning US, started to lose its national identity. The essential connective links to the grassroots constituency were gone. The network on-air spokesperson role had been discontinued and the national hotline had been shut down in the later stages of the literacy campaign. Some of the on-air spot positions that we had fought so hard to create were surrendered to other departments in the company, diminishing much of the national PLUS exposure. Some ABC affiliated stations discontinued their local PLUS initiatives. PBS remained a partner in name only. There was no longer any substantive coordination between the "two huge battleships."

Further, literacy lost its powerful national voice when Barbara Bush left the White House, and Harold McGraw, Jr., the founder of the Business Coalition for Effective Literacy, retired from his company. And PLUS had changed its name and its direction.

The real losers were the national literacy momentum and potential new learners all across America. The literacy movement is still growing, little by little, city by city, every year and will continue because it is still fueled by the tremendous momentum that was established in the mid-and late-eighties. But the loss of the continuity of national and local broadcast messages for literacy, including the call to action, was crippling.

In 1993, Capital Cities/ABC announced a new phase of Project Learning US called *Children First*. This campaign was dedicated to the premise that by understanding the issues and the many ways that Americans can become involved in helping our children, we will effectively and conclusively put children in the forefront. It is a very important issue and project, as was the emphasis on life-long learning and the visibility that it brought to key issues.

But the Project Learning campaign and *Children First* program did not maintain the focus, continuity, cohesiveness, and intensity that PLUS had created from 1985 to 1992. Unlike Project Literacy US, Project Learning and *Children First* became primarily awareness-raising campaigns, much like traditional broadcasting public service activities, and abrogated the action center – the massive grassroots connection.

Questions have often been asked about the accomplishments of PLUS. Was it successful and why? What did it accomplish? Are there statistics that show what it accomplished?

Project Literacy US was successful by any measurement. Its success was based on a simple bottoms-up, top-down theory. The coupling of continuing national and local television and radio messages with grassroots efforts by service providers and literacy organizations was unprecedented and it worked.

Here are a few statistics:

* Approximately 800,000 calls were made to the National Literacy Hotline from potential new learners and a like number were received by regional and local hotlines.

* The volunteer programs, basically the Literacy Volunteers of America and Laubach services, doubled and even tripled new student enlistments.

* Service provider organizations, including LVA and Laubach, more than doubled the number of volunteer tutors.

* The Adult Basic Education (ABE) programs, under the jurisdiction of the US Department of Education, had increases of over 33%, going from some 2.8 million students in 1985 to approximately 4 million by 1991.

* Federal funding for literacy programs increased from a little over $98 million in 1985 to over $200 million in 1991.

* There have been further funding increases in most of the federal literacy programs since the 1992 report.

* State funding for literacy programs increased from $240 million to $750 million from 1985 to 1991.

* The Even Start Literacy Program increased funding from $15 million to approximately $60 million in 1992.

* Project Literacy US was a strong force in helping to get the National Literacy Act of 1991 passed, which established the National Institute for Literacy.

* The National Workplace Literacy Coalition increased its budget from $9.5 million in 1988 to an estimated $19 million in 1992.

I believe that PLUS's greatest accomplishment was as catalyst – a visible and powerful national entity – that others could rally around. It became the common ground where literacy coalitions and agencies, who had been in competitive turf battles for years, could finally come together, join hands, and work toward a common goal.

I know that the national and local reach and impact of Project Literacy US made millions of citizens more aware of the educational crisis in our country. With the expanding realization that there are millions of functionally illiterate young people, even many with high school diplomas, many began asking why and how. I believe PLUS played a major role in triggering the current educational reformation in America. I believe because PLUS illuminated the far-reaching hidden problem of illiteracy, a significant consensus was formed and determined that drastic measures were needed to reverse an obvious downslide in American education. Everyone who worked in the literacy movement can take great pride in that landmark achievement!

Project Literacy US was the most widely acclaimed and honored of any broadcasting public service campaign in history. In l987, PLUS received President Reagan's Volunteer Action Award, and in l988, The American Legion Distinguished Service Award, The Gabriel Award for individual achievement, The Department of Health and Human Services' Private Sector Initiative Award, the

President's Award of the American Association for Adult and Continuing Education, and the SER Jobs for Progress Presidential Award. The Correctional Educational Association honored PLUS in 1989 with its Executive Board Award, and many other citations have been received from literacy service organizations.

Those of us who worked with Project Literacy US had many experiences and learned many lessons that I think can be important to others in the future.

We learned that media, and especially broadcasting, can play a role – a significant role – in bringing awareness and common cause to major social issues.

We learned that a particular issue or campaign will get much more involvement and recognition from media members if they are included as full partners at the inception and not just looked to for reportorial coverage once a campaign begins.

We learned that a long-term commitment to the cause, working hand in hand with many partners across the country, can bring results.

We learned that illiteracy is a problem in its own right, but it is also fundamental to the resolution of an entire range of other social ills. This is not to say that literacy is a panacea, but it is a key point of entry, a way of gaining different perspectives, even new ideas to pursue.

We found that illiteracy is a seamless web. We tend to think of illiteracy primarily as it affects adults. But there is an alarmingly growing number of young people without proper education and basic skills. What we are really dealing with is the human resources agenda for this nation's future generations.

Perhaps the most important lesson we learned is that the best strategy for accomplishing the mission is to build partnerships, linkages, coalitions, and cooperative action.

We learned that in this pluralistic society, no one sector can do it all. There is no single way to solve problems, be it illiteracy, crime and violence or drug abuse. We need the involvement of all sectors. Within each sector we need serious, long-term commitments. And those commitments must include a willingness to rise above special interests and turf battles to build partnerships. We don't have time to keep reinventing the wheel. We are beyond individual or group isolationism. We do not need bureaucracy.

As we look to the future, it is important to note that in this great country we have found that democracy has worked because it has expanded to include more and more people as active participants.

We now understand and recognize that education and learning is more than a problem of the classroom. It belongs to the entire society: the family with intergenerational illiteracy, the work force with a lack of productivity, the justice system with illiterate inmates, probationers and parolees; the welfare system with illiterate parents; and our schools with high dropout rates and inadequate resources.

And with all of that, there is one more fundamental lesson that we learned regarding the empowerment of literacy:

There is a burgeoning uneasiness in almost every quarter of America about the question of values, or the lack thereof. We witness the continuing decay of our inner cities with crime and violence becoming an everyday occurrence, with guns in the hands of children, with a definite bent toward a nation of haves and have nots. This anxiety is being expressed in many ways, publicly through media messages claiming, "There is a hole in our moral ozone." Or that we are at a "value crisis as a nation." Perhaps more telling are the private conversations and whispers and questions and fears as we wonder what happened to the basic values that built this great nation, or as so many of us say – especially the old-timers – the "values and virtues that we were taught."

We as a nation are coming to the realization that literacy for all of our people goes to the heart of that value system. Knowledge is the cornerstone of individuality and spiritual and emotional values. Without it, individuals are lost and eventually so may we be as a nation.

And we learned through our experiences with Project Literacy US that broadcasting can be a key partner in helping to identify and establish that need for knowledge.

Twenty-One

Farewell ABC

The spring of 1995 brought a big change – the end of my 46-year association with ABC.

It was really not a surprise. I had known for over a year that my agreement as a consultant as the National Spokesperson for Project Literacy US would not be renewed since I learned that Capital Cities/ABC was discontinuing the use of consultants. At the time I had started to cherish my freedom in my semi-retirement. I did have more time to spend with the wonders of nature at the farm. More importantly, I had more time to visit with my daughters. Marcia was doing very well at Devereux, and Corinne, just graduated from Roger Williams University in Bristol, Rhode Island, had blossomed into a sincere, dependable and beautiful young woman. I was at peace with the world. As the year wore on and I saw the PLUS activity lessen and falter and the company's leadership position in public service start to slip away, I hoped that the new management would rethink their decision regarding outside consultants. It wasn't that I needed a job for financial reasons or any reason other than my strong feeling for the importance of broadcasting's involvement in public service, especially for literacy and education.

It was a crystal-clear spring day early in May when I traveled to New York to meet with the powers-that-be at Capital Cities/ABC. I had set up several meetings to discuss the state of the industry and the programming and financial outlook for the television network and to learn of the future of PLUS.

One of the first sessions was with David Weston, the newly appointed president of the ABC Television Network Division. Weston's responsibilities included overseeing the TV network and all that goes with it. A few days after his appointment, at the annual network meeting with TV press critics in Los Angeles, Weston had stated, "I would like people to be able to say about ABC that we have a sense of our role in our society, of our sense of social responsibility."

When I read Weston's remarks I was excited. It was rare that a network executive made such statements. I immediately sent him a note and applauded his sentiments. I told him that "social responsibility" had been one of our goals during my tenure as the head of the network and that if there was any way at all that I could be helpful, to please let me know. I received a return note in a matter of days, thanking me for my thoughts and asking that I stop in and see him on my next trip to New York.

When I turned up at his office soon afterwards, Weston greeted me in his shirtsleeves with a big smile and a firm handshake. I had met him briefly on one other occasion, but I had not remembered how really young he looked. He had experienced a spectacular rise on the Capital Cities/ABC ladder, having joined the company just four years earlier from Wilmer, Cutler and Pickering, a law firm in Washington, D.C. Weston's experience in broadcasting included a brief stint as general counsel, two years as the administrative assistant to the president of the TV division and two years as a senior vice president in charge of program production.

As we chatted pleasantly, I had empathy for the young man and the enormous responsibility he had inherited. Weston is a lean, fairly tall, nice-looking man in his late thirties who exudes an aura of intelligence and concern as he speaks. As bright as he is, I was concerned that his lack of experience would not bode well for the future of the company.

After exchanging pleasantries, I reiterated my feelings regarding his comments to the press.

"The debate on program content is going to continue to heat up," I said. "It goes hand in hand with the 'what has happened to our values?' issue."

Weston agreed. "I had meetings with the program people on this very subject during my trip to the coast. It's of great concern to us. I meant what I said to the press critics. But it's easier said than put into practice, as you know."

After a pause, he looked at me sharply and asked, "If you were in charge of the network now, what is the one thing you would do?"

I thought for a moment because there are several things I would do. My first impulse was to suggest the reinstatement of Project Literacy US but I knew it would fall on deaf ears since Weston had been far removed from our public service activities. His question was concerned with the business of television. I know he expected me to propose something definitive about program content and the company's responsibility or a monumental statement about the revolution in technology.

Instead, I said, "The first action I would take is to do everything in my power to put a multi-faceted audience measurement and program assessment system in place as quickly as humanly and technologically possible."

Weston's face fell. Broadcasting executives don't want to wrestle with the ratings problems, especially when his or her network is in a leading position.

"I am convinced that TV program performance has to be measured in several ways," I continued, "Certainly beyond just the size of audience. I believe that a new, comprehensive system, an accurate assessment of the scope and effects of television programming will provide the industry its own means of accountability. It can bring most of the medium's problems into perspective – including problems of program content, proper programming for children, and all the rest."

"Isn't that being worked on, Jim?" Weston asked. "It seems the Nielsen meter system is being more widely accepted and I believe there is a group working on alternatives."

"I understand that the Television Network Association (consisting of representatives of the TV networks) is working on various proposals." I said. "But these studies I am told are to get a more accurate assessment of viewership and demographics. That's essential for scheduling and selling, but they ignore any assessment of the sociological effects, pro and con, of certain types of programs and their messages. I guarantee you that nothing can or will happen with any of that until a leader, a network, makes it happen."

I should have added, "It won't happen until the government threatens to step in and do it for you."

Weston just looked at me. I had the feeling he wanted to go on to other subjects in his busy day.

I did not go into great detail on the system I had in mind during my conversation with Weston. The concept of an accurate measurement system had been a primary issue for me for several years. I believe that a comprehensive measurement system of this scope is absolutely essential for the broadcasting industry in order to validate its dominance and to ensure presentation of the facts about the impact of programs. Granted, the idea of restructuring broadcasting's audience measurement and program assessment is bold and difficult (mainly because of resistance from powerful members of the industry). But it can, in time, be accomplished. The technology and the research techniques are already in place.

A meaningful and comprehensive measuring system would not simply measure the number of households and age groups watching a show. It would accurately reflect the emotional and psychological impact on viewers. It is only this type of measuring system that would support or negate the ambiguous attributes and criticisms that many people haphazardly attach to television.

I have a full proposal for such a system, too detailed to outline in these pages, but one I am convinced would be workable and effective. As with any research, the results of the survey would be intended as guide posts – not as a means of censorship – to build more meaningful, more entertaining and informative programs.

The reason I feel so strongly about the need for a new research method is that the current measurement system is simply not representative of the ever-expanding, increasingly competitive, multi-billion-dollar, modern-day broadcasting industry. The time for the broadcasting industry to self-regulate and be held accountable for the effects of its programs is long overdue.

The current people meter system was introduced in 1991 by the Nielsen Company in response to the obvious inadequacies of in-home audimeter measurement. It has several problems that have not been worked out, as I pointed out earlier, including a high percentage of refusals for the people meter sample (only 55% of the preselected sample by Nielsen actually agrees to take the meter in their home), immediately tilting the balance in the sample (and a still-to-be-accepted button-pressing technique by viewers in the sample) and yet, this system is still in place. Astoundingly, researchers report that the meter system has a margin of error as high as 32%.

Talk about the education system in the United States being antiquated! Broadcasting has allowed itself to become the object of continual criticism and suspicion through an error-prone system. There is no company, organization, institution or agency that accepts a one-third statistical margin of error in marketing or reporting. But television – a multi-billion-dollar industry that has become the greatest marketing tool for goods and services ever known, accepts it and employs it daily as a matter of course. Based on this erroneous system, programs are canceled, people are fired, companies go out of business, and every show on television is affected. Critics constantly fire salvos about the lack of quality and too much violence and the broadcast industry has no ammunition to dispute criticism.

As an adjunct to a new survey system, I would establish a board of consultants comprised of leaders from various segments of our society. Again, this would not be for approval of content or to restrict creative freedom, but simply for guidance to create higher-quality programming.

Further, I would conduct confidential screening sessions with members of this board, hosted by the programming department, to view and discuss the many programs in development. The comments and reactions from these screening sessions would give the program executives some needed insights on the effects and influences of the programs and impressions left by the TV screen – perhaps even a new, enlightened attitude toward their audience.

The importance of these three factors – a new assessment system, a program content counseling board, and meetings of network management and programmers with that board – is a strong, definitive statement that the company and the network not only believe in being responsible, but actually practice self-regulation. The accountability would be where it should be.

During my meeting with David Weston, we also discussed the constantly changing technological advancements and what they can mean to the company and the television network. Capital

Cities/ABC seems more focused on the audience and the product than on the technology that will deliver the product to that audience.

Robert Iger, the youthful president and chief operating officer of Capital Cities/ABC appointed in 1994, was clearly pointing the company in a "the show's the thing" direction. Iger had an unprecedented rise and become the head of a major communications company. In 1982, he was a program coordinator with ABC Sports. He was quoted in a 1995 interview in *Broadcasting* magazine:

> *As I look ahead I'm much more focused on the consumer than I am on the technology, and as we as a company focus on the consumer, we believe that the consumer will always want to consume product. Whether that product is consumed by way of a telephone line, a cable line, a home satellite dish, an over-the-air broadcast experience, a home computer or something else, there will be a demand for a certain product. And what we are exploring is where we think the demand will be focused.*

I agree with Iger's assessment and the company's direction. However, I do believe that consideration of the distribution of that product is essential in a successful system. The effects on commercial broadcasting of the widely discussed communications superhighway are still very fuzzy, with many companies and individuals expanding or experimenting in the constantly changing technological environment.

In my view, over-the-air commercial television and radio will enjoy the same reach and influence in the next ten to fifteen years that they enjoy in 2001, if the network and program executives don't accelerate the tendency to aim their basic fare at specific demographics (i.e. the teenage and youth market). Broadcasting, and especially television, can further be enhanced by interactive initiatives with other media. Meanwhile the networks had best keep a sharp eye on their affiliated stations and build mutually rewarding relationships or their reach and influence can diminish quickly, as history has shown.

The inherent strength of television and radio commercially has been demonstrated with dramatic increases in advertising sales figures year after year as I outlined in an earlier chapter. (Radio went from total revenues of $8.7 billion in 1990 to over $19.8 billion in 2000.) Twenty-five years ago, the thought of radio advertising delivering such high volume revenue was out of the question.

The television advertising figures are even more dramatic. Total TV revenues grew from $26.6 billion in 1990 to $31.3 billion in 1994. (In 2000, the revenues surpassed $41 billion.)

Just prior to my meeting with Weston, the advance sales figures for TV advertising in prime time on the four major broadcast networks for the 1995-1996 season had been reported. "Up front prime-time sales are expected to reach as high as $5.4 billion, a stunning jump from 1994-1995's record $4.4 billion," according to a *Broadcasting* magazine story.

"We are really excited," Weston said. "It is the best up front season in our history. It's a great signpost for the future." In 2000, *the up front sales figures for the television networks collectively were approximately 8.5 billion.*)

The robust sales picture in the nineties was in contrast to the industry's problems of the late seventies and early eighties. At that time, the broadcasting industry, especially – but not exclusively – television, was infiltrated by business interests whose principle priority was profit, profit and more profit. Gradually, the character of the industry evolved.

In the mid-eighties, all three major networks were sold to new owners. Only one of these new owners, Capital Cities, Inc., had any appreciable experience in broadcasting, having owned a number of television and radio stations for years. The other two, General Electric and Loews Theaters, had little or no history with broadcasting, and it showed from the onset. All three of the company managements had determined that far too much fat had grown on all areas of their acquired properties, including compensation to the television affiliates. A rather ruthless period of downsizing and adjusting was instigated that put all three networks in precarious positions at one time or another. Meanwhile, Rupert Murdoch, with

Barry Diller at the helm, started the Fox Television Network, which meant more competition for ratings, affiliated stations, and advertising dollars – and more cost cutting.

As we watched from the sidelines, the result of all of this shuffling was very disturbing to those of us who had spent our entire careers in broadcasting. The new "leaders" seemed determined to start over and plow the same fields, make the same mistakes, reinvent the same wheels and generally tinker with the foundation that had already brought the industry to a position of power and prominence. Frankly, the "messing," trying to run the broadcasting business with widget factory mentality, set the business back several years as illustrated earlier with the affiliate compensation example. Thank goodness, the innate structure of the system, fueled by supply and demand, persevered, and despite the blundering, the over-the-air commercial broadcast business survived, even stronger, but different. The positions of the networks changed, characterized by the painful demise of the once-mighty CBS, thanks to the expedient philosophy of its chairman, Larry Tisch. But the industry, based on demand, sustained its strength to the point that the marketplace could support four major networks. The Fox Network finally emerged as a major one, through the strength of obtaining the rights to NFL Football from CBS and a consequent stronger, more competitive station lineup. And two other entertainment organizations, Paramount Pictures and Warner Brothers, joined the national competition, debuting in January of 1995 with television networks. All in contrast to the struggling two-and-a-half network economy of just twenty-five years ago.

The "profit at all costs" philosophy damaged the traditional business of broadcasting and also affected many loyal employees who were released in the process. Thousands of dedicated and capable workers, many of whom had devoted their entire professional lives to a respective broadcasting network or individual radio or television station, were suddenly dismissed. It is a devastating process that disrupted many fine people and their families. Granted, most of the dismissed employees were given decent severance packages, and many of the workers, in time, did get other jobs. But that does not dispel the shattering idea that, after many years of helping build a company, these long-time employees were told by new owners – people they don't know or respect – that they are no longer wanted.

Management passed this off as "That's the price of doing business, besides, they had a good, long run and the company paid them well...."

This process, of course, is not exclusive to the broadcasting and communications industry. This ruthlessness in business is seemingly growing and is pervasive.

There is a better way, and most of the CEOs and so-called "leaders" know it. It takes modern human resources counseling and planning. Many corporations are putting a new emphasis on their human resources. As it happens, Capital Cities/ABC developed one of the best human resources departments in any business. It was forged through the pain of the 1985 merger. Other acquiring companies can learn from the Cap Cities, GE/NBC, and CBS experiences.

At the close of our meeting, I mentioned to David Weston that I hoped in the so-called "new morality" of the late twentieth century and on into the twenty-first century that a new spirit of humanness might prevail. I hope that the new leaders of the communications industry, whatever its transformation in the next century, will put its employees – its human resources – on the same line as its thirst for profit. That does not mean to say that companies should not release incompetents and trim down the work force when the economy dictates it, but greater consideration should be given to those long-time employees who helped build the company and made it profitable.

Weston nodded and we exchanged a few thoughts on how the television industry seems to be "in play", with almost daily rumors about NBC or CBS merging or being bought out by any number of companies. I remarked how stable our company seemed to be as the leader in the field. Capital Cities/ABC had never been mentioned in the constant rumors of possible takeovers or buy-outs. All in all, the meeting was very informative and pleasant. Weston stood up and thanked me for my thoughts.

After several other sessions, including stopping by to see some of my old pals in the sales department, and Laurie Byrne, my secretary and executive assistant for over ten years, I had the last meeting of the day with Patti Matson, the corporate vice president for communications. With Charlie Keller's retirement in January, Patti had taken the Capital Cities/ABC Office of Corporate Initiatives under her wing and became ultimately responsible for the company's public service activities including Project Learning US and *Children First*. Patti had been with ABC for almost twenty years, having joined the ABC News Department in Washington, D.C., after serving on Betty Ford's staff during the Ford presidency.

I had known and worked with Patti through those years, including the last few years when she handled public relations for Tom Murphy and Dan Burke. She had worked closely with us during the banner years of PLUS and she was very aware of the accomplishments.

Patti was extremely gracious when I entered her office. She came around the desk and sat in one of the chairs in front of her desk facing me as I sat in the other. We talked for a long time about the business and how it had changed and the fact that so many of our friends and former associates had left the company. She asked my opinion on the abilities of the people and the management structure in the corporate initiatives office. I was very candid with her and told her the department needed a renewed sense of leadership and energy, and that in my judgment, the staff was overly reactive, and not active enough in forging new initiatives and partnerships. I strongly reiterated the value of the literacy/learning projects to the company.

Finally, I posed the key question. "Patti, my arrangement with Dan Burke was on a year-to-year basis. When Dan retired last year, Charlie Keller said that this would probably be my last as the national spokesperson since the company was eliminating outside consultants. As you know, I founded the communications department and helped build the public service programs from scratch. My interest is in seeing them work and seeing them continue. I'm not interested in being on the outside looking in – as I said to Leonard Goldenson many years ago, 'I don't want to be a voice in the wilderness' – but if we can give new energy to the literacy and *Children First* campaigns, I can be helpful, especially in Washington."

"Jim, you have already made a difference," she said. Her eyes fell and she continued softly. "The company is simply not going to continue to use outside consultants. We are tightening budgets once again, including cutting back on the corporate initiatives funds. We hardly have enough funds to handle our current plans." She paused.

"I guess what I'm saying is," she said with a smile, "we can't afford you."

I told Patti that I didn't agree with the "downsizing" posture in such a strong economic climate, but that I could understand the company's position as far as I personally was concerned. There is a time to bid and a time to fold. The time for me to pass on the baton was probably overdue, I opined, but I reiterated that I thought it was a mistake for the company to diminish the public service activities. As I studied her carefully, and I thought about the comments in the previous meetings that day, I realized once again that most broadcast executives think of public service as putting announcements on the air, raising awareness, and thus fulfilling their responsibility.

Public service to most broadcasters has always been an obligation that has little to do with their core business of news, sports and entertainment. Even at Capital Cities/ABC, some members of management felt that the company was doing enough public service with its announcements and occasional social-issue segments on *Good Morning, America, Nightline*, the *American Agenda* on *World News Tonight*, any number of documentaries and occasional story lines in daytime and prime-time shows. These occasions were very important, but they were sporadic, without notice to the audience and especially the constituents working on a particular social issue. While the stories or announcements were helpful in calling awareness to a problem, they were not part of a cohesive force to find solutions to the problem.

As Capital Cities/ABC President Bob Iger stated in his interview in *Broadcasting* magazine, "I think the public is well served by our company, specifically in our broadcast of public service announcements. No other broadcast entity distributes more public service announcements to the viewer than we do."

Iger was right about the number of announcements. What he overlooked is the medium's unique ability to bring visibility to social issues *and* to be the connective link with national and local organizations for action at the community level.

I thanked Patti Matson for her good efforts. I told her that I intended to continue with my literacy activities and my work with children's groups on my own and through several board associations, and that if I could ever be helpful, to please let me know. Old soldiers never die; they just look for new horizons.

I know Patti could sense my concern, my sense of loss, as I headed for the door. She touched my arm and said, "Jim, the literacy project is one of a kind, and only you could have done it."

I have been asked many times, why, if Project Literacy was so successful, other networks have not emulated it and set up their own long-term public service campaigns. The other networks do have other public service programs, of course, but none on a single issue over a sustained period of time. I think the principal reason that others did not emulate, or even join (they were invited), PLUS was that they never assessed the real and enormous impact at the grassroots level of broadcasting's role in the literacy movement. They didn't really assess the impact of the continuity of national messages tied into action points in local communities. They didn't and don't realize the number of lives that have been positively changed – in some instances, even saved. That's what PLUS did accomplish. That is what *can* be done for any number of ills that are plaguing our country – teenage pregnancy, kids dropping out of school, poverty, alcoholism, homelessness, crime and on and on. That is the lesson and legacy of PLUS. That, to me, must be the broadcasting public service vision for the twenty-first century. God knows we have enough problems crying out for solutions and too few resources and people trying to find the answers.

As I left the handsome, towering Capital Cities/ABC building on West 66th Street, I thought again how it stood on the very same spot as the old two-story building where I worked in radio thirty-five years before. I looked back rather ruefully, realizing that it would be one of the last times that I would leave it as a consulting associate of the company, let alone a full-time employee. When I had entered the building that morning the security guard at the desk asked for identification. It was a long way from the days when I knew all the ABC security people by their first names.

Reflecting on the day's meetings, despite my disappointment, I certainly had no complaints about the company's decision to end our agreement. I had been a full-time employee of ABC for over forty years and a consultant for over six years as a spokesperson for the company. I had been well rewarded for my efforts. And Capital Cities, with new management at the top of the company and in several key departments, had every right to retrench and move in whatever directions it wanted. The *Children First* initiative has enormous potential if it receives the proper guidance and priority. But I still feel, all personal gains aside, that Capital Cities/ABC, from a status and good business standpoint, made a mistake in abandoning the literacy and education campaign.

Despite the fact that I had known that my long association with ABC was coming to an end – one that I had triggered by taking a semi-retirement in 1989 – I was nonetheless, frankly, a bit unnerved.

It was strange to think that ABC would no longer be part of my name, let alone my life. For years I introduced myself by saying, "I am Jim Duffy with ABC." It literally became part of my name – Duffywithabc; we became, as silly as it sounds, one and the same. When I left the presidency of the TV network in 1985, the Hall of Fame Broadcaster Bob Bennett from Station WCVB in Boston, a former chairman of the Affiliate Board of Governors, wrote me a letter that opened by saying, "Jim Duffy and ABC. ABC and Jim Duffy. They are synonymous."

I thought about the Capital Cities/ABC future in the increasingly complex world of communications. Despite the inexperience of some of its management, the company was in a solid position. It had done remarkably well, thanks to the management philosophy of Murphy and Burke. I marveled at their gentlemanly but tough and effective approach. I'm sure in the first couple of years following the merger, the Capital Cities management wondered what they had let themselves in for and even if they had made a good decision in making a $3.5 billion purchase. In the mid-eighties the economy had weakened, ABC continued to have problems in prime-time television programming, and the word from many industry observers was that commercial over-air broadcasting was becoming obsolete. But despite being somewhat overwhelmed with the complexities of the network business, both radio and TV, Murphy and Burke believed in the power and reach of broadcasting – just as Leonard Goldenson had before them – and charged straight ahead. Of the many attributes the Capital Cities management showed, the most meaningful to me was that they are dead honest. As the old adage goes, "Their word is their bond." A well-known Cap Cities working philosophy is that you are allowed to make mistakes as long as they are honest mistakes. If you are discovered to be dishonest or deceitful in performing your duties, no matter what your position, you will be dismissed quickly.

Murphy, Burke and the others in management were certainly honest and forthright with me. As I noted earlier, Dan Burke was as straightforward and supportive as a person can get in allowing us to continue with Project Literacy US. I don't know of any other person in broadcasting, or any other business for that matter, who would have had Dan's vision and compassion in helping us with literacy and other public service initiatives. I only wish he had not retired.

As for me, I knew I was going to continue my literacy and education activities through my work on several boards. My years of experience in media had brought several calls from start-up cable networks that needed some guidance with specific program ideas. And I had been asked to be on two or three company boards as a paid director. It wasn't that I wouldn't be plenty busy; it was just that I no longer had the long-time ABC anchor.

Reality finally set in: on August 1, 1995, after forty-six years and twelve days, my marriage with ABC would be finished.

But first, in the heat of summer of 1995, a bombshell of seismic proportions landed on the broadcasting landscape that was destined to change the dimensions of communications in the next century.

Michael Eisner, the chairman of the Walt Disney Company, announced on Monday, July 31, 1995, that his company was purchasing Capital Cities/ABC, Inc. for $19 billion. It was a total surprise to the entire broadcasting community and shook it to its very foundations. Capital Cities/ABC was the last company that people, including experts, considered likely to be purchased or merged. Astoundingly, the twenty or so executives who had negotiated the merger for a number of weeks, including Eisner and Tom Murphy, maintained absolute secrecy until the moment it was announced.

The Walt Disney-Capital Cities/ABC merger was the second largest in the history of acquisitions and far and away the largest single merger in the history of the communications industry.

The next day, Michael Jordon, the chairman of the Westinghouse Electric Company, and Larry Tisch, the beleaguered chairman of CBS, announced a merger between their two companies for approximately $5.4 billion.

In two excitement-filled days, the superhighway of communications for the twenty-first century started to take on synergy and dimension. A few weeks later, Time-Life announced its acquisition of Turner Broadcasting, potentially putting Ted Turner, chairman of the Turner Properties, in a subordinate position to the Time-Life chairman, Gerald Levin. This multi-billion-dollar merger could create a powerful competitor in the communications race but the explosiveness of its leaders may dampen its potential. More coalescing by diverse companies will have happened by the time you read this book. Other major entertainment and communications mega forces will be formed to keep pace with the leading pioneers in the global communications empire.

The Walt Disney/Capital Cities/ABC announcement had obvious significance for me and other long-time employees of ABC. But beyond the financial boost for stockholders, it really brought home the end of an era that, to my mind, will never be recaptured.

As I watched the television coverage of the Eisner and Murphy press conference announcing the merger, I could not help but reflect over the years when I was associated with both of these men. Is this powerful multi-millionaire the same tall, gangly, extremely bright

Michael Eisner who almost sailed out to sea in a rudderless Sunfish in Martinique in 1972? Is it the same young man who worked in movie acquisitions, daytime and prime-time programming for ABC? Is this the same fellow who would excitedly come up with twenty new ideas an hour, only two of which made good business sense? But, in reflection, those two were extraordinarily good ideas. And this surely is the same calm, thoughtful Tom Murphy who bought a television station in Albany, New York, in 1954, believed in the power and influence, and went on to become an industry giant. He is the same frugal Murphy who painted only the two front sides of that first dilapidated station building in order to save money.

Eisner dropped another bombshell two weeks later when he announced that Michael Ovitz, the super-agent and founder of Hollywood's dominant Creative Artists Agency (CAA), would become the president of the Walt Disney Company. This news also shocked the show business community because in many quarters Ovitz was considered more powerful than Eisner. The two Michaels were reportedly close friends and both are power players. It was a most interesting and intriguing development.

The timing of the announcement of the Disney and Capital Cities merger was ironic for me. It was made the morning of the last day of my association with ABC. For me, at least, it truly was the end of an era and of a long, memorable adventure.

Twenty-Two

Coming Home

One of the great joys in my new-found freedom was to be able to walk with our dogs – we have six, of all varieties and sizes, most of them rescues from abuse – through the farm's back pastures and woods whenever I pleased. It was a time of freedom, too, for the dogs romping through the fields and a time of "clearing the air" for me. It was my opportunity to listen to the wind in the trees; a chance to get my thoughts straight and get a perspective on the things that troubled me.

Our usual route was to walk through the meadows, around the small lake and into the woods with its pine trees and hardwoods towering over several acres. Often we walked down to little Seneca Creek deep in the woods where the beavers had sawed off trees, constructed a dam and formed their own village. The woods were magnificently filled with the wonders of nature.

I took the dogs for a long walk in mid-August on a late, hot Sunday afternoon, after the news of the Walt Disney Company/ABC merger and the other changes had been made and debated and analyzed by the experts. The summer day was humid and very still except for the chorus of crickets incessantly chirping as we walked past the hedges around the horse paddocks. The pasture grass was dry and, while still green, was bent over and turning brown. I could feel it snap under my feet as I got into the taller grass. It reminded me how badly we needed rain. The tree leaves, too, were starting to droop and look heavy and slightly tarnished.

The paddocks were empty except for our two old burros, Jacques and Pierre. Standing in the far corner of the field, they looked like statues except for the occasional swishing of their tails. Jacques and Pierre seemed to quietly contemplate returning to their stall where the shade provided relief from the sun and the annoying flies. The emptiness was so different from the springtime, when the

471

pastures are full of horses, dancing and strutting with their tails flying. The daytime summer heat and the insects had chased our horses into the barns, where they were settled in, nodding off and waiting for their evening feed. During the day, they were comfortable in their stalls, resting and enjoying the cool shade of the stone-based bank barn. Once the day turned to dusk, the horses were let out to enjoy the cooler night air.

I looked ahead into the low western sun across the lake and saw the outline of seven deer standing still at the far corner of a field next to the woods. I was surprised because deer usually stay in the cooler shadow of the woods in the summer daylight hours. They must have heard the distant cracking of the underbrush because they suddenly came alive and leaped into the woods as the dogs and I headed for the beaver creek. As we walked on, I tried to sort out my thoughts on the impact of the new powers and influences in the broadcasting business where I had spent my entire professional life.

The story of the financial growth of the American Broadcasting Company is truly amazing. Leonard Goldenson bought the company from Edward Noble in 1953 for $25 million against the advice of his board of directors. Tom Murphy, on behalf of Capital Cities, bought ABC for $3.5 billion in 1985. Ten years later, Capital Cities/ABC sold the company to Disney for $19 billion – a rather tidy profit by any calculation.

The Capital Cities/ABC/Disney merger would make the new Walt Disney Company the largest entertainment distribution company in the world. Its key properties included a TV network, TV stations, radio networks, radio stations, motion picture studios, cable channels (including ESPN – the dominant sports channel), record companies, theme parks, Disney interests in Europe and Asia, publishing companies, newspapers and magazines and a partnership with three telephone companies to provide video programming and interactive services.

The company's ability to produce and distribute entertainment, news and sports programming at that point in time was unparalleled and could easily dominate the industry.

From my own point of view, the new Disney Company, especially the broadcasting arm, had infinite possibilities. The new technology plus the merging of resources and the talent from the various divisions had limitless potential.

Yet we must not confuse potential with the actual. Although the possibilities were endless, the new mega company was bound, not by technology, which could only enhance the possibilities, but it was ultimately charted by the people at the helm of this giant. Clearly, in their hands rested the latent power of the mega-media source, the scope of which the modern world has never experienced. It is people, not technology, who will make history that will carve the future. It is people, not technology, who will write the next chapter in defining influence and molding the force of change that is broadcasting's reach and potential. And therein lies the source of my anxiety and unrest on that quiet summer afternoon.

On this point, I do believe that in the next few years commercial broadcasters will gradually reduce the amount of violence in their shows. The four major networks (ABC, CBS, NBC and Fox), at least, will cut back on the more violent action scenes and leave the blood and gore to the fringe elements of the motion picture business that thrive on the bizarre thirsts of a particular audience. I also believe that in the future, cablecasters will also start to edit some of the extreme violence in their offerings since the cable business has achieved a firmer footing with a somewhat broader audience. However, I predict that broadcasters will attempt to get more sex and suggestiveness into their prime-time story lines. It will be an attempt to compete better with cable and consequently *all* of the networks will drop to cable's level in appealing to the seamier side of the viewing audience. We are already seeing this change in the schedules for all networks, including WB and UPN, and it will escalate until citizens' groups, religious leaders and concerned members of Congress intercede with threatened regulations.

As I walked further in the woods, I found myself shaking my head about the entire idea. You would think that the smarter commercial broadcasters would have learned from the experience of the pitfalls of permissive programming, but apparently they haven't.

I feel the move to more sex and suggestiveness in commercial TV and radio programming is a very expedient move (motivated by the devil ratings, once again) that will be short term and a ticket to unnecessary misery. There is no question in my mind that the first years of the new century will see a massive movement toward the reestablishing of moral values in America. Why is the industry flying directly in the face of that movement? In my view, broadcasters should be in the forefront, leading it.

This raises a question that I have often been asked. What makes a successful television or radio network? The answer undoubtedly is the character and quality of the people who run it.

A successful television (or radio) network is a finely tuned system where *all* of the elements and departments – programming, sales, distribution (affiliates), promotion and marketing, operations and engineering, public relations, community relations and public service, administration, standards and practices, legal counsel, and financial – are focused on a common goal, all working effectively in unison.

In speeches to college students, I have described a successful operation in business as one that is like a well-lubricated chain. The links of the chain are the areas that I just described. If any one of those links weakens and starts to sag, it can slow down the entire operation and render it inoperative.

The most prominent and crucial operating links in that chain are the programs, the sales operation and the distributors. If the programming is bad, many stations won't clear it and sales can't reach their quotas. If the programming is good, but a poor sales staff can't sell it, then funds dwindle so that the network can't continue with competitive-quality programming. And if affiliated stations, the distribution system, feels slighted because of low compensation or a lack of recognition and preempts the programming, the sales department can't sell the programs because the possible viewing audience is restricted, and the programs are canceled.

Every department and person in that chain link process must be regarded as a partner. It takes compassion, understanding, experience, intelligence and patience from the network leadership to make that chain work smoothly and successfully.

It is important to note, too, that management in broadcasting is not dealing with a product that is manufactured, packaged and then shipped to consumers. Broadcasters deal with ideas and concepts that are produced into audio and video programs and aired to a very diverse audience in every corner of the country. If a sufficient number of people reject those programs and ideas, all the links in the operational chain slow down and will eventually stop.

In my judgment, a certain element of ruthlessness in management practices has crept into the broadcasting industry in the past few years. Ruthlessness in handling employees and customers and expediency in programming and sales are not qualities that bring long-range acceptance, respect and distinction. They are disruptive in any chain of events and will take their toll.

Despite these danger signs, there is little question that the coming decades will be the most rewarding and exciting ones in the history of entertainment and communications. The new leaders have untold opportunities in the new century. The course that they chart will ripple across all sectors of America and the world.

In terms of better serving the public in the future, consider what a massive, continuous public service campaign on literacy or mentoring or any number of issues could accomplish tied in through the new Walt Disney Company system. Activities could be included in theme parks, movie trailers, recordings, sporting events, newspapers, magazines, the Internet, as well as television and radio programs and announcements. Celebrities in every area of the entertainment and information worlds could be linked to the messages. Partner organizations dealing with the respective issues could be coordinated not only in this country, but around the world. What is the old Indian saying? It takes an entire village to raise a child. The possibilities are thrilling and monumental, yet troubling.

As I watched the dogs splash around in the beaver creek, my thoughts turned to my own adventures and opportunities in broadcasting, to the business that had consumed so much of my life. Those years have left me with many memories of experiences I have had and the people I have met. They are indelible, and most of them I wouldn't erase even if I could. They come in different hues and in different places in the world, and they, the memories, come back to me often. They are a source of joy and of pride.

I remember so clearly my first days at ABC: my initial meeting with Ell Henry, the *Breakfast Club* broadcasts, my early radio sales calls throughout the Midwest, and my early struggle as a television salesman in Chicago. I remember my first meeting with Leonard Goldenson and how impressed I was with his clear-cut vision for broadcasting and his directness. There are hundreds of memories of my experiences representing the network in New York, across America and, indeed, many parts of the world.

I simply can't put out of my mind the fairyland setting in Innsbruck, Austria, in 1974 when we arrived for the Winter Olympic Games. A soft snow was falling at sunset and the athletes and guests from nations all around the world had gathered in the downtown streets, some dressed in bright costumes, some dancing, others singing, many carrying skis over their shoulders, all merrily providing a canvas of human togetherness that the most skilled artist could not capture.

But that warm memory quickly evolves to the tension and concern as I recall sitting in a client's booth watching Jim McKay in the studio directly in front of us, reporting on the terrorist raid on the Israeli village at the 1974 Summer Olympic Games in Munich.

Or how can I forget the once-in-a-lifetime thrill of standing at the podium in Las Vegas in front of more than two thousand of my peers as I received the National Association of Broadcaster's Distinguished Service Award in 1989; or the distinction of introducing President and Mrs. Bush from the East Room of the White House on two separate occasions for the *National Literacy Honors* telecast; or seeing the pride and tears of joy in the eyes of Estel Sizemore, the fifty-two-year-old truck driver from Cincinnati, Ohio, when he told me how he had finally learned to read and was now fulfilling his dream of reading to his granddaughter?

I will always remember strolling the beautiful white sand beach in Maui with several of our network people and affiliates when we discussed the possibility of a long-term public service campaign between the network and the affiliates, planting the seed for Project

Literacy US. And then two years later when we gathered under the stars at the Mona Launi Hotel on the big island of Hawaii and listened spellbound as Maureen McGovern, standing at the top of the atrium steps with the full Hawaiian Symphony Orchestra playing below, sang *That Special Place*, a touching and romantic song written especially for ABC. The evening and the performance were in honor of Elton and Betty Rule, since Elton was retiring from the company at the end of the year. There were few dry eyes among those Maui stars that special evening at that special place, now a special place in our memory.

The reflections and the visions of people, especially those wonderful, loyal men and women who helped me in my journey, and flashes of the places and events, go on and on and are a mosaic of my adventures with the American Broadcasting Company. I could fill volumes with those indelible moments that colored my life and gave it meaning.

One of my most meaningful memories is walking the streets of Moscow, wrapped in its grayness and drabness and cold exterior, with my fifteen-year-old son, Jay, as we headed to participate in the first American sports telecast from behind the Iron Curtain in the summer of 1965. That trip has special significance for me. Jay died in March of 1994. As I described earlier, he was a handsome, talented and charming guy who grew up in the drug culture of the sixties. He died of a drug overdose at forty-three. There had been many trips to rehabs...several family interventions...many heartbreaks. He almost made it. God bless him. How can I forget?

For his funeral in Bridgeport, I asked my friend Anderson Clark, an ordained minister, to conduct the service. He read the following poem that I had written in honor of Jay, the day after he died.

TO MY SON JAY

You are my son as you will forever be,
young and lusty and bold and strong,
but at times tempted and troubled
as we mortals are when things go wrong.

Now that you are past the final hill,
I know it is not so very far away,
That we will hear your laughter still
rise above the burdens of each day
and help us all better understand,
that in your own courageous way,
through even the darkest shadows
and all the bitter and hurtful tears,
your life had spirit and meaning,
through many happy years.

As you join our other loved ones
in our Maker's warm and waiting arms,
do not look back at life in anger,
but with contentment, and restful calm.
Reach back, one day we will join you
and our most precious family above,
and know that in your current journey,
you have my deepest, soulful love.

We planted a beautiful dogwood tree in Jay's memory on the north yard of the chapel at St. Luke's Episcopal Church in Darien, Connecticut. On the other side of the chapel is a matching tree, now strong and flowering, that was planted in the spring of 1981 in honor of my son Terry. Not far away, on the Greenwich High School lawn, Diane has a beautiful oak tree planted in her memory. It is almost inconceivable that trees represent three of my five children's lives. Maybe that's why I love trees so much. Maybe that's why I get a very special sense of peace when I walk in the woods. Maybe that's why I hug my remaining daughters, Marcia and Corinne, extra tight when I am with them. I know it is why I listen so intently to the wind in the trees.

Two of my children died from alcohol or drug related incidents. They both grew up in the drug culture of the sixties. I am even more frightened today when I read the statistics about the increase in drug and alcohol use by young people, including among preteens. I am convinced that the power and influence of broadcasting can be a catalyst to help find solutions to these insidious problems, just as it did for the problems of illiteracy.

Bill Brock in *The New American Revolution Essay* writes, "If sex, drugs, and violence are seen as the norm in the messages American children receive, and those messages are so pervasive as to be almost overwhelming, then we have to start asking ourselves, who is responsible for the message and how do we change it? There is no ducking this one: we are the ones responsible for the message."

All of us, especially parents, have a tremendous responsibility in guiding young people to happy and successful lives. I think about it every day. That responsibility includes watching TV with our children and explaining the myriad of information on the screen; it also includes turning off the set when the programming is not appropriate. And it includes mentors, in that growing and important movement, giving their charges, certainly those underprivileged youngsters, a sense of the difference between fantasy and reality – fiction and fact and realizing potential.

Certainly the leaders, the writers, the producers, the programmers in every facet of the entertainment world have an unquestioned responsibility for the message. I pray that they recognize it and live up to that responsibility.

I met a woman from India recently who said, "You are fortunate to have your freedoms in America, but you also have other things that are destructive. You have greed and dishonesty. So many people want to take so much instead of giving to others. Americans have so much that is taken for granted. If you want to see what life is really like, go to my country or other countries in the Third World. Children are starving. They are dying on the streets."

"What good is all of the new super high technology," she asked, "if we allow the human race to disintegrate?"

As I walked back out of the woods into the lowering sun and carefully counted all six dogs, the heat of the August day was starting to wane. I looked at my watch. I must have been walking for almost two hours. The walk had helped me sort things out; it helped clear the air. With the dogs now following me, getting ready to head home, I stopped and watched a flock of Canada geese flying toward the sun, wending their way eventually south, getting an early start on their fall migration. Then, flying in a perfect "V" pattern, they suddenly dipped and glided into perfect landings, one by one, on the lake near the pine grove, honking all the time, letting the dogs and all other living creatures know that they were heading home. The cawing of the crows in the trees around the house grew louder as we approached.

As I looked at the landscape just ahead of me, it was like a painting. Off to the left was a grove of pine trees that partially hid the gazebo and the large, yellow farmhouse. The rugged, native red stone fireplace and chimney stood prominently at the back of the house between two screened-in porches. To the right was the back of the old smokehouse, covered with ivy, and further to the right, the carriage house, shaded by oak and walnut trees. Further still to the right were the white-fenced paddocks and the imposing stone-based bank barn, accented by the smaller tractor and equipment sheds behind it. There were no automobiles, or airplanes, or telephone lines to be seen. The picture could have been out of the eighteenth century, save for the satellite dish camouflaged behind the smokehouse.

I thought about how much we have gained during the twentieth century, as a nation and as individuals; and I thought about how much we have lost. I also thought how fortunate I have been as one individual to be able to lead the life that I have led, despite the deaths and the heartbreaks and the times of frustration and despair. I don't say that out of any sense of theatrics or bravado or protocol. I know I have been blessed to have the opportunities I was given. I learned some very hard but simple principles from them. One is never, whatever your circumstance, give up. And, I learned that trust is a precious commodity that must never be compromised. And, I also learned to give of myself to others in need. I learned that there is no greater satisfaction in life than in giving to others. I am a firm believer that in order to really feel the breeze at the top of the mountain, we must, somewhere along the line, have struggled at the bottom of the hill. I believe that in order to feel the full sweetness of a morning rain, we must have felt the tears of loss and pain and regret.

Yes, I am blessed. And I thank God for each tomorrow.

When I got to the side porch door, I suddenly paused for some inexplicable reason. I looked down the two-lane country road that leads to Eminence Farm. The shadows of the trees around the barn were lengthy across the road, now west to east. I started to go in the door and then paused and looked again. I stopped dead in my tracks. There was a sudden slight wind and it brushed the leaves of the black walnut trees. I heard the sound of a train whistle, low and winsome off in the distance, and the hum of a distant farm machine. The August symphony of the cicadas in the trees in the still, warm afternoon seemed ageless. The sounds, even the smells, were the very same as at The Old Homestead sixty years before. I shaded my eyes from the sun once again and looked way down the road through the shadows, wondering if I saw a small boy running toward me on that road, calling from a long way off, "Grandpa....Grandpa, I'm coming home." Tears came to my eyes. Six dogs sat watching me, tongues hanging out from their long run through the fields, cocking their heads to see what was wrong. I shook myself out of my reverie and picked up the smallest of our Jack Russell terriers and gave her a big hug. "Let's go, puppy," I said. "Our day is almost over."

Here is my young family on the steps of our home on Mimosa Drive in Cos Cob, Connecticut in the fall of 1966. L to R - Marcia, 8; Diane, 9; Jay, 15; and Terry, 11. Jay is holding our beloved Golden Retriever, Sandy. Jay, Terry and Diane are all gone. My youngest, Corinne (not shown), was born in 1970.

Top - Corinne, 29, and Marcia, 41, at Christmas in Virginia, 1999. They are hold-ing our Jack Russell Terriers, Endy and Emmy.

Bottom - With Leonard Goldenson, chairman of the board of ABC, at a reception in New York in 1985.

Commentary

In February 1999, Leonard Goldenson, the founder, chairman, and visionary for the American Broadcasting Company, died. He was 94 years old. Goldenson was a gentle, compassionate and brilliant man. He was also a visionary in the field of communications and a mentor and counselor to so many of us who worked under his guidance to build ABC into the media giant that it is today. At his memorial service, in newspaper articles about his death, and at industry gatherings subsequent to his death, numerous people referred to Goldenson's death as the end of an era.

Certainly, it was the end of an era for ABC. Goldenson, as founder and chairman, was a significant force in directing the ABC network, its executives, its programs and its growth. Goldenson was a master at strategy and a pioneer in convergence, or the interlacing of various media sources to capitalize power. Goldenson understood the power of television and most important, he had respect for the paramount role that programming played in defining television, its impact and viability.

Without question, Goldenson was a hard-fisted businessman. Also without question was the fact that Goldenson was always concerned, and we knew our jobs depended on it, with the profit and loss, the dollars and cents of the American Broadcasting Company. But in retrospect, I have come to realize that what separated Goldenson's management of television from today's chairmen and boards of directors of media entities, was the attention to and oversight of programming and a recognition and concern for its immense impact on our culture, our values as a society, and our future generations.

Television, in its amazing growth, has provided our nation with entertainment and information that has surpassed our wildest dreams, certainly those dreams and visions I had when I was a young boy on the farm at The Old Homestead. Thanks to the visions and courage of many leaders, the medium of television has been an uplifting gift to America and the world in its first fifty years.

Now, there is widespread public opinion that television has entered a new era. Many media analysts define this new era by the technology that has afforded television new reach, expanded audiences and the overlap and convergence of media that are now invasive to every aspect of our lives. Having been in the business for fifty years and a witness to the growth and influence of the broadcast media, in my view, the new era of television is better defined as the transfer of power from the message (programming) to the messenger (the corporate entity).

Coming from an advertising background, I sold television on its impact and ability to sway, influence and bring to action, millions of consumers across America. I wholeheartedly believe, more so even today, in that power. I saw it day after day. And day after day, companies such as Procter and Gamble, Chevrolet, Texaco, Anheuser-Busch, McDonald's, Coca Cola and hundreds more were the beneficiaries of television's ability to influence. There are volumes of credible evidence that document that television advertising accounted for huge percentages of the growth of these and numerous other companies. The foundation of ABC's and all other broadcast media sales presentations were based on "cost per thousands," a reference to the numbers of people the message would impact. And that's exactly what we delivered … impressions, influence, action.

The power of the message was clearly evident in the PLUS campaign, which prompted millions to respond to the public service announcements, taking their first step to become literate. And I saw the power and influence of television messages as Jim Burke, chairman of Johnson and Johnson, re-established consumer trust in J&J's products after the Tylenol tampering episode. For decades, the power of the television message has elected presidents and has helped promote accepted codes of behavior. "Just Say No to Drugs," "Don't Drink and Drive," and "A Mind is a Terrible Thing to Waste," are just a few examples of the tremendous and measurable influence that television messages have had on our social behavior and mores.

Yet clearly, in today's world of corporate mergers, venture capitalists, stock portfolios, and bottom-line business strategy, the potential of the power of the message has been overshadowed by the quest for power of the messenger. We have media conglomerates today, Time-Warner/AOL, Disney/ABC, and GE/NBC, Viacom/CBS, and others, that concentrate solely on the power of the stock price of the deliverer of the message. Programming is now designed to bring audience to the messenger with little regard for the impact of the message itself.

Leaders in the broadcast industry now focus on the power of the media conglomerate to reach more audience. The competition of media sources has reordered priorities. Larger audiences, more subscribers, increased advertising revenue by whatever means necessary are the new benchmarks of success. Profit margins, stockholder dividends, and position on the NYSE have eradicated our sense of responsibility to programming, to the message.

What has defined the end of the era for television is actually a loss of respect for the message that television is broadcasting. In the battle of the mega-media corporations, we have lost sight of the broad-based influence of the messages we transmit, and we are paying the ultimate price of this transfer of power.

The increase in crime and violence, especially by our youth, is just one manifestation of this transfer of power. I am convinced, beyond the shadow of a doubt, that television programming is the most influential element for our youth, for our society, and for the development of social values. In television lives the power for social change.

This transfer of power and its effect has not gone totally undetected. In 1997, Congress passed a bill requiring each of the networks to program a minimum of three hours of educational shows for children each week. The language in the bill, once the lobbyists had their influence on what constitutes educational, was so vague and nebulous that it was meaningless.

The standard of measurement for children's programming is so antiquated and so distorted that it will never be viable until a new system for measurement is developed, and that is just not on the agenda of the new mega-media entities. Sadder still is that the television industry, which is so quick to assure toy manufacturers that it can create market demand for their toys, is not using that immense influence to responsibility assist in the development of our children.

The new era in broadcasting has also signaled an abrupt change in the relationship between the television networks and their affiliated stations. The networks have decreased their compensation to the affiliates. Leverage for this decrease is created by the possibility of an alternate system of delivery such as cable and satellite options. The once proud 'ABC spirit of partnership' with its affiliates is sadly waning, and in the near future, communities across the US will come to realize that loss.

There are now 105 million television homes in America, and advertisers attempting to influence the American television audience spend almost 50 billion dollars annually. Messages of questionable attitudes and values are being presented every day to young people via programs that blatantly convey that violence, permissiveness, and anti-social behavior are acceptable and are the norm. Our social fabric is being altered.

In the past, the message that television and media delivered was a product of the leadership of key individuals at the top of the television industry who recognized their responsibility for delivering high-quality programming. Names such as Goldenson, William Paley and Dr. Frank Stanton of CBS, General David Sarnoff and Grant Ticker of NBC, Don McGannon of Group W, Bob Bennett of Metromedia, and a few others were synonymous with control of the programs that networks or station groups would offer. But as we move into the age of the media conglomerate, personal responsibility and individual leadership have vanished. Leaders in the television industry now are defined by stock prices and profit margins.

The staunch defenders of the creative process and programming in the entertainment industry claim we cannot stifle creativity for the sake of true drama and the art of comedy. Media agents are quick to respond that we must not sanitize the medium and put networks and stations at a competitive disadvantage. These are valid issues, but these media monoliths must not be allowed to operate without guidance and without finite parameters of what is responsible.

There is no disputing that we are in the midst of multiple environments: the age of communication, the information age and the technology-driven new millennium. This intersection contains unprecedented significance to our lifestyle, to our children, and to our future. Most importantly, we need to recognize that media will play a paramount role in channeling us through this intersection.

The ultimate question that we must address is simple, yet crystal clear: From whence will come the vision?

If the forces of media, under the guise of today's corporate conglomerates, are so powerful and are now the primary agents of social change and social mores, where is the check and balance required to ensure they act responsibly and with integrity? Who is the gatekeeper? Under whose influence and regulation do media fall? Who will provide the leadership that is desperately needed for an industry that has become so powerful?

I have been extremely blessed in my life. I have had many personal triumphs and many personal tragedies. I had a wonderful opportunity to play a role, to influence the direction of an industry that now holds great promise and potential for our future. Having had the time now to look back, to reflect and to analyze the industry, I realize that my influence on ABC Television and ABC Radio can be traced directly to the principles I learned in Moweaqua from Grandpa Adams at an early age.

During my career at ABC, I spent hundreds of hours with other key staff members pondering the responsible thing to do, the important road to take, and the consequences of the messages that we were selling and delivering. We understood that it was inherent in our job to consider the social as well as the financial consequences. And there were many hours sitting alone, contemplating how to maximize the power and reach of the ABC Television Network. Many of those times, it was the wind in the trees that provided the backdrop for my evaluations and decisions

The terrorists' bombing of the World Trade Center in New York and the Pentagon in our nation's capital on Tuesday, September 11, 2001 brought a terrible awakening to America and to the world. It brought home to each of us how mortal and fragile we really are. It made us stop with many tears and heavy hearts and cherish the blessings we have been given. And it made us understand and appreciate the need for great, moral and responsible leadership in our land. I am proud to say that the communications forces, especially television and radio, were the catalysts for bringing instantaneous information to all of us, and, most importantly, to bringing a renewed sense of unity and purpose to the American spirit.

When the ashes settle and the economy strengthens once again, I wonder if in the new and different America, we will all feel the need to reflect, to listen to our conscience, and to ensure that all of us, especially the commerce and communications giants, are positive forces on our society and our youth.

I can only hope that those who will lead the television and broadcast industry into the next decade will consider how the Maori tribe answered the dilemma of their future:

> *It seems that the elders of a Maori tribe in New Zealand, concerned over their future, over the generations to come, met in long, soul-searching sessions over the single question...How to have noble children. And after all the tiring hours, days, even weeks...after all the words and the thousand-and-one ideas...after endless debate and conflict...they finally came to a conclusion. And that conclusion, through all the complexities, was remarkably simple. The only way to have noble children is to be noble men and women.*